FROMMER'S

COMPREHENSIVE TRAVEL GUIDE

MADRID & THE COSTA DEL SOL '93-'94

by Darwin Porter
Assisted by Danforth Prince

PRENTICE HALL TRAVEL

NEW YORK • LONDON • TORONTO • SYDNEY • TOKYO • SINGAPORE

FROMMER BOOKS

Published by Prentice Hall General Reference
A division of Simon & Schuster Inc.
15 Columbus Circle
New York, NY 10023

ISBN 0-671-84705-8
ISSN 0899-2932

Design by Robert Bull Design
Maps by Geografix Inc.

FROMMER'S MADRID & THE COSTA DEL SOL '93-'94

Editor-in-Chief: Marilyn Wood
Senior Editors: Alice Fellows, Lisa Renaud
Editors: Charlotte Allstrom, Thomas F. Hirsch, Peter Katucki, Sara Hinsey
    Raveret, Theodore Stavrou
Assistant Editors: Margaret Bowen, Lee Gray, Ian Wilker
Managing Editor: Leanne Coupe

SPECIAL SALES

Manufactured in the United States of America

CONTENTS

LIST OF MAPS

LIST OF MAPS

INVITATION TO THE READERS

In researching this book, I have come across many wonderful establishments, the best of which I have included here. I am sure that many of you will also come across appealing hotels, inns, restaurants, guest houses, shops, and attractions. Please don't keep them to yourself. Share your experiences, especially if you want to comment on places that have been included in this edition that have changed for the worse. You can address your letters to:

Darwin Porter
Frommer's Madrid & the Costa del Sol '93–'94
c/o Prentice Hall Travel
15 Columbus Circle
New York, NY 10023

A DISCLAIMER

Readers are advised that prices fluctuate in the course of time and travel information changes under the impact of the varied and volatile factors that affect the travel industry. Neither the author nor the publisher can be held responsible for the experiences of readers while traveling. Readers are invited to write to the publisher with ideas, comments, and suggestions for future editions.

SAFETY ADVISORY

Whenever you're traveling in an unfamiliar city or country, stay alert. Be aware of your immediate surroundings. Wear a moneybelt and keep a close eye on your possessions. Be particularly careful with cameras, purses, and wallets, all favorite targets of thieves and pickpockets.

CHAPTER 1

INTRODUCING MADRID

1. CULTURE, HISTORY & BACKGROUND

• **WHAT'S SPECIAL ABOUT MADRID**

• **DATELINE**

2. FOOD & DRINK

3. RECOMMENDED BOOKS, FILMS & RECORDINGS

The city of Madrid lies land-locked on a windswept and often arid plain, the color of whose skies has been described as "Velásquez blue." Certain poets have even labeled Madrid as "the gateway to the skies." Madrid is populated by adopted sons and daughters from virtually every region of Spain, a demographic fact which adds to its cosmopolitan gloss. Despite its influence as the cultural beacon of the Spanish-speaking world and its quintessentially Spanish nature, the city lacks such all-important Iberian features as a beach, an ancient castle and cathedral, and an archbishop. In compensation for the lack of these amenities, the always-practical Madrileños long ago learned to substitute long strolls through the city's verdant parks and along its paseos. They built an airy and elegant palace (which the Spanish king and queen use mainly for ceremonial purposes), and erected countless churches, many glistening with baroque ornamentation and gilt. As for an archbishop, Madrileños are content with falling under the jurisdiction of the archbishop in nearby Toledo.

1. CULTURE, HISTORY & BACKGROUND

Madrid has been called "the Brasilia of Europe," its location chosen as a national symbol rather than for any particular historic or cultural reason. Despite the city's eventual transformation into the stately capital of an immensely powerful empire, some of the most famous Spaniards in history never lived there, preferring instead the plains and hills of Andalusia or the more ancient cities of Zaragoza, Barcelona, Toledo, Segovia, and Granada. Regardless of Madrid's relative lack of cultural antecedents, the Spanish monarchs and the city's residents have vigorously overcompensated for this ever since. Rulers as diverse as the Hapsburgs, their Bourbon replacements, and Franco have poured architectural bounties, priceless artworks, and the profits from many generations of businesses into the city. An observation made by a resident in 1644 is equally true today: "Each day, new houses are being built, and those that once were on the outskirts are now in the middle of the town." This unbridled building program has helped to transform Madrid into a stellar capital city, home to almost 4.5 million people, and focus of the social and career ambitions of many millions more.

Known as a melting pot for individualists, an entity which Spain

☑ WHAT'S SPECIAL ABOUT MADRID

Museums
☐ The Prado, the number-one attraction in Spain.

☐ Museum of Lázaro Galdiano, filled with old masters, many from the Golden Age of the Spanish Empire.

☐ Convento de las Descalzas Reales, a 16th-century royal convent, with many art treasures.

Parks and Gardens
☐ Parque del Retiro, a verdantly landscaped refuge in the heart of Madrid.

Architectural Highlights
☐ Plaza Mayor, the main square of the old town and quintessential symbol of Hapsburg Madrid.

☐ Palacio Real, Philip V's colossal palace, with 2,000 opulent rooms.

☐ The Moorish arcades of Madrid's Plaza de Toros, architectural attractions in their own right.

Shopping
☐ El Rastro, one of the largest open-air flea markets in Europe, best visited on a Sunday morning.

☐ Mercado Puerta de Toledo, a shopping mall with 150 of Spain's most glamorous merchandisers.

Events/Festivals
☐ The *corrida*, a spectacle of death, which has been both celebrated and condemned in Spanish art and literature.

☐ Fiesta de Sant' Isidro, 10 days of fairs, parades, and bullfights honoring the city's patron saint.

Cool for Kids
☐ Casa de Campo, a festive fun park filled with amusements.

After Dark
☐ Flamenco, the incomparable Spanish art form, presented at late-night clubs throughout the city.

Literary Shrines
☐ Casa de Lope de Vega, long-ago home (now a museum) of the 16th-century author whose work is most frequently compared to that of Shakespeare.

---

seems to produce in profusion, Madrid is without question a world-class capital. Gone are the censorship, the fears, the armed guards, and the priggish morality of the Franco years, whose influence often impelled Spain's artists, such as Picasso, to ply their crafts in such neighboring countries as France.

Today, artists and writers gravitate to the newly revitalized Madrid, whose allures, freedoms, and promises of acclaim and fiscal recognition pull them into one of the most fertile artistic climates in the world. Whether or not you agree with its expression—artists and art movements, like discos, will come and go—Madrid is alive, passionate, and richly able to spearhead the *movida* (the "action") of a newly liberated Spanish culture. The legendary propensity of Spaniards to celebrate their nightlife is observed with something approaching passion in the new Madrid, as Madrileños stay awake till the wee hours, perhaps congregating in the very early morning over hot chocolate and *churros*. Standing at the same countertop with them might be representatives of the hundreds of businesspeople and bankers whose zeal and imagination have revitalized the business landscape of Madrid, transforming its hypermodern office towers into well-respected and often feared entrepreneurial forces. For despite Madrid's many pleasures, Madrileños recognize that their city is a place for work as well as for play, as evidenced by the spate of new industries, services, and products emerging from Spain today.

Its inhabitants are enormously proud of their well-endowed city. If you approach it with indulgence, affection, and a sense of humor, you'll be richly rewarded. Capital of the Spanish-speaking world, and the object of travel fantasies for thousands of residents of Central and South America, Madrid is at the same time a monolithic big city, as well as a tapestry of small villages. Each of these developed an identity throughout the various expansions of the capital. Each neighborhood offers countless numbers of subcultures that thrive within its precincts. The result is an almost inexhaustible supply of diversions and distractions, some of them potent enough to justify spending almost all your Spanish holiday within the confines of Madrid.

GEOGRAPHY

In the geographic center of the Iberian peninsula, Madrid lies amid the southern *mesetas* (tablelands) of Castilla la Nueva, close to the base of the heavily eroded Sierra de Guadarrama (maximum altitude around 8,000 feet) and the slightly more distant mountain ranges of Somosierra and Gredos.

Far from the tempering effects of the ocean, the city endures a hot and arid climate, but there are scattered pockets of verdancy thanks to the city's principal river (the Manzanares, a minor tributary of the Tagus). The terrain to the north and west of Madrid rises upward to the rocky, birch- and pine-studded tablelands of the previously mentioned mountain ranges, while to the east, south, and southwest sprawl hot and arid flatlands that eventually lead to the plains of Extremadura and La Mancha. (A notable exception to this dry terrain appears in the historic resort of Aranjuez, where alluvial flatlands and massive irrigation contribute to a greater verdancy.)

Madrid, as well as the entire country that contains it, defines its position in relation to the Puerta del Sol. This crescent-shaped plaza has traditionally considered itself the starting point for every road and highway in Spain. A milepost in the center identifies the distance (in kilometers) to dozens of cities throughout Iberia, Europe, and the world.

Madrid is divided into three distinct geographical zones, which include Old Madrid, the Ensanche, and the modern sections of the city built up since the vast expansion that began in the 1950s.

Old Madrid incorporates the compact medieval core which housed a Muslim settlement around the year 800. This small but historic district once contained freshwater supplies and thick fortifications. Much altered by later Christian monarchs, its heart lies around the Palacio de Oriente, site of major rebuilding during the 18th century. Old Madrid also includes the city's medieval Christian neighborhoods as well as districts erected by the Hapsburgs. Originally centered around the Plaza de la Villa and the Plaza de la Paja, the population of that era eventually gravitated after about 1650 to the Plaza Mayor. Old Madrid also incorporates the grandiose 18th- and 19th-century neighborhoods of Spain's most recent royal dynasty, the Bourbons, whose most visible architectural symbol remains the neighborhoods near and along the paseo del Prado.

The areas that comprise the Ensanche developed during the 19th century after the old city ramparts were demolished to release the pressure on an urban infrastructure almost bursting at its seams. Thus developed the wide leafy boulevards of the Salamanca and Arguelles districts, and the extension of the world-famous paseo de la Castellana. Populated shortly after their development with members of Spain's newly affluent bourgeoisie, they have remained ever since as symbols of the fiscal prosperity of certain segments of Spanish society.

Modern Madrid—known for its acres of angular but anonymous apartment dwellings, as well as for some of the most exciting postmodern architecture anywhere—developed as the population of the city continued to burgeon after the end of the Spanish Civil War. Its boundaries have crept inexorably over such formerly independent villages as Chamartín (site of the city's largest and most modern railway station), Hortaleza, Villaverde, and many others.

In efforts to channel some of the endless traffic, which some observers consider the curse of Madrid, during the 1960s and 1970s city architects encircled all three of the city's divisions with the M-30 beltway. This super-ring-road today encloses the capital with as many as 16 lanes of endless traffic that funnel travelers and their vehicles onto the six superhighways, each of which radiates outward from its central junction at Madrid.

PEOPLE

No city in Spain figures more prominently in the imaginations of its people than Madrid, and as such, it has always exerted a kind of magnetic lure for newcomers from the countryside. Seeking employment, the fulfillment of personal dreams, and/or freedom from the social restrictions of their villages, natives of each of the other Spanish provinces have flooded into Madrid since its original establishment in 1561.

During the past century the population of the city has grown astonishingly: from 400,000 people in 1880 to more than 4.5 million today. This surge of newcomers (many of whom arrived since the 1940s from such relatively impoverished districts as Galicia, Castile, Extremadura, and Andalusia) has created a cosmopolitan mixture well accustomed to the assimilation of new ideas. This trend has been especially apparent in Madrid since the end of the repressive regime of Franco.

The Spanish exodus from rural to urban areas presents particular ironies to anyone looking at the landscapes around Madrid: Some of the most sparsely inhabited and least productive areas of Europe lie within an hour's drive of the city limits of the Spanish capital. Today, scattered around any typical Madrileño scene, you're as likely to see tall, blue-eyed Spanish-speaking blondes, descendants of the Visigothic Celts, as olive-skinned Mediterranean types. Regardless of their looks, they indulge in the single and omnipresent Madrileño characteristic: Everyone seems to work very hard during the day, and play very hard until late into the night. Both facets of the Madrileño character exist simultaneously, a duality that sometimes baffles

IMPRESSIONS

It may truly be affirmed that as God worked six days, and rested on the seventh, Madrileños rest the six and on the seventh . . . go to the bull-fight.
—H. O'SHEA, 1865

---

newcomers. It all contributes to the nickname attached to residents of Madrid: *gatos* (cats), who are best remembered for their nocturnal activities.

Madrileños are known for their friendliness and gregariousness. To citizens, the *ambiente* of a place—the amount of noise, people, visual distractions, and joy—is very important to the definition of a successful evening. City residents, especially young ones, tend to flee from calm and tranquil places, grouping instead in enclaves of often boisterous energy and noise. In the course of any ordinary night, a Madrileño might stop at four or five bars, some of them requiring some effort to reach, more on the expectation of meeting acquaintances and friends than for the drinks themselves.

Today the hard-working, hard-driving residents of Madrid seem awake with a gregarious sense of excitement, racing toward the 21st century with a freedom and abandon denied to them during the stifling decades of the Franco years.

HISTORY

A LATE ARRIVAL Far younger than many other cities of Spain—dozens of which can document their histories to before the ancient Romans—Madrid is the glittering parvenue of Spanish cities, imposed upon the populace by autocrats and embraced ever since as the most frequently discussed and most controversial city in the country.

Despite its present-day dominance of Spanish life, Madrid (except for a small settlement first of Muslims and later of Christians, both of lackluster importance) didn't exist during most of the crucial events that defined modern Spain.

The *Reconquista* (the wresting of the Iberian peninsula from the Moors) had ended in triumph for the Catholic monarchs long before Madrid became important. Preferring their more ancient bastions in Aragón and other parts of Castile, and their newly conquered territories around Granada and Seville, Isabella and Ferdinand did not particularly favor Madrid. Columbus probably never visited it, and as a landlocked village it never played any role in the crucial discoveries of the New World.

At least a century before Madrid soared into the consciousness of the world, the Pacific had been discovered, the Jews had

DATELINE

- **800s** Moors establish a fortified settlement, naming it Majrít, on the site of today's Royal Palace.
- **932** Majrít is demolished by Ramiro I, but soon after is reconquered by the Moors.
- **1202** Alfonso VII grants Madrid specific privileges, including a municipal charter.
- **1309** The Castilian Parliament (*Cortés*) chooses Madrid as its meeting place, setting a precedent for future meetings.
- **1492** Catholic monarchs conquer the last Moorish stronghold, Granada; Columbus discovers the New World.

(continues)

DATELINE

- **1519** Cortés seizes Mexico; Spain rushes to colonize the New World.
- **1525** Francis I, Renaissance King of France, is imprisoned briefly in Madrid after a humiliating military defeat.
- **1561** Philip II declares Madrid capital of the Spanish Empire.
- **1563** Philip retires from Madrid to his monastery at El Escorial.
- **1580** Spain annexes Portugal, combining both empires into a vast landmass ruled from Madrid for 60 years.
- **1588** Sinking of the Spanish Armada by an increasingly powerful England.
- **1598** Death of Philip II; Spain is close to bankruptcy; the new monarch continues to embellish Madrid.
- **1606** Completion of the Plaza Mayor; rapid growth of Madrid's population.
- **1700** The death of Charles II provokes a dynastic battle; the War of the Spanish Succession involves most of Europe and leaves a French-born Bourbon on the Spanish throne.
- **1713** The Treaty of Utrecht sets terms for an uneasy
  (continues)

already been expelled from Spain and scattered across North Africa and southern Europe, the Philippines had been colonized, and Buenos Aires had been founded. And at least 50 years prior to the establishment of Madrid, the Incas, the Aztecs, the Taínos, and many other cultures of Central and South America were well on the way to annihilation. In other words, Madrid entered late into the ongoing drama of Spanish history, but when it did, it immediately became the most important character in the play.

MOORS & MEDIEVAL CHRISTIANS

The Moors first inhabited the city's site during the 800s, building thick fortifications near the Plaza de l'Oriente, on the site of today's Royal Palace. First mentioned in a historical document in 932, the settlement was demolished by the Catholic leader Ramiro II. The Moorish occupants, however, almost immediately regained control, only to be ousted again in 1083 by Alfonso VI of Castile. The settlement's Arabic name (Majrít) would, over time, become the most evocative place name in the Spanish language.

In 1202, partly to strengthen it against continuing Moorish raids, King Alfonso VII granted the settlement specific privileges, as well as a *Fuero* (municipal charter). This designation encouraged the meeting there, in 1309 and again in 1478, of the fledgling Castilian Parliament (*Cortés*). In 1419, Juan II was proclaimed King of Castile there. Three kings—Portugal's John IV, Enrique (Henry) III of Castile (famous for conquering the Canary Islands), and the weak-willed and dissolute Enrique IV of Castile—each spent prolonged periods in Madrid, perhaps setting a favorable royal precedent. Enrique IV also contributed to the town's fame by marrying Juana of Portugal there in 1464, and then again, unwittingly, by dying there in 1474. Even the very powerful and very canny French King, François I (sometimes dubbed the first Renaissance king of northern Europe) was briefly imprisoned within Madrid's Torre de Los Lujanes, after his army's defeat at the Battle of Pavia in 1525. Today that building is carefully preserved as one of Madrid's only surviving examples of Gothic architecture.

MADRID, CENTER OF THE SPANISH EMPIRE   By the mid-1500s, however,

Spain was a very different political entity from that of the previous century. Firmly in control of a united Spain, with little interference from the popes in Rome, Philip II (1556–98) developed into one of the most influential, and perhaps the most obsessive, monarchs in European history. Committed to his ambition of forever uniting the Iberian peninsula into a single political entity under a strong Catholic monarchy, and surrounded by the staggering wealth produced by the gold and silver mines of the New World, Philip proclaimed the unpretentious town of Madrid in 1561 as the capital of Spain. Although he cited its healthful climate and central position as his reasons, some historians have suggested that he was also interested in escaping the avaricious power of the rich and solidly entrenched cities of Andalusia. Another incentive was the avoidance of the potentially dangerous archbishops in neighboring Toledo as well.

Many of Philip's contemporaries believed that he would abandon Madrid when faced with the discomfort, inconvenience, and expense of transforming a simple Castilian village into a glittering capital, although that was not to be the case. Importantly, the designation of Madrid as the empire's capital encouraged the eventual dominance of the Castilian dialect and cultural presuppositions upon all the rest of what is now known as Spain. This trend would be especially emphasized 380 years later, under the regime of Franco, when dialects and the cultural ambitions of other regions were suppressed, often brutally.

Although architectural embellishments, including the layout of the Plaza Mayor, slowly transformed Madrid's allure, Philip almost immediately chose to sequester himself within the vast and somber confines of his monastery and palace, El Escorial, 30 miles west of Madrid, from which he ruled the Spanish Empire in semi-ascetic isolation. Ironically, his retreat began a scant two years after his designation of Madrid as his capital, ensuring that he would never have to personally endure the inconvenience of ruling from a half-finished city.

Despite his other successes, his greatest was the acquisition of Portugal in 1580, the result of the disappearance of the Portuguese heir in a Moroccan battle in 1578, as well as the targeted and insidious diplomacy of Philip himself and the threat of all-out

DATELINE

peace; Philip V packs the government with non-Spanish administrators.

- **1734** The medieval Alcázar burns to the ground and is replaced within a few years with the neoclassical Royal Palace.

- **1760s–1800** Sewers and paved roads are built, along with other municipal improvements; many buildings are designed in the French-inspired Bourbon style.

- **1746–88** Spain is ruled by enlightened monarchs who enact liberal reforms.

- **1798** Goya paints the frescoes in the Chapel of San Antonio de la Florida.

- **1808** Forces of Napoleon invade Spain; King Ferdinand abdicates and is replaced immediately by Napoleon's much-hated brother.

- **1808–14** War of Spanish Independence; Europe is once again deeply involved in Spain's internal problems; in 1812, aided by Wellington's English forces, Madrid evicts the French.

- **1814** Ferdinand VII rules Spain while buttressed by French troops; retracting promises of clemency, he eventually butchers hundreds
(continues)

DATELINE

of his opponents.

1822 Colombia is recognized as an independent nation by the United States; the loss of Spain's South and Central American colonies accelerates rapidly.

1833 Isabella II ascends the throne, and promises libertarian reforms, but soon retracts them; riots sweep through Madrid.

1850 The first railroad is built within Spain.

1868 A revolution sends the unpopular Isabella II into exile in France; two years later a republic is established to replace the monarchy.

1875 The Republic collapses after five years of civil unrest; the army restores power to the Bourbon monarchs in the person of Alfonso XII.

1880 The beginning of a decade of unrest; rebellions in Cuba are suppressed by Spanish forces; Madrid expands both its borders and its population.

1885 Death of Alfonso XII; his heir, Alfonso XIII, is born six months later, and during his minority (1886–1902), his mother rules as Queen Regent.

1898 The Spanish-American War

(continues)

war. This union, although it was undone by a Portuguese rebellion 60 years later, served to join—from headquarters in Madrid—the second-largest colonial empire in the world in union with the largest of them all. For more than 50 years Madrid controlled the entire Iberian peninsula, including Portugal's valuable Atlantic ports, the armadas of skilled navigators for whom Portugal was at the time famous, and the infinite riches of Portugal's colony of Brazil as well.

Many of these benefits were undone by the growing tensions between Spain and England, whose officially sanctioned pirates had consistently plundered the convoys of Spanish treasure ships from the New World. England had also strewn discontent within Spain's possessions in the Netherlands, and vigorously persecuted Catholics within England. All of Spain had been horrified by the confiscation by the English monarchs of lands, buildings, and treasuries once belonging to the Catholic religious orders. Relations between Madrid and London couldn't have been worse, escalating into the showdown of 1588. Using naval techniques never before tested in large-scale battles, England utterly destroyed the largest group of warships assembled to date, the Spanish Armada, in one of the most decisive battles in naval history. Its destruction was a blow from which Spain never really recovered.

Though the destruction of the Armada was endlessly humiliating, a deeper malaise was already widespread within the government at Madrid. The expenses of Philip's vast empire were greater than the income produced by the gold and silver mines of Mexico and Peru, and no program of industrial or commercial development was ever promulgated to offset the deficits. As bullion flooded through Madrid into the moribund Spanish economy, hyper-inflation followed, leading to virtual declarations of bankruptcy three times during Philip's reign. Inefficient and often corrupt administration of Spanish commerce and industry—which was being taxed almost out of existence—led to a staggering decline in revenues and an unwillingness of moneylenders to advance any further capital. When the influx of gold slowed substantially during the early 1700s, the result was disastrous.

Despite Philip's failures, during his reign the prodigious output of science, literature, and the arts is viewed today as partial compensation for many of his shortcomings. His tenure, in fact, is viewed as the Golden Age of Spanish literature, much of which made oblique, satirical, or honorific references to the epic scale of what was happening in Madrid.

MADRID'S EXPANSION & THE EMPIRE'S DECLINE When Philip died in 1598, Madrileños clung desperately to their hopes that royal favor would continue to be shown their city from the new regime. Strewn with muddy excavations and lofty dreams, the city was filled with adventurers, courtesans, impoverished members of the nobility, soldiers, priests, and laborers sweating to erect buildings to house them all.

Under the subsequent ruler, Philip III (1598–1621), Madrid reinforced its role as capital of the largest power base since the fall of the Roman Empire. Despite the empire's chronic fiscal imbalances, Madrid continued to grow, often at the expense of the heavily taxed Spanish populace. (During one chapter of the new city's most intense construction, the government moved briefly and temporarily to Valladolid.) Though the city's life had originally been established around the Plaza de la Paja, and later the Plaza de la Villa, it surged northward with the completion in 1606 of the new city's most visible showcase, the Plaza Mayor. Rhythmic in its gracefully repetitive classicism, and large enough to conceivably cram most of the populace within its perimeter, it functioned as Madrid's nerve center and open-air living room for almost 300 years, at least until vast expansions of the city's borders diminished its crucial importance sometime in the 19th century.

BOURBON MADRID A major era in the history of Madrid came to a violent end upon the death of Charles II (1665–1700), the last of the Spanish Hapsburgs. A disputed inheritance led to simultaneous claims upon the throne by contenders from two separate dynasties. The first was Charles of Hapsburg, the preferred candidate of England, Portugal, Holland, Austria, and some of the German states. The second candidate was Philip of Anjou, a France-based member of the powerful Bourbon dynasty then ruling in Versailles, and the grandson of the fiercely ambitious Louis XIV. Madrid almost instantly became a crucible of intense

DATELINE

reduces the once-majestic Spanish Empire to an empty shell; Spain is once again close to fiscal ruin; Madrid continues to expand.

• **1902** Elevation of Alfonso XIII as king at age 16; every pronouncement he makes infuriates libertarians throughout Spain.

• **1914** World War I; Spain avoids direct European confrontation, but finds Morocco increasingly troublesome.

• **1921** Madrid's Mayor Eduardo Dato, an influential conservative, is assassinated, leading to massive repression and massive strikes; the Spanish army suffers a brutalizing and scandal-ridden defeat in North Africa.

• **1923–30** Dictatorship of Primo de Rivera, with full support of Alfonso XIII.

• **1931** More unpopular than ever, the king informally abdicates and goes into exile in France; hours after his departure, the Second Republic is established.

• **1933** The right to vote is granted to Spanish women.

• **1936–39** The Spanish Civil War; on March 28, 1939, Madrid, the last Re-

(continues)

politicking as the fate of European power hung in the balance. The city was twice invaded by military forces, although the allegiance of the capital's most influential politicians with the Bourbon side (and the deathbed designation of the Bourbon candidate by the previous king as his heir) eventually helped to sway the election in favor of Philip of Anjou. Many modern historians interpret this period of Madrid's history as crucially important in defining the presuppositions of Europe's colonial expansions of the 18th and 19th centuries. It was also to begin a repetitive pattern which frequently designated Madrid as the fulcrum of European power politics, with its events closely watched (and often manipulated) by the other powers of Europe.

Although the war's winner, Philippe of Anjou, had made his first (aborted) triumphal entry into Madrid in 1701 as Philip V, his real reign began a dozen years later, in 1713. In that year the Treaty of Utrecht more or less rearranged the power balance of Europe, and set peace terms that would almost immediately be bitterly contested. One act of self-preservation that the new king almost immediately enacted was the promulgation of the Salic Laws of 1713, whose intention was never again to allow one of his Hapsburg rivals to gain the throne of Spain through marriage.

Impressed with the formal neoclassicism then sweeping over the architecture of both France and the rest of Europe, Philip V initiated an energetic building program whose monuments and palaces are among the most memorable buildings in Madrid today. Although to an increasing degree he retreated from political involvement of any kind, his 33-year reign was punctuated with the construction of monuments which included the Hospicio de San Fernando, the Montserrat Church, the Cuartel del Conde-Duque, and the Toledo Bridge, all in the baroque style. For his vacation home, the French-born king commissioned a smaller version of the palace at Versailles on the fertile alluvial plain of Aranjuez, 29 miles south of Madrid, beginning in 1721.

On Christmas night of 1734, the medieval Alcázar, used for centuries as the king's residence in Madrid, was destroyed by fire, leaving a gaping hole in the city landscape that was filled in three years later by the 2,000-room Royal Palace (Palacio Real). During the 1760s up until the early 19th century, the city received such amenities as drains, paved streets, street lighting, the neoclassical brick-and-stone building that today houses the Prado (originally built as a natural science museum but converted into an art museum in 1819), the lavish but since-destroyed Palacio de Buenavista, the Botanic

Gardens, the post office in the Puerta del Sol, the Puerta de Alcalà, and the Church of San Francisco el Grande.

Despite the architectural glories transforming the face of Madrid, the French-born monarch—a frequent victim of what his contemporaries referred to as "religious melancholia"—eventually abandoned Madrid almost completely in favor of his vast residence at La Granja. During his reign, court records recorded almost 800 executions, often by burning, for heresy, and more than 14,000 imprisonments and/or tortures for religious reasons. By the time of Philip's death in 1746, Spain had been at war for 40 of the 46 years of his reign, his will promulgated by French and Italian administrators, each of whom maintained an iron hand on the politics of Madrid.

During the short reign of Ferdinand VI (1746–59) and the somewhat longer and more enlightened reign of Charles III (1759–88), Spain attained peace at last as its rulers worked to improve the society at large. Artists and artisans flocked to Madrid to further embellish its monuments. Both the population of Spain and the relative importance of Madrid increased greatly. Between 1700 and 1788 the country's population increased from 5.7 million to almost 10.25 million. The brutal actions of the Inquisition were moderated greatly, and persecution of religious heresy was no longer considered an essential part of government policy. In 1773 a decree issued from Madrid ordained the distribution of large tracts of government-owned land to peasants and the colonization of many uninhabited areas of the Spanish peninsula. For this purpose, more than 6,000 Bavarians were invited to establish farms in the Sierra Morena. New industries were established, often with encouragement from Madrid and advice from foreign experts. The national lottery, which is today an almost inescapable sight at any Madrid streetcorner, was initiated for the first time.

THE DECLINE OF THE MONARCHS   During the reign of the sluggish and stupid Charles IV (1788–1808), the Plaza Mayor was reconstructed and reembellished. Goya reached some of his greatest artistic heights with the frescoes in the Chapel of San Antonio de la Florida in 1798. A series of entangling alliances and military compromises, however, soon placed Spain at the mercy of the revolutionary government of France, whose armies under Napoleon threatened to conquer all of Europe.

After persuading Spain (through diplomatic and military pressure and appeals to the monarch's greed and fear) to pay large cash settlements to France, and then to initiate abortive attacks against both England and Portugal, Napoleon and his French armies invaded Spain in 1808. Almost immediately the unpopular Charles IV abdicated his throne, to be replaced immediately by the French-controlled puppet, Joseph Bonaparte, brother of Napoleon.

Within a few weeks the people of Madrid rose up against the French invaders, signalling the debut of the War of Independence (1808–14). Although the revolt was suppressed and Madrid remained a captive of the French, many Madrileños joined their guerrilla counterparts in the surrounding provinces, proving themselves a serious deterrent to the French invaders. Spain proved once again a theater for the power politics of the rest of Europe.

Joseph Bonaparte fled from Madrid, but was soon thereafter returned to power after his brother arrived from France to personally direct military operations. The English and the Portuguese both sent forces onto Spanish soil for operations against Napoleon's forces. Complicating matters was the support for Bonaparte of well-equipped bands of liberal Spaniards, who saw in Napoleon's revolutionary policies the hopes of ridding Spain of its traditional dynasties of despotic kings. Much aided by the English—and especially Wellington, who recaptured Madrid from the French in 1812 and has remained a hero in Spain ever since—the Spaniards eventually pushed Napoleon, who faced greater problems in Central Europe and on the Russian front, out of Spain altogether in 1813.

To power came Ferdinand VII (1814–33), who was said to have done only one thing consistently and well—persecuting and punishing liberal Spaniards. In the wake of one of the many rebellions that punctuated his reign (this one in 1823), he was captured by his subjects, who came very close to reinitiating the series of liberal reforms that he had repeatedly sabotaged. Horrified at what they considered impertinent behavior toward a king, the other monarchies of Europe opted to send a French army in to release him, which it did, ironically, under the pretext of liberal enlightenment. Once released by the embarrassed French forces, Ferdinand retracted the promises of clemency that he had made, and ordered the execution of many hundreds of liberal Madrileños.

Madrid's hold on its South and Central American colonies had already been severely weakened by around 1800. By 1822 Colombia was recognized as an independent nation by the United States, and Mexico and Colombia were recognized by Great Britain in 1824. Other Spanish-speaking colonies began their wars of independence in droves, drawing fertile propaganda from real and imagined stories of monarchical repressions manifested upon the people of Madrid. Upon the death of Ferdinand VII in 1833, his daughter was declared Queen Isabella II, an act which immediately provoked armed rebellions in the streets of the capital. So potent were the demands of the liberals that she—partly to save her throne—called for the revision of the Spanish constitution in 1837 and the establishment of parliamentary models of government. Later she retracted these positions, an act that led to further armed conflicts.

The year 1833 is also marked by the formal beginnings of the Catalán *renaixença,* wherein a resurgence of Catalonian pride in literature, architecture, language, and politics began to whittle away at the unrivaled monolith of Madrid's supremacy in Spain.

Concrete examples of the new queen's works included the establishment of the Canal de Isabella II, which still supplies much of Madrid with its water, and the introduction of gas lighting. In 1850 the railway was introduced into Spain, connecting Madrid to the regal but not-very-distant resort of Aranjuez. A year later Queen Isabella opened the Teatro Real, dedicated to the presentation of Spanish drama and music. A larger-than-life bronze statue in her honor still graces the park in front of the theater today.

Isabella's reign was accented with endless fears on the part of both Britain and France that her political and matrimonial flirtations would upset the European balance of power. These fears proved correct when she and her younger sister, in defiance of a series of carefully orchestrated diplomatic agreements, both married French-born members of the Bourbon family in 1846 on the same day—an event that infuriated both Lord Palmerston in London and the growing numbers of Spanish liberals. The final quarter century of her reign was marked by endless changes within her ministries, countless intrigues, and continuing civil strife. It ended in defeat after a revolution in 1868 sent her fleeing from Madrid over the border into France. A republic was born to replace her.

THE FIRST REPUBLIC Despite its initial euphoria caused by the departure of Spain's controversial and not-very-bright queen, the five-year life span of Spain's First Republic (1870–75) was also punctuated with repetitive bouts of civil strife. During 1870 alone, four different presidents held office in Madrid, each deposed after only a few months or weeks. It soon became very clear to all observers that only the army could restore order. Many regions of Spain during this era rejected all authority from Madrid and instituted interim governments of their own. After crushing opposition in Andalusia, the Basque country, and Catalonia, the army disbanded Madrid's Parliament and imposed military authority under General Serrano, who eventually restored power, in 1875, back to the Bourbons.

THE LATER BOURBONS First of the later Bourbons was Alfonso XII (1875–85), who enjoyed almost immediate support. He initiated a new Parliament (Cortés) in 1876 based on universal suffrage, and negotiated a well-intentioned peace treaty with Basque separatists in the north. With peace in effect, Madrid was able to send large armies of Spanish soldiers to quell the increasingly violent revolutions occurring in such New World colonies as Cuba. Meanwhile, the socialist theories of Marx and the Anarchist views of Bakunin gained strong footholds among workers in both Madrid and Barcelona, as disputes arose regarding which of the political philosophies would exercise ideological control. Between 1880 and 1900 Madrid endured endless and usually violent protests, each of which was followed by harsh repression from the increasingly beleaguered government. Simultaneous with these upheavals, Madrid acquired its first tram lines, electric lights, and telephones.

Alfonso XII died in 1885, leaving two daughters and a pregnant second wife, who unwittingly revived the Madrileños' traditional fears of the Hapsburgs because of her lineage as second cousin to Archduke Ferdinand of Austria. Six months later a son was born to the newly widowed Queen Regent and named Alfonso XIII.

During the time of Alfonso's infancy, much of which was spent in and around Madrid, Spain swung like a pendulum between liberal and conservative governments—a process that eventually bankrupted the treasury and led to massive unrest. A misguided series of stiff import duties benefited only a handful of wealthy industrialists, throwing many laborers out of work.

Armed conflicts in the Spanish colonies of Cuba and nearby Morocco sapped Spain of both its human and fiscal resources. In 1898 the Spanish-American War stripped Spain of all but a handful of its colonies—specifically Puerto Rico, Cuba, the Philippines, the larger of the Mariana Islands, and the Sulu Islands—leaving the once-mighty Spanish Empire a ghostly shred of its former grandeur. All that remained under Madrid's control were a handful of impoverished and sun-baked territories in north and northwest Africa, including sections of Morocco and what was referred to at the time as the Spanish Sahara. Even these were soon to prove enormously troublesome.

Alfonso XIII, a spoiled and willful child, was crowned king of Spain at the age of 16 in 1902, shortly after the population of Madrid had reached 500,000. Very much under the influences of the Catholic church and ultra-right-wing reactionary forces, Alfonso's decisions were both conservative and controversial, often aimed at the sabotage of any hope of libertarian reform. Even his marriage to a descendant of Britain's royal family, Victoria Regina of Battenburg, in 1906, caused a major political upheaval—as did his symbolic proclamations in defiance of libertarian models. General strikes in 1912 threatened the country with chaos.

Although Spain was spared a direct role in the horrors of World War I, civil strife and increasing hostilities in Morocco were almost as painful as the ravages suffered by the rest of Europe. All parties agreed in theory to avoid an active participation in World War I, but the country was divided further between the conservatives, who favored Germany, and the liberals, who favored Britain and the Allies. As ideological walls were made ever stronger between Monarchists and Republicans, Spain grew increasingly tense and distraught as political rages swept through the corridors of power in Madrid.

During this era, the landscape of Madrid continued to grow and expand. The Gran Vía was laid out in 1910 and ultimately completed in 1931, whereupon it became the focus of much that was fashionable and worldly. Vast new districts, including the Salamanca and Argüelles districts, were opened as the city's borders expanded to cope with its growing population. In 1919 the first commercial air flight was initiated between Madrid and Barcelona, and in 1921 Madrid's metro (subway) system was inaugurated. On March 8 of the same year, Eduardo Dato—mayor of Madrid and an influential mediator who had been working to achieve unity among the Conservatives of Spain—was assassinated in Madrid, sending waves of fear through the Spanish establishment and resulting in harsh crackdowns by the government. The same year, the Spanish army— motivated by the passionate endorsement of Alfonso XIII— embarked impetuously on a course of military action against Moroccan insurgents in the Rif Mountains of North Africa. The almost-immediate result was a crushing and humiliating defeat at the Battle of Anual, as well as the loss of vast territories in eastern Morocco. The general in charge of the Spanish army (Manuel Silvestre) committed suicide; and in the wake of his death, a republican-sponsored enquiry unearthed massive fiscal improprieties, which caused an even greater uproar.

DICTATORS VERSUS ANARCHISTS   In 1923, fears of continued anarchy led to the establishment of a conservative dictatorship of military strongman Primo de Rivera, which lasted from 1923 to 1930, and with whom Alfonso XIII closely associated himself. De Rivera's son, José Antonio Primo de Rivera, significantly, went on to establish the Spanish Fascist party in 1933. After the collapse of the elder Primo de Rivera's dictatorship in 1930, the king reluctantly agreed to municipal elections, which resulted in an overwhelming victory of the Republicans over the Monarchists. Bereft of supporters but refusing to formally abdicate, King Alfonso XIII left Spain on April 14, 1931, for the French border to live forever in exile. On the day of his departure the provisional government of the second republic was established. Alfonso XIII had bequeathed one of the most inept monarchical records in Spanish history to the people of Madrid. His tenure had witnessed the arrival and departure of 33 different finance ministers—none of whom was ever able to accumulate enough power or credibility to effect lasting change. Perhaps more important, the distrust of government that his unyielding policies engendered were to have lasting effects on Spain.

THE SECOND REPUBLIC From its base in Madrid, Spain's second attempt at democratic government did what it could to hold together the country's entrenched factions. On the right stood the Catholic church, the army, and the landed aristocracy. On the left stood the "anarcho-syndicalists," the socialists, and the regional autonomists, who saw in the left greater chances for their eventual independence. As riots from both the left and the right disrupted the social fabric of Spanish life, the country's economy withered. In January 1933, women (who were at the time perceived as a conservative bastion within Spain) were given the right to vote, more as an incentive for the retention of power by the right, according to cynics, than as a libertarian reform.

THE CIVIL WAR Although the Spanish Civil War originated among military officers in Morocco, it was in Madrid that much of the drama unfolded. In 1936, frustrated at the fragmentation of their platforms, a wide spectrum of leftist and trade-union groups formed a unified and powerful voting block that incorporated anarchists, republicans, Trotskyites, socialists, and Marxists into one coherent whole. Their United Front swept the 1936 elections, a victory that immediately sparked a wholesale murder of perceived capitalists; the opening of prisons throughout Spain; almost 350 labor strikes; the burning of almost 200 churches, many of them in Madrid; and the attempted arson of 250 other churches throughout Spain.

Spain ran wild, with the elected popular-front coalition wholly unable to cope with the trauma. On July 18, 1936, in reaction to what was perceived as a dangerous threat to law and order, an army mutiny led by Gen. Francisco Franco took command of Spanish troops stationed in Morocco. Within two days the mutiny had spread throughout the entire Spanish army, an act that sparked the Spanish Civil War and some of the most passionately defended ideological platforms of the 20th century.

Franco's strongholds incorporated virtually all of Spain except Madrid, Barcelona, and sections of the north and northwest. Some historians claim that if Madrid had capitulated, there would have been no civil war at all, only a peaceable takeover of the government. Franco and his forces labeled themselves Nationalists, claiming that theirs was no mere *pronunciamiento* by a corrupt monarch, but a *movimiento nacional*. In opposition were the leaders of the previously elected popular front, who at great disadvantage fought against virtually the entire armed elite of Spain. To make matters even more difficult for the popular front (thereafter known as the Republicans), their unified coalition soon began to break apart, thus losing its claim to legality and the popular vote.

Suddenly, amid massive international publicity, hordes of volunteers—many of them communist sympathizers—came to the aid of the beleaguered Republicans, who held out in Madrid and certain cities of the east and north. Simultaneously, well-equipped and well-trained Franco-led Nationalists received massive supplies and modern weapons from Fascist-run Germany and Italy— supposedly the result of prior clandestine agreements. Contemporary participants such as Antonio Machada (a meditative and austere

Spanish poet who died in the conflict in 1939) declined to label the conflict a civil war, but rather an all-out German-Italian invasion.

Some of the most notorious massacres of the 20th century were committed by members of both sides. These included priests and everyday citizens from towns as diverse as Guernica, Badajoz, Toledo, Barcelona, and Bilbao. Saved from immediate conquest because of a last-minute detour by the nationalists to help comrades beleaguered in the Alcázar at Toledo, Madrid rallied its forces and endured 28 months of siege. The government moved from Madrid first to Valencia then briefly to Barcelona, and eventually to the Costa Brava resort of Figueres. Madrid was left in charge of a defense council headed by Gen. José Miaja. Real power was held in siege-ridden Madrid by the unions, who adhered to communist doctrines by banning all forms of religious worship in Madrid churches—a ban lifted only after the entry of Franco into the city three years later.

Residents of Madrid survived on two ounces of food daily, and as hundreds of city residents died of starvation, attack from Franco's forces eventually proved almost unnecessary. On March 28, 1939, Madrid, the last bastion of Republicanism, collapsed as 200,000 Nationalist troops entered the city without a struggle. The war had lasted two years and nine months, ruined Spain, and cost an estimated million lives.

THE FRANCO YEARS With very few other options to choose from, France, Britain, and the United States all formally recognized Franco's government—which had set up headquarters in Madrid—before the end of 1939. Franco's Italian and German troops marched triumphantly out of Madrid during a massive parade there on May 19, 1939. Franco immediately granted strong financial credits for the reconstruction of ruined houses and public buildings. Spain began rebuilding its industry, which eventually transformed Madrid into one of Europe's great industrial powers.

When World War II erupted, Franco immediately disassociated himself with the Fascists of Germany and Italy, declaring Spain at first nonbelligerent and later neutral. A few days later he signed, and later reinforced, a treaty of nonaggression with Portugal, thereby ensuring peace with one of Britain's strongest and oldest allies. The conquest of Catholic Poland by the combined efforts of Germany and the Soviet Union greatly offended the deeply Catholic Spain. Spain did, however, send troops to fight in the Ukraine, in 1942, with the Nazis against the dreaded Communists. In a speech he made in 1942, Franco reiterated a line from which he never wavered: "Yesterday, today, and tomorrow, for the countries of Europe there exists only one danger—Communism."

Throughout World War II, Franco, in one of the most amazing diplomatic feats of the 20th century, managed to avoid too close an association with Fascist Germany and Italy, despite the many philosophies and scandals he shared with their leaders: One of these was the almost complete suppression of most civil liberties. Although

---

IMPRESSIONS

In winter especially she seems a capital half-frozen in the attitudes of a past generation.
—JAMES MORRIS, 1964

industry and the beginnings of tourism grew during the Franco years, Spain slumbered—a repressed and reactionary head of a once-great empire, dozing in the streaming Iberian sunlight. Street crime was almost nonexistent, yet so was intellectual and artistic expression as many of the country's greatest artists and scientists chose to take up residence elsewhere.

MODERN SPAIN Franco's death in 1975 has been defined as Spain's "national tragedy" coming to an end. An intricate series of events brought back to power a member of the Bourbon monarchy, King Juan Carlos I, a sophisticated member of Franco's inner circle and grandson of the much-despised Alfonso XIII. Sensing the shift in the national mood—and determined to be a better spokesman than his grandfather—he has skillfully directed the path of his country along libertarian lines that have made Madrid one of the most admired capitals of Europe.

In 1978 the Centrist government of Adolfo Suarez adopted a new constitution as part of a national referendum that restored parliamentary government, with strong doses of autonomy for Spain's far-flung regions.

In 1982 the charismatic and articulate Felipe González brought new vigor to the Spanish Socialist Workers' Party (PSOE) by reviving Spain's role within Europe and by administering its membership into the EEC (European Economic Community) in 1986.

The *movida madrileña* (Madrid happening) of the late 1980s was a cultural, social, and intellectual renaissance that poured a surge of creative energy into the city skyline, making Madrid a lot of fun to be in—the envy of creative circles throughout the world.

In 1992 Madrid was named "cultural capital of Europe," a heady recognition of the rebirth of its self-confidence after the years of unhappy repression.

FAMOUS SPANIARDS

Miguel de Cervantes Saavedra (1547–1616) The reigning figure of Spanish letters led a life of more adventure than his fictional characters. A former soldier who participated in the Armada, he was later captured and sold into slavery in Algiers. In unrelated incidents, he was twice imprisoned: accused of murder and for failure to pay his debts. During his lifetime he wrote 20–30 plays, only two of which have survived. During one of his prison sojourns, he began a tale of an idealist chasing windmills across the plains of La Mancha. Later released as *Don Quixote,* it reigns today as the most superlative work of literature ever produced in the Spanish language.

Mariano José de Larra ("Le Figaro"; 1809–37) The most self-destructive of the Madrileño romantics of the early 19th century. De Larra's lofty ideals and abortive imbroglios have sometimes been compared to those of Byron. Educated in France, he returned to Madrid at the age of 17 as a drama critic and political analyst. Increasingly revered as a famous personality (whose plays, ironically, were resounding critical failures), he maintained a rigidly entrenched opposition to the absolutist kings. Mourning his unfulfilled love for a much older married woman and the frustrations of his political stalemates, he shot himself at the age of 27 in what might be the most romanticized suicide in Spanish history.

Tirso de Molina (Fray Gabriel Téllez; 1584–1648) Often

compared to Shakespeare, he is considered one of the three great dramatists of the Golden Age of Spanish literature. (The other contenders include Lope de Vega and Pedro Calderón de la Barca.) Designated as the official historian of the monastic order of Mercedarians, he spent most of his time writing comedies and plays, perhaps 300 in all, although only a few have survived. His first work, *Los Cigarrales de Toledo,* was published in 1621. His most famous plays were *El Burlador de Sevilla* and *El Condenado por Desconfiado.* In his day he was a great favorite with audiences in Madrid.

Tomás de Torquemada (1420–98)   A "name that will live in infamy," he became the inquisitor-general to Isabella and Ferdinand in 1483. An impassioned (and probably insane) fanatic, he hated everything that wasn't Catholic or Spanish. As confessor to the Catholic monarchs, he was instrumental in the expulsion of the Jews and *Moriscos* (converted Muslims) from Spain. Torquemada tried people for sorcery, witchcraft, heresy, necromancy, bigamy, blasphemy, and usury. He obtained "evidence" through torture. At least 2,000 people were executed by this man, who, legend says, never ate unless the tongue of a scorpion was placed beside his plate.

Félix Lope de Vega y Carpio (1562–1635)   The most prolific writer in the history of Spain, boasting between 1,500 and 1,800 plays (only a few hundred of which have survived), he is viewed as the creator of Spanish comedy and the greatest playwright of the Golden Age of Spanish literature. Vega led an adventurous early life and served in the Spanish Armada. Ordained as a priest after the sudden death of his son and wife, he moved to Philip II's new capital, where he spent the remaining 25 years of his life, many of them tragically. His most famous surviving plays include *El Caballero de Olmedo, Peribañez,* and *Fuenteovejuna.*

El Greco (Domenikos Theotokópoulos; 1541–1614)   Born in Crete, he emigrated, as did hundreds of other artists of his era, to the Spanish Empire with its wealth of commissions. He was trained in Italy under Titian, but his greatness was not acknowledged by critics until late in the 19th century. Spain's best-known adherent of Mannerist painting (a stylized evolution of the late baroque), El Greco painted his masterpiece, *The Burial of Count Orgaz* in Toledo, 42 miles southwest of Madrid. Preferring colors which Philip II, among others, considered lurid, he became famous for the elongated limbs of his subjects, as well as his highly evocative pictorial depictions of mystical ecstasy. Considered insane by local residents, he was fond of publicly declaring that Michelangelo had no talent.

Francisco Bahamonde Franco (1892–1975)   *El Generalísimo* or *El Caudillo,* as he was called, Franco was the fascist dictator of Spain from the end of the Spanish Civil War until his death. A soldier from the age of 15, Franco, as all-powerful ruler of Spain, imposed rigid censorship and a stifling grip on the country's arts and commerce throughout his reign. Siding with Hitler during World War II, he declared neutrality when the tides of victory turned toward the Allies, thereby managing to retain his position during the unsettling years of the late 1940s and 1950s. Declared "Head of State for Life" in 1947, he eventually designated King Juan Carlos I as his successor, passing over Juan Carlos's less malleable father, whom Franco publicly referred to as "the pretender."

St. Teresa of Ávila (originally Teresa de Cepeda y Ahumada;

1515–82) Disgusted with what she considered the corruption of the early 16th century church, she is known today as the most pragmatic and down-to-earth mystic in the history of the Catholic church. Inspired to found a religious order (Las Discalced) in which the original rules of the Carmelite Order were strictly observed, she was eventually assigned to write her spiritual autobiography by her religious superiors. Until very recent times this was reputedly the third most widely read book (after the Bible and *Don Quixote*) in Spain. Upon her death in Ávila, it is said that a fragrant, violet-hued oil poured forth from her tomb. She was canonized in 1622 and was made a doctor of the church in 1970.

Consuelo Vello ("La Fornarina"; 1884–1915) This turn-of-the-century darling of the *zarzuela* theaters of the Gran Vía was revered for her beauty, talent, and charm. The daughter of a washerwoman and a member of the Guardia Civil, she became the most famous Spanish actress to date. Giuseppe Verdi was numbered among her fans. After a life of much-publicized melodrama, she died at the age of 31, the result of a botched surgical procedure. Her grave at Madrid's cemetery of San Isidro is still visited by well-wishers today.

ART

By the time of Madrid's establishment in 1561, many of the great artists of the Spanish medieval age had wrought their influence upon the country's aesthetic landscape. Philip II—conscious of his status as a Hapsburg, with distinct links and possessions in faraway Flanders (Belgium)—espoused the Hispano-Flemish style of painting, with its penchant for verdant landscapes, rich depictions of fabrics and jewelry, and its elevated presentation of subjects in both group and individual portraits.

Simultaneously, a strong tradition had already been established whereby Spanish artists embarked for training in heroic painting in Italy, returning with an altered sense of perspective, classical references, sophisticated interplays of light with shadow, and a sense of heroic grandeur. Italian Mannerism—a development of late baroque painting identified by its nervously stylized depictions of mystical events—became fashionable in Spain and was at the time of Madrid's establishment best exemplified by the works of El Greco (Domenico Theotokópoulos; 1540–1614). Born on the island of Crete (in Greece), he emigrated with the flood of other artists and artisans to Spain, looking for the many commissions that the newly monied kingdom was prepared to pay for abundantly. Although he chose to settle in Toledo, 42 miles southwest of Madrid, his work and influence slowly affected the sense of dignity and grandeur that were associated with the newly developing capital. Unfortunately, El Greco's unusual and very strong colors and the elongated limbs of his subjects did not please Philip II, who preferred more conservative— and more Italianized—artworks to adorn the chapels and endless anterooms of El Escorial.

The construction and embellishments of Madrid coincided with what is today referred to as the Golden Age of Spanish painting (1550–1650). The Royal Collections—which later comprised the foundation of the collection in the Prado—was established during the reigns of Charles V, the previously mentioned Philip II, and Philip IV. At least some of these were acquired from the fiscally embarrassed English monarch Charles II during some of the most spectacular art sales of all time. Especially popular were works by the Venetian painter Titian, whose formal settings and mythical/heroic subject matter appealed to the empire-building Spanish monarchs.

Several talented Spaniards, most notably Juan Fernández Navarrete "El Mudo" (1526–79), rushed to emulate Titian's style, infusing Italian mannerism with a Spanish flavor. From this developed the Escorial School of *tenebrist* painters, whose style quickly spread to faraway Seville. One devoted member of this school who defined many of its terms was the Andalusia-born painter Francisco Pacheco (1564–1654), best known for his patronage of the young Velásquez, who eventually married Pacheco's daughter.

Velásquez (1599–1660), later accepted as the finest painter to emerge from Spain, is said to have prefigured certain tenets of 19th-century impressionism with his use of light to illuminate and define the space around his figures. Today entire wings in the Prado are devoted to his works, which include *Christ in the House of Martha and Mary, Musical Trio,* and an entire and very fascinating series of portraits of the royal family. Ironically, many of Velásquez's portraits were copied by talented artisans for presentation to foreign dignitaries. Today even well-trained experts are hard-pressed to tell the copies from the originals.

Meanwhile, only Seville competed with Madrid for supremacy in painting. Famous Seville artists included Zurbarán (1589–1664), known for his dramatic use of bright light and shadow in the style of Caravaggio; and Bartolomé Esteban Murillo (1617–82), noted for the truthful yet relaxed postures of his subjects. Murillo modified baroque themes with occasional doses of sentimentality. Also important was Juan de Valdés Leal (1622–90), known for the sometimes-confusing sense of violence which often mars his works.

Meanwhile, other important painters in the School of Madrid included Juan Bautista Maino (1578–1649), Antonio de Pereda (1608–78), and José Antolinez (1635–75). Painting in religious contexts, they were also known as skilled draftsmen and colorists, often emulating the Flemish style of van Dyck. The most unusual, and perhaps the most insecure, member of the school included Claudio Coello (1642–93), who spent seven laborious years on a portrait of Charles II worshipping the Sagrada Forma. Today that work hangs in the Sacristy of El Escorial.

With the takeover of the throne of Spain by the French-born Bourbon dynasties, the official tastes in Spanish art turned distinctly toward Spain's Gallic neighbor. From Paris were imported such artists as Michel-Ange Houasse, Michel Van Loo, and Jean Ranc, who were immediately feted and officially promoted as the artistic saviors of Spanish painting. Fueled by the then-prevalent French tastes, official Spanish art became increasingly preoccupied with the heroic and mythological themes popular at Versailles. Many Spanish painters simply mimicked these themes mindlessly, producing little of enduring value until a Czech-born artist, Anton Rafael Mengs (1728–79) moved to Madrid to execute a series of fine portraits whose conceptions were much emulated for years to come.

One of Mengs's most prominent students and admirers became the most famous Spanish painter of his era, the heavily politicized Francisco de Goya (1746–1828). During the 14 years he spent designing cartoons (designs and themes) for wall hangings in the Royal Tapestry Factory, he was deeply influenced by the bucolic outdoor scenes of the English artist Hogarth and the Italian artist and decorator G. B. Tiepolo. Later, his portraits, usually in grays, of famous Madrileños helped him attain the rank of court painter to Charles IV. Unfortunately, the unvarnished realism of his subsequent portraits of the far-from-attractive king and members of his family caused a considerable flutter from the courtiers and gossips. The controversial portraits were followed by a satirical series of engravings depicting ignorant and licentious priests and gluttonous and unprincipled aristocrats; these earned Goya powerful enemies who would plague him all his life.

The political betrayals and bloody atrocities in Madrid during Napoleon's occupation provided subject matter for some of the most enduring paintings in the history of Europe. One of Goya's particularly graphic series, *The Disasters of War,* prefigured the scope and scale of the genocides and military horrors that would follow in the next century. These artistic, and perhaps psychic, visions occurred simultaneously with the artist's increasing deafness, which began at the age of 47. These factors probably contributed to the anguish of his world-famous "Black Paintings." Today displayed in the Prado, they are probably the best visual depiction of paranoia, rage, and despair ever created.

Goya died, a political exile, in Bordeaux, France. His body was reinterred in 1919, placed in a vault of Madrid's Church of San Antonio de la Florida, whose interior he had frescoed. Today it is a site of pilgrimage for art lovers from around the world.

The 19th century produced an array of genre, portrait, and landscape artists who catered to the demands of Madrid's growing number of newly rich capitalists. Among the most famous of these were **Eduardo Rosales** (1836–74), and **Mariano Fortuny** (1838–74), a resident of Rome and Madrid and famous for his occasionally frivolous dominance in Spanish art before the rise of impressionism. Also important was **Joaquín Sorolla** (1862–1923), known for his beach scenes of the Costa Brava and for his portraits of everyday workers. A resident of Madrid from 1912 until his death, he is also closely associated with the city of Valencia.

By the end of the century, as impressionism and the roots of modern art took hold of the artistic psyche of Madrid, such artists as the cubist **Juan Gris** (1887–1927) and muralists such as **José María Sert** (1874–1945) and **Daniel Vazquez Diaz** (1882–1969) made indelible impressions on the way the world looks at line and color.

Among 20th-century artists, the most incontestably famous of them all was **Pablo Ruiz Picasso** (1881–1973). Long exiled from Spain for his political views and the fame of his sometimes-politicized paintings, he created his own stereotype of the brilliant Spanish artist living and working in an exiled and heroic isolation. Likewise, **Joan Miró** (1893–1983), whose brightly colored masterpieces helped create a poetic vision of the subconscious, moved from Madrid to the more liberalized artistic scene of Paris. Later he spent increasing amounts of time in Barcelona as well.

Finally, Barcelona native **Salvador Dalí** (1904–88) was the most influential surrealistic painter of all time, famous for his personal idiosyncracies and his iconoclastic ways of viewing reality. Unfortunately, many critics cite the decline of his work into sales-related gimmickry and exhibitionism toward the emotionally unbalanced end of his life.

During the late 1980s, Madrid reemerged as the undisputed centerpiece of all artistic production in Spain. Postmodern artists who fed (and still feed) upon the city's vivid cultural life have included painters **Féderico Amet** and **Miguel Barcelo,** and such sculptors as **Jorge de Oteiza, Pablo Serrano,** and **Miguel Ortiz Berrocal.**

ARCHITECTURE

Many of the major currents in Spanish architecture were already well-entrenched by the time Philip II decided to establish his capital at Madrid. What awaited him was a small provincial town with a scattering of fortifications originally laid by the Moors, and an unpretentious core of Gothic buildings. The most noteworthy of these includes the Torre de los Lujanes, site of the imprisonment of the French king François I in 1525. Much blackened by time, it still stands in the heart of Madrid's tiny Gothic neighborhood, near the Plaza de la Villa.

Inspired by lofty dreams of a capital worthy of the size and wealth of the Spanish Empire, Philip immediately approved the classical revival style whose columns, porticoes, and proportions emulated the grandeur of ancient Rome. One of his preferred architects, Herrera, designed parts of the new capital, as well as the somber majesty of the king's semi-monastic retreat at El Escorial, 30 miles west of Madrid. Inspired by these precedents, royal architect Juan Gomez de Mora laid out the dignified symmetry of the era's most visible remaining landmark, the Plaza Mayor, completed in 1606.

The Bourbons, whose first member ascended the throne after much bloodshed in 1700, opted for a graceful neoclassicism of the type then sweeping through their homeland in France. Today many of the monumental buildings that line the showcase boulevards of Madrid, including those near the Prado Museum and the Alcala Gate, are derivatives of the Bourbon taste for the symmetry and restrained opulence of the French aesthetic. Ample use was made at this time, incidentally, of the rose-pink brick that the region produced in such abundance.

Surprisingly, although many of the buildings from these eras are dignified and, at their best, even graceful, Madrid possesses relatively few monuments erected to the glories of Spain's imperial empire. Considering the size of that empire, and the wealth produced by it, the city's architecture—though splendid—is surprisingly unpretentious. (London, Paris, and Vienna, also seats of empire, have many more grandiose monuments than Madrid, for example.) At least part of Madrid's human scale is because of the many political upheavals that punctuated the city's 19th-century history. Much of this is probably also because of the Spanish appreciation of street life on an intimate and personalized scale. The combined effect seems to divide Madrid's vast precincts into a series of well-defined, and often very charming, villagelike neighborhoods.

After around 1850, the wealth and growing power of the newly prosperous Madrileño bourgeoisie called for the construction of hundreds of new villas, town houses, and elegant apartment buildings. The result was the knocking down of the 17th-century ramparts that ringed the city's core and the creation of several new districts, which are today collectively referred to as the Ensanche. These districts incorporated each of the different styles of Iberia, including mudéjar/Neo-Andalusian, neoclassical, Neo-Gothic, art nouveau, Neo-Renaissance, and a scattering of the iconoclastic and organic styles then springing up in Catalonia. These districts are among the most architecturally interesting in Madrid. Specific neighborhoods that are still considered upscale embodiments of 19th-century capitalistic wealth include the Salamanca and Argüelles districts, set to the northwest and northeast, respectively, of the city's 16th- and 17th-century core.

Since the end of World War II, Madrid's population has grown so rapidly that the city has almost split its architectural seams. In response, vast new neighborhoods bristling with all descriptions of modern buildings have sprung up. Their design ranges from insipid and angular blocks of low-cost apartment buildings erected during the Franco years to recently completed examples of some of the most dramatic modern and postmodern design in Europe.

LITERATURE

One of Spain's most worthwhile by-products has been its fertile outpouring of literature. Roots of the art form were already flourishing long before Madrid was established, although, significantly, the city's foundation and subsequent population explosion coincided almost exactly with what is considered the Golden Age of Spanish literature.

The cultural streams that contributed to Madrid's eventual dominance of Spanish literature began with the ancient Romans. Ancient writers who composed on what is now Spanish soil included **Seneca the Elder** (54 B.C.–A.D. 39), **Seneca the Stoic** (4 B.C.–A.D. 65), the epic poet **Lucan** (A.D. 39–65), and the epigrammist **Martial** (42–104).

The next surge of literary output in Spain came from Muslim, not Christian, sources. By 800 the Hispano-Arabic homeland of Al Andalus was considered one of the Mediterranean's most brilliant beacons of culture. Astronomy, medicine, architecture, and literature flourished as Córdoba became the largest city in Europe (with an estimated population of 500,000), with both Seville and Granada following close behind. Notable poets included **Yosef the Scribe** (c. 1000), **Ibn Quzman** (c 1100), **Muccadam ben Muafa** (c. 900), **Ibn Rushd** (Averröes; 1126–1198), and the Jewish mystic **Maimonides** (1135–1204). Considered among the most brilliant philosophers of their era, both Averröes and Maimonides (writing, ironically, in Arabic) forged landmark reconciliations of Aristotelian logic with the tenets of their respective faiths.

By the 1200s, Christian Spain was beginning to assert its own literary identity. In Barcelona, whose merchants flourished as competitors of Venice, Catalán poetry fed richly off Provençale models in neighboring France. In the heartland of Spain (Castile, the then-independent province that contains what is now Madrid) **Alfonso X the Wise** (1252–84) repressed the use of Latin, favoring instead the vernacular dialect of Castilian. This preference had been established during the mid-1100s by the fame of the epic poem *El cantar del mio Cid* (*The Song of My Cid*), set down in writing from what might have been a long-standing oral tradition. Its subject, dear to the hearts of the Catholic monarchs, involved the reconquest of Iberia from the Moors. A noted poet and scholar in his own right, Alfonso gathered the literary traditions of ancient Rome, the Arabic world, medieval Christianity, and mystical Judaism into his Castilian court.

The almost-immediate result was a surge of original literary creativity. **Juan Ruiz,** a prominent archbishop, compiled *The Book of Spiritual Love* around 1300, a semi-satirical/semi-mystical tract exposing ecclesiastic corruption, set in the context of both lyrical and narrative verse.

By the time Madrid was selected as the center of the Spanish Empire, Castilian had entrenched itself as the literary language of a united Spain. **Bartolomé de las Casas** (1474–1566) defended the dignity of the New World's native peoples in his tract *The Tears of the Indians.* Late in the 1400s, a religiously motivated mystery play, *Misteri d'Elch,* offered hordes of Christian pilgrims an insight into Catholic spiritualism.

The real sophistication of the era's literary output, however, dealt with secular rather than religious themes. One of the earliest of these was the raucous and earthy novel *The Comedy of Calixto and Melibea (La Celestina),* by **Fernando de Rojas** (1465–1541). Even more prominent was a particularly prolific playwright, **Félix Lope de Vega y Carpio** (1562–1635). A participant in the humiliating defeat of the Spanish Armada in 1588, and an adventurer in both the romantic and military sense of the word, he produced more than 1,800 plays, 400 of which have survived. Flawed by their sometimes hasty execution, they are nonetheless considered seminal to the beginnings of a purely Madrileño repertoire of plays.

Lope de Vega shares his literary stardom with two other famous Madrileños: **Tirso de Molina** (1584–1648), and **Pedro Calderón de la Barca** (1600–81). Tirso de Molina, in one of the 300 plays he wrote, was the original creator of the amorous character of Don Juan, whose fame spread instantly throughout Europe, assisted greatly by the musical efforts, a century later, of Mozart.

The Golden Age, fueled by the excitement and wealth of Spain's expanding colonial empire, produced such disparate writers as **St. Teresa of Ávila** (1515–82) and her follower, **St. John of the Cross** (1542–91); and a series of poets who included **Luis de Góngora** (1561–1627), whose Castilian verse adopted the poetic models of the ancient Romans. Also noteworthy was the bitterly satirical social critic **Francisco de Quevedo** (1580–1645).

Each of these writers paved the way for the greatest author in Spanish history, **Miguel de Cervantes** (1547–1616). His *Don Quixote de la Mancha* remains one of the most enduring classics of world-class literature, avidly read by contemporaries who included Shakespeare, and by such modern novelists as Proust, Nabokov, James Joyce, and virtually every notable author of the Hispanic world today.

With the arrival of the French-derived Bourbon dynasty on the throne of Spain, authors drew more and more of their inspiration from the neoclassical models then popular in the literary salons of Paris and in such power centers as Versailles. **Llandro de Moratín** (1760–1828), chief librarian to Joseph Bonaparte, the puppet ruler placed on the throne by French intervention, produced plays and poems based without apology on French precedents. **Gaspar Melchor de Jovellanos** (1744–1811), poet, economist, and politician, kept his finger on the pulse of the Enlightenment through his frequent experiments with French models.

A contemporary, however, who broke the elevated tone of the

salon-inspired writing of his day, was **Juan Ramón de la Cruz** (1731–94); his characters elevated Madrid's working classes to the status of cultural heros. An avowed enemy of the materialistic and social-climbing bourgeoisie, he penned one of his era's most famous satirical works, *The Tertulias of Madrid.*

During the 19th century Spanish Romanticism led to the development of many dozens of dashingly theatrical literary heroes—flamboyant in their personal lives and endlessly controversial in the then-prevalent climate of monarchical absolutism. Spanish writers—in trends which paralleled those in the rest of Europe—rejected the reason and objectivity of neoclassicism and embraced instead the emotionalism and subjectivity of Romanticism.

The beginning of the Romantic movement in Spanish art and literature is today defined as the accession to the Spanish throne of Isabella II in 1833. The brief period of freedom that preceded her eventual, and much-resented, autocratic crackdown permitted the return from exile of many politically active writers and politicians. The art of satire became increasingly fine-tuned, exemplified by such writers as **Mariano José de Larra** (1809–37), **José Zorilla** (1817–93), and the pugnacious political dissident **José de Espronceda** (1808–42). Despite the beauty of Espronceda's poetry, his most famous work was a novel, *El estudiante de Salamanca* (The Student of Salamanca), which was based, as were many other literary works of the Romantic age, on the inexhaustible implications of the Don Juan legend.

In 1904 post-Romantic dramatist **José Echegaray** (1832–1916) was the first Spaniard to win the Nobel Prize for literature. Other famous Spanish writers—many of whom returned to the cultural wellsprings of Madrid—included **Vicente Blasco Ibañez** (1867–1928), author of *La barraca* (The Cabin), *Blood and Sand,* and *The Four Horsemen of the Apocalypse.* Also important (and prolific) was **Benito Pérez Galdós** (1843–1920), whose vast output (46 volumes of historical romances) led to frequent comparisons with both Balzac and Dickens.

The loss of power, money, and prestige caused by Spain's defeat during the Spanish-American War of 1898 led to a loose coalition of writers known as the Generation of 1898. Well-respected members of this group included **Ramón Valle Inclán** (1866–1936), author of four novellas (called *Sonatas*), each named after one of the seasons; the Basque-born philosopher **Miguel de Unamuno** (1864–1936), and winner of the 1922 Nobel Prize for literature; and **Jacinto Benavente** (1866–1954), author of *Los intereses creados* (Bonds of Interest). Two other major figures included **Federico García Lorca** (1898–1936), author of some of the most hauntingly beautiful drama, prose, and poetry in the history of Spain, and **Antonio Buero Vallejo** (1916–). Although many writers and poets were killed on active duty during the Spanish Civil War, the bludgeoning to death of García Lorca by Franco supporters in an Andalusian graveyard was particularly horrible.

Since the end of the Civil War, one of Madrid's most prevalent literary movements was *modernismo.* Two winners of the Nobel Prize (in 1956 and 1977, respectively) included **Juan Ramón Jiménez** (1881–1958), author of *Platero y Yo,* and **Vicente Aleixandre** (1898–1984). Also important was **José Ortega y Gasset** (1883–1955), author of *La rebelión de las masas* (Revolt of the Masses; 1930). A more recent winner of the coveted prize, this time in 1989, was **Camilo José Cela** (1916–   ), author of *La Colmena* (The Hive), who evocatively described Madrid during the artistic bleakness of the Franco years.

Since the death of Franco in 1975, new writers have cropped up on the literary landscape of Spain. They are often preoccupied with the advancement of their native regions (examples include Catalonian authors **Miguel Delibes, Carmen Laforet,** and **Monserrat Roig**). Despite the attraction of these authors for themes relating to their specific regions, they nonetheless continue to look toward the omnipresent *movida* of Madrid for their publishing contacts and at least part of their artistic inspiration.

MUSIC

Easy to recognize, Spanish music is passionate, moody, and rhythmical; and although each region of Spain produced its own distinctive variety of music, they can all be unearthed in the richly diverse nightclubs, concert halls, and theaters of Madrid.

A common thread that seems to run through the country's music is its shimmering nationalism, its pride of place, and its subliminal expression of Spain's proud and richly nuanced national identity. Spanish music is a composite of more than two millennia of cultural influences, incorporating elements from the Phoenicians, Greeks, Romans, Visigoths, Moors, Jews, Aryan gypsies, and residents of the former Spanish colonies in the Americas and Asia.

Today many of the country's musical forms are inseparable from the dance forms meant to accompany them. Joyful, exuberant, or disturbingly evocative of either collective or personal anguish, Spanish dances and the music that accompanies them are archetypically Spanish—and one of the country's most famous cultural exports.

The first written music of Spain sprang from the early Christian era, when church liturgies evolved into Visigothic chants. Before the Arab invasion, church music flourished in such population centers as Toledo, Zaragoza, and Seville, and it continued as Christian Spain developed hymns and liturgical chants in its dozens of cloistered convents and monasteries.

To this rich tapestry were added the chants and love poetry of the Arabs. From their North African kingdoms they brought with them many interesting instruments, which included the square tambourine (*adufe* in Spanish), the standard tambourine (*panderete*), drum (*atabal*), and metal castanets (*sonajas de azófar*).

During the Renaissance—whose first glimmerings arrived in Spain during the late 1400s—instrumental music became an important art form. This was especially true of pieces written for an early six-string guitar called the *vihuela*, which was later replaced by the five-string guitar during the 17th century, and eventually by the six-string Spanish guitar that is famous today.

Shortly after the establishment of Madrid in 1561, the capital began to dominate the musical life of Spain. Opera—brought to Spain from Italy during the 17th century—was encouraged by the Portuguese-born Queen Barbara of Braganza, wife of Ferdinand VI; the queen organized major operatic performances for her courtiers. Domenico Scarlatti, son of the better-known Alessandro Scarlatti, benefited from the royal patronage of the Bourbon monarchs. Living in Madrid from 1728 to 1757, he composed some of his 500 harpsichord sonatas there and taught his operatic techniques to new generations of Spanish musicians. Another composer who enjoyed Bourbon patronage was Luigi Boccherini (1743–1805), who composed part of his vast repertoire of string quartets and quintets—more than 230 in all—in Madrid beginning in 1768.

From the formal contexts of opera—which many Spaniards justifiably considered a cultural imposition from France and Italy—came the **zarzuela.** Light and sometimes sentimental musical entertainments similar to Gilbert and Sullivan operettas, they richly fulfilled the 19th century Madrileño penchant for singing, dancing, social satire, and inconsequential romantic imbroglios. Later, zarzuelas developed into a type of variety show, where plots of any kind were abandoned in favor of singing and dancing for their own sake. The art form was greatly encouraged when the Teatro de Zarzuela opened in 1856.

Shortly afterward, Queen Isabella II opened the Teatro Real for serious opera, and the Sociedad de Conciertos, established in 1865, welcomed visiting orchestras from around the world. Despite the civil unrest and general strikes that continued to plague Madrid during the late 19th century, an array of theaters catering to zarzuela and popular taste flourished—holding such foreign visitors as Nietzsche, Camille Saint-Saëns, and Giuseppe Verdi in thrall during their occasional visits to the Spanish capital.

Meanwhile, **flamenco,** a musical expression of the collective despair of Andalusia, reached widespread prominence as Spain's growing sense of nationalism embraced it as a national art form. Famous throughout the world, but with diminishing numbers of skilled performers, it incorporates rhythmic hand-clapping with guitar playing, shrill and not-very-melodious singing, and—at its best—a cathartic form of dancing. Incorporating a mixture of Jewish liturgical chanting, the calls to prayer of the Muslim *muezzin,* and Byzantine Christian rituals, it has been called a seductive blend of fierce personal passion and technical discipline. The art form's most renowned dancers have included personalities as famous as any of the country's legendary bullfighters, including La Niña de los Peines, Antonio Mairena, Antonio Chacón, and Antonio Gades.

Into this rich cultural stewpot stepped some of Spain's most enduring classical musicians, whose efforts used the above-mentioned musical forms in new and dramatic orchestral modes. Foremost among them was **Manuel de Falla** (1876–1946), who achieved international fame with such compositions as *El amor brujo* (Love, the Magician), *Nights in the Gardens of Spain,* and *El sombrero de tres picos* (The Three-Cornered Hat). Some of Falla's works were composed expressly for Spanish guitarist **Andrés Segovia;** their joint efforts set a world-class level of acceptance of the classical guitar on the concert-hall circuit.

Other important classical composers include **Joaquín Turina** (1882–1949), best defined as a musical nationalist. His most famous works include *Mujeres españolas, Danzas gitanas,* and *La procesión del Rocio.* **Isaac Albéniz** (1860–1909) carried the zeal of Spanish nationalism even further during the three years it took to compose his *Iberia Suite.* Comprised of a dozen different piano pieces derived from the ancient musical idioms of Spain, they are among the most original piano works of the late 19th century. Simultaneously, **Enrique Granados** (1867–1916), composer of the piano suite *Goyescos,* derived his inspiration from works of the quintessentially Spanish painter Francisco Goya.

Today the musical scene in Madrid includes a wide array of influences from both the Spanish past and the electronic present. This is reflected in the works of **Frederic Mompou** (1893–1987), **Joaquín Rodrigo** (1902–   ), **Lluis de Pablo** (1930–   ), and **Cristobal Halffter** (1930–   ), a musical disciple and former protégé of Falla.

The tradition of the Spanish guitar has been handed down from the previously mentioned Andrés Segovia to such new musical stars as **Narcisco Yepes** (1927–   ), although the position of premier cellist is today in dispute since the demise in 1973 of Spanish-born **Pau (Pablo) Casals.** As for singers, Spain has produced such world-class stars as **Montserrat Caballé** and **José Carreras.** Madrid has enjoyed an especially strong link to the legendary **Plácido Domingo,** who traces his birth to an address in the Spanish capital: calle Ibiza 34, which seems on the verge of becoming an impromptu site of musical pilgrimage.

RELIGION

With the exception of Poland, and perhaps Italy and Portugal, Spain has been the most staunchly and unwaveringly Catholic country in all of Europe. The Catholic church has vastly influenced world events through its cooperation with the Spanish monarchs, who dubbed themselves *Los Reyes Católicos* (the Catholic Monarchs) as proof of their devotion. Much of the passion for cultural and political expansion, and much of the inspiration for Spain's greatest buildings, were derived from the country's often-unquestioned acceptance of the tenets of the Catholic church.

The history of Spanish liberalism has usually included opposition to church presuppositions and power. Much of the social history of 19th-century Madrid reads like a series of liberal reforms with their subsequent retraction by the absolutist monarchs. Major inroads were made against church power during constitutional reforms of 1868–74 and 1931, although many of the church prerogatives and privileges were reinstated by Franco after his victory in the Civil War and his subsequent 36-year stranglehold on organized dissent within Spain. In 1953 an official concordat between the Roman Catholic church and the Franco regime reinforced many of the church's rights in exchange for its declaration of fealty and allegiance to the Spanish state.

Today Roman Catholicism is the country's established religion, with 10 metropolitan and 64 suffragan sees. The primate of all Spain is the archbishop of Toledo. Since the liberal reforms that followed the death of Franco, church authority is no longer as ironbound as before, and many otherwise devoted Catholics are openly challenging such church tenets as restrictions concerning divorce, among others.

FOLKLORE

Drawing richly on the dim prehistory of its Celtiberian past, Spain is practically awash with folkloric festivals whose mystical significance lies deep within the country's collective unconscious. Some religious historians cite the cult of bull worship as one of the most enduring mystical rituals in the Mediterranean world. Although Spain long ago embraced Catholicism with something approaching passion, the folkloric significance of the bullfight is much older, sociologists claim, than the Christian tradition.

Additionally, the Spanish folklore associated with rituals involving flamenco, cult worship of the Virgin, wedding or funeral ceremonies, and the legendary frenzies of religious processions in such places as Rocío, has preoccupied psychologists and sociologists for many years.

Despite its relatively late arrival in 1561 onto the landscape of Spain, many of the country's most famous legends concern the city of Madrid. One of them concerns the Virgen de la Almudena, one of the city's patron saints, a likeness of whom was concealed in a niche of the city's medieval fortifications during the 9th century, just before the city's capture by the Moors. Two hundred years later, the legend goes, just prior to Madrid's Christian reconquest, a local beauty of impeccable character named María (*La Beata*) recited stories told by local gossips that the long-forgotten statue had requested liberation from the masonry that surrounded it. King Alfonso immediately organized a massive religious procession around the periphery of the walls and announced his intention of demolishing the city's fortifications so that the supposed image might be released.

Terrified that her information might have been false, but believing nonetheless in the existence of such a statue, María La Beata offered her life to the Virgin in exchange for a rescue of the statue. The next day, during the procession, an avalanche of stones fell from the wall, revealing the image of the Virgin. María La Beata, struck dead on the spot by the intensity of her religious ecstasy, was found in a position of prayer, near the newly exposed niche, from which the statue of the Virgin seemed to be smiling at her. Since then, November 9 has been reserved as a special Madrid-based celebration of the Virgen de Almudena, whose legend is a particular favorite of impressionable teenaged girls.

Madrid's other patron saint was a humble servant and farmhand, San Isidro, who was happily married (the legend goes) to an endlessly patient peasant woman named María de la Cabeza. A historical resident of a house opposite the Church of San Miguel, on calle del Doctor Letamendi in Madrid, Isidro is credited with the ability to perform such miracles as making water gush from barren rocks, healing the blind and the sick, and convincing a team of angels to descend from heaven to plow his master's fields while he was either absorbed in prayer or sleeping (the stories differ). Not without mystical powers of her own, María de la Cabeza performed her best-publicized miracle after throwing her cloak upon the raging currents of the Jarama River; instantly transformed into a bridge, it permitted her and Isidro an easy passage across.

Today Madrid's most famous annual event involves parties, processions, and an almost continuous run of bullfights, all of which are collectively known as the Festival of San Isidro. Scheduled to fall during a three-week period beginning on or around May 15, the day which the Catholic church specifically designates in honor of San Isidro, it includes an array of almost obsessive taurine activities that are considered among the most skilled and elegant in the entire world.

The celebrations of both Christmas (Navidad) and New Year (Año Nuevo) are observed with both public and private parties throughout Madrid. At midnight on New Year's Eve, the Puerta del Sol is the site of a gathering of thousands of celebrants, each of whom amusedly pops a grape into his or her mouth with each midnight chime of the plaza's main clock. The Christmas season culminates in parties on the night of January 5 and the Procession of the Three

Kings (Cabalgata de los Reyes Magos). Winding through the streets of Madrid, replete with Middle Eastern costumes of long ago, it especially appeals to children.

In January, during the fiesta of San Antón, lovers of animals lead their pets to the San Antonio Abad church, where a priest blesses them in honor of the patron saint of animals, San Antón.

Madrid offers its own distinctive version of carnival. Replete with parades, elaborate costumes, and lots of civic brouhaha, it ends on the Tuesday before Ash Wednesday, just before the enforced piety of Semana Santa, or Holy Week, the seven days before Easter. Modern Madrid seems about equally divided between those observers who spend long hours in church or on religious pilgrimages, and those who use the holidays to depart for long and very secular vacations.

Many other folkloric celebrations occur at annual intervals in Madrid, some of which are concerned with past military victories. Most important of these is the 2 de Mayo (May 2), an observation of the 1802 revolt of the Madrileños against the French forces of Napoleon. Naturally, the bulk of Madrid's parties, parades, and celebrations emanate outward from the Plaza 2 de Mayo.

DANCE

From Madrid's lowliest *taberna* (tavern) to its poshest nightclub, you are likely to hear heel clicking, foot stamping, castanet rattling, hand clapping, and the sound of sultry guitar music. This is *flamenco*. Its origins lie deep in Asia, but the Spanish gypsy has given it an original and unique style of its own. It is a dance dramatizing inner conflict and pain. Performed by a great artist, flamenco can tear your heart out.

Flamenco has no story line. The leader sets the pace, drawing each of the performers forward. He or she lurks behind and around the group at all times, trying to infuse them with rhythm and the moody passions of the art form. It can be contagious, so don't be surprised if you end up with the castanets yourself.

Other regional dances you're likely to see in Madrid include the *sardana* of Catalonia, the *muineira* of Galicia, and the fiery, colorful dances of León, Castile, and Valencia. The *jota* of Aragón is also renowned. When this dance is presented in a more sensuous Arabic fashion, it is transformed into the fandango. The *seguidilla* has much in common with the jota and fandango. Described by Cervantes as "the quicksilver of all senses," the seguidilla gave birth to the music and dancing of the *bolero*, popular in the taverns of the 18th and 19th centuries. The exoticism of many of these dances has been amplified by such non-Spanish composers as Bizet, and with such classical Spanish composers as Ibañez and Falla, who infused their orchestral music with the passions and rhythms of these native music and dance forms.

Today the most popular dance, especially in Madrid, is the *sevillana*. In the classic tradition, music and rhythm would be provided exclusively by either one or two flamenco guitars to accompany the dancers. Today, however, as part of the expanding horizons of a Spain eager to assimilate its cultural classics with new input from abroad, the dancers might perform to the music of mariachi-derived brass band and/or conga drums. Regardless of their degree of historic accuracy, and irrespective of their formality, all these dances can appropriately end with *Olé!*

BULLFIGHTS — THE SPECTACLE OF DEATH

Many consider bullfighting to be cruel and shocking; others consider it a cathartic representative of the mystery of life and death. As Ernest Hemingway pointed out in *Death in the Afternoon*, "The bullfight is not a sport in the Anglo-Saxon sense of the word, that is, it is not an equal contest or an attempt at an equal contest between a bull and a man. Rather, it is a tragedy; the death of the bull, which is played, more or less well, by the bull and the man involved and in which there is danger for the man but certain death for the bull." Hemingway, of course, was an aficionado.

When the symbolic drama of the bullfight is acted out, some think that both actors and its observers can reach a higher emotional (and sometimes spiritual) plane. Some people argue that it is not a public exhibition of cruelty at all, but rather a highly skilled art form requiring great human qualities: survival, courage, showmanship, and gallantry.

Regardless of how you view it, this spectacle is an authentically Spanish experience, and as such has much to reveal about the character of the land and its people.

The season of the *corridas* (bullfights) lasts from early spring until mid-October, or earlier. Fights are held in a *plaza de toros* (bullring). The oldest ring in Spain lies in Andalusia's remote town of Ronda, although many of those in Spain's larger cities are stadium-sized architectural wonders, often built (as in the case of Madrid) in a richly embellished mudéjar/Andalusian style. Unless you happen to arrive during a bullfighting festival (as in the case of Madrid's Festival of San Isidro, when fights are held every day during a three-week period in late springtime), fights are usually held every Sunday afternoon. Madrid, however, because of its size and the devotion of its fans, often holds corridas on Thursday as well.

Tickets fall into three classifications: *sol* (sun), the cheapest and sometimes the most stiflingly hot; *sombra* (shade), the most expensive; *sol y sombra* (a mixture of sun and shade), the medium-priced range.

The corrida begins with a parade. For many viewers, this may be the high point of the afternoon's festivities, as all the bullfighters are clad in their *trajes de luce* or "suits of light."

Bullfights are divided into *tercios* (thirds). The first is the *tercio de capa* (cape), during which the matador tests the bull with various passes and gets acquainted with him. The second portion, the *tercio de varas* (sticks), begins with the lance-carrying *picadores* on horseback, who weaken, or "punish," the bull by jabbing him in the shoulder area. The horses are sometimes gored, even though they wear protective padding, or the horse and rider may be tossed into the air by the now-infuriated bull. The picadores are followed by the *banderilleros*, whose job it is to puncture the bull with pairs of boldly colored darts.

In the final *tercio de muleta*, the action narrows down to the lone fighter and the bull. Gone are the fancy capes. Instead, the matador uses a small red cloth known as a *muleta*, which, to be effective, requires a bull with lowered head. The picadores and banderilleros have already worked, through the wounds inflicted upon the animal, to achieve this. Using the muleta as a lure, the matador wraps the bull around himself in various passes, the most dangerous of which is the *natural*; here, the matador holds the muleta in his left hand, the sword in his right. Right-hand passes pose less of a threat, since the sword can be used to spread out the muleta, making a larger target for the bull. After a number of passes, the time comes for the kill, the "moment of truth." In a moment that, depending on your reaction, might be a moment of deeply emotional high tragedy, a truly skilled fighter may dispatch the bull in one thrust, traditionally aiming to sever the animal's spinal cord just behind its skull.

After the bull dies, the highest official at the ring may award the matador an ear from the dead bull, or perhaps both ears, or ears and tail. For a really extraordinary performance, the hoof is sometimes added. The bullfighter may be carried away as a hero, or if he has displeased the crowd, be chased out of the ring by an angry mob. At a major fight, six bulls are usually killed by three matadors in one afternoon.

2. FOOD & DRINK

Madrid manages to incorporate within its borders a gastronomic sampling of each of the country's best-loved dishes. The city's highly varied cuisine seems to hold one thing in common: The portions are immense, and though the prices are not as moderate as in recent years, they can still be moderate by North American standards. Whenever possible, try to sample some of Spain's regional specialties, abundantly offered at restaurants throughout the city. Many of these, such as Andalusian gazpacho and Valencian paella, have transcended their region and are now considered great dishes of the world.

MEALS Breakfast In Madrid, the day starts with a continental breakfast of hot coffee, hot chocolate, or tea, with assorted rolls, butter, and jam. A typical Spanish breakfast often includes *churros* (fried fingerlike doughnuts) and a hot chocolate that's very sweet and thick. The coffee is usually strong and black, served with hot milk. Some Americans consider it too strong and bitter for their tastes, and therefore ask for instant coffee instead.

Lunch An important meal in Spain, comparable to the farm-style noonday "dinner" in America. It usually includes three or four courses, beginning with a choice of soup or several dishes of hors d'oeuvres called *entremeses.* Often a fish or egg dish is served after this, then a meat course with vegetables. Wine is always on the table. Dessert usually consists of pastry, custard, or assorted fruit; this is followed by coffee. Lunch is served from 1 to 3:30pm, with "rush hour" at 2pm.

Tapas After an early-evening promenade, many Spaniards head for their favorite *tascas,* or bars, where they drink wine and sample assorted *tapas,* such as bits of fish, eggs in mayonnaise, or olives.

Dinner Another extravaganza. A typical meal starts with a bowl of soup, followed by a second course, often a fish dish, and by another main course, usually veal, beef, or pork, accompanied by vegetables. Again, desserts tend to be fruit, custard, or pastries.

Wine is always available. Afterward, you might have a demitasse and a fragrant Spanish brandy. The chic dining hour, even in one-donkey towns, is 10 or 10:30pm. In well-touristed districts of

Madrid, as well as in hard-working Catalonia, you can usually dine by 8pm. In most middle-class establishments, people dine no later than 9:30pm. Your choice.

THE CUISINE Soups and Appetizers Soups are usually served in big bowls. Cream soups, such as asparagus and potato, can be fine; sadly, however, they are too often made from powdered ingredients in foil packets from such companies as Knorr and Liebig. The chilled gazpacho, on the other hand, is tasty and usually made fresh. Served year round, it's particularly refreshing during the hot months. The combination of ingredients is pleasant: olive oil, garlic, ground cucumbers, and raw tomatoes with a sprinkling of croutons. Madrid also offers a sampling of the many varieties of fish soup (*sopa de pescado*) which seem to derive from each of Spain's many provinces, and many of these are superb.

In Madrid's top restaurants, as many as 15 tempting hors d'oeuvres might be offered, often among the best of their kind anywhere. In lesser-known places, including restaurants without an active turnover of clients or inventories, avoid these entremeses, which often consist of last year's sardines and shards of sausage left over from the Moorish conquest.

Eggs These are served in countless ways. A Spanish omelet, a *tortilla española*, is made with potatoes. A simple omelet is called a *tortilla francesa*. A *tortilla portugésa* is similar to the American version of a Spanish omelet.

Fish Madrid gathers into its periphery both the raw ingredients and the regional recipes for some of the finest fish dishes in Spain. One of the most common varieties is hake (*merluza*), sweet and white. *Langosta,* a variety of small-clawed lobster, is seen everywhere, particularly on ice or in refrigerated display cases. Although it's a treat, it's also terribly expensive. The Portuguese in particular, but some Spaniards too, go into raptures at the mention of barnacles. Gourmets relish their seawater taste; others find them tasteless. *Rape* is the Spanish name for monkfish, a sweet, wide-boned ocean fish with a texture like that of scallops. Also try a few dozen half-inch baby eels. They rely heavily on olive oil and garlic for their flavor, but they're great-tasting. Squid cooked in its own ink is suggested only for those who want to go native. The city's frequent offerings of charcoal-broiled sardines, a particular treat in the Basque provinces but occasionally available in Madrid, however, are a culinary delight. Trout Navarre is one of the capital's most popular fish dishes, carefully deboned and usually stuffed with bacon or ham.

Paella You can't go to Madrid without sampling what might be the most famous dish to ever emerge from Spain. Originally a specialty of the seacoast city of Valencia, and now considered the property of Spaniards around the world, it's an aromatic rice-and-saffron dish usually topped with shellfish, chicken, sausage, peppers, and local spices. Served authentically, it comes steaming hot from the kitchen in a metal pan called a *paellera*. (Incidentally, what is known in America as Spanish rice isn't Spanish at all. If you ask an English-speaking waiter for your Spanish rice, he'll probably serve you paella.)

Meats Don't expect Kansas City steak, but do try the spit-roasted suckling pig, so sweet and tender it can often be cut with a fork. The veal is also good, and the Spanish *lomo de cerdo* (loin of pork) is unmatched anywhere. As for chicken, it will sometimes qualify for the Olympics in that it's stringy and muscular. Spit-roasted chicken, however, can often be flavorful.

Vegetables and Salads Except in summer, Spanish vegetables are not the greatest. In some places, fresh vegetables are hard to come by, and the diner is often served canned (and often overcooked) string beans, peas, or artichokes. Potatoes are also a staple. Salads are usually fresh, made with crisp lettuce and vine-ripened tomatoes in summer.

Desserts The Spanish don't emphasize dessert. Flan, a home-cooked egg custard, appears on all menus—sometimes with a burnt-caramel sauce. Ice cream appears on nearly all menus as well. The best bet is to ask for a basket of fresh fruit, which you can wash at your table in the bowl of water that's usually provided. Homemade pastries are usually moist and not too sweet. As a dining oddity, many restaurants serve fresh orange juice for dessert. Madrileños love it!

Olive Oil and Garlic Olive oil is used lavishly in Madrid and throughout Spain. Despite its well-documented health effects, you may not want it in all dishes. If, for example, you prefer your fish fried in butter, the word for butter is *mantequilla* (in some instances you'll be charged extra for the butter). Garlic is also an integral part of the Spanish diet, and even if you love it, you may find the Spaniard loves it more than you do, and uses it in the oddest dishes.

NONALCOHOLIC BEVERAGES Water Tap water is usually considered safe to drink in Madrid, and in tourist resorts along the Costa del Sol. Despite that, many frequent travelers opt for drinking bottled water instead, simply because it usually tastes better. If you'd like your water with a little kick, then ask for *agua mineral con gas*. Note that in some remote hamlets, bottled water transported from a faraway district of Spain sometimes costs more than the locally bottled regional wine.

Soft Drinks In general, avoid the carbonated citrus drinks on sale everywhere—most of them never saw an orange, much less a lemon. If you want a citrus drink, order old, reliable Schweppes. An excellent noncarbonated drink for the summer is called Tri-Naranjus and comes in lemon and orange flavors. Your cheapest bet is a liter bottle of *gaseosa*, which comes in various flavors. In summer you should also try a drink I've never seen outside Spain, *horchata*, a nutty, sweet milklike beverage made of tubers called *chufas*. Its flavor is vaguely reminiscent of liquefied almonds.

Coffee Even if you're a dedicated coffee drinker, you may find the *café con leche* (coffee with milk) a little too strong. I suggest *leche manchada*, a little bit of strong, freshly brewed coffee in a glass, filled with lots of frothy hot milk.

Milk Even though some old-time aficionadoes in rural districts claim that some of milk's flavor is lost during the pasteurization process, always avoid untreated milk and milk by-products. Most of the milk sold in Madrid, fortunately, is bottled and properly sterilized. One of the city's popular brands of fresh and pasteurized milk is Lauki, and is sold in food stores throughout the city.

ALCOHOLIC BEVERAGES Beer Although not native to Spain, beer (*cerveza*) is now drunk everywhere. Domestic brands include San Miguel, Mahou, Aguila, and Cruz Blanca.

Wine Sherry (*vino de Jerez*) has been called "the wine with a hundred souls." Drink it before dinner (try the topaz-colored *finos*, a very pale sherry) or whenever you drop in to some old inn or bodega for refreshment; many of them have rows of brimming kegs with spigots. Manzanilla, a golden-colored, medium-dry sherry, is extremely popular. The sweet cream sherries (Harvey's Bristol Cream, for example) are favorite after-dinner wines (called *olorosos*). While the French may be disdainful of Spanish table wines, they can be truly noble, especially two leading varieties, Valdepeñas and Rioja, both from Castile. If you're fairly adventurous and not too demanding in your tastes, you can always ask for the *vino de la casa* (wine of the house) wherever you dine. The Ampurdan of Catalonia is a heavy and somewhat coarse, but flavorful wine. From Andalusia comes the fruity Montilla. There are also some good Spain-derived champagnes (*cavas*) widely available in Madrid, such as Freixenet. One brand, Benjamin, also comes in individual-sized bottles.

Sangría This is the all-time favorite refreshing drink in Spain. It's red-wine punch that combines wine with oranges, lemons, seltzer, and sugar.

Whisky and Brandy Imported whiskies are available at most Madrileño bars, but at a high price. If you're a drinker, switch to brandies and cognacs, where the Spanish reign supreme. Try Fundador, made by the Pedro Domecq family in Jerez de la Frontera. If you're seeking a smooth cognac, ask for "103" white label.

3. RECOMMENDED BOOKS, FILMS & RECORDINGS

BOOKS

Historically, Spain's Golden Age lasted from the late 15th to the early 17th century; this era is well surveyed in J. H. Elliot's *Imperial Spain 1469–1716* (New American Library, 1977).

Most accounts of the Spanish Armada's defeat are written from the English point of view. For a change of perspective, try David Howarth's *The Voyage of the Armada* (Penguin, 1981).

One of the best accounts of Spain's earlier history is found in Joseph F. O'Callaghan's *History of Medieval Spain* (Cornell University Press, 1983).

In the 20th century, the historical focus was almost dominated by the tragedies of the Spanish Civil War, recounted in the classic by Hugh Thomas, *The Spanish Civil War* (Harper & Row, 1977). For a personal account of the war, read George Orwell's *Homage to Catalonia* (Harcourt Brace Jovanovich, 1969). The poet García Lorca was murdered during the Civil War; the best account of the brutality of his death is found in Ian Gibson's *The Assassination of Federico García Lorca* (Penguin, 1983).

If you like more contemporary history, read John Hooper's *The Spaniards* (Penguin, 1987). Hooper provides insight into the events of the post-Franco era.

The Moors contributed much to Spanish culture, leaving Spain with a distinct legacy that's documented in Titus Burckhardt's *Moorish Culture in Spain* (McGraw Hill, 1972).

Antoni Gaudí is the Spanish architect who most excites many

first-time visitors. Among the many illustrated books on his work, *Gaudí* (Escudo de Oro's "Collection of Art in Spain," 1990) contains 150 photographs of some of the most unusual early 20th-century architecture in Europe. It's sold at newsstands throughout Madrid.

Spain's most famous artist was Pablo Picasso. The most controversial recent book about the late painter is *Picasso, Creator and Destroyer* by Arianna Stassinopoulos Huffington (Simon & Schuster, 1988).

Spain's other headline-grabbing artist was Salvador Dalí. In *Salvador Dalí: A Biography* (E. P. Dutton, 1986), author Meryle Secrest asks: Was he a mad genius or a cunning manipulator?

Andrés Segovia: An Autobiography of the Years 1893–1920 (Macmillan, 1976), translated by W. F. O'Brien, is useful for understanding the demands placed upon professionals in the world of Spanish classical music.

For the most intimate glimpse into the world of a Spanish film director, read *Mi ultimo suspiro (My Last Sigh)*, the autobiography of Luis Buñuel, whose films mirrored the social, political, and religious conflicts that tore Spain apart during the 20th century.

Passed over by some as superficial, James A. Michener's *Iberia* (Random House, 1968) remains the classic travelogue on Spain.

The most famous Spanish novel of all time is *Don Quixote* by Miguel de Cervantes. Exploring the conflict between the ideal and the real in human nature, it has been one of the most artistically influential novels in literary history.

The collected works of the famous dramatist of Spain's Golden Age, Pedro Calderón de la Barca, can be read in *Plays* (University Press of Kentucky, 1985).

The major works of one of the most lyrically evocative authors in pre–Civil War Spain, Federico García Lorca, can be enjoyed in *Five Plays: Comedies and Tragicomedies* (New Directions, 1964).

Ernest Hemingway, an avid Hispanophile, completed many works on Spain, none more notable than his novels of 1926 and 1940, respectively, *The Sun Also Rises* (Macmillan, 1987) and *For Whom the Bell Tolls* (Macmillan, 1988), the latter based on his experiences in the Spanish Civil War. Don Ernesto's *Death in the Afternoon* (various editions) remains the English-language classic on bullfighting.

The Life of Saint Teresa of Ávila by Herself (Penguin, 1987) is reputedly the third most widely read book in Spain, after the Bible and *Don Quixote*. The translation is by J. M. Cohen.

FILM

One of the biggest names in Spanish cinema is Luis Buñuel, whom some regard as the ultimate genius of Spanish cinema. In 1928, Salvador Dalí and Buñuel cooperated on the director's first movie, *Un Chien Andalou* (An Andalusian Dog), considered the most important surrealist film ever made. Two years later, sadistic scenes in *L'Age d'Or* (The Golden Age)—again written with Dalí's help—led to riots in some movie houses. Buñuel also directed *La Mort en ce Jardin* (Death in This Garden) with Simone Signoret (1957). In 1960 he made *Viridiana*, which supposedly won the prize for best picture at Cannes, even though Franco banned the film in Spain.

Today's *enfant terrible* is Pedro Almodovar, whose *Women on the Verge of a Nervous Breakdown* won an Academy Award nomination in 1990. Ostensibly the film is the story of a woman's abandonment, but its madcap proceedings deal with everything from spiked gazpacho to Shiite terrorists. An iconoclast like Almodovar, who has publicly declared his homosexuality, flourishes in the contemporary liberalized Spain, which abolished censorship in 1977, two years after the death of Franco.

In 1982, José Luís Garci became the first Spaniard to win an Oscar for best foreign film, with *Volver a Empezar* (To Begin Again).

One of the biggest box-office hits in Spanish film history, and still available in video, is *El Crimen de Cuenca* (The Crime in Cuenca), directed by Pilar Miró, who went on to become "chief of state of Spanish television." The film, which details Civil Guard torture, caused a furor when it was released. It was suppressed until the coup attempt of 1981.

RECORDINGS

As residents of the premier cultural bastion of Spain, Madrileños cultivate their tastes in a wide variety of music. Here is a list of recordings that the city's critics consider important.

Don Odilo Cunill directs the Cor Monastic de Abadia de Montserrat in *Cantos Gregorians de la Missa Per Els Fidels Missa orbis Factor,* Gregorian chants recorded in the chapel of the monastery at Montserrat.

In the album *Andrés Segovia, España,* the late master plays guitar versions of fandangos and *tonadillas.* In a more classical vein the same artist plays Bach, Scarlatti, and music by the Czech composer Benda (1722–95) in *Recital Intimo.*

The Orquesta de Conciertos de Madrid performs Falla's *El Amor Brujo* and *El Sombrero de Tres Picos.* The same group, conducted by Enrique Jorda, can be heard in Albéniz's *Suite Española* and *Dos Piezas Españoles.*

Isabel Pantoja, widow of the late bullfighter, sings soulful interpretations of Andalusian ballads in *Se Me Enamora el Alma.* Rocio Jurado renders them smolderingly in *Punto de Partida* and *Canciones de España.*

Carlos Cana performs popular interpretations of Spanish Argentinian tangos, habañeras, and sevillanas on *Luna de Abril.* In *Canalla,* Antonio Cortés Chiquetete is heard performing 19th-century folk melodies. Felipe Campuzano gives piano interpretations of Andalusian folk music in *Cadiz: Andalucía Espiritual.*

Pasodobles Famosos, performed by the Gran Banda Taurina, is popular with older Spaniards, partly for its nostalgic value. This was the music played until very recently at every Spanish gathering, from bullfights to weddings to christenings.

In *Siroca,* Paco de Lucía combines traditional flamenco guitar in its purest form with modern influences, including tangos, *bulerías,* and *tanquillos.* You can also hear Paco de Lucía on *Fantasía Flamenca,* interpreting authentic flamencas in a traditional manner.

The brilliance of the late virtuoso Narcisco Yepes can be heard on *Musica Española para Guitarra,* performing traditional favorites.

The Spanish beauty Ana Belén sings contemporary love ballads in *A la Sombra de un León.* She is married to the somewhat less popular singer Victor Manuel, known for his collection of contemporary ballads, *Tiempo de Cerezas.*

In Madrid, an outstanding local band is called Radio Futura. They have been called "the Einsteins of Spanish rock music." Reviewers usually cite the Mecano, a Madrid band, as "pretty boys." They're sort of a Spanish version of New Kids on the Block, and they sell records by the ton. Borrowing a name from a famous old German movie, the Gabinete Caligari, in the words of one reviewer, is a band that represents "macho Hispano-pop." From Catalonia comes a duo with a unique sound, a band recording rock music as El Ultimo de la Fila.

One of the biggest record sellers in Spain is Joan Manual Serrat, a singer-songwriter recording more traditional popular music in both Catalán and Castilian.

In Madrid, traditional Spanish music is also offered by singer-songwriter Luis Eduardo Aute, who has thousands of fans throughout the Spanish-speaking world.

In current Spanish jazz, Tete Montoliu's recordings represent some of the best the country has to offer. All, or most, of these records are available at Spanish music stores in the United States. They are available in Madrid and throughout Spain as well.

PLANNING A TRIP TO MADRID

This chapter is devoted to the where, when, and how of your trip—the advance-planning issues required to get it together and take it on the road. After deciding where to go, most people have two fundamental questions: What will it cost? and How do I get there? This chapter will answer both of those questions, and resolve other important issues such as when to go, what insurance coverage is necessary, and where to obtain more information about Madrid.

1. INFORMATION, ENTRY REQUIREMENTS & MONEY

SOURCES OF INFORMATION

IN THE U.S. For information before you go, contact the **Tourist Office of Spain,** 665 Fifth Ave., New York, NY 10022 (tel. 212/759-8822). Other tourist information offices are Spanish Tourist Office, 8383 Wilshire Blvd., Suite 960, Beverly Hills, CA 90211 (tel. 213/658-7188); Tourist Office of Spain, Water Tower Place, Suite 915 East, 845 N. Michigan Ave., Chicago, IL 60611 (tel. 312/642-1992); and Tourist Office of Spain, 1221 Brickell Ave., Miami, FL 33131 (tel. 305/358-8223).

OUTSIDE THE U.S. Tourist offices include Spanish Tourist Information, 203 Castlereagh St., Suite 21A (P.O. Box 675), NSW 2000 Sydney, South Australia (tel. 612/264-7966); Tourist Office of Spain, 102 Bloor St. W., 14th Floor, Toronto, ON M5S 1M8, Canada (tel. 416/961-3131); and Spanish Tourist Office, 57–58 St. James's St., London SW1 (tel. 071/499-1169).

OTHER SOURCES Other useful sources are **newspapers and magazines.** To find the latest articles that have been published on your destination, go to your library, ask for the *Guide to Periodical Literature,* and look under the city/country for listings.

You may also want to contact the U.S. State Department for their **background bulletins.** Contact the Superintendent of Documents, U.S. Government Printing Office, Washington, DC 20402 (tel. 202/783-3238).

A good **travel agent** can also be a good source of information. If you use one, make sure he or she is a member of the American Society of Travel Agents (ASTA). If you get poor service from a travel agent, contact ASTA's Consumer Affairs Department, 1101 King St., Alexandria, VA 22314 (tel. 703/739-2782).

And finally, we come to the best source of all—friends and **other travelers** who have just returned from your destination.

ENTRY REQUIREMENTS

PASSPORTS A valid passport is all an American, British, or Canadian citizen needs to enter Spain. You don't need an international driver's license if you're renting a car; your local license from back home should suffice.

VISAS For visits of less than three months to Spain, visas are not required by citizens of the United States, Canada, and Great Britain. Citizens of Australia, New Zealand, and South Africa do need to obtain a visa when visiting Spain and should apply in advance at the Spanish Consulate in their home countries.

CUSTOMS Spain permits you to bring in most personal effects and the following items duty free: two still cameras with 10 rolls of film each, one movie or video camera, tobacco for personal use, one bottle of wine and one bottle of liquor per person, a portable radio, a tape recorder, a typewriter, a bicycle, golf clubs, tennis racquets, fishing gear, two hunting weapons with 100 cartridges each, skis, and other sports equipment.

Upon leaving Spain, American citizens who have been outside the U.S. for 48 hours or more are allowed to bring in $400 (U.S.) worth of merchandise duty free—that is, if they have claimed no similar exemption within the past 30 days. Beyond this free allowance, the next $1,000 worth of merchandise is assessed at a flat rate of 10% duty. If you make purchases in Spain, keep your receipts.

MONEY

To give you an idea of what Madrid costs, consult the "What Things Cost" chart below in this chapter.

CASH/CURRENCY The basic unit of Spanish currency is the **peseta (pta.),** currently worth about 1¢ in U.S. currency. One U.S. dollar is worth about 100 pesetas. (*Warning:* This is subject to change, of course, because the dollar and the peseta fluctuate on the world market. Check with your bank for up-to-date quotations.)

Pesetas are distributed in coin denominations of 1, 2, 5, 10, 25, 50, 100, and 200 pesetas. Paper money comes in bills of 100, 200, 500, 1,000, 5,000, and 10,000 pesetas.

Hotels usually offer the worst rate of exchange, while banks generally offer the best. But even banks charge a commission for the service, often $2 or $3, depending on the transaction.

TRAVELER'S CHECKS Traveler's checks are the safest way to carry cash while traveling. Most banks will give you a better rate for traveler's checks than for cash. The list of suppliers of these checks has grown somewhat shorter in recent years because of the mergers of traveler's check facilities at several major banks. Checks denominated in U.S. dollars are accepted virtually anywhere, but in some cases

THE PESETA & THE DOLLAR

At this writing, $1 equals approximately 100 ptas. (or 1 pta. =1¢), and this was the rate of exchange used to calculate the dollar values given throughout this book, rounded to the nearest nickel. This rate fluctuates from time to time and may not be the same when you travel to Spain. Therefore, the following table should be used only as a guide:

Ptas.	U.S.$	Ptas.	U.S.$
5	.05	1,500	15.00
10	.10	2,000	20.00
15	.15	2,500	25.00
20	.20	3,000	30.00
25	.25	4,000	40.00
30	.30	5,000	50.00
40	.40	6,000	60.00
50	.50	7,000	70.00
75	.75	8,000	80.00
100	1.00	9,000	90.00
150	1.50	10,000	100.00
200	2.00	15,000	150.00
250	2.50	20,000	200.00
500	5.00	25,000	250.00
1,000	10.00		

(perhaps for ease of conversion into local currencies), travelers might want checks denominated in other currencies.

Each of the agencies listed below will refund your checks if they are lost or stolen, provided you produce sufficient documentation. When purchasing your checks, ask about refund hotlines.

- **American Express** (tel. toll free 800/221-7282 in the U.S. and Canada) charges a 1% commission. Checks are free to members of the American Automobile Association.
- **Barclays Bank/Bank of America** (tel. toll free 800/221-2426 in the U.S. and Canada).
- **Citicorp** (tel. toll free 800/645-6556 in the U.S., or 813/623-1709 collect in Canada).
- **MasterCard International/Thomas Cook International** (tel. toll free 800/223-9920 in the U.S., or 609/987-7300 collect).

Purchase checks in a variety of denominations—$20, $50, and $100—and divide them up in your luggage to avoid losing everything if you're robbed.

Foreign banks may charge up to 5% to convert your checks into Spanish pesetas. Note that you'll get the best rate if you cash traveler's checks at the banks issuing them: VISA at Barclays, American Express at American Express, and so forth.

CREDIT & CHARGE CARDS   You'll find that carrying credit and charge cards is useful in Spain. **American Express, VISA,** and **Diners Club** are widely recognized. If you see the Eurocard or

Access sign on an establishment, it means that it accepts **MasterCard.**

Credit and charge cards can save your life when you're abroad. With American Express and VISA, for example, not only can you charge purchases in shops and restaurants that take the card, but you can also withdraw pesetas from bank cash machines at many locations in Spain. Check with your card company before leaving home.

Keep in mind that the price of purchases is not converted into dollars until notification is received in the United States, so the price is subject to fluctuations in the dollar. If the dollar declines by the time your bill arrives, you'll pay more for an item than you expected. But those are the rules of the game. It can also work in your favor if the dollar should rise.

WHAT THINGS COST IN MADRID	U.S. $
Taxi from the airport to the Puerta del Sol	18.20
Public transportation within the city	1.40
Local telephone call	.16
Double room at the Palace Hotel (deluxe)	450.00
Double room at the Hotel Residencia Carlos V (moderate)	105.00
Double room at the Hostal Principado (budget)	50.00
Lunch for one, without wine, at Alkalde (moderate)	28.00
Lunch for one, without wine, at Hollywood (budget)	10.00
Dinner for one, without wine, at Cabo Mayor (deluxe)	50.00
Dinner for one, without wine, at Sobrino de Botín (moderate)	30.00
Dinner for one, without wine, at La Plaza (budget)	15.00
Coca-Cola in restaurant	1.95
Cup of coffee	1.95
Glass of wine	1.80
Admission to the Prado	4.15
Roll of color film, 24 exposures	7.90
Movie ticket	6.50
Theater ticket	6.00

2. WHEN TO GO — CLIMATE, HOLIDAYS & EVENTS

CLIMATE In Madrid, climate is subject to rapid change. July and August are the most uncomfortable months—in fact, the government virtually shuts down in August, except for a skeleton crew, and goes into "exile" at the northeast Atlantic resort of San Sebastian. The temperature can often reach a high of 91° Fahrenheit in July, 76° in September. In winter, it can plunge to 34°F, although it averages around 46°.

In October (average temperature: 58°F), Madrid enjoys its "season." Hotel space is at a premium. Every bullfighter, doll manufacturer, Galician hotelier, Andalusian olive grower, or Santander vineyard keeper having business with the government descends on Madrid at this time. In the same month, wealthy Spanish aristocrats flock here from the secluded ducal palaces in Andalusia and Castile to savor the sophistication of the capital, its opera, theater, and endless rounds of parties and dinners. The air is clear, the sun kind; the restaurants and *tascas* (bars) overflow with Iberian *joie de vivre*.

In my view, however, the balmy month of May (average temperature: 61°F) is the best time for making your own descent on the capital.

Madrid's Average Daytime Temperature and Rainfall

	Jan	Feb	Mar	Apr	May	June	July	Aug	Sept	Oct	Nov	Dec
Temp. (°F)	43	45	49	54	61	68	75	74	68	58	48	43
Rainfall (in.)	2	2	1.6	2	1.5	1.2	0.4	0.3	1.3	2	2.4	2

HOLIDAYS National holidays in Spain include January 1 (New Year's Day), January 6 (Epiphany), March 19 (Day of St. Joseph), Good Friday, Easter Monday, May 1 (May Day), June 10 (Corpus Christi), June 29 (Day of St. Peter and St. Paul), July 25 (Day of St. James), August 15 (Feast of the Assumption), October 12 (Spain's National Day), November 1 (All Saints' Day), December 8 (Immaculate Conception), and December 25 (Christmas).

No matter how large or small, every city or town in Spain also celebrates its local saint's days. In Madrid, it's on May 15 (Saint Isidro).

MADRID CALENDAR OF EVENTS

FEBRUARY

☐ **Arco Art Exhibit,** held at IFEMA (the Madrid Trade Fair Organization), avenida de Portugal, daily noon to 9pm. The best in contemporary art from Europe and America is lavishly presented. Metro: Lago. Dates vary.

☐ **Madrid Carnival** The carnival kicks off with a big parade along paseo de la Castellana, culminating in a masked ball at the Círculo de Belles Artes the following night. Fancy-dress competitions last until Ash Wednesday, when the festivities end with a tear-jerking "burial of a sardine" at the Fuente de los Pajaritos in the Casa de Campo; the evening is topped off with a concert in the Plaza Mayor. Dates vary.

MAY

✪ *FIESTAS DE SAN ISIDRO* Madrileños run wild with a 10-day celebration honoring their patron saint. Food fairs, Castilian folkloric events, street parades, parties, music, dances, bullfights, and other festivities mark the occasion.
    Where: Madrid. *When:* May 12–21. *How:* Make hotel reservations early. Expect crowds and traffic (beware of pickpockets). For information, write the Comisión de Festejos del Excmo, Ayuntamiento de Madrid, Plaza Mayor, 28014 Madrid.

JULY

☐ **Veranos de la Villa** Called "the summer binge" of Madrid, this summer-long program presents folkloric dancing, pop music, classical music, zarzuelas, and flamenco at various venues throughout the city. Open-air cinema is a feature in the Parque del Retiro. Ask at the various tourist offices for complete details (which change every summer). Sometimes admission is charged, but often these events are free.

AUGUST

☐ **Fiestas of Lavapiés and La Paloma** These two fiestas—the most traditional in Madrid—begin with the Lavapies on August 1 and continue through the hectic La Paloma celebration on August 15, the day of the Virgen de la Paloma. Tens of thousands of residents and visitors race through the narrow streets. Apartment dwellers above hurl buckets of cold water onto the crowds below to cool them off. Children's games, floats, music, flamenco, and zarzuelas, along with street fairs, mark the occasion. August 1–15.

OCTOBER

✪ *AUTUMN FESTIVAL* Both Spanish and international artists participate in this cultural program, with a series of operatic, ballet, dance, music, and theatrical performances. From Strasbourg to Tokyo, this event is a premier attraction, yet tickets are reasonable, costing 1,500 ptas. ($15) and up per event.
    Where: Madrid. *When:* Usually in October. *How:* Make hotel reservations early, and write for tickets to the Festival de Otoño, paseo de la Castellana, 101, 28046 Madrid (tel. 91/556-24-12).

3. HEALTH & INSURANCE

HEALTH

Madrid should not pose any major health hazards. Many travelers suffer from diarrhea, generally caused by the overly rich cuisine—garlic, olive oil, and wine. Take along some antidiarrhea medicine, moderate your eating habits, and—even though the water in most parts of Madrid is considered safe—consume mineral water only. Milk and milk products are pasteurized and generally considered safe. The Mediterranean, a horrendously polluted sea, washes up on Spain's shores, and fish and shellfish from it should only be eaten cooked. Try to make sure it's fresh; sometimes inadequate refrigeration of fish and shellfish—especially in the hot summer months—can lead to what some foreign visitors to Spain call "the Toledo trot," the equivalent of Mexico's "Montezuma's revenge."

Sometimes travelers find that the change of diet in Madrid leads to constipation. If this occurs, eat a high-fiber diet and drink plenty of mineral water. Avoid large lunches and dinners with wine. Consult your doctor before you go about taking Colace, a stool softener, or Metamucil.

Doctor   If you need a doctor, ask your hotel to locate one for you. You can also obtain a list of English-speaking doctors in Spain from the **International Association for Medical Assistance to Travelers (IAMAT),** in the United States at 417 Center St., Lewiston, NY 14092 (tel. 716/754-4883); in Canada, at 40 Regal Rd., Guelph, ON N1K 1B5 (tel. 519/836-0102). Getting medical help in Spain is relatively easy, compared to many countries, and competent doctors are found in each of the country's widely scattered regions.

Chronic Illness   If your medical condition is chronic, always talk to your doctor before taking an international trip. He or she may have specific advice to give you. For conditions such as epilepsy, a heart condition, diabetes, and some other afflictions, wear a Medic Alert Identification Tag, which will immediately alert any doctor to the nature of your condition. It also provides the number of Medic Alert's 24-hour hotline, so that a foreign doctor can obtain your medical records. For membership, the cost is a well-spent $30. Contact the **Medic Alert Foundation,** P.O. Box 1009, Turlock, CA 95381-1009 (tel. toll free 800/432-5378).

Prescription Drugs   Take along an adequate supply of any prescription drugs that you need and prescriptions with the generic name—not the brand name—of the drugs as well. Carry all vital medicines and drugs (the legal kind only) with you in your carry-on luggage, in case your checked luggage is lost.

Also, take your own personal medical kit. Include first-aid cream, insect repellent, aspirin, nose drops, and Band-Aids. If you're subject to motion sickness on a plane or train, remember to bring along motion-sickness medicine as well.

It's also a good idea to take along a good sunscreen, one that has a high enough protection factor to block out most of the dangerous ultraviolet rays of the sun, which can be intense in Spain. In case you do find yourself overexposed to the sun, have some liquid solution of the aloe plant with you for soothing relief.

Vaccinations   You aren't required to have any particular inoculations to enter Spain (except for yellow fever if you're arriving from an infected area).

INSURANCE

Before purchasing any additional insurance, check your homeowner, automobile, and medical-insurance policies. Also check the membership contracts issued by automobile and travel clubs and by credit-card companies. If, after close examination, you feel you still need insurance, consider the following.

Health/Accident Many credit-card companies insure their users in case of a travel accident, provided a ticket was purchased with their card. Sometimes fraternal organizations have policies that protect members in case of sickness or accidents abroad. The best policies provide advances in cash or transfers of funds so that you won't have to dip into your travel funds to settle any medical bills you might incur while away from home. To submit a claim, you'll need documentation from a medical authority.

Another insurance option is **Travel Assistance International**, 1133 15th St. NW, Suite 400, Washington, DC 20005 (tel. 202/331-1609, or toll free 800/821-2828), which offers travel coverage up to $15,000 for urgent hospital care and medical evacuation back to the United States if necessary. For an additional fee you can be covered for trip cancellation, lost luggage, and accidental death and dismemberment. The fee depends on how long you plan to stay. Fees begin at $40 per person ($60 for a family) for a one- to eight-day trip. You can call a 24-hour "hotline" number (tel. 202/347-7113 in Washington, D.C., or toll free 800/368-7878 in the U.S. and Canada) that will put you in touch with agents all over Europe, including Spain.

Loss/Theft Many homeowner insurance policies cover theft of luggage during foreign travel and loss of documents—your Eurailpass, your passport, or your airline ticket, for instance. Coverage is usually limited to about $500. To submit a claim on your insurance, you'll need police reports; such claims can be filed only when you return from Spain.

Cancellation If you've booked a charter flight, you'll probably have to pay a cancellation fee if you cancel a trip suddenly, even if it's due to an unforeseen crisis. It's possible to get insurance against such a possibility; some travel agencies provide this coverage. Often flight insurance against a canceled trip is provided by credit-card companies when you use the card to pay for the ticket. Most tour operators or insurance agents can provide cancellation insurance.

Among the companies offering such health, loss, and cancellation policies are:

- **Access America, Inc.** (an affiliate of Blue Cross/Blue Shield), 101 W. 31 St., New York, NY 10001 (tel. 212/465-0707, or toll free 800/825-3633).
- **Travel Guard International,** 145 Clark St., Stevens Point, WI 54481 (tel. toll free 800/826-1300 in the U.S.).
- **Wallach & Company, Inc.,** 243 Church St. NW, Suite 100-D, Vienna, VA 22180 (tel. 703/281-9500, or toll free 800/237-6615 in the U.S.).

4. WHAT TO PACK

Always pack as light as possible. Sometimes it's hard to get a porter or a baggage cart at rail and air terminals. And airlines are increasingly strict about how much luggage you can take along, not only as carry-on but also as checked baggage.

It depends on where you're going in Spain and at what time of year, but as a general rule, pack the same clothes that you might wear in the southeastern United States. That is, dress as if you were visiting Virginia or the Carolinas at the same time of year as your trip to Spain. Buildings in Spain tend not to be very well heated, so you might want to take an extra sweater.

Dress is casual in Madrid. A jacket and tie are required in only first-class establishments. For special occasions, men should pack a suit. For women, skirts and sweaters, suits, simple dresses, and dress slacks are never out of place.

For sightseeing, casual clothes and comfortable shoes (two pairs) are best. When touring churches and cathedrals, dress appropriately: Head coverings are not required, but you'll be denied entry if you're wearing shorts. After sunning at the beach, both men and women should wear a cover-up over their bathing suits when on the street. If you plan to visit a casino or nightclub, dress up—casual but chic is best.

Finally, pack only items that travel well. Don't count on being able to get your clothes pressed at hotels, especially budget hotels. Take clothes that you can wash out in your bathroom sink and hang up to dry overnight. Pack a plastic bag for clothes that are still damp when you move on to your next destination.

5. TIPS FOR SPECIAL TRAVELERS

FOR THE DISABLED Because of its many hills and endless flights of stairs, getting around Spain can be difficult for the disabled. Despite the lack of adequate services, more and more disabled travelers are taking on the challenge of Spain, and conditions are slowly improving.

The newer hotels are more sensitive to the needs of the disabled, and in general, the more expensive restaurants are wheelchair accessible. However, since most places have very limited, if any, facilities for the disabled, it would be best to consider an organized tour especially designed to accommodate the disabled.

For information, contact the **Travel Information Service,** Moss Rehabilitation Hospital, 1200 W. Tabor Rd., Philadelphia, PA 19141-3099 (tel. 215/456-9600 for voice phone, or 215/456-9602 TTD for the hearing impaired). There's a nominal charge to cover postage and handling costs for information packages that are mailed.

The U.S. government publishes "Air Transportation of Handicapped Persons" for free; write to **U.S. Department of Transportation,** Distribution Unit, Publications Division, M-4332, Washington, DC 20590, and ask for Free Advisory Circular No. AC12032.

You might want to consider joining the **Federation of the Handicapped,** 211 W. 14th St., New York, NY 10011 (tel. 212/747-4268), which offers summer tours for members. The annual fee is $4. The names and addresses of other tour operators can be obtained from the **Society for the Advancement of Travel for the Handicapped,** 347 Fifth Ave., New York, NY 10016 (tel. 212/447-7284). Yearly membership dues are $45 ($25 for seniors and students). Send a self-addressed stamped envelope.

The best source of information for the vision-impaired is the **American Foundation for the Blind,** 15 W. 16th St., New York, NY 10011 (tel. 212/620-2000, or toll free 800/232-5463), which issues ID cards for the legally blind for $6.

FOR SENIORS Many discounts are available for seniors, but often you need to be a member of an association to obtain them.

For information, write away for "Travel Tips for Senior Citizens" (publication no. 8970), distributed for $1 by the **Superintendent of Documents, U.S. Government Printing Office,** Washington, DC 20402 (tel. 202/783-3238). Another booklet—this one distributed free—is called "101 Tips for the Mature Traveler." Write or phone **Grand Circle Travel,** 347 Congress St., Suite 3A, Boston, MA 02210 (tel. 617/350-7500, or toll free 800/221-2610).

One of the most dynamic travel organizations for seniors is **Elderhostel,** 75 Federal St., Boston, MA 02110 (tel. 617/426-7788), established in 1975, which operates an array of programs throughout Europe, including Spain. Most courses last around three weeks, and represent good value, since they include airfare, accommodations in student dormitories or modest inns, all meals, and tuition. Courses involve no homework, are ungraded, and are often liberal arts oriented. These are not luxury vacations but they are fun and fulfilling. Participants must be at least 60 years old; however, if two members go as a couple, only one member need be "of age." Write or call for a free newsletter and a list of upcoming courses and destinations.

SAGA International Holidays, 120 Boylston St., Boston, MA 02116 (tel. 617/451-6808, or toll free 800/343-0273), is known for its inclusive tours for seniors. The company prefers that joiners be at least 60 years old. Tours encompass dozens of locations in Europe, including Spain, and usually last for an average of 17 nights.

In the United States, the best organization to belong to is the **American Association of Retired Persons,** 601 E St. NW, Washington, DC 20049 (tel. 202/434-2277). Members are offered discounts on car rentals, hotels, and airfares. The association's group travel is provided by the AARP Travel Experience from American Express. Tours may be purchased through any American Express office or travel agent or by calling toll free 800/927-0111. Cruises may be purchased only by telephone (tel. toll free 800/745-4567). Flights to the various destinations are handled by either of these toll-free numbers as part of land arrangements or cruise bookings.

Information is also available from the **National Council of Senior Citizens,** 1331 F St. NW, Washington, DC 20004 (tel. 202/347-8800). A nonprofit organization, the council charges $12 per couple, for which you receive a monthly newsletter that is in part devoted to travel tips. Reduced discounts on hotel and auto rentals are previewed.

FOR FAMILIES Advance planning is the key to a successful oversees family vacation.

- If you have very small children you should discuss your vacation plans with your family doctor and take along such standard supplies as children's aspirin, a thermometer, Band-Aids, and the like.
- On airlines, a special menu for children must be requested at least

24 hours in advance, but if baby food is required, bring your own and ask a flight attendant to warm it to the right temperature.

- Take along a "security blanket" for your child (a pacifier, a favorite toy or book) or, for older children, something to make them feel at home in different surroundings (a baseball cap, a favorite T-shirt, or some good-luck charm).
- Make advance arrangements for cribs, bottle warmers, and car seats if you're driving anywhere.
- Ask the hotel if it stocks baby food, and if not, take some with you and plan to buy the rest in local supermarkets.
- Draw up guidelines on bedtime, eating, keeping tidy, being in the sun, even shopping and spending—they'll make the vacation more enjoyable.
- Babysitters can be found for you at most hotels, but you should always insist, if possible, that you secure a babysitter with at least a rudimentary knowledge of English.

Family Travel Times is a newsletter about traveling with children. Subscribers can also call in with travel questions, but only on Wednesday from 10am to 1pm eastern standard time. Contact TWYCH, which stands for *Travel With Your Children,* 14 W. 18th St., New York, NY 10011 (tel. 212/206-0688).

FOR SINGLE TRAVELERS   It's no secret that the travel industry caters to people who are not traveling alone. Double rooms, for example, are usually much more reasonably priced than singles. One company has made heroic efforts to match single travelers with like-minded companions. Founder Jens Jurgen charges $36–$66 for a six-month listing in his well-publicized records. New applicants desiring a travel companion fill out a form stating their preferences and needs. They then receive a list of people who might be suitable. Companions of the same or opposite sex can be requested. For an application and more information, write to **Jens Jurgen, Travel Companion,** P.O. Box P-833, Amityville, NY 11701 (tel. 516/454-0880; fax 516/454-0170).

  Singleworld, 401 Theodore Fremd Ave., Rye, NY 10580 (tel. 914/967-3334, or toll free 800/223-6490), is a travel agency that operates tours for solo travelers. Some, but not all, are for people under 35. Annual dues are $25.

  Since single supplements on tours usually carry a hefty price tag, a way to get around paying the supplement is to find a travel agency that allows you to share a room with a hitherto-unknown fellow traveler. One company offering a "guaranteed-share plan" for their tours in Spain is **Cosmos** (an affiliate of Globus Gateway Tours), 9525 Queen's Blvd., Rego Park, NY 11374 (tel. toll free 800/221-0090), or 5301 S. Federal Circle, Littleton, CO 80123 (tel. toll free 800/221-0090). Upon arrival in Spain, a suitable roommate will be assigned from among the tour's other participants.

FOR STUDENTS   The largest educational travel service for students is **Council Travel,** a subsidiary of the Council on International Educational Exchange, 205 E. 42nd St., New York, NY 10017 (tel. 212/661-1414), providing details about budget travel, study abroad, work permits, and insurance. Council Travel offices are located throughout the United States. Call toll free 800/GET-AN-ID to find out where the closest office is to you. The organization produces a number of publications, and offers the Student Travel Catalogue, available free. It also issues to bonafide students an **International Student Identity Card** ($14); this card gets you such benefits as special student airfares to Europe, medical insurance, and many special discounts. In Spain the card secures you free entrance into state museums, monuments, and archeological sights. Domestic train fares in Spain are also reduced for students.

For real budget travelers it's worth joining the **International Youth Hostel Federation (IYHF).** For information, write AYH (American Youth Hostels), P.O. Box 37613, Washington, DC 20013-7613 (tel. 212/783-6161). Membership costs $25 for 12 months; children under 18 pay $10.

6. ALTERNATIVE/ADVENTURE TRAVEL

Offbeat, alternative modes of travel often cost less and can be an enriching way to travel to Madrid.

EDUCATIONAL TRAVEL   An international series of programs for those over 50 years of age who are interested in combining travel and learning is offered by **Interhostel,** developed by the University of New Hampshire. Each program lasts two weeks, is led by a university faculty or staff member, and is arranged in conjunction with a host college, university, or cultural institution. Participants may stay longer if they wish. Programs in Spain include field trips to museums and other centers of interest. For information, contact the **University of New Hampshire,** Division of Continuing Education, 6 Garrison Ave., Durham, NH 03824 (tel. 603/862-1147, or toll free 800/733-9753).

A good source of information about courses in Spain is the **American Institute for Foreign Study (AIFS),** 102 Greenwich Ave., Greenwich, CT 06830 (tel. 203/869-9090, or toll free 800/727-2437). This organization can set up transportation and arrange for summer courses, with bed and board included.

The biggest organization dealing with higher education in Europe is the **Institute of International Education,** 809 United Nations Plaza, New York, NY 10017 (tel. 212/883-8200). A few of its booklets are free, but for $26.95, plus $3 for postage, you can purchase the more definitive *Vacation Study Abroad*. Visitors to New York may use the resources at the institute's information center, which is open to the public Monday through Friday from 10am to 4pm. The institute is closed on major holidays.

One well-recommended clearinghouse for academic programs throughout the world is the Milwaukee-based **National Registration Center for Study Abroad (NRCSA),** 823 N. 2nd St. (P.O. Box 1393), Milwaukee, WI 53201 (tel. 414/278-0631). The organization maintains language-study programs in Madrid and about nine other cities in Spain. With lodgings in private homes included as part of the price and part of the experience, tuition begins at around $700 for an intensive two-week language course. Courses of six weeks, eight weeks, a semester, and a full academic year are also available. (Some colleges do accept successful completion of the curriculums as independent studies.) Courses accept participants over age 17 (many are senior citizens).

A clearinghouse to contact for information on Spain-based language schools is **Lingua Service Worldwide,** 2 W. 45th St., Suite 500, New York, NY 10036 (tel. toll free 800/394-5327). It represents organizations devoted to the teaching of Spanish in 11 cities of Spain, including one in Madrid.

The **Education Office of Spain,** 150 Fifth Ave., Suite 918, New York, NY 10011 (tel. 212/741-5144), whose funding comes from the Spanish Ministry of Education, offers information on language schools in the universities and privately funded schools of Spain, including Madrid. Information is provided free.

For more information about study abroad, contact the **Council on International Educational Exchange (CIEE),** 205 E. 42nd St., New York, NY 10017 (tel. 212/661-1414).

HOMESTAYS The **Friendship Force,** 575 South Tower, 1 CNN Center, Atlanta, GA 30303 (tel. 404/522-9490), is a nonprofit organization existing for the sole purpose of fostering and encouraging friendship among people around the world. Group visits are arranged to a given host country, where each participant is required to spend two weeks—one of those weeks with a family.

Servas, 11 John St., New York, NY 10038 (tel. 212/267-0252)—the name means "to serve" in Esperanto—is a nonprofit, nongovernmental, international, interfaith network of travelers and hosts whose goal is to help promote world peace, goodwill, and understanding. Servas travelers stay at people's homes without charge for up to two days. Visitors pay a $45 annual fee, fill out an application, and undergo an interview for suitability. They then receive a Servas directory listing the names and addresses of Servas hosts.

The **International Visitors Information Service,** 733 15th St. NW, Suite 300, Washington, DC 20005 (tel. 202/783-6540), will mail you a booklet that, for example, can tell you how to find lodgings with a Spanish family. Checks in the amount of $5.95 should be made out to Meridian/IVIS.

HOME EXCHANGES One of the most exciting breakthroughs in modern tourism is the home exchange, whereby the Diego family of Madrid can exchange their home with the Brier family in North Carolina. Sometimes the family automobile is included. Of course, you must be comfortable with the idea of having relative strangers in your home, and you must be content to spend your vacation in one place.

Home exchanges cut costs. You don't pay hotel bills, and you can also save money by shopping in markets and eating in.

Intervac, U.S., P.O. Box 590504, San Francisco, CA 94159 (tel. 415/435-3497), is part of the world's largest home-exchange network. It publishes three catalogs a year, containing listings of more than 8,000 homes in more than 36 countries, including Spain. Members contact each other directly. The $57 cost buys all three of the company's catalogs, including mailing costs, and provides a listing of your home in one of the three catalogs; seniors over 62 pay $52. Hospitality and youth exchanges, as well as rentals, are also offered.

Vacation Exchange Club, P.O. Box 820, Haleiwa, HI 96712 (tel. toll free 800/638-3841), has around 100 listings for Spain, including Madrid. The annual dues of $50 entitle subscribers to receive spring and winter listings, and the placement of a member's listing in one of these directories.

The Invented City, 41 Sutter St., Suite 1090, San Francisco, CA 94104 (tel. 415/673-0347), is another international home-exchange agency. Home-exchange listings are published three times a year: in February, May, and November. A membership fee of $50 allows you to list your home; you can state your preferred time to travel, your occupation, and your hobbies.

COOKING SCHOOLS Thanks to Spain's colonies in the New World, Spanish cuisine may have been more widely diffused than that of any other country. One organization devoted to training Hispanophiles in the fine art of the nation's cuisine is the **Escuela de Cocina Juan Altimiras,** 2 Plaza de la Incarnación, Madrid (tel. 91/247-4220). Established by chef Juan Altimiras in 1973, it offers a series of lectures and demonstrations that benefit even professional chefs.

7. GETTING THERE

BY PLANE

Flights to Madrid from the U.S. East Coast take six to seven hours, depending on the season and prevailing winds. The major airlines servicing Madrid from North America are Iberia, Trans World Airlines, American Airlines, United Airlines, and Continental Airlines.

Standard Fares

Most airlines divide their year roughly into seasonal slots, with the least expensive fares between November 1 and March 14. The shoulder season (spring and early fall) is only slightly more expensive—and includes October, which many western tourists consider the ideal time to visit Spain. Summer, of course, is the most expensive time.

DISCOUNT APEX FARES Most airlines offer a consistently popular advance-purchase excursion (APEX) fare that often requires a 14-day advance payment and an obligatory stay of between 7 and 90 days, depending on the carrier. In most cases this ticket is not completely refundable if you change flight dates or destination, so it pays to ask lots of questions before you book.

Iberia Airlines (tel. toll free 800/772-4642), the national carrier of Spain, offers more routes into and within Spain than any other carrier. Iberia's fares are lowest if you reserve an APEX ticket and travel midweek (Monday through Thursday). From June 1 to August 31, round-trip tickets from New York to Madrid cost $934 midweek ($984 if you travel Friday through Sunday), plus $18 tax. Round-trip flights from Los Angeles to Madrid during the same season cost $1,182 midweek, and $1,232 on weekends, plus tax. Fares, which are subject to change, are lower during off-season.

American Airlines (tel. toll free 800/433-7300) offers daily nonstop service to Madrid from its massive hub at Dallas/Fort Worth, with excellent connections to the rest of the airline's impressive network. With a 14-day advance purchase, and a scheduled return between 7 and 90 days after your departure, American's

---

**Ⓕ FROMMER'S SMART TRAVELER:
AIRFARES**

1. Shop all the airlines that fly to your destination.
2. Always ask for the lowest fare, not just for a discount fare.
3. Keep calling the airline—availability of cheap seats changes daily. Airlines would rather sell a seat than have it fly empty. As the departure date nears, additional low-cost seats become available.
4. Ask about frequent-flyer programs when you book a flight.
5. Check bucket shops for last-minute discounts even greater than their advertised slashed fares.
6. Ask about discounted land arrangements. Sometimes they're cheaper when booked with an air ticket.
7. Ask if standby fares are offered.
8. Fly for free or at a heavy discount as a courier.
9. Look for special promotional fares offered by major carriers or airlines struggling to gain a foothold in the market.

---

least expensive round-trip ticket during high season from Dallas to Madrid costs $1,204 for travel on weekdays and $1,254 for travel Friday through Sunday. Imposing more flexible restrictions than those of years gone by, American charges a $125 penalty for any changes in itinerary once you've used the outbound portion of your ticket. American offers a youth fare for travelers aged 12–24. Priced at $560 each way for travel Monday through Thursday, and $585 each way for travel Friday through Sunday, it's not substantially less than the APEX fare. It does, however, favor last-minute departures, since its restrictions bypass the usual 14-day advance-booking requirements. The youth fare cannot be reserved more than three days before departure in either direction.

Trans World Airlines (tel. toll free 800/221-2000) operates separate daily nonstop flights to both Barcelona and Madrid from New York's JFK. The airline's cheapest APEX tickets require a 14-day advance purchase, and a delay of between 7 and 90 days before activating the return portion of your flight. Depending on the day of flight (Monday through Thursday is the least expensive), round-trip passages during high season cost $932–$982. Changes are permitted in departure dates for $125 each. TWA also offers a limited number of youth fares, which must be arranged three days or less before any particular flight. Available only for passengers aged 12–24, they cost $366–$391 each way, depending on the day of flight.

One of the newer possibilities for transatlantic flights into Spain is offered by **United Airlines** (tel. toll free 800/538-2929). Inaugurated in 1991, these routes fly passengers nonstop every day from Washington, D.C.'s Dulles airport into Madrid. With a 14-day advance purchase, and a stay abroad of between 7 and 90 days, United charges high-season rates of $1,004–$1,154 round-trip during the midsummer high season, depending on flight dates. United also offers youth fares similar to those at its competitors, charging $435–$485 each way for travelers aged 12–24. These are bookable only three days or less prior to departure.

Continental Airlines (tel. toll free 800/525-0280) offers daily nonstop flights to Madrid from Newark, N.J., which many New York residents prefer to other area airports. Round-trip APEX fares during high season, with restrictions very similar to those at each of the competitors listed above, run $932–$982, plus tax, depending on the days of travel. A youth fare, available to travelers aged 12–25 with a valid student ID card, costs $366–$391 each way, depending on the day of travel, and can be arranged within three days or less of any departing flight. Likewise, Continental offers discounts of 10% to anyone aged 62 or older, as well as to a senior citizen's companion, regardless of his or her age.

SPECIAL PROMOTIONAL FARES   Since the airlines are now deregulated, expect announcements of promotional fares to Europe. This means that you'll have to have a good travel agent, or do a lot of shopping around yourself, to learn what's available at the time of your intended trip.

REGULAR FARES   If your schedule doesn't permit you one of the options discussed above, you can opt for a regular fare. **Economy class** is the lowest regular fare, followed by **business class,** and then by **first class,** the most expensive ticket. In first class, increased amenities are the rule: The food is better, the seats extend backward into something resembling a bed, and drinks are free. You'll also get free drinks and better meals in business class, but in economy class you pay for alcoholic beverages. All three of these fares have one thing in common: You can book them at the last minute, and can depart and return when you wish. Of course, you'll pay more for the lack of restrictions.

Other Good-Value Choices

CHARTER FLIGHTS   A charter flight is one reserved months in advance for a one-time-only transit to a predetermined destination. For reasons of economy, some travelers choose this option.

Before paying for a charter, check the restrictions on your ticket or contract. You may be asked to purchase a tour package and pay far in advance. You'll pay a stiff penalty (or forfeit the ticket entirely) if you cancel. Charters are sometimes canceled if the tickets don't sell out. In some cases the charter-ticket seller will offer you an insurance policy for your own legitimate cancellation (hospital stay or death in the family, for example).

There's no way to predict whether a charter flight or a bucket-shop (see below) flight will be cheaper. You'll have to investigate this at the time of your trip. Charter operators and bucket shops used to perform separate functions, but today many perform both functions.

Among charter-flight operators is **Council Charters,** a subsidiary of the Council on International Educational Exchange (tel. 212/661-0311, or toll free 800/800-8222). This outfit can arrange charter seats to most major European cities, including Madrid, on regularly scheduled aircraft.

BUCKET SHOPS   Sometimes referred to as "consolidators," bucket shops exist in many shapes and forms. In their purest form they act as clearinghouses for blocks of tickets that airlines discount and consign during normally slow periods of air travel. Ticket prices vary, sometimes going for as much as 35% off full fare. Terms of payment can be anywhere from 45 days before departure to the last minute.

Bucket shops abound from coast to coast, but just to get you started, here are some recommendations (look also for ads in your local newspaper's travel section):

Access International, 101 W. 31st St., Suite 1104, New York, NY 10001 (tel. 212/465-0707, or toll free 800/825-3633), may be the country's biggest consolidator. It specializes in thousands of discounted tickets to the capitals of Europe, including Madrid. Flights are usually on regularly scheduled U.S.-based airlines.

Out west, you can try **Sunline Express Holidays, Inc.,** 607 Market St., San Francisco, CA 94105 (tel. 415/541-7800, or toll free 800/SUNLINE); or **Euro-Asia, Inc.,** 4203 E. Indian School Rd., Suite 210, Phoenix, AZ 85018 (tel. 602/955-2742, or toll free 800/525-3876).

Travel Avenue, 180 N. Des Plains, Chicago, IL 60661 (tel. toll free 800/333-3335), is a national agency with headquarters in Chicago. Its tickets are often cheaper than most shops, and it charges the customer only a $25 fee on international tickets, rather than taking the usual 10% commission from an airline.

STANDBYS A favorite with spontaneous travelers who have absolutely no scheduled demands on their time, a standby fare leaves them dependent on the whims of fortune—and hoping that a seat will be open at the last minute. Not all airlines offer standbys.

GOING AS A COURIER This cost-cutting technique has lots of restrictions, and tickets may be hard to come by, so it's not for everybody. Couriers are hired by overnight air-freight firms hoping to skirt the often tedious Customs hassles and delays that face regular cargo on the other end. With a courier, the checked freight sails through Customs just as quickly as the passenger's luggage. Don't worry—the courier service is absolutely legal; you won't be asked to haul in illegal drugs, for example. For performing this service, the courier gets a great discount on airfare, and sometimes even flies for free. You're allowed one piece of carry-on luggage only (your usual baggage allowance is used by the courier firm to transport its cargo). As a courier, you don't actually handle the merchandise you're "transporting" to Europe; you just carry a manifest to present to Customs. Upon arrival, an employee of the courier service will reclaim the company's cargo.

Incidentally, as a courier you fly alone; a friend may be able to arrange a flight as a courier on a consecutive day, but don't count on it. Most courier services operate from Los Angeles or New York, but some operate out of other cities, such as Chicago or Miami.

Courier services are often listed in the *Yellow Pages* or in advertisements in travel sections of newspapers. One such firm is **Halbart Express,** 147-05 176th St., Jamaica, NY 11434 (tel. 718/656-8189 from 10am to 3pm daily). Another is **Now Voyager,** 74 Varick St., Suite 307, New York, NY 10013 (tel. 212/431-1616). Call daily to speak with someone from 11:30am to 6pm; at other times you'll get a recorded message.

The **International Association of Air Travel Couriers,** P.O. Box 1349, Lake Worth, FL 33460 (tel. 407/582-8320), for an annual membership of $35, will send you six issues of its newsletter, *Shoestring Traveler,* and about half a dozen issues of *Air Courier Bulletin,* a directory of air courier bargains around the world.

REBATORS To confuse the situation even more, rebators also compete in the low-cost air-travel market. Most rebators offer discounts that run 10%–25% (but this could vary from place to place), plus a $20 handling charge. They're not the same as travel agents, although they sometimes offer similar services, including discounted land arrangements and car rentals.

Rebators include **Travel Avenue,** 180 N. Des Plaines, Chicago, IL 60661 (tel. 312/876-1116, or toll free 800/333-3335), and **The Smart Traveller,** 3111 SW 27th Ave., Miami, FL 33133 (tel. 305/448-3338, or toll free 800/226-3338 in Florida and Georgia only).

BY TRAIN

If you're already in Europe, you may want to go to Spain by train, especially if you have a Eurailpass. Even if you don't, the cost is moderate, depending on where you are. Rail passengers who visit from Britain or France should make couchette and sleeper reservations as far in advance as possible, especially during the peak summer season.

Because Spain's rail tracks are a wider gauge than those used for French trains (except for the TALGO and Trans-Europe-Express trains), it's necessary to change trains at the border. For long journeys on Spanish rails, seat and sleeper reservations are mandatory.

The most comfortable and the fastest trains in Spain are the TER, TALGO, and Electrotren. However, you pay a supplement to ride on these fast trains. Both first- and second-class travel is available on Spanish trains. Tickets can be purchased in either the United States or Canada at the nearest office of FrenchRail, Inc., or from any reputable travel agent. Confirmation of your reservation will take about a week.

If you want your car carried, you must travel Auto-Expreso in Spain. This type of auto transport can be booked only through travel agents or rail offices once you arrive in Europe.

BY BUS

Bus travel to Spain is possible, but not popular—it's slow. Coach services do operate regularly from major capitals of Western Europe to Madrid and Barcelona.

The busiest routes are from London. **Eurolines,** 52 Grosvenor Gardens, Victoria, SW1 (tel. 071/730-0202), provides bus service to Spain. Schedules depend on the season, so call in advance if you're planning to travel by bus, which involves a sea crossing, of course, at some point in the journey.

BY CAR

FROM EUROPE Motor approaches from Europe to Spain are across France on expressways. The most popular border crossing into Spain is east of Biarritz. To Madrid, the best route to take is the E70 west to Bilbao; then cut south on the E804 to the junction with the E05, which heads southwest to Burgos. Bypass Burgos and continue south on the route to Madrid, which is also known as the N-I.

FROM BARCELONA If you're driving from Barcelona to Madrid, connect with the E90 heading west to Zaragoza; from there continue west to Madrid along the E90 via Guadalajara.

PACKAGE TOURS

Some people prefer that a tour operator take care of all their travel arrangements. There are many such companies, each offering transportation to and around Spain, prearranged hotel space, and such extras as a bilingual tour guide and lectures. Often these tours to Spain include excursions to Morocco or Portugal.

There are many different tour operators eager for a share of your business, but one of the most unusual is **Abercrombie & Kent International, Inc.,** 1520 Kensington Rd., Oak Brook, IL 60521 (tel. 708/954-2944, or toll free 800/323-7308), a Chicago-based company established some 30 years ago. Known as a specialist in glamorous tours around the world, it offers deluxe 12-day tours of the Iberian peninsula by train, which—despite all the extras—still costs less than any personally arranged tours with equivalent facilities and services.

Abercrombie and Kent's "Great Spain & Portugal Express" tour is a carefully organized guided first-class rail trip through the tourist gems of Spain and its historical neighbor, Portugal. Tour participants spend the night in some of the most elegant *paradores* of Spain. (Run by the government and chosen for their historic and/or cultural interest, these include some of the most famous castles and medieval monasteries). Tours depart in May and September; the cost is from $4,323 per person, double occupancy, with single supplements of around $900 per person. (Holders of rail passes receive a slight discount.)

America Express Vacations, 300 Pinnacle Way, Norcross, GA 30071 (tel. 404/368-5100, or toll free 800/241-1700), offers some of the most comprehensive programs available to Spain with Madrid as the major stopover.

Sun Holidays, 26 6th St., Suite 603, Stamford, CT 06905 (tel. 203/323-1166, or toll free 800/243-2057), has been a specialist in extended vacations for senior citizens since 1980. The company regularly features fully escorted motorcoach tours of Spain and Portugal, and pays special attention to retired Americans.

The best fly-drive operation is available from **Kemwel Car Rental,** 106 Calvert St., Harrison, NY 10528-3199 (tel. 914/835-5555, or toll free 800/678-0678). If you purchase a round-trip ticket from Iberia Airlines, you'll receive a $69 Kemwel car for one week with unlimited mileage, all taxes and collision-damage waiver included. There are no hidden extras—you pay only for the gas you use. The offer is based on at least two passengers traveling together; single travelers pay a supplement of $75. You can call **Iberia Airlines** year round about its fly-drive programs in Spain (tel. toll free 800/772-4642).

Welcome Tours Hispanidad, 99 Tulip Ave., Floral Park, NY 11001 (tel. 516/488-4700, or toll free 800/274-4400), offers a number of attractive features on its tours. These include car rentals, accommodations at *paradores,* prepackaged and independent travel options, and "stay-put" land and air vacations at resort areas. It offers escorted motorcoach tours, as well. Its fly-drive program—called "A la Carte"—allows travel anywhere in Spain for those wishing to make their own itineraries. Compact budget cars are included in the program. Hotels or apartments can be arranged along the Costa del Sol.

GETTING TO KNOW MADRID

In *The Sun Also Rises,* Hemingway described Madrid as "a white sky-line on the top of a little cliff away off across the sun-hardened country." Papa would not know the city today. The little pueblo that was Madrid continues to grow at a dramatic rate, expanding rapidly in land area and industrial development, sprouting suburbs of apartment houses for the burgeoning population.

On a plateau of the Sierra de Guadarrama, the capital of Spain is the highest in Europe, reaching a peak of 2,373 feet above sea level at its loftiest point. The sierra air is dry, almost crystal pure, the sky cerulean as painted by Velázquez.

As Spanish cities go, Madrid is still young. *Don Quixote* was already known throughout the world when in 1561 Philip II decided to make Madrid the capital of Spain. The location was apt: Geographically, it was the heart of the Iberian peninsula.

On your way into Madrid from Barajas Airport, you're likely to see an aging *dueña* shrouded in black—perhaps mourning for her husband who died in the Spanish Civil War in the late 1930s. The scene is one of the *tableaux vivants,* frozen in time and space.

As you near the center of the city, however, skyscrapers herald tomorrow's world. Flashy billboards implore everybody to "*bebe* Coca-Cola," or to wear Yankee-style Levi's for greater sex appeal.

It's impossible to separate Madrid or Castile from the saga of the nation as a whole. It was from the barren, undulating plains of the country's heartland that the proud, sometimes arrogant, Castilians emerged. They were destined not only to unify the country, but to dominate it—and to go even further, carving out an empire that was to embrace the Aztecs and Incas, even the far-away Philippines.

In Castile you'll meet a survival-sharpened people. One scholar put it this way: "The Spaniards are a fierce, idealistic, generous people, capable of great sacrifice and heroism when driven by their proud and burning passions, but they are also intolerant, dogmatic, and individualistic." Regardless, know that Mardrileños—whatever their backgrounds—are generally friendly, especially to their well-behaved guests. As hosts, they have great style and graciousness, and Madrid today is among the most hospitable capitals in Europe.

---

1. ORIENTATION

No one ever claimed that knowing or getting around Madrid was easy. Many taxi drivers (usually from the provinces) are unfamiliar with the city as well, once they branch off the main boulevards.

Everything in the Spanish capital is spread out, and this may cause you difficulty until you get the feel of it. For example, on one typical night you may want to sample the *tapas* (hors d'oeuvres) at a *tasca* on the Ventura de la Vega, dine at a restaurant that opens onto the fairly far-off Plaza Mayor, witness an evening of flamenco near the Ritz Hotel, then head for your hotel at the gateway to Toledo. The easiest, most sensible and practical means of getting around to all these widely scattered places is by taxi (see "Getting Around," below in this chapter).

ARRIVING/DEPARTING

BY PLANE   The international airport for Madrid is **Barajas,** and it's divided into two separate terminals—one for international flights, another for domestic. A shuttle bus runs between the two. For Barajas Airport information, telephone 205-43-72; for Iberia Airlines information, dial 411-25-45.

Air-conditioned yellow buses take you from right outside the arrivals terminal at Barajas to the underground bus depot under the Plaza Colón. You can also get off at several points along the way, provided you don't have your suitcases stored in the hold. The fare is 250 ptas. ($2.50), and buses leave about every 20 minutes, either to or from the airport.

If you go by taxi into town, the fare will run about 1,800–2,100 ptas. ($1.80–$2.10), depending on traffic. The driver is entitled to assess a surcharge (in either direction) not only for the trip but also for baggage handling. If you should step into a nonmetered limousine, it's important to negotiate the price in advance.

BY TRAIN   Madrid has three major railway stations. At the **Atocha,** Glorieta de Carlos V (Metro: Atocha RENFE), you can book passage for Lisbon, Toledo, Andalusia, and Extremadura. For trains to Barcelona, Asturias, Cantabria, Castilla-León, País Vasco, Aragón, Cataluna, Levante, Murcia, and the French frontier, go to **Charmartín** in the northern suburbs, at Agustín de Foxa (Metro: Charmartín). The third is the **Estación del Norte** (Príncipe Pío; Metro: Norte), which is the main gateway for trains to northwestern Spain (Salamanca and Galicia). For railway information, telephone 429-02-02.

Warning: In Madrid, don't wait to buy your rail ticket or make a reservation at the train station. By this time there may be no tickets left—or at least no desirable tickets. For most tickets, go to the principal RENFE office at Alcalá 44 (tel. 429-05-18). It's open Monday through Friday from 9am to 3pm and 4 to 7:30pm, and on Saturday from 9am to 1:30pm. Metro: Banco de España.

BY BUS   Madrid has at least eight major bus terminals, including the large **Estación Sur de Autobuses,** Canarias 17 (tel. 468-42-00; Metro: Palos de Moguer). Buses to the environs of Madrid, such as Toledo and Segovia, leave from numerous other stations; it's best to call 401-99-00 for current information about departures.

BY CAR   The following are the major highways into Madrid:

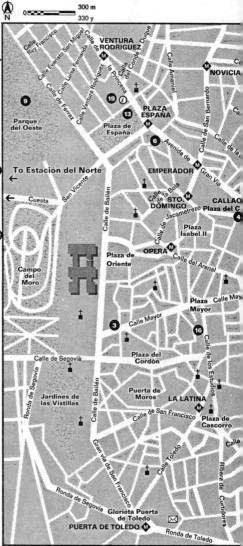

Route	From	Distance to Madrid
N-I	Irún	315 miles (505km)
N-II	Barcelona	389 miles (622km)
N-III	Valencia	217 miles (347km)
N-IV	Cádiz	400 miles (640km)
N-V	Badajoz	253 miles (450km)
N-VI	Galicia	374 miles (598km)

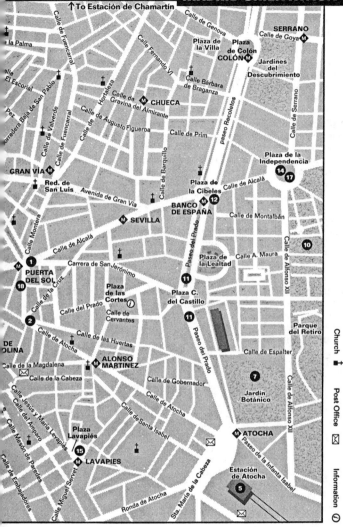

To Estación de Chamartín

Calle de Genova

SERRANO
Calle de Goya M

Plaza de
la Villa

Plaza
de Colón M
COLÓN M

Jardines
del
Descubrimiento

Calle Fernando VI

Calle de Fuencarral

la Palma

El Escorial

Calle Bárbara
de Braganza

Calle de
Gravina

CHUECA

Calle del Almirante

Calle de Hortaleza

rredera Baja de San Pablo

Calle de Augusto Figueroa

Calle de Prim

Paseo Recoletos

Calle de Serrano

GRAN VÍA M

Red. de
San Luis

Avenida de Gran Vía

Calle de Barquillo

Plaza de la
Independencia

14

17

Plaza de
la Cibeles

Calle de Alcalá

Calle de Valverde

Calle de Fuencarral

Calle Montera

BANCO
DE ESPAÑA

12

M SEVILLA

Calle de Montalbán

Calle de Alcalá

Carrera de San Jerónimo

Paseo del Prado

Plaza de
la Lealtad

Calle A. Maura

10

Calle de Alfonso XII

1

M
PUERTA
DEL SOL

18

Calle de la Cruz

Plaza
de las
Cortes

Calle del Prado

Plaza C.
del Castillo

11

11

Calle de
Cervantes

Parque
del Retiro

2

Calle de Atocha

Calle de las Huertas

Paseo del Prado

Calle de Espalter

DE
OLINA

Calle de la Magdalena

ALONSO
MARTÍNEZ

Calle de Gobernador

7

Calle de la Cabeza

Calle de Atocha

Jardín
Botánico

Calle de Alfonso XII

Calle Jesús y María

Calle del Amparo

Calle de Santa Isabel

Plaza
Lavapiés

15

M LAVAPIÉS

ATOCHA

Calle Mesón de Paredes

Calle Miguel Servet

Sta. María de la Cabeza

Estación
de Atocha

5

Calle de Embajadores

Ronda de Atocha

Paseo de la Infanta Isabel

Church ■✝

Post Office ⊠

Information ⓘ

The most convenient tourist office is on the ground floor of the 40-story **Torre de Madrid,** Plaza de España (tel. 91/541-23-25; Metro: Plaza de España). It's open Monday through Friday from 9am to 7pm and on Saturday from 9:30am to 1:30pm. The staff here can give you a list of hotels and hostales, but cannot recommend any particular establishment.

If you're heading on to another city after your visit to Madrid, ask for a street map of the next destination on your itinerary, especially if you're driving.

CITY LAYOUT

The Spanish capital, as mentioned, is a fast-growing city, its development sporadic and largely haphazard. It can be described in many ways and from many points of view.

If you're interested in "Royal Madrid," you'll think of the **Palacio Real,** which fronts the handsome **Plaza de Oriente,** with its Velázquez-inspired equestrian statue of Philip IV. The gardens, parks, and wide avenues—all appropriate for state receptions and parades—took new significance with the restoration of the Spanish monarchy.

If you're a romanticist nostalgic for the 19th century, you'll watch in sadness as the mansions along the **paseo de la Castellana** and its satellite streets are torn down to make way for modern offices and shops, deluxe hotels, and apartment buildings. Thankfully, a few are still preserved and used today by foreign embassies.

If you're an artist or devotee of art, you'll spend most of your time at the great old **Prado,** the treasure house of Spanish masterpieces that shelters a once-royal collection of European art.

If you're on a shopping spree, you'll gravitate to the **Gran Vía,** called the avenida José Antonio during the long dictatorship of Franco. The Gran Vía is the main street of Madrid, with its stores, cinemas, and hotels—the latter both luxury and budget. The wide avenue—flanked with sidewalk cafés—ends at the **Plaza de España** with its Edificio España, one of the tallest skyscrapers in Europe. Or you'll wander past the multitude of shops, boutiques, coffeehouses, and couturiers' salons of the more prestigious **calle de Serrano.**

If medieval Madrid intrigues you, you'll seek out the Moorish towers of the old quarter, looking for the *mudéjar* style of architecture. You'll photograph (in your mind, if not with your camera), the **Plaza de la Villa,** and focus especially on the **Torre de los Lujanes.** According to tradition, François I of France was held captive at the tower after he was taken prisoner in Pavia, Italy.

The colonnaded and rectangular **Plaza Mayor,** one of the most harmoniously designed squares in Europe, recalls the Madrid of the 17th century. The scene of many an *auto-da-fé* (burning of a heretic), bullfight, or execution of a traitor, it is today one of the best spots in the city for a *paseo* (stroll), especially if you take time out from your outing to explore the adjoining shops, some of which sell sombreros. Later you can select a restaurant, perhaps one with a table that opens right on the square.

If you walk through one of the vaulted porticoes of the Plaza Mayor to the south, down the street of *típico* restaurants and taverns—**calle de Cuchilleros**—you'll reach the **calle de Toledo.** Then you'll be entering a special world of Old Madrid, still preserved. Known as the *barrios bajos,* it is home to the Madrileño lowest on the economic scale. In some cities it would be called a ghetto or slum. But in Madrid the area abounds with such style—screaming gypsy *niños,* arcaded markets stuffed with meats and vegetables, shops, *tascas, cuevas*—that it retains great punch.

The City Center and Main Avenues

The real center of the city is the **Puerta del Sol** (the Gateway of the Sun). Despite its grand appellation, it's a dull terminus of considerable traffic congestion and crime. Beginning at the Puerta del Sol, **calle de Alcalá** is the most traffic-choked artery in Madrid, a street that runs for more than 2½ miles. It's the avenue of Spanish bankers, and houses the Escuela y Museo de la Real Academia de Bellas Artes de San Fernando.

Madrid's greatest boulevard, its Champs-Elysées, begins at Atocha Railway Station. Heading north, it's called the **paseo del Prado,** and it passes on its right the Botanical Gardens and the Prado museum. It doesn't end, but changes its name at the **Plaza de la Cibeles,** dominated by the "cathedral of post offices" and a fountain honoring Cybele, "the great mother of the gods."

At Cibeles, the boulevard is henceforth the **paseo de Carvo Sotelo,** and leads into the **Plaza de Colón.** At Colón, the **paseo de la Castellana** begins. Seemingly endless, paseo de la Castellana stretches through a posh area spreading out on both sides and featuring apartment houses, restaurants, department stores, and hotels; it continues past the public ministries, up to the flourishing **Plaza de Castilla,** and then on to the huge La Paz hospital complex.

FINDING AN ADDRESS   In Madrid this can be a problem: The city is noted for its long boulevards—one stretching for 2½ miles—so knowing the street number and cross street is very important. The rule about street numbers is that there is no rule. Most streets begin their numbering on one side, running in order until the end, then running back in the opposite direction on the other side. Therefore, no. 50 could be opposite no. 308. But there are many exceptions to this, so be prepared.

STREET MAPS   Arm yourself with a good map before setting out. The best is published by **Falk,** and it's available at most newsstands and kiosks in Madrid. Those given away free by tourist offices and hotels aren't adequate, as they don't show the maze of little streets.

Neighborhoods in Brief

Madrid can be divided into three principal districts—Old Madrid, which holds the most tourist interest; Ensanche, the new district, often with the best shops and hotels; and the periphery, which is of little interest to visitors.

Plaza Mayor/Puerta del Sol   This is the heart of Old Madrid, often called "the tourist zone." Filled with taverns and bars, it is bounded by carrera de San Jerónimo, calle Mayor, cava de San Miguel, cava Baja, and calle de la Cruz. From the Plaza Mayor, the arco de Cuchilleros is filled with Castilian restaurants and taverns; more cuevas (wine bars) lie along cava de San Miguel, cava Alta, and cava Baja. To the west of this old district is the Manzanares River. Muslim Madrid centers on the present-day Palacio de Oriente and Las Vistillas. What is now the Plaza de la Paja was the heart of Madrid and its main marketplace during the medieval and Christian period. In 1617 the Plaza Mayor became the hub of Madrid, and it remains the nighttime center of tourist activity, more so than the Puerta del Sol.

The Salamanca Quarter Ever since Madrid's city walls came tumbling down in the 1860s, the district of Salamanca to the north has been a fashionable address. Calle de Serrano cuts through it, a street lined with stores and boutiques. The U.S. Embassy is also here.

Gran Vía/Plaza de España The Gran Vía is the city's main street, lined with cinemas, department stores, and the headquarters of banks and corporations. It begins at the Plaza de España, with its bronze figures of Don Quixote and his faithful Sancho Pancho.

Argüelles/Moncloa The university area is bounded by Pintor Rosales, Cea Bermúdez, Bravo Murillo, San Bernardo, and Conde Duque. Students haunt its famous ale houses.

Chueca An old and decaying area north of the Gran Vía. Its main streets are Hortaleza, Infantas, Barquillo, and San Lucas. It's the center of gay nightlife, with many clubs and cheap restaurants. It can be dangerous at night, however.

Castellana/Recoletos/Paseo del Prado Not really a city district, this is Madrid's north-south axis, its name changing along the way. The Museo del Prado and some of the city's more expensive hotels are found here. Many restaurants and other hotels are located along its side streets. In summer the several open-air terraces are filled with animated crowds. The most famous café is the Gran Café Gijon.

---

2. GETTING AROUND

BY PUBLIC TRANSPORTATION **Discount Passes** You can save money on public transportation by purchasing a 10-trip ticket—known as a *bonos*—for the Metro (subway) for 450 ptas. ($4.50) at any Metro station. The center of the system is the Puerta del Sol; call 435-22-66 for more information.

For 450 ptas. ($4.50) you can also purchase a 10-trip ticket (but without transfers) for Madrid's bus system. It's sold at Empresa Municipal de Transportes, Plaza de la Cibeles (tel. 401-99-00), where you can also purchase a guide to the bus routes. It's open daily from 8am to 8:30pm.

Subway [Metro] The Metro system, first installed in 1919, is quite easy to learn, and you can travel if not comfortably at least without any congestion or crushing as in former years.

Line 7 is completely different from the rest, and as modern as some of Europe's newest subway systems. The future lines under construction will be the same type as no. 7.

The central converging point of the Metro is at the Puerta del Sol. The subways begin their runs at 6am and shut down at 1:30am. It's best to try to avoid traveling on the subways during the rush hours, of course. The fare is 115 ptas. ($1.15). For information, call 435-22-66.

Bus A network of buses traverses the city, fanning out to the suburbs. The route of each bus is clearly marked at each stop on a schematic diagram. Buses are fast and efficient, and travel down special lanes made for them all over the city. Both red and yellow

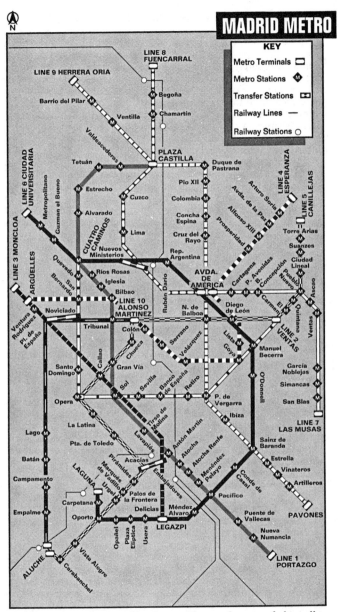

buses charge 115 ptas. ($1.15) per ride—and most of the yellow buses have the advantage of being air-conditioned. (For information on buses from the airport into Madrid, see "Arriving/Departing" in "Orientation," above.

Madrid has at least eight principal bus terminals, including the large **Estación Sur de Autobuses,** Canarias 17 (tel. 468-42-00; Metro: Palos de Moguer). Buses to the environs of Madrid, such as Toledo and Segovia, leave from numerous stations.

BY TAXI Fortunately, cabs are moderately priced. At the start of a ride, the meter registers 125 ptas. ($1.25)—this was at press time, but that fare will surely have gone up by the time of your visit. An average ride costs about 600 ptas. ($6). There are extras as well. Trips to the railway station or the bullring carry a supplement, plus an additional fee tacked on to the fare on Sunday and holidays. A ride to Barajas Airport carries a 250-pta. ($2.50) surcharge, plus 100 ptas. ($1) per bag. It's customary to tip at least 10% or more of the fare.

A ride is usually an adventure, as Madrileño drivers go fast, occasionally (but not always) stopping at red lights.

Taxi-riding has some minor traps that visitors will do well to avoid. There are two major types of taxis: black with horizontal red bands and white with diagonal red bands. Their rates are usually the same. However, many unmetered, unbanded taxis also abound in Madrid; the drivers rent their services as guides for the day or half day. But when business is slow, these guides sometimes operate as "gypsy" cabs and pick up unsuspecting passengers, take them to their destinations, and charge them whatever they think the market will bear. Beyond that pitfall, you must be careful to require that your driver start the meter when you enter the cab. Otherwise, the driver may "assess" the cost of the ride to your disadvantage.

To call a taxi, dial 445-90-08, 247-82-00, or 404-90-00.

BY CAR Rentals You won't want to drive in Madrid; it's too congested. But if you're touring the environs of Madrid, you'll find that a rented car will come in handy, allowing you to stop off at that *típico* roadside tavern for *tapas* or to make that side detour to a medieval village. You'll be your own guide, exploring at your leisure places not covered—or covered too hurriedly—on an organized tour.

Many of North America's biggest car-rental companies, including Avis, Budget, and Hertz, maintain offices throughout Spain. Though several Spain-based car-rental companies will try to entice you to their facilities, letters from readers have shown that the resolution of billing irregularities and insurance claims tends to be less complicated with the U.S.-based car-rental firms.

To qualify for the best rates, you should reserve a car at least two weeks prior to your departure from North America.

- **Avis** (tel. toll free in the U.S. 800/331-2112).
- **Budget Rent-A-Car** (tel. toll free in the U.S. 800/427-3325).
- **Hertz** (tel. toll free in the U.S. 800/654-3001).

Insurance Insurance options at each of the companies are complicated; some companies will, for a higher net rate, include the insurance and taxes in a car's weekly rental fee. Others, such as Budget, prefer to quote the insurance as a separate add-on fee. A collision-damage waiver (CDW) costs around $13 a day for most small and medium-sized cars. Unless you're covered through independent insurance (such as that offered by some credit-card companies), it's usually an excellent idea to take the extra insurance.

Gas Gas is easily obtainable and is the usual fuel for rented cars in Spain. The average Spanish vehicle—predominantly Seats or Fiats—gets close to 45 miles per gallon. At time of press, a liter of gas costs about 98 pesetas—this works out to about $4 per U.S. gallon.

Parking This is a nightmare! Street parking is not readily available. As spaces become free, motorists often compete fiercely for the vacancy. If you're driving into Madrid—the only time you should use your car, really—you should call your hotel and ask if it offers a space. If not, ask the location of the nearest garage. Stop first at your hotel, unload your luggage, and then follow directions to the nearest parking garage. Parking prices depend on the neighborhood. Those in the very center of Madrid are the most expensive, of course.

Driving Rules   Madrileños drive on the right side of the road. Drivers should pass on the left; local drivers sound their horns when passing another car. Autos coming from the right have the right-of-way.

If you must drive in Madrid, try to do so between 3 and 5pm, when many motorists are having a siesta. Never park your car facing oncoming traffic, as that's against the law. If you're fined by the highway patrol (Guardia Civil de Tráfico), you must pay on the spot. Penalties for drinking and driving are very stiff. The speed limit is 35 m.p.h. (55kmph).

BY BICYCLE   Ever wonder why you see so few people riding bicycles in Madrid? Those who tried were overcome by the traffic pollution. It's better to walk.

ON FOOT   Walking is the perfect way to see Madrid, especially the ancient narrow streets of the old town. If you're coming to the old town from another district—and chances are that your hotel will be outside the old town—you can take the bus or Metro. For such a large city, Madrid can be covered amazingly well on foot, because so much of what will interest a visitor lies in various clusters.

BY HITCHHIKING   This is no longer smiled upon as much as it used to be. Although it's technically legal, I don't recommend that you stick out your thumb in the presence of the Civil Guard. More important, hitchhiking is an increasingly dubious and unsafe way to travel, with the inherent danger of simply not knowing what maniac is likely to pick you up. Take the bus or train—it's safer, easier, and faster.

 FAST MADRID

How do you find what you're seeking quickly and conveniently? In an emergency, of course, your hotel is your best bet. But some of the smaller hotels aren't staffed with personnel entirely fluent in English; and sometimes—even if they are—the person at the desk can be apathetic about something of vital interest to you.

American Express   For your mail or banking needs, try the American Express office at the corner of the Marqués de Cubas and Plaza de las Cortés 2 (tel. 429-57-75), across the street from the Palace Hotel. The office is open Monday through Friday from 9am to 5:30pm and on Saturday from 9am to noon. Metro: Gran Vía.

Area Codes   The telephone area code for Madrid is 91 if you are calling from within Spain. If you're dialing Spain from North America, the country code for Spain is 34 and the area code for Madrid is 1. (Don't dial 91 when calling Madrid from the United States.)

Babysitters   Nearly all major hotels in Madrid can arrange for babysitters, called *canguros* in Spanish. Usually the concierge keeps a list of reliable sitters and will put you in touch with one of them, provided you give adequate notice. Rates vary considerably, but tend to be reasonable. More and more babysitters in Madrid speak English, but don't count on it. Chances are yours won't—although you can request it, of course.

Bookstores   Aguilar, calle de Serrano 24 (tel. 577-36-74; Metro: Serrano), sells English and Spanish editions. It has two other outlets at Goya 18 (tel. 575-06-40; Metro: Velázquez) and paseo de la Castellana 154 (tel. 259-09-67; Metro: Cuzco). Open Monday through Saturday from 10am to 1pm and 5 to 8pm.

Turner's, Génova 3 (tel. 410-29-15; Metro: Alonso Martínez), has one of the largest collections of English and French titles in Madrid. Lots of touring aids are available. Open Monday through Friday from 9:30am to 2pm and 5 to 8pm, and on Saturday from 10am to 2pm.

Business Hours   **Banks** are open Monday through Friday from 9:30am to 2pm and on Saturday from 9:30am to 1pm. Most **offices** are open Monday through Friday from 9am to 5 or 5:30pm; the longtime practice of early closings in summer seems to be dying out. In **restaurants,** lunch is usually served from 1 to 4pm and dinner is 9 to 11:30pm or midnight. There are no set rules for the hours of **bars and taverns:** Many open at 8am, others at noon; most stay open until 1:30am or later. Major **stores** are open Monday through Saturday from 9:30am to 8pm; smaller establishments, however, often take a siesta, doing business from 9:30am to 1:30pm and 4:30 to 8pm. Hours can vary from store to store.

Currency Exchange   For the best rate when changing your money from dollars into pesetas, you should go to a bank. Banks are open Monday through Friday from 9:30am to 2pm; it's best to go after 10am. Many banks are also open on Saturday from 9:30am to 1pm. The currency exchange at Chamartín railway station (Metro: Charmartín) is open 24 hours a day.

Dentist   For an English-speaking dentist, contact the U.S. Embassy, calle de Serrano 75 (tel. 577-40-00), which has a list of recommended ones. If you have a dental emergency, you may have to call several dentists before you can get an immediate appointment. Or else, for both medical and dental services, consult **Unidad Médica,** Conde Aranda 1 (tel. 435-18-23), in back of the Plaza de Colón. Office hours are Monday through Friday from 9am to 8pm and on Saturday from 10am to 2pm, although there is a daily 24-hour answering service.

Doctor   See "Dentist," above.

Drugstores   Drugstores are scattered all over Madrid. If you're trying to locate one at an odd hour, look for a list of open pharmacies posted outside the door of any closed drugstore. The Spanish government requires drugstores to operate on the rotating system of hours—thereby assuring you that some will be open at all times, even on Sunday at midnight.

Two of the capital's largest pharmacies are in districts heavily visited by foreign travelers: Farmacia Gayaso, Arenal 2 (tel. 521-28-60; Metro: Puerta del Sol), and the Farmacia del Globo, Atocha 46 (tel. 239-46-00; Metro: Tirso de Molina), usually have at least one employee who speaks English. For a 24-hour pharmacy, phone 098.

Electricity   Many North Americans find that the plugs of their hairdryers and razors won't fit into the sockets in Madrid, where the electricity is 200 volts AC, 50 cycles. In the unlikely event that you manage to force the plug of your appliance into the outlet, you will destroy your appliance, upset the hotel management, and possibly cause a fire, so don't try. Many hardware stores in North America sell the appropriate transformers (often called converters), and the concierge desks of most hotels will either lend you a transformer and an adapter for your plugs or tell you where you can buy them nearby. If you have any doubt about whether you have the appropriate transformer, ask questions at your hotel desk.

Embassies/Consulates If you lose your passport, fall seriously ill, get into legal trouble, or have some urgently serious problem, your embassy or consulate located in Madrid will probably have a mechanism to help you.

- **The United States Embassy,** calle Serrano 75 (tel. 577-4000; Metro: Núñez de Balboa), is open Monday to Friday 9:30am to 1pm.
- **The Canadian Embassy,** Núñez de Balboa 35 (tel. 431-43-00); Metro: Núñez de Balboa) is open Monday to Friday 9am to 1pm.
- **The United Kingdom Embassy,** Fernando el Santo (tel. 319-02-00; Metro: Rubén Darío), is open Monday to Friday 10am to 1pm.
- **The Republic of Ireland Embassy,** calle Claudio Coello 73 (tel. 576-35-00; Metro: Núñez de Balboa) open Monday to Friday 10am to 2pm.
- **The Australian Embassy,** paseo de la Castellana 143 (tel. 279-85-04; Metro: Cuzco), is open Monday to Friday 10am to 1pm.
- **New Zealand,** citizens should contact the U.K. embassy for assistance or advise, see address above.

Emergencies If you need the police, call 091. In case of fire, dial 080. For an ambulance, as in the case of an accident, telephone 588-44-00.

Etiquette Women often kiss each other once on both cheeks when they meet. Men extend a hand when introduced; if they are good friends, they will often embrace. In general, women (except young moderns) expect men to open doors for them and to rise when they enter a room. The elderly are often treated with great respect and courtesy. When it comes to lining up for something—say, for a bus—you should step forward or you may find yourself the last one on. As a foreign guest, avoid all unfavorable references to Spain; Spanish nationalist pride often asserts itself vigorously in the face of criticism by a foreigner.

Eyeglasses A reasonably priced place to purchase eyeglasses (prescription variety) or have eyeglasses repaired is Visionalab, Orense 24 (tel. 556-44-15; Metro: N. Ministerios). It's open Monday through Friday from 10am to 9pm and on Saturday from 10am to 3pm.

Film Negra makes both black-and-white and color film. Valca is another popular brand. Also see "Photographic Needs," below.

Hairdressers/Barbers A good salon for women is Galico, Velázquez 89 (tel. 563-47-63; Metro: Núnez de Balboa), open Monday through Saturday from 10am to 6pm; call for an appointment. For men, a fine choice is Jacques Dessange, O'Donnell 9 (tel. 435-32-20; Metro: Príncipe de Vergara), open Monday through Saturday from 10am to 6:30pm. All the El Corte Inglés department stores have good barbershops (see "Department Stores" under "Shopping A to Z" in Chapter 8).

Hospitals The British-American Medical Unit, Conde de Aranda 1 (tel. 435-18-23; Metro: Usera), has a staff of doctors, dentists, and even optometrists. However, this is not an emergency clinic, although someone is available on the staff at all times. The normal daily hours are 9am to 8pm. For a real medical emergency, call 588-44-00 for an ambulance.

Hotlines Call 559-13-93 to reach an English-language "helpline," providing practical information daily from 7pm to 11pm. During other hours, you get an answering machine.

Language Spanish is the official language of the land, of course, and French is also widely spoken in parts. In Madrid, more and more people, especially the younger ones, are learning English. Nearly all major hotels and top restaurants are staffed with English-speakers. However, out in the country it will help a lot if you were a language major in school. The best phrase book is *Spanish for Travellers* by Berlitz; this pocket dictionary has a menu supplement and a 12,500-word glossary of both English and Spanish.

Laundry/Dry Cleaning In most first-class hotels recommended in this guide, you need only fill out your laundry and dry-cleaning list and present it to your maid or valet. Same-day service usually costs 25%–50% more. Madrid has a number of launderettes. Try, for example, Lavandería Marcenado, calle Marcenado 15 (tel. 416-68-71; Metro: Prosperidad), which is full service and open Monday through Friday from 9:30am to 1:30pm and 4:30 to 8pm. There's also Lavandería Donoso Cortés, calle Donoso Cortés 17 (tel. 446-96-90; Metro: Quevedo), which is self-service. It's open Monday through Friday from 8:30am to 7:30pm and on Saturday from 8:30am to 1pm.

A good dry-cleaning service is provided by the El Corte Inglés department store at calle Preciados 3 (tel. 532-18-00), where the staff speaks English.

Libraries A large selection of American magazines and other material is available at the Washington Irving Center, Marqués de Villamagna 8 (tel. 435-6922; Metro: Rubén Darío), open Monday through Friday from noon to 7pm. The British Cultural Center, Almagro 5 (tel. 337-35-00; Metro: Alonso Martínez), also has a large selection of English reading material; it's open Monday through Friday from 9am to 7pm.

Liquor Laws The legal drinking age is 18. Bars, taverns, and cafeterias usually open at 8am, and many serve alcohol until around 1:30am or later. Generally, you can purchase alcoholic beverages in almost any grocery.

Lost Property If you've lost something on a Madrid bus, go to the municipal office at Alcántara 26 (tel. 401-31-00; Metro: Goya), open Monday through Friday from 9am to 2pm and on Saturday from 9am to 1pm. If you've lost something on the Metro, go anytime to the Cuatro Caminos station (tel. 233-20-00). For objects lost in taxis, go to Plaza de Chamberí (tel. 448-79-26; Metro: Chamberí), open Monday through Friday from 9am to 2pm and on Sat from 9am to 1pm. For objects lost anywhere else, go to the Palacio de Communicaciones at the Plaza de la Cibeles (tel. 531-93-52; Metro: Banco de España), open Monday through Friday from 9am to 2pm and on Saturday from 9am to 1pm. Don't call—show up in person.

Luggage Storage/Lockers   These can be found at both the Atocha and Chamartín railway terminals, as well as the major bus station at the Estación Sur de Autobuses, Canarias 17. Storage is also provided at the air terminal underneath the Plaza de Colón.

Mail   To send either an airmail letter or postcard to the United States it costs 75 ptas. (75¢) for 15 grams. Allow about a week for delivery; in some cases, two weeks. Rates change frequently, so check at your hotel before mailing anything.

Newspapers/Magazines   Most newsstands along the Gran Vía or kiosks at the major hotels carry the latest edition of the *International Herald Tribune.* Spain also has an American weekly, a magazine known as the *Guidepost,* packed with information about late-breaking events in the Spanish capital, tips on movies shown in English, musical recitals, and more. You may also want to become a regular reader of the *Iberian Daily Sun,* an English-language newspaper containing stories and listings of interest to visitors from North America and Britain as well as expatriates. If you're traveling south, look out for *Lookout* magazine, a quality production in English with stories focused primarily on Spain's Costa del Sol along with some articles of general interest to the traveler to Spain.

Pets   It's best to leave them at home. If you don't, you must bring any licenses and proof of vaccinations to your nearest Spanish consulate before you leave. Normally pets aren't welcome in public places; certain hotels will accept them, however—but these arrangements should be made in advance. Don't forget to check quarantine regulations affecting your animal upon your return. Guide dogs, however, are always excluded from such rigid rules. For the pamphlet "Pets," write the U.S. Customs Service, P.O. Box 7407, Washington, DC 20044; or call 202/566-8195 for a recorded message concerning Customs rules about pets.

Photographic Needs   Film is expensive in Spain; take in as much as Customs will allow. I suggest that you wait to process it until you return home. However, if you can't wait, you can take your undeveloped film to the leading department store, Galerías Precíados, calle Precíados 28, right off the Gran Vía (tel. 222-47-71), where you can have your film developed in two hours. Your photographic needs can also be serviced by the El Corte Inglés department store at calle Precíados 3 (tel. 532-18-00).

Police   Dial **091.**

Post Office   If you don't want to receive your mail at your hotel or the American Express office, direct it to *Lista de Correos* ("General Delivery") at the central post office in Madrid. To pick up mail, go to the window marked Lista, where you'll be asked to show your passport. Madrid's central post office is in "the cathedral of the post offices" at the Plaza de la Cibeles (tel. 521-81-95).

Radio/TV   During the day on shortwave radio you can hear the Voice of America and the BBC. An English-language radio program in Madrid called "*Buenos Días*" (Good Morning) airs many useful hints for visitors; it's broadcast Monday through Friday from 6 to 8am on 657 MegaHertz. Radio 80 broadcasts news in English Monday through Saturday from 7 to 8am on 89 FM. Some TV programs are broadcast in English in the summer months. Many hotels—but, regrettably, not most of our budget ones—also bring in satellite TV programs in English.

Religious Services   Most churches in Madrid are Catholic, and they're all over the city. Catholic masses in English, however, are given at Alfonso XIII no. 165; for information, call 233-20-32 in the morning. The British Embassy Church of St. George is at Núñez de Balboa 43 (call 576-51-09 for worship hours). The interdenominational Protestant Community Church, Padre Damian 23 (tel. 446-26-81), offers weekly services in the Colegio de los Sagrados Corazones, while the Immanuel Baptist Church offers English-speaking services at Hernández de Tajada 4 (tel. 407-43-47). A Christian Science church is at Pinilla del Valle 5 (tel. 259-21-35), and you'll find a Jewish synagogue at Balmes 3 (tel. 445-98-35), with services on Friday at 7:30pm and on Saturday at 9:30am.

Restrooms Some are available, including those in Retiro Park in Madrid and on the Plaza del Oriente across from the Royal Palace. Otherwise, you can always go into a bar or *tasca,* but you really should order something—perhaps a small glass of beer or even a bag of peanuts.

The Spanish designations for restrooms are *aseos* or *servicios. Caballeros* are for men and *damas* are for women.

Safety Because of increased thefts in Madrid, the U.S. Embassy urges American visitors to leave passports and valuables in a hotel safe or other secure place while visiting sights of the city. Purse-snatching is prevalent, with the criminals working in pairs, grabbing purses from pedestrians, cyclists, and even from cars. If your car is standing still, a thief may open the door or break a window in order to snatch a purse or package, even from under the seat. A popular scam against Americans in Madrid involves one miscreant's smearing the back of the clothing of the victim, perhaps with mustard or chocolate; an accomplice pretends to help the victim clean off the mess, meanwhile picking all pockets of valuables. The embassy statement advises: Don't carry a purse; keep your valuables in front pockets; carry only enough cash for the day's needs; be aware of who is around you; and keep a separate record of your passport number, traveler's check numbers, and credit-card numbers.

Every car can be a target, parked or just stopped at a light. Don't leave anything in sight in your car. Place valuables in the trunk when you park, and always assume that someone is watching you to see whether you're putting something away for safekeeping. Keep the car locked while you're driving and even for a one-minute stop.

Whenever you're traveling in an unfamiliar city or country, stay alert. Be aware of your immediate surroundings. Wear a money belt and keep a close eye on your possessions. Be particularly careful with cameras, purses, and wallets—all favorite targets of thieves and pickpockets. It's your responsibility to be aware and be alert, even in the most heavily touristed areas.

Shoe Repairs In an emergency, go to one of the "Mister Minit" shoe-repair centers at any El Corte Inglés department store. The flagship store of this chain is at calle Preciados 3 (tel. 532-81-00), near the Puerta del Sol (also the Metro stop); it's open Monday through Saturday from 10am to 9pm.

Smoking In Spain virtually everyone smokes—on buses, in the Metro, everywhere. NO FUMA signs are often ignored.

Taxes Since Spain joined the Common Market (EEC) on January 1, 1986, it committed itself to gradually eliminating most tariff barriers between itself and the rest of Europe. In consequence, internal sales taxes (known in Spain as I.V.A.) were immediately adjusted upward to between 6% and 33%, depending on the commodity being sold. Most of the basic necessities of the Spaniard's life, including food and most wines, are taxed at 6%. The majority of goods and services, as well as rental cars, are taxed at the "ordinary" rate of 12%. Luxury goods such as jewelry, furs, motor yachts, and private airplanes also carry a 12% tax. The rental of rooms in hotels with government ratings of four or five stars is subject to a 12% tax; rooms in hotels rated three stars or fewer are levied a 6% tax. These taxes are usually (but not always) quoted as part of the hotel rates.

For drinkers and smokers, all imported liquors and all tobaccos (whether Spanish or foreign) are taxed at 6% or 12% (depending on the store), making the prices of vices just a little bit higher. Most drinkers solve the problem by switching from scotch to Spanish wines, Spanish beers, or Spanish brandies with soda.

If you buy goods worth a total of more than 25,000 ptas. ($250), you're eligible for a tax rebate of 6% or 12%, depending on the type of purchase. Major department stores will deduct the tax from your bill if you present your passport. Small stores may provide you with a form to fill out that you must show with your purchase to the Spanish Customs I.V.A. desk at your departure point. If a shop does not have a form, save your receipts to show at the I.V.A. desk. The government will refund by mail the amount due in pesetas. Refunds take between two and three months.

Telegrams/Telex/Fax   Cables may be sent from the central post office building in Madrid on the Plaza de la Cibeles (tel. 521-81-95). To send a telegram by phone, dial 522-20-00. In Spain it's cheaper to telephone within the country than to send a telegram. You can send telex and fax messages from the same central post office and from all major hotels.

Telephones   If you don't speak Spanish, you'll find telephoning from your hotel the easiest. Know, however, that this is often a very expensive way of doing it, as hotels impose a surcharge on every operator-assisted call. If you're more adventurous, you'll find street phone booths, known as *cabinas,* with dialing instructions in English. A three-minute local call can be made by inserting three coins of 5 ptas. (5¢) each. For long-distance calls—especially transatlantic ones—it may be best to go to the main telephone exchange, Locutorio Gran Vía, Gran Vía 30, or Locutorio Recoletos, paseo Recoletos 37-41. However, you may not be lucky enough to find an English-speaking operator. You'll have to fill out a simple form that will facilitate placing your call.

Time   Spain is six hours ahead of eastern standard time in the U.S. Daylight saving time (one hour ahead of standard time) is in effect from the last Sunday in March to the last Sunday in September.

Tipping   Don't overtip. The government requires that restaurants and hotels add their service charges (usually 15%) to the bill. However, that doesn't mean you should skip out of a place without dispensing some extra pesetas. Following are some guidelines:

In **hotels,** tip the porter 50 ptas. (50¢) per bag, but never less than 100 ptas. ($1), even if you have only one suitcase; for the maid, 100 ptas. ($1) per day; the doorman, 100 ptas. ($1) for assisting with baggage and 25 ptas. (25¢) for calling a cab. In top-ranking hotels the concierge will often submit a separate bill, showing charges for newspapers and other services; if he or she has been particularly helpful, tip extra.

For **cab drivers,** add about 10%–15% to the fare as shown on the meter. However, if the driver personally unloads or loads your luggage, add 25 ptas. (25¢) per bag.

At **airports** such as Barajas in Madrid and major terminals, the porter who handles your luggage will present you with a fixed-charge bill, usually 75–100 ptas. (75¢–$1) per bag.

In both **restaurants and nightclubs,** a 15% service charge is added to the bill. To that, add another 3%–5%, depending on the quality of the service. Waiters in deluxe restaurants and nightclubs are accustomed to the extra 5%, which means you'll end up tipping 20%. If that seems excessive, you must remember that the initial service charge reflected in the fixed price is distributed among all the help.

In addition, barbers and hairdressers expect 10%–15%; tour guides expect 200 ptas. ($2), although it's not mandatory; and theater/bullfight ushers get 25–50 ptas. (25¢–50¢).

Transit Information   For Metro information, call 401-99-00.

Useful Telephone Numbers   For telegrams by phone, dial 522-20-00; for Iberia Airlines information, call 411-25-45.

Water   It's generally safe to drink the tap water in Madrid; however, if you have a delicate stomach, it's better to switch to mineral water instead.

Weather   Dial 094 for the latest reports.

3. NETWORKS & RESOURCES

FOR STUDENTS   Contact **TIVE,** calle José Ortega y Gasset 71 (tel. 401-95-01; Metro: Becerra), which provides data on low-cost transportation in Spain and also Europe. Always check their discounts against those of other airlines to see just how great a reduction you're getting.

FOR GAY MEN & LESBIANS   Before you go to Spain, you can order *Spartacus,* the international gay guide ($27.95), from **Giovanni's Room,** 1145 Pine St., Philadelphia, PA 19107 (tel. 215/923-2960).

Madrid is now one of the gay capitals in Europe. Besides Madrid, the major gay centers in Spain are Barcelona, Sitges, and Torremolinos on the Costa del Sol (although that resort attracts a mixed crowd). Madrid's gay life centers on the **Chueca district,** north of the Gran Vía, where the bar life begins around 11pm and often lasts until dawn.

In Madrid the Gay Switchboard is **Solidaridad Gay,** Tortosa 4 (tel. 468-50-32), and it's open 24 hours a day with support, legal advice, and information. The best source for gay travel in Spain is **Sky Tours, S.A.,** calle Mayor 80 (tel. 241-04-03; Metro: Opera or Puerta del Sol); it's open Monday through Saturday from 9am to 2pm and 4:30 to 8pm.

Lesbian life remains much more underground in Spain than does male gay life. The best source of information is the **Librería de Mujeres** (see below), a feminist bookshop with much useful data. The best women's entertainment center in Madrid (attracting men too) is **No Sé los Digas a Nadie** ("Don't Tell Mama"), which will be recommended in Chapter 9.

FOR WOMEN   The **Women's Medical Hotline** in Madrid is 419-94-41, receiving calls Monday through Friday from 3:30 to 6:30pm. A women's center is the **Librería de Mujeres,** calle San Cristóbal 17 (tel. 521-70-43), near the Plaza Mayor (Metro: Puerta del Sol). Poetry readings, concerts, talks, and a good international bookstore with some English-language editions are part of the activities and offerings of this group. Open Monday through Saturday from 10am to 2pm and 5 to 8pm.

MADRID ACCOMMODATIONS

The hotel boom in Madrid has been spectacular: Three-quarters of my recommendations are modern. Yet many guests prefer the landmarks of yesteryear, including those grand old establishments, the Ritz and the Palace (ca. 1910–12). However, many other older hostelries in Madrid haven't kept abreast of the times. A handful haven't added improvements or overhauled bedrooms substantially since the 1960s.

Traditionally, hotels in Madrid were clustered around the Atocha Railway Station and the Gran Vía. In my search for the most outstanding hotels in the upper brackets, I've almost ignored these two popular but noisy districts. The newer hotels have been erected away from the center, especially on residential streets jutting off from paseo de la Castellana. However, bargain-seekers will still find great pickings along the Gran Vía and around the Atocha station.

RESERVATIONS Most hotels require at least a day's deposit before they will reserve a room for you. Preferably, this can be accomplished with an international money order, or, if agreed to in advance, with a personal check. You can usually cancel a room reservation one week ahead of time and get a full refund. A few hotelkeepers will return your money three days before the reservation date, but some will take your deposit and never return it, even if you cancel far in advance. Many budget hotel owners operate on such a narrow margin of profit that they find just buying stamps for airmail replies too expensive by their standards. Therefore, it's most important that you enclose a prepaid International Reply Coupon with your payment, especially if you're writing to a budget hotel. Better yet, call and speak to the hotel of your choice, or send a fax.

If you're booking into a chain hotel, such as Hyatt or Forte, you can call toll free in North America and easily make reservations over the phone. Toll-free 800 numbers, when available, are indicated in the individual hotel recommendations in this guide.

If you arrive without a reservation, begin your search for a room as early in the day as possible. If you arrive late at night, you may have to take what you can get, often in a much higher price range than you'd like to pay.

PRICE CLASSIFICATIONS The following prices are for a double room with private bath. Hotels rated "Very Expensive" charge 30,000 ptas. ($300) and up for a double—some establishments in this bracket, including the Villa Magna, the Santo Mauro, and the Ritz, can ask twice that price. Hotels judged "Expensive" ask 17,300–30,000 ptas. ($173–$300) for a double. "Moderate" hotels—at least moderate in the sense of Madrid's hotel price scale—charge 10,000–17,300 ptas. ($100–$173) for a double room. Hotels considered "Inexpensive"—again, by Madrid's pricing standards—ask 6,000–10,000 ptas. ($60–$100) for a double. Any double under 6,000 ptas. ($60) is definitely "Budget" in today's high-priced Madrid.

THE STAR SYSTEM Spain officially rates its hotels by star designation. Five stars is the highest rating in Spain, signaling a deluxe establishment, complete with all the amenities and high tariffs associated with such accommodations.

Most of the establishments recommended in this guide are three- and four-star hotels falling into that vague "middle-bracket" category. Hotels granted one and two stars, as well as pensions (guest houses), are far less comfortable, although they may be perfectly clean and decent places, but with limited plumbing and other physical facilities. The latter category is strictly for dedicated budgeteers.

For easy reference, see the Accommodations Index.

Reminder: The telephone area code for Madrid is 91 if you're calling from within Spain. If you're dialing from North America, the country code is 34 and Madrid's area code is 1.

1. NEAR THE PLAZA DE LAS CORTÉS

VERY EXPENSIVE

HOTEL VILLA REAL, Plaza de las Cortés 10, 28014 Madrid. Tel. 91/420-37-67. Fax 91/420-25-47. 115 rms, 19 suites. A/C MINIBAR TV TEL Metro: Plaza de la Cibeles.

$ Rates: 28,000 ptas. ($280) single; 35,000 ptas. ($350) double; from 65,000 ptas. ($650) suite. Breakfast 1,650 ptas. ($16.50) extra. AE, DC, MC, V. **Parking:** 1,500 ptas. ($15).

Until 1989 the Villa Real was little more than a run-down, 19th-century apartment house auspiciously located across a three-sided park from the Spanish Parliament (Congreso de los Diputados). Its developers poured billions of pesetas into renovations to produce a charming and stylish hotel that's working hard to catch on with the cognoscenti of Spain. The eclectic facade combines an odd mixture of neoclassical and Aztec motifs, and in front of it wait footmen and doormen dressed in buff and forest-green uniforms. The interior contains a scattering of modern paintings amid neoclassical moldings and details.

Each of the accommodations contains televisions with video movies and satellite reception, a safe, soundproofing, a sunken salon filled with leather-upholstered furniture, and built-in furniture accented with burlwood inlays.

Dining/Entertainment: The social center is the high-ceilinged, formal bar. The hotel doesn't have a formal restaurant, but does offer a cafeteria for light meals.

Services: 24-hour room service, laundry/valet, babysitting, express check-out.

Facilities: Sauna, solarium, health club, currency exchange, business center.

THE PALACE, Plaza de las Cortés 7, 28014 Madrid. Tel. 91/429-75-51. Fax 91/429-86-55. 487 rms, 31 suites. A/C MINIBAR TV TEL **Metro:** Banco de España or Anton Martín.

$ Rates: 23,500–34,500 ptas. ($235–$345) single; 30,000–41,000 ptas. ($300–$410) double; from 55,000 ptas. ($550) suite. Breakfast 2,100 ptas. ($21) extra. AE, DC, MC, V. **Parking:** 1,200 ptas. ($12).

The Palace is known as "the grand *dueña*" of Spanish hotels. The establishment had an auspicious beginning, inaugurated by the late King Alfonso XIII in 1912. Covering a city block, it is superbly located, facing the Prado museum and Neptune Fountain, in the historical and artistic area, within walking distance of the main shopping center and the best antiques shops. Some of the city's most intriguing tascas and restaurants are only a short stroll away.

Architecturally, it captures the elegant pre–World War I "Grand Hotel" style, with an emphasis on space and comfort. Even though it's one of the largest hotels in Madrid, it retains a personal atmosphere. The hotel is fully air-conditioned, with an impressive lobby. The rooms are conservatively traditional, with plenty of space for leisurely living and large bathrooms with lots of extra amenities.

Dining/Entertainment: The elegant dining choice here is the Grill Neptuno, serving an international cuisine, with many Spanish specialties. Meals here begin at 6,500 ptas. ($65). However, those on more modest budgets can patronize the Ambigu, offering buffet dining; the salad buffet costs 2,000 ptas. ($20) and the full buffet is 4,000 ptas. ($40). Piano music or other entertainment is provided in the hotel lobby every day.

Services: 24-hour room service, laundry/valet, babysitting, express checkout.

Facilities: Currency exchange, business center.

INEXPENSIVE

HOSTAL CERVANTES, Cervantes 34, 28014 Madrid. Tel. 91/429-27-45. 12 rms (all with bath). **Metro:** Banco de España.

$ Rates: 5,000 ptas. ($50) single; 6,000 ptas. ($60) double. No credit cards.

One of Madrid's most pleasant family-run hotels, the Cervantes has been widely appreciated by our readers for years. Take a tiny birdcage-style elevator to the immaculately maintained second floor of this stone-and-brick building. Each accommodation contains a bed, spartan furniture, and a private bath. No breakfast is served, but the Alfonsos will direct you to a nearby café. The establishment is convenient to the Prado, Retiro Park, and the older sections of Madrid.

2. NEAR THE PLAZA DE ESPAÑA

EXPENSIVE

PLAZA HOTEL, Plaza de España 8, 28013 Madrid. Tel. 91/247-12-00. Fax 91/248-23-89. 260 rms, 40 suites. A/C MINIBAR TV TEL **Metro:** Plaza de España.
$ Rates: 19,500 ptas. ($195) single; 24,500 ptas. ($245) double; from 32,000 ptas. ($320) suites. Breakfast 1,200 ptas. ($12) extra. AE, DC, MC, V. **Parking:** 1,300 ptas. ($13).

The Plaza Hotel could be called the Waldorf-Astoria of Spain. A massive rose-and-white structure, it soars upward to a central tower 26 stories high. It's a landmark visible for miles around and one of the tallest skyscrapers in Europe.

The hotel's accommodations include conventional singles and doubles as well as luxurious suites, each of which contains a sitting room and lots of amenities. Each of the accommodations, regardless of its size, contains an expansive marble-covered bathroom. Furniture is usually a standardized modern style, in such carefully harmonized colors as gray and mulberry.

Dining/Entertainment: The hotel has a traditional restaurant, the Toledo, and a smaller, somewhat less expensive eatery, the Acelea. There's also a piano bar.

Services: 24-hour room service, laundry/valet, concierge, babysitting.

Facilities: The swimming pool and sun terrace on the top floor provide sweeping views over the architectural symmetry of one of Madrid's largest squares (the Plaza de España).

MODERATE

CASÓN DEL TORMES, calle Río 7, 28013 Madrid. Tel. 91/541-97-46. Fax 91/541-18-52. 63 rms (all with bath). A/C MINIBAR TV TEL **Metro:** Plaza de España.
$ Rates: 7,900 ptas. ($79) single; 11,000 ptas. ($110) double. Breakfast 600 ptas. ($6) extra. MC, V. **Parking:** 1,200 ptas. ($12).

The attractive three-star Casón del Tormes is around the corner from the Royal Palace and the Plaza de España. Set behind a red-brick four-story facade with stone-trimmed windows, it overlooks a quiet one-way street. The long narrow lobby contains vertical wooden paneling, a marble floor, and a bar opening into a separate room. Motorists appreciate the public parking lot near the hotel. Laundry service is provided.

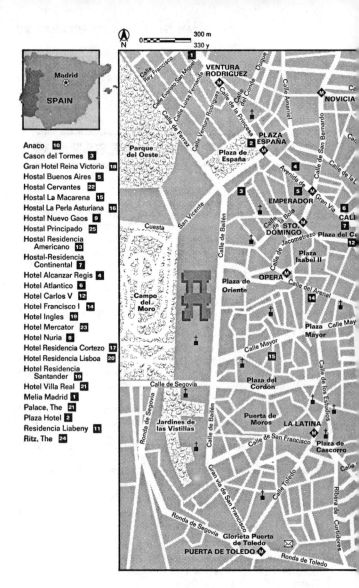

Anaco 10
Cason del Tormes 3
Gran Hotel Reina Victoria 18
Hostal Buenos Aires 5
Hostal Cervantes 22
Hostal La Macarena 15
Hostal La Perla Asturiana 16
Hostal Nuevo Gaos 9
Hostal Principado 25
Hostal Residencia
    Americano 13
Hostal-Residencia
    Continental 7
Hotel Alcanzar Regis 4
Hotel Atlantico 6
Hotel Carlos V 12
Hotel Francisco I 14
Hotel Ingles 19
Hotel Mercator 23
Hotel Nuria 8
Hotel Residencia Cortezo 17
Hotel Residencia Lisboa 20
Hotel Residencia
    Santander 19
Hotel Villa Real 21
Melia Madrid 1
Palace, The 21
Plaza Hotel 2
Residencia Liabeny 11
Ritz, The 24

3. ON OR NEAR THE GRAN VÍA

MODERATE

ANACO, Tres Cruces 3, 28013 Madrid. Tel. 91/522-46-04. Fax 91/531-64-84. 39 rms (all with bath). A/C TV TEL **Metro:** Gran Vía, Callao, or Puerta del Sol.

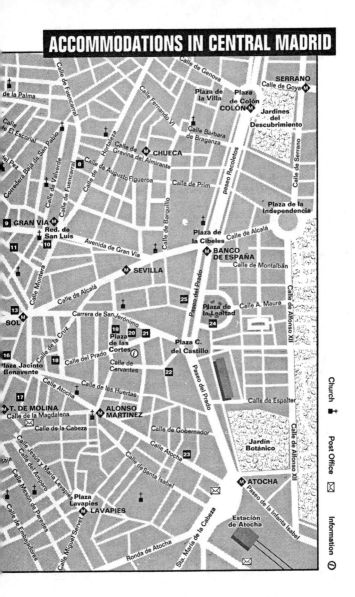

ACCOMMODATIONS IN CENTRAL MADRID

Church ✚ **Post Office** ⊠ **Information** ⓘ

$ Rates: 7,800 ptas. ($78) single; 11,500 ptas. ($115) double. Breakfast 700 ptas. ($7) extra. AE, DC, MC, V.

A modestly modern hotel, the Anaco is just off the shopping thoroughfare, the Gran Vía. Opening onto a tree-shaded plaza, it attracts those seeking a resting place featuring contemporary appurtenances and cleanliness. The bedrooms are compact, with built-in headboards, reading lamps, and lounge chairs. Useful tip: Ask for one of the five terraced rooms on the top floor, which rent at no extra charge. English is spoken. A municipally operated garage is nearby.

HOTEL ATLÁNTICO, Gran Vía 38, 28013 Madrid. Tel. 91/522-64-80 or toll free in the U.S.A. 800/528-1234. Fax 91/531-02-10. 62 rms (all with bath). A/C MINIBAR TEL **Metro:** Gran Vía.
$ Rates (including continental breakfast): 7,000 ptas. ($70) single; 10,000 ptas. ($100) double; 12,800 ptas. ($128) triple. AE, DC, MC, V.

Newly refurbished, this hotel occupies the third and fourth floors of a grand turn-of-the-century building on a corner of Madrid's major artery. Established in 1989 as a Best Western affiliate, it offers security boxes in its well-furnished bedrooms. Off the third-floor lobby, where you register, is an English-inspired bar open 24 hours a day. Snacks are also available.

HOSTAL BUENOS AIRES, Gran Vía 61, 28013 Madrid. Tel. 542-01-02. Fax 91/542-28-69. 25 rms (all with bath). TEL **Metro:** Plaza de España. **Bus:** 1, 2, or 44.
$ Rates: 8,500 ptas. ($85) single; 11,000 ptas. ($110) double. Breakfast 450 ptas. ($4.50) extra. AE, DC, MC, V.

To reach this place, you pass through the marble-covered street-floor lobby of a 1955 building, then take the elevator to the second floor. The freshly decorated hostal occupies two floors. One of its best features is a wood-sheathed café bar, open daily from 8am to midnight. Bedrooms are comfortable, modern, and clean. There's a safety-deposit box in each room.

RESIDENCIA LIABENY, Salud 3, 28013 Madrid. Tel. 91/532-52-06. Fax 91/532-74-21. 219 rms (all with bath). A/C MINIBAR TV TEL **Metro:** Puerta del Sol, Callao, or Gran Vía.
$ Rates: 9,500 ptas. ($95) single; 14,000 ptas. ($140) double. Breakfast 900 ptas. ($9) extra. AE, MC, V. **Parking:** 1,200 ptas. ($12).

Behind a stone-sheathed rectangular facade, this hotel is in a prime location midway between the tourist highlights of the Gran Vía and the Puerta del Sol. Named after the original owner of the hotel, it contains seven floors and comfortably contemporary bedrooms, each of which has a private bathroom.

INEXPENSIVE

HOSTAL NUEVO GAOS, calle Mesonero Romanos 14, 28013 Madrid. Tel. 91/532-71-07. Fax 91/522-70-98. 23 rms (all with bath). MINIBAR TV TEL **Metro:** Callao. **Bus:** 1, 2, or 44.
$ Rates: 6,500 ptas. ($65) single; 8,000 ptas. ($80) double. AE, DC, MC, V.

On the second, third, and fourth floors of a building just off the Gran Vía, this hostal offers guests the chance to enjoy a comfortable standard of living at moderate rates. It lies directly north of the Puerta del Sol, across the street from the popular flamenco club Torre Bermejas. Breakfast can be taken at a nearby café. Eight rooms are air-conditioned.

BUDGET

HOSTAL-RESIDENCIA CONTINENTAL, Gran Vía 44,

(F) FROMMER'S SMART TRAVELER: ACCOMMODATIONS

VALUE-CONSCIOUS TRAVELERS SHOULD
TAKE ADVANTAGE OF THE FOLLOWING:

1. Reductions in rates for rooms without private bath. Usually a
   room with a shower is cheaper than a room with a private
   bath, and even cheaper is a room with a basin only.
2. Reductions at some hotels if you pay cash instead of with a
   credit card.
3. Long-term discounts if you're planning to spend more than
   one week in Madrid.

QUESTIONS TO ASK IF YOU'RE ON A BUDGET:

1. If there's a garage, what's the parking charge?
2. Is there a surcharge for local or long-distance telephone
   calls? Usually there is, and it can be as high as 40%; in that
   case, make your calls at the nearest post office.
3. Is service included or will it be added to your final bill?
   Likewise, are all taxes included, or will you be billed extra?
4. Is a continental breakfast included in the rate? After a stay of
   three or four days, the cost of breakfast alone can make a big
   difference in your final bill.

28013 Madrid. Tel. 91/521-46-40. 29 rms (all with bath).
TEL **Metro:** Callao. **Bus:** 1, 2, 36, or 46.
$ Rates: 3,800 ptas. ($38) single; 4,800 ptas. ($48) double.
Breakfast 300 ptas. ($3) extra. AE, DC, MC, V.

 Sprawling handsomely over the third and fourth floors of Gran
Vía 44, this hostal is a bit more expensive than the other
accommodations in the building, but the rooms are comfortable, tidy, and newly renovated. The desk clerk speaks English. The
Continental is in a virtual "casa of budget hotels," a 19th-century
building filled exclusively with small hotels and pensions. If no room
is available at the Continental, you can ring the doorbells of the other
establishments, as this house of hotels is a good bet for the budget
tourist.

**HOTEL ALCÁZAR REGIS, Gran Vía 61, 28013 Madrid. Tel.
91/247-93-17.** 25 rms (none with bath). **Metro:** Plaza de
España or Santo Domingo.
$ Rates: 2,000 ptas. ($20) single; 4,000 ptas. ($40) double.
Breakfast 350 ptas. ($3.50) extra. AE.
Conveniently perched on a corner in the midst of Madrid's best
shops is this post–World War II building, complete with a circular
Greek-style temple as its crown. In a captivating atmosphere, you'll
find long and pleasant rooms, wood paneling, leaded-glass windows,
parquet floors, crystal chandeliers, and graciously proportioned
bedrooms, each with hot and cold running water.

HOTEL NURIA, Fuencarral 52, 28004 Madrid. Tel. 91/

531-92-08. Fax 91/532-90-05. 80 rms (all with bath). TEL
Metro: Gran Vía or Quevedo. **Bus:** 3, 7, or 40.

$ Rates (including breakfast): 4,000 ptas. ($40) single; 5,600 ptas.
($56) double. AE, DC, MC, V.

The Hotel Nuria, just three blocks from the Gran Vía, has some
bedrooms with especially interesting views of the capital. Furnishings
are simple and functional. The hotel was renovated in the late 1960s.

---

4. NEAR THE PUERTA DEL SOL

EXPENSIVE

**GRAN HOTEL REINA VICTORIA, Plaza Santa Ana 14,
28012 Madrid. Tel. 91/531-45-00.** Fax 91/522-03-07. 187
rms, 9 suites. A/C MINIBAR TV TEL **Metro:** Tirso de Molina or
Puerta del Sol.

$ Rates: 19,500 ptas. ($195) single; 24,000 ptas. ($240) double;
from 32,000 ptas. ($320) suite. Breakfast 1,200 ptas. ($12) extra.
AE, DC, V. **Parking:** 1,400 ptas. ($14).

This establishment is about as important to the legends of Madrid as
the famous bullfighter Manolete himself. He used to stay here, giving
lavish parties in one of the reception rooms and attracting mobs in
the square below when he went out on his balcony for morning
coffee. Since the recent renovation and upgrading of this property by
Spain's Tryp Hotel Group, it's less staid and more impressive than
ever.

Originally built in 1923, and named after the grandmother of the
present King of Spain, Juan Carlos, the hotel sits behind an ornately
eclectic stone facade which the Spanish government protects as a
historic monument. Although it's located in a congested neighborhood in the center of town, it opens onto its own verdant and sloping
plaza, rich in tradition as a meeting place of intellectuals during the
17th century. Today the area is usually filled with flower vendors,
older people catching rays of midafternoon sun, and young people
resting between bouts at the dozens of neighborhood tapas bars.
Almost anything is available within a few minutes' walk.

Each of the hotel's bedrooms contains sound-resistant insulation,
a safe for valuables, and a private bathroom with many amenities.

Dining/Entertainment: Guests enjoy the hotel's stylish and
popular lobby bar, the Manuel Gonzalez Manolete, whose lavishly
displayed bullfighting memorabilia and potent drinks add another
attraction to an already memorable hotel. The in-house restaurant is
the El Ruedo.

Services: 24-hour room service, concierge, babysitting.

MODERATE

**HOTEL CARLOS V, Maestro Vitoria 5, 28013 Madrid. Tel.
91/531-41-00.** Fax 91/531-37-61. 67 rms (all with bath). A/C
TV TEL **Metro:** Puerta del Sol or Callao.

$ Rates: 9,000 ptas. ($90) single; 11,500 ptas. ($115) double.
Breakfast 750 ptas. ($7.50) extra. AE, DC, MC, V.

The Hotel Carlos V has long been a favorite of mine—I stayed here when I researched the original *Spain on $5 a Day* back in the 1960s. The seven-story art nouveau building dating from 1904 has been altered over the years. Rooms have been upgraded and now contain such amenities as music and personal safes; bathrooms have been modernized. What hasn't changed is the unbeatable location: around the corner from the Galerías Preciados and just a short walk from the Gran Vía and the Puerta del Sol. The lobby retains its air of elegance.

INEXPENSIVE

HOTEL FRANCISCO I, Arenal 15, 28013 Madrid. Tel. 91/248-43-14. Fax 91/531-01-88. 58 rms (all with bath). TEL **Metro:** Puerta del Sol or Ópera.
$ Rates (including breakfast): 5,500 ptas. ($55) single; 7,500 ptas. ($75) double. MC, V.
Here you can rent modern, clean rooms. There's a pleasant lounge and a bar, and on the sixth floor you'll find a comfortable, rustically decorated restaurant where a fixed-price meal costs around 1,800 ptas. ($18). The hotel provides 24-hour room service and laundry and valet.

HOTEL INGLÉS, calle Echegaray 8, 28014 Madrid. Tel. 91/429-65-51. Fax 91/420-24-23. 58 rms (all with bath). TEL **Metro:** Puerta del Sol or Seville.
$ Rates: 5,600 ptas. ($56) single; 8,200 ptas. ($82) double. Breakfast 500 ptas. ($5) extra. AE, DC, MC, V.

You'll find the Hotel Inglés on a central street lined with *tascas* (bars). It's perhaps more modern and impersonal than when Virginia Woolf made it her address in Madrid. Behind its red-brick facade you'll find unpretentious and contemporary bedrooms, each well maintained. The comfortable armchairs in the TV lounge are likely to be filled with avid soccer fans. The lobby is air-conditioned, but the rooms are not. Guests who have to open the windows at night are likely to hear noise coming from the enclosed courtyard, so light sleepers should be aware of this problem.

HOTEL RESIDENCIA SANTANDER, calle Echegaray 1, 28014 Madrid. Tel. 91/429-95-51. 38 rms (all with bath). TV TEL **Metro:** Puerta del Sol.
$ Rates: 6,800 ptas. ($68) single; 8,500 ptas. ($85) double. Breakfast 400 ptas. ($4) extra. No credit cards.
A snug little hotel just off the Puerta del Sol, the Santander is a refurbished 1930s house with adequate rooms. Although it's on a teeming street, you might appreciate the local atmosphere. Restaurants and bars in the area are active day and night.

BUDGET

HOSTAL LA MACARENA, cava de San Miguel 8, 28005 Madrid. Tel. 91/265-92-21. 18 rms (all with bath). **Metro:** Puerta del Sol, Ópera, or La Latina.
$ Rates: 3,500 ptas. ($35) single; 5,000 ptas. ($50) double. Breakfast 350 ptas. ($3.50) extra. AE, MC, V.

Known for its reasonable prices and praised by readers for the warmth of its reception, this unpretentious, clean hostal is run by the Ricardo González family. Its 19th-century facade ornamented with Belle Epoque patterns offers an ornate contrast to the chiseled simplicity of the ancient buildings facing it. The location is one of the hostal's assets, on a street (admittedly noisy) immediately behind the Plaza Mayor, near one of the best clusters of *tascas* (bars) in Madrid.

HOSTAL LA PERLA ASTURIANA, Plaza de Santa Cruz 3,
   28012 Madrid. Tel. 91/266-46-00. 32 rms (all with bath).
   Metro: Puerta del Sol.
$ Rates: 3,800 ptas. ($38) single; 4,800 ptas. ($48) double.
   Breakfast 300 ptas. ($3) extra. AE, DC, MC, V.
Ideal for those who want to stay in the heart of Old Madrid (one block from the Plaza Mayor and two blocks from the Puerta del Sol), this small family-run establishment has a courteous staff member at the desk 24 hours a day for security convenience. You can socialize in the small, comfortable lobby adjacent to the reception desk. The bedrooms are clean, with fresh towels supplied daily. Many inexpensive restaurants and *tapas* bars are nearby.

HOSTAL PRINCIPADO, Zorilla 7, 28014 Madrid. Tel. 91/
   429-81-87. 15 rms (all with bath). **Metro:** Puerta del Sol,
   Seville, or Banco de España. **Bus:** 5, 9, or 53.
$ Rates: 4,000 ptas. ($40) single; 5,500 ptas. ($55) double. AE,
   MC, V.
Unassuming and unpretentious, this two-star hotel offers clean and simple accommodations at attractive rates. In a well-kept town house, it's run by a gracious owner who keeps everything renovated and well maintained. New tiles, attractive bedspreads, and curtains give it a fresh look. No breakfast is served, but many nearby cafés serve whatever you might want.

HOSTAL RESIDENCIA AMERICANO, Puerta del Sol 11,
   28013 Madrid. Tel. 91/522-28-22. 43 rms (all with bath).
   TEL **Metro:** Puerta del Sol.
$ Rates: 4,000 ptas. ($40) single; 5,800 ptas. ($58) double. No
   credit cards.
The Hostal Residencia Americano, on the third floor of a five-story building, is suitable for those who want to be in the Puerta del Sol area. Owner/manager A. V. Franceschi has refurbished all rooms, most of them outside chambers with balconies facing the street. Mr. Franceschi promises hot and cold running water 24 hours a day. No breakfast is served.

HOTEL RESIDENCIA LISBOA, Ventura de la Vega 17,
   28014 Madrid. Tel. 91/429-98-94. Fax 91/369-41-96. 23
   rms (all with bath). **Metro:** Puerta del Sol.
$ Rates: 4,000 ptas. ($40) single; 5,400 ptas. ($54) double. AE,
   DC, MC, V.
The Lisboa, on Madrid's most famous restaurant street, can be a bit noisy, but that's my only complaint. The hotel is a neat, modernized town house with compact rooms, and central heating in the cooler months. The staff speaks five languages. The Lisboa does not serve

breakfast, but it's surrounded by budget dining rooms, cafés, and *tascas* (bars).

5. NEAR ATOCHA STATION

MODERATE

HOTEL MERCATOR, calle Atocha 123, 28012 Madrid. Tel. 91/429-05-00. Fax 91/369-12-52. 89 rms (all with bath), 3 suites. MINIBAR TV TEL **Metro:** Atocha or Antón Martín.

$ Rates: 7,000 ptas. ($70) single; 10,000 ptas. ($100) double; from 12,000 ptas. ($120) suite. AE, DC, MC, V. **Parking:** 1,000 ptas. ($10).

Only a three-minute walk from the Prado, the Mercator draws a clientele seeking a good, modern hotel—orderly, well run, and clean, with enough comforts and conveniences to please the weary traveler. The public rooms are simple, outfitted in a vaguely modern type of minimalism. Some of the rooms are more inviting than others, especially those with desks and armchairs. Twenty-one units are air-conditioned. The Mercator is a *residencia*, that is, it offers breakfast only, and doesn't have a formal restaurant for lunch and dinner. However, it has a bar and cafeteria serving light meals such as *platos combinados* (combination plates). Happily, the hotel has a garage, and is within walking distance of American Express and the Iberia Airlines office. Laundry is provided, plus room service from 7am to 11:30pm.

HOTEL RESIDENCIA CORTEZO, Doctor Cortezo 3, 28012 Madrid. Tel. 91/369-01-01. Fax 91/369-37-74. 90 rms (all with bath). A/C MINIBAR TV TEL **Metro:** Tirso de Molina.

$ Rates: 7,000 ptas. ($70) single; 10,500 ptas. ($105) double. Breakfast 800 ptas. ($8) extra. AE, MC, V.

Just off calle de Atocha, which leads to the railroad station of the same name, the hotel is a short walk from the Plaza Mayor and the Puerta del Sol. The accommodations are comfortable and attractive, with contemporary baths. The beds are springy, the colors well chosen, the furniture pleasantly modern; often there is a sitting area with a desk and armchair. The public rooms match the bedrooms in freshness.

6. NEAR RETIRO/SALAMANCA

VERY EXPENSIVE

PARK HYATT VILLA MAGNA, paseo de la Castellana 22, 28046 Madrid. Tel. 91/261-49-00, or toll free 800/233-1234 in North America. Fax 91/575-3158. 166 rms, 16 suites. A/C MINIBAR TV TEL **Metro:** Rubén Darío.

$ Rates: 50,000 ptas. ($500) single, Sun–Thurs, 25,500 ptas.

F FROMMER'S COOL FOR KIDS: ACCOMMODATIONS

Novotel Madrid *(see page 90)* Children under 16 stay free in their parents' room, where the sofa converts into a comfortable bed. Kids delight in the open-air swimming pool and the offerings of the bountiful breakfast buffet.

Plaza Hotel *(see page 79)* Kids like the rooftop swimming pool and sun terrace so much it might be hard to get them to leave for the Prado. The Plaza is a landmark, a skyscraper for Madrid.

Tirol *(see page 98)* This centrally located three-star hotel is a favorite of families seeking good comfort at moderate prices. Kids like the cafeteria.

($255) Fri–Sat; 61,000 ptas. ($610) double, Sun–Thurs; 30,500 ptas. ($305) Fri–Sat; from 90,000 ptas. ($900) suite. Weekend discounts apply to Sunday-night stopovers only if the room has been rented for a Saturday night as well. Breakfast from 2,000 ptas. ($20) extra. AE, DC, MC, V. **Parking:** 1,650 ptas. ($16.50)

⭐ Considered one of the finest and most sought-after hotels in Europe, the Park Hyatt is clad in slabs of rose-colored granite and set behind a bank of pines and laurels on the city's most fashionable boulevard. It was already legendary as a supremely comfortable and elegant modern hotel when Hyatt International took over its management in 1990. Today it's getting still better.

The hotel was originally conceived when a handful of Spain's elite teamed up to create a setting in which their special friends, along with an increasing array of discriminating international visitors, would be pleased to live and dine. They hired an architect, imported a French decorator (whose style has been described as a contemporary version of neoclassicism), planted exquisitely arranged gardens, and put the staff through a rigidly intensive training program. The result is elegant and appropriately expensive.

Separated from the busy boulevard by a parklike garden, its facade has severely elegant contemporary lines. In contrast, its opulent interior recaptures the style of Carlos IV, with richly paneled walls, marble floors, and massive bouquets of fresh flowers. Through the lobby and elaborate drawing rooms passes almost every film star shooting on location in Spain.

This luxury palace offers plush but dignified bedrooms, decorated in Louis XVI, English Regency, or Italian provincial style. Each has fresh flowers and televisions with video movies and satellite reception (including news broadcasts beamed in from the U.S.).

Dining/Entertainment: In the lobby-level champagne bar, the bartender can mix any drink you might fancy, as a piano provides soothing and highly drinkable entertainment. The in-house restaurant, the Berceo, serves international food in a glamorous and sophisticated setting.

Services: 24-hour room service, concierge, same-day laundry and dry cleaning, limousine service, babysitting.

Facilities: Business center, car rentals, barber and beauty shop, boutique Villa Magna; tennis and golf available 15 and 25 minutes from the hotel, respectively.

THE RITZ, Plaza de la Lealtad 5, 28014 Madrid. Tel. 91/521-28-57, or toll free 800/225-5843 in the U.S. Fax 91/532-87-76. 156 rms, 24 suites. A/C MINIBAR TV TEL **Metro:** Banco de España.

$ Rates: 50,000–60,000 ptas. ($500–$600) single; 60,000–70,000 ptas. ($600–$700) double; from 105,000 ptas. ($1,050) suite. Breakfast 2,500 ptas. ($25) extra. AE, DC, MC, V. **Parking:** 2,000 ptas. ($20).

The most famous hotel in Madrid is the Ritz, which offers all the luxuries and special attentions that world travelers have come to expect of a grand deluxe hotel. The director suggests that guests book very, very early, as rooms are hard to come by at this veritable citadel of gracious and snobbish living. An international rendezvous point, it has been handsomely updated and modernized, although efforts have been made to retain its Belle Epoque character, unique in Europe. Acquired by Forte, the Ritz has undergone millions of dollars of "refreshing" to maintain its position as one of the leading hotels in the world.

No other hotel, except perhaps the Palace, has a more varied history. One of *Les Grand Hôtels Européens,* the Ritz was built at the command of King Alfonso XIII, with the aid of César Ritz, in 1908. It looks out onto the big circular Plaza de la Lealtad in the center of town, near the 300-acre Retiro Park, facing the Prado museum and its extension, the Palacio de Villahermosa, and the Stock Exchange. The Ritz was constructed when costs were relatively low, and when spaciousness, luxury, and comfort were the order of the day. The facade of the hotel is classed as a historic monument. The new hotels going up in Madrid simply can't match its elegance.

Like the cognoscenti of old, who have long had a liking for the Ritz, today's guest likes its grandeur, comfort, service, and gracious living. It's not only elegant in this thick-carpeted sense, but also quiet.

Each of the bedrooms contains masses of fresh flowers and televisions with video movies and satellite reception. The marble baths are some of the finest I've seen in years of inspecting hotels in Europe.

Dining/Entertainment: The five-star Ritz Restaurant is one of the most attractive in Europe. It's decorated in cream, blue, and gold, with paneled mirrors and 16th-century Flemish tapestries. Its chefs present an international menu, and its paella is said to be the best in Madrid. Except for champagne, the wine list is staunchly Spanish. Guests can also dine in the casual Terraza Ritz.

In these days of casual attire, it's important to know that guests at the Ritz dress up, even for breakfast. This is not a "resort" hotel.

Services: 24-hour room service, laundry/valet, express check-out.

Facilities: Car-rental kiosk, business center, currency exchange.

WELLINGTON, Velázquez 8, 28001 Madrid. Tel. 91/575-44-00. Fax 91/576-4164. 270 rms, 10 suites. A/C MINIBAR TV TEL **Metro:** Retiro or Velázquez.

$ Rates: 21,000 ptas. ($210) single; 31,500 ptas. ($315) double; from 49,000 ptas. ($490) suite. Breakfast 1,950 ptas. ($19.50) extra. AE, DC, MC, V. **Parking:** 1,800 ptas. ($18)

The Wellington, with its impressive antique-tapestried entrance, is one of Madrid's more sedate deluxe hotels, built in the mid-1950s but substantially remodeled since. Set in the affluent Salamanca residential area near Retiro Park, the Wellington offers redecorated rooms, each with cable TV and movie channels, music, two phones (one in the bathroom), and a guest-operated combination safe. Units are furnished in English-inspired mahogany reproductions, and the bathrooms (one per accommodation) are modern and immaculate, with marble sheathing and fixtures. Doubles with private terraces (at no extra charge) are the most sought-after accommodations.

Dining/Entertainment: An added bonus here is the El Fogón grill room, styled like a 19th-century tavern, where many of the provisions for the typically Spanish dishes are shipped in from the hotel's own ranch. The pub-style Bar Inglés is a warm and hospitable rendezvous spot. Lighter meals are served in the Las Llaves de Oro (Golden Keys) cafeteria.

Services: 24-hour room service, same-day dry cleaning and laundry.

Facilities: Outdoor swimming pool, garage, beauty parlor.

EXPENSIVE

GRAN HOTEL TRYP VELÁZQUEZ, calle de Velázquez 62, 28001 Madrid. Tel. 91/275-28-00. Fax 91/575-28-09. 144 rms (all with bath). A/C MINIBAR TV TEL. **Metro:** Retiro.
$ Rates: 14,800 ptas. ($148) single; 18,500 ptas. ($185) double. Breakfast 1,200 ptas. ($12) extra. AE, DC, MC, V. **Parking:** 1,200 ptas. ($12).

On an affluent residential street near the center of town, this hotel has an art deco facade and an interior so filled with well-upholstered furniture and richly grained paneling that it shows more of its 1947 origin than any 1930s kinship. Several public rooms lead off a central oval area; one of them includes a warm bar area. As in many hotels of its era, the bedrooms vary, some large enough for entertaining, but all have piped-in music. This is one of the most attractive medium-size hotels in Madrid, with comfort and convenience. Parking is available on the premises.

HOTEL ALCALÁ, Alcala 66, 28009 Madrid. Tel. 91/435-10-60. Fax 91/435-11-05. 153 rms (all with bath). A/C MINIBAR TV TEL **Metro:** Príncipe de Vergara.
$ Rates: 12,500 ptas. ($125) single; 17,800 ptas. ($178) double. Breakfast 1,000 ptas. ($10) extra. AE, DC, MC, V. **Parking:** 1,200 ptas. ($12).

The Hotel Alcalá enjoys an enviable position on a busy boulevard near the northern edge of Retiro Park. It has tastefully modern bedrooms, each with voluminous draperies, tile and wooden headboards, coordinated colors, private bathroom, and TV with reception of many different European channels.

Facilities in the hotel include a two-level public lounge dotted with comfortable chairs, the ornate Restaurant Basque, a lower-level coffee shop, an underground garage, and a bright Toledo-red American bar opening off the lounge.

NOVOTEL MADRID, calle Albacete 1, 28027 Madrid. Tel. 91/405-46-00, or toll free 800/221-4542 in North America. Fax 91/404-11-05. 236 rms (all with bath). A/C MINIBAR TV TEL **Metro:** Concepción. **Directions:** Exit from the M-30 at Barrio de la Concepción/Parque de las Avenidas, just before reaching the city limits of central Madrid; then look for the chain's trademark electric-blue signs.

$ Rates: 14,000 ptas. ($140) single; 17,500 ptas. ($175) double. Children under 16 stay free in parents' room. Breakfast 1,500 ptas. ($15) extra. AE, DC, MC, V. **Parking:** Free.

The Novotel was originally intended to serve the hotel needs of a cluster of multinational corporations with headquarters 1½ miles east of the center of Madrid, but its rooms are so comfortable and its prices so reasonable that tourists have begun using it as well. It opened in 1986, with an enthusiastic staff. Its position on the highway, at the corner of calle Albacete and avenida Badajoz, away from the maze of sometimes confusing inner-city streets, makes it especially attractive to motorists. Kids delight in the open-air pool and the offerings of the bountiful breakfast buffet.

Bedrooms are designed in a standardized format whose popularity in Europe has made it one of the hotel industry's most notable success stories. Each contains a well-designed bathroom, in-house movies, radio, TV, and soundproofing. The sofa, once bolster pillows are removed, can be transformed into a comfortable bed, where children can sleep. The English-speaking staff is well versed in both sightseeing attractions and solutions to most business-related problems.

MODERATE

EMPERATRIZ, López de Hoyos 4, 28006 Madrid. Tel. 91/563-80-88. Fax 91/563-98-04. 170 rms (all with bath), 1 suite. A/C MINIBAR TV TEL. **Metro:** Rubén Darío.

$ Rates: 9,500–12,000 ptas. ($95–$120) single; 15,500–17,000 ptas. ($155–$170) double; from 20,000 ptas. ($200) suite. Breakfast 1,200 ptas. ($12) extra. AE, DC, MC, V. **Parking:** 1,600 ptas. ($16).

The Emperatriz lies just off the wide paseo de la Castellana, only a short walk from some of Madrid's most deluxe hotels, but it charges relatively reasonable rates. It contains comfortably unpretentious bedrooms, each of which has a TV receiving many different European channels, a private bathroom, and a mixture of both traditional and modern furniture. If one is available, ask for a room on the eighth floor, where you'll get a private terrace at no extra charge. On the premises are a beauty salon, barbershop, and well-upholstered lounges where you're likely to meet fellow globetrotting Americans.

GRAN HOTEL COLÓN, Pez Volador 11, 28007 Madrid. Tel. 91/573-59-00. Fax 91/573-08-89. 390 rms (all with bath). A/C MINIBAR TV TEL **Metro:** Conde Casal.

$ Rates: 10,500 ptas. ($105) single; 15,000 ptas. ($150) double. Breakfast 800 ptas. ($8) extra. AE, DC, MC, V. **Parking:** 1,200 ptas. ($12).

West of Retiro Park, the Gran Hotel Colón is a few minutes from the center by subway. It offers comfortable yet moderately priced accommodations in one of the city's modern hotel structures. More than half the accommodations have private balconies, and each contains comfortably traditional furniture, much of it built-in.

To literally top everything off, there's a swimming pool on the roof, 11 stories up, where you can sunbathe with a view of the skyline of Madrid. Other assets of the hotel include two dining rooms, a covered garage, and Bingo games. One of the Colón's founders was an accomplished interior designer, which accounts for the unusual stained-glass windows and murals in the public rooms and the paintings by Spanish artists in the lounge.

HOSTAL RESIDENCIA DON DIEGO, calle de Velázquez 45, 28001 Madrid. Tel. 91/435-07-60. 58 rms (all with bath). TEL **Metro:** Colón.
$ Rates: 7,000 ptas. ($70) single; 10,000 ptas. ($100) double. Breakfast 600 ptas. ($6) extra. MC, V.

On the fifth floor of a building with an elevator, this hostal is in a combination residential/commercial neighborhood that's relatively convenient to many of the monuments of the city. The vestibule contains an elegant winding staircase accented with iron griffin heads supporting its balustrade. The hotel is warmly inviting, filled with leather couches and a kind of comfortable, no-nonsense style of angular but attractive furniture. A bar stands at the far end of the main sitting room. Laundry service is provided, and room service is on call from 8am to midnight daily.

HOTEL CLARIDGE, Plaza Conde de Casal, 6, 28007 Madrid. Tel. 91/551-94-00. Fax 91/501-03-85. 150 rms (all with bath). A/C TV TEL **Metro:** Conde Casal.
$ Rates: 8,200 ptas. ($82) single; 10,700 ptas. ($107) double. Breakfast 750 ptas. ($7.50) extra. AE, MC, V. **Parking:** 1,000 ptas. ($10).

This contemporary building is beyond Retiro Park, about five minutes from the Prado by taxi. The bedrooms are well organized and styled: small, compact, with coordinated furnishings and colors, and with private bathrooms. You can take your meals in the hotel's cafeteria or just relax in the modern lounge.

7. CHAMBERÍ

VERY EXPENSIVE

CASTELLANA INTER-CONTINENTAL HOTEL, paseo de la Castellana 49, 28046 Madrid. Tel. 91/410-02-00, or toll free 800/327-0200 in North America. Fax 91/319-58-53. 270 rms, 35 suites. A/C MINIBAR TV TEL **Metro:** Rubén Darío.
$ Rates: 31,000–44,000 ptas. ($310–$440) single; 39,000–53,000 ptas. ($390–$530) double; from 60,000 ptas. ($600) suite. Breakfast 1,600 ptas. ($16) extra. Midsummer discounts (whose rates usually include breakfast) are sometimes available, with many restrictions, through the toll-free number listed above. AE, DC, MC, V. **Parking:** 1,100 ptas. ($11).

Solid, spacious, and conservatively modern, this is one of the more reliable and stylish hotels in Madrid. Originally built in 1963 as the then-most-prestigious hotel on the famous boulevard, it lies behind a barrier of trees in a neighborhood of elegant apartment houses and luxury hotels. The hotel's sunny and high-ceilinged public rooms provide a cool and welcome refuge from the Madrileño heat. Surprisingly spacious, they're considered a tribute to the art of Spanish masonry, with terrazzo floors, and a large-scale collection of angular abstract murals laboriously pieced together from multicolored stones and tiles. Most of the accommodations have private balconies and traditional furniture, and each contains a color TV with in-house video and channels from across Europe. The hotel is affiliated with the Inter-Continental hotel chain.

Dining/Entertainment: The La Ronda Bar offers soothing drinks near the elegant Los Continentales restaurant. (Attached to Los Continentales is a cost-conscious coffee shop with the same name.)

Services: There's a helpful concierge and a travel agent who will book theater tickets, rental cars, and airline connections; 24-hour room service, laundry, babysitting.

Facilities: A scattering of kiosks and boutiques, hairdresser/barber, business center.

HOTEL PALACIO SANTO MAURO, calle Zurbano 36, 28010 Madrid. Tel. 91/319-69-00. Fax 91/308-54-17. 31 rms, 6 suites. AC MINIBAR TV TEL **Metro:** Rubén Darío or Alonso Martínez.

$ Rates: 39,200 ptas. ($392) single; 58,800 ptas. ($588) double; from 66,500 ptas. ($665) suite. Breakfast from 2,500 ptas. ($25) extra. AE, DC, MC, V. **Parking:** 1,950 ptas. ($19.50).

One of the most exciting new hotels of Madrid opened in 1991 in the once-decrepit neoclassical walls of a villa that was originally built in 1894 for the Duke of Santo Mauro. In a verdant garden, and reminiscent of the kind of architecture you'd have expected to find in France, it contains an elegant mixture of rich fabrics, art deco art and furnishings, and an impressive number of polite staff members who exceed the number of accommodations by two to one. Each of the bedrooms has a sophisticated audio system with wide choice of tapes and CDs, and many sophisticated decor notes which might include curtains of raw silk, Persian carpets, and a daringly postmodern array of jewel-toned colors.

Dining/Entertainment: The Belagua Restaurant is recommended separately (see Chapter 5). There's also an elegant bar located off the main lobby, and tables set up beneath the garden's large trees for drinks and snacks.

Services: 24-hour room service, laundry/valet, a reception staff trained in the procurement of practically anything.

Facilities: Indoor swimming pool, health club with sauna and massage.

MIGUEL ANGEL, Miguel Angel 29-31, 28010 Madrid. Tel. 91/442-81-99. Fax 91/442-53-20. 278 rms, 26 suites. A/C MINIBAR TV TEL **Metro:** Rubén Darío.

$ Rates: 20,500–23,600 ptas. ($205–$236) single; 30,000 ptas. ($300) double; from 42,000 ptas. ($420) suite. Breakfast 1,800 ptas. ($18) extra. AE, DC, MC, V. **Parking:** 1,800 ptas. ($18).

Just off paseo de la Castellana, the Miguel Angel is sleekly modern and has quickly built a reputation for providing some of the finest accommodations in the Spanish capital. It has much going for it—location, contemporary styling, imaginative furnishings and art objects, an efficient staff, and plenty of comfort. Behind its facade is an expansive sun terrace on several levels, with clusters of garden furniture, surrounded by semitropical planting.

The bedrooms contain color-coordinated fabrics and carpets and, in many cases, reproductions of classic Iberian furniture. Each is soundproof and has a radio and TV. Tax and breakfast are extra.

Dining/Entertainment: The Farnesio bar is decorated in a Spanish Victorian style, and piano music is played from 8pm. A well-managed restaurant on the premises is the Florencia, which serves a fixed-price lunch or dinner for 6,000 ptas. ($60). In the Zacarias boite restaurant until around 3am dinner is also served, which you can enjoy while watching an occasional cabaret or musical performance.

Services: 24-hour room service, same-day laundry/valet.

Facilities: Indoor heated swimming pool, sauna, hairdresser, drugstore; art exhibitions are sponsored in the arcade of boutiques.

EXPENSIVE

CONDE DUQUE, Plaza Conde Valle de Súchil 5, 28015 Madrid. Tel. 91/447-70-00. Fax 91/448-35-69. 136 rms (all with bath). TEL **Metro:** San Bernardo.

$ Rates: 14,250 ptas. ($142.50) single; 20,850 ptas. ($208.50) double. Breakfast 1,450 ptas. ($14.50) extra. AE, DC, MC, V.

The modern three-star Conde Duque, near a branch of the Galerías Preciados department store, opens onto a tree-filled plaza in a residential neighborhood near the Glorieta Quevado. The hotel is located 12 blocks north of the Plaza de España, off calle de San Bernardo, which starts at the Gran Vía—too long a walk, but a subway stop is nearby. The furnishings include modern built-in headboards and reproductions of 19th-century English pieces. There are bedside lights and telephones.

HOTEL ESCULTOR, Miguel Angel 3, 28010 Madrid. Tel. 91/410-42-03. Fax 91/319-25-84. 45 rms, 20 suites. A/C MINIBAR TV TEL **Metro:** Rubén Darío.

$ Rates: 19,000 ptas. ($190) single; 23,500 ptas. ($235) double; from 35,000 ptas. ($350) suite. Breakfast 1,150 ptas. ($11.50) extra. AE, DC, MC, V. **Parking:** 1,700 ptas. ($17) at a nearby public garage.

Originally built in 1975, this comfortably furnished hotel provides fewer services and offers fewer facilities than other hotels in its category, but compensates with larger accommodations. Each unit has its own charm and contemporary styling. Each has video films, a private bathroom, and a layout that's well organized, efficient, and logical. The hotel is fully air-conditioned, and the staff usually provides useful information about facilities in the surrounding neighborhood.

Dining/Entertainment: The hotel has a small but comfortable bar, open nightly from 7pm to 1am, and a traditional restaurant, the Señorio de Erazu, which closes on Saturday at lunchtime and all day on Sunday.

Services: Room service at breakfast only (7–11am).

RESIDENCIA BRÉTON, Bréton de los Herreros 29, 28003 Madrid. Tel. 91/442-83-00. Fax 91/441-38-16. 56 rms (all with bath). A/C MINIBAR TV TEL **Metro:** Ríos Rosas.

$ Rates: 12,700 ptas. ($127) single; 20,000 ptas. ($200) double. Breakfast 1,050 ptas. ($10.50) extra. AE, DC, MC, V. **Parking:** 1,000 ptas. ($10).

You'll find this modern hotel on a side street several blocks from paseo de la Castellana. It's well furnished with reproductions of Iberian pieces. As a residencia it doesn't offer a major dining room, but it does have a little bar and breakfast room adjoining the reception lounge. Each of the rooms has attractive wooden beds, wrought-iron electric fixtures, comfortable chairs, and tilework painted with ornate designs in the bathrooms.

8. CHAMARTÍN

VERY EXPENSIVE

EUROBUILDING, calle Padre Damian 23, 28036 Madrid.
   Tel. 91/345-45-00. Fax 91/457-97-29. 440 rms, 100 suites.
   A/C MINIBAR TV TEL. **Metro:** Cuzco.
$ Rates: 25,000 ptas. ($250) single; 32,000 ptas. ($320) double;
   from 40,000 ptas. ($400) suite. Breakfast 1,900 ptas. ($19.00)
   extra. AE, DC, MC, V. **Parking:** 1,800 ptas. ($18).

Even while it was on the drawing boards, the rumor was that this five-star sensation of white marble would provide, in the architect's words, "a new concept in deluxe hotels." The Eurobuilding long ago lived up to its advance billing, reflecting a high level in taste and design. It's two hotels linked by a courtyard, away from the city center but right in the midst of apartment houses, boutiques, nightclubs, first-class restaurants, tree-shaded squares, and the heart of the modern Madrid business world.

The more glamorous of the twin buildings is the main one, containing only suites, each of which was recently renovated in luxurious pastel shades and named Las Estancias de Eurobuilding. Drinks await you in the refrigerator. Gold-and-white ornately carved beds, background music, a roomwide terrace for breakfast and cocktail entertaining—all are tastefully coordinated. Across the courtyard, the sister Eurobuilding contains less impressive—but still very comfortable—single and double rooms, many with views from private balconies of the formal garden and swimming pool below. All the accommodations have televisions with video movies and satellite reception, security doors, and individual safes.

Dining/Entertainment: Shared by both buildings is the luxury restaurant, Balthasar, on the lower level behind a Turkish-inspired spindle screen. La Taberna, also on the premises, offers more rapid dining. Perhaps the ideal way to dine here is al fresco by the pool, enjoying a buffet luncheon.

Services: 24-hour room service, concierge, laundry/valet, babysitting.

Facilities: Outdoor swimming pool, health club with sauna.

MELÍA CASTILLA, calle Capitán Haya 43, 28020 Madrid.
   Tel. 91/571-22-11, or toll free 800/336-3542 in North America. Fax 91/571-22-10. 951 rms, 16 suites. A/C MINIBAR TV TEL
   Metro: Cuzco.
$ Rates: 25,000–30,500 ptas. ($250–$305) single; 31,000–
   36,000 ptas. ($310–$360) double; from 63,000 ptas. ($630) suite.
   Breakfast 1,950 ptas. ($19.50) extra. AE, DC, MC, V. **Parking:**
   1,850 ptas. ($18.50).

This mammoth hotel qualifies, along with the Palace, as one of the largest hotels in Europe. Loaded with facilities and built primarily to accommodate huge conventions, the Meliá Castilla also caters to the needs of the individual traveler. Everything is larger than life here: You need a floor plan to direct yourself around its precincts. The lounges and corridors of pristine marble are vast—there's even a landscaped garden and a showroom full of the latest-model cars.

Each of the twin-bedded rooms comes equipped with private bath, radio, color TV, and modern furniture. The Meliá Castilla is in the north of Madrid, about a block west of paseo de la Castellana, a short drive from the Chamartín railway station.

Dining/Entertainment: The hotel has a coffee shop, a seafood restaurant, a restaurant specializing in paella and other rice dishes, cocktail lounges, and the Trinidad nightclub. In addition, there's the restaurant/show, Scala Meliá Castilla.

Services: 24-hour room service, hairdresser/barber, concierge, babysitting, laundry/valet.

Facilities: Swimming pool, a shopping arcade with souvenir shops and a bookstore, saunas, gymnasium, parking garage.

EXPENSIVE

CUZCO, paseo de la Castellana 133, 28046 Madrid. Tel. 91/556-06-00. Fax 91/556-03-72. 330 rms. A/C MINIBAR TV TEL **Metro:** Cuzco.
$ Rates: 16,850 ptas. ($168.50) single; 21,000 ptas. ($210) double. Breakfast 1,300 ptas. ($13) extra. AE, DC, MC, V. **Parking:** Free.

Popular with businesspeople and American tour groups, the Cuzco is in a commercial neighborhood of big buildings, government ministries, spacious avenues, and the main Congress Hall. The Chamartín railway station is a 10-minute walk north of the hotel, so it's a popular and convenient address.

This 15-story structure, set back from Madrid's longest boulevard, has been redecorated and modernized since it was completed in 1967. The architect of the Cuzco allowed for spacious bedrooms, each with a separate sitting area, video movies, and a private bathroom.

There's a bilevel snack bar and cafeteria. The lounge is a forest of marble pillars and leather armchairs, the ambience enhanced by contemporary oil paintings and tapestries. Facilities include a beauty parlor, sauna, massage, gymnasium, and cocktail bar.

HOTEL CHAMARTÍN, Agustín de Foxa, Estación de Chamartín, 28036 Madrid. Tel. 91/323-30-87. Fax 91/733-02-14. 378 rms, 18 suites. A/C MINIBAR TV TEL **Metro:** Chamartín. **Bus:** 5.
$ Rates: 12,500 ptas. ($125) single; 17,300 ptas. ($173) double; from 28,000 ptas. ($280) suite. Breakfast 1,000 ptas. ($10) extra. AE, DC, MC, V. **Parking:** Nearby for 1,000 ptas. ($10).

This brick-sided hotel soars nine stories above the northern periphery of Madrid. It's part of the massive modern shopping complex attached to the Chamartín railway station, although once you're inside your soundproof room, the noise of the railway station will seem far away. The owner of the building is RENFE, Spain's government-owned railway system, but the nationwide hotel chain that administers it is Entursa Hotels. The hotel is 15 minutes by taxi from both the airport and the historic core of Madrid, and is conveniently close to one of the capital's busiest Metro stops. Especially oriented to the business traveler, it offers a currency-exchange kiosk, a travel agency, a car-rental office, and a video screen in the lobby that posts the arrival and departure of all of Chamartín's trains. A coffee bar serves breakfast daily, and room service is available from 7am to midnight. The hotel restaurant, Cota 13, serves an international cuisine. A short walk from the hotel lobby, in the railway-station complex, are a handful of shops and movie theaters, a roller-skating rink, a disco, and ample parking.

MODERATE

ARISTOS, avenida Pío XII no. 34, 28016 Madrid. Tel. 91/457-04-50. Fax 91/457-10-23. 24 rms (all with bath). A/C TV TEL **Metro:** Pío XII.
$ Rates: 8,500 ptas. ($85) single; 12,900 ptas. ($129) double. Breakfast 650 ptas. ($6.50) extra. AE, DC, MC, V.

This three-star hotel is in an up-and-coming residential area of Madrid, not far from the Eurobuilding. Its main advantage is a garden in front, where you can lounge, have a drink, or order a complete meal. The hotel's restaurant, El Chaflán, is frequented by residents of the neighborhood in addition to hotel visitors. Each of the bedrooms has a small terrace and an uncomplicated collection of modern furniture.

9. ARGÜELLES/MONCLOA

VERY EXPENSIVE

HUSA PRINCESA, Serrano Jover 3, 28015 Madrid. Tel. 91/542-35-00. Fax 91/559-46-65. 320 rms, 38 suites. A/C TV TEL **Metro:** Argüelles.
$ Rates: 26,000 ptas. ($260) single; 32,000 ptas. ($320) double; from 64,000 ptas. ($640) suite. Breakfast 1,900 ptas. ($19) extra. AE, DC, MC, V. **Parking:** 2,500 ptas. ($25).

Originally built during the mid-1970s, and radically renovated after its takeover in 1991 by the Spanish HUSA chain, the Princesa is a sprawling hotel designed like a series of massive rectangular solids clustered into an angular whole. The concrete-and-glass facade overlooks busy boulevards in the city center. The Princesa is well patronized by both businesspeople and groups of visiting tourists. Each of the bedrooms contains comfortable contemporary furniture and a modernized bathroom.

Dining/Entertainment: The hotel has a restaurant, (Marguerita), a bar (El Chic), and a disco (Delfin) that opens every night at 8pm.

Services: 24-hour room service, concierge, babysitting.

Facilities: Conference rooms, underground garage; at press time, plans were in effect for an as-yet-uncompleted health club and hairdressing salon.

MELÍA MADRID, Princesa 27, 28008 Madrid. Tel. 91/541-82-00, or toll free 800/336-3542 in North America. Fax

91/541-19-05. 260 rms, 5 suites. A/C MINIBAR TV TEL **Metro:** Rodríguez.

$ Rates: 25,000–32,000 ptas. ($250–$320) single; 32,000–38,000 ptas. ($320–$380) double; from 45,000 ptas. ($450) suite. Breakfast 1,900 ptas. ($19) extra. AE, DC, MC, V. **Parking:** 1,600 ptas. ($16).

Here you'll find one of the most modern, yet uniquely Spanish, hotels in the country. Its 23 floors of wide picture windows have taken a permanent position in the capital's skyline. Each of the bedrooms is comfortable, spacious, and filled with contemporary furnishings, and usually offers sweeping views over the rooftops of Madrid. Each contains a TV with video movies and many different channels from across Europe. The chalk-white walls dramatize the flamboyant use of color accents; the bathrooms are sheathed in snow-colored marble.

Dining/Entertainment: The Restaurant Princesa is elegant and restful. Equally popular is the Don Pepe Grill. The cuisine in both restaurants is international, and includes an array of Japanese and Indian dishes. There are also three bars and a coffee shop.

Services: 24-hour room service, concierge, babysitting, hairdresser/barber, laundry.

Facilities: A commercial gallery which includes souvenir shops, bookstores, and a health club with sauna and massage.

INEXPENSIVE

TIROL, Marqués de Urquijo 4, 28004 Madrid. Tel. 91/248-19-00. 97 rms (all with bath), 4 suites. A/C TEL **Metro:** Argüelles. **Bus:** 2 or 21.

$ Rates: 6,500 ptas. ($65) single; 8,500 ptas. ($85) double; 12,000 ptas. ($120) suite. Breakfast 400 ptas. ($4) extra. MC, V. **Parking:** 1,300 ptas. ($13).

A short walk from the Plaza de España and the swank Meliá Madrid Hotel is a good choice for clean, unpretentious comfort. A three-star hotel, the Tirol offers only nine singles, and eight of the hotel's accommodations have a private terrace. Furnishings are simple and functional. There's a cafeteria and a parking garage in the hotel.

MADRID DINING

It's the custom in Madrid to consume the big meal of the day from 2 to 4pm. After a recuperative siesta, Madrileños then enjoy *tapas* (snacks) in hundreds of *tascas* (bars) scattered throughout the capital.

All this nibbling is followed by dinner—more likely a light supper—in a restaurant, usually beginning about 9:30pm to as late as midnight. Many restaurants, however, start serving dinner at 8pm, to accommodate visitors from other countries.

Madrid restaurant prices shock first-time visitors—that is, those who don't live in such expensive cities as Tokyo, Oslo, London, or Paris. Restaurants listed in this chapter as "Very Expensive" charge 5,500 ptas. ($55) and up per person for a meal. Meals include service and tax (ranging from 6% to 12% depending on the restaurant), but this doesn't include drinks, which add to the tab considerably. Restaurants rated "Expensive" charge 3,500–5,500 ptas. ($35–$55) per person for a meal, "Moderate" establishments ask 2,000–3,500 ptas. ($20–$35), and "Inexpensive" eateries offer meals under 2,000 ptas. ($20) per person.

BUDGET DINING If you can't afford the prices charged by most first-class restaurants of Madrid, you'll find a variety of budget dining options to keep the bill down.

Menu del Día and Cubierto Order the *menu del día* (menu of the day) or *cubierto,* both of which are fixed-price menus based on what's fresh at the market that day. They're the finest dining bargains in Madrid. Usually, each will include a first course, such as fish soup or hors d'oeuvres, followed by a main dish, plus bread, dessert, and the wine of the house. Though you won't have a large choice, you will dine well.

Menu Turistico The *menu turistico* is a similar fixed-price menu, but for many it's too large, especially at lunch. Only those with large appetites find it the best bargain.

Cafeterias These are not self-service establishments, but restaurants serving light, often American, cuisine. Go to one for breakfast instead of dining at your hotel, unless breakfast is included in the room price. Some cafeterias offer no hot meals, but many feature combined plates of fried eggs, french fries, veal, lettuce-and-tomato salads, or light fare like hot dogs and hamburgers.

Tapas An option is to dine well at lunch and then stop by a *tasca* (local tavern) for an evening meal of appetizer-size *tapas*, which might be eggs in mayonnaise, potato omelets, codfish salad, cured ham, Russian salad, octopus in garlic-mayonnaise sauce, grilled mushrooms, stuffed peppers, potato croquettes, etc.

Don't overtip. Follow the local custom. Theoretically, service is included in the price of your meal, but it's customary to leave 10% additional.

For more details on dining (such as when and what to eat) see "Food and Drink" in Chapter 1.

1. NEAR THE PLAZA DE LAS CORTÉS

EXPENSIVE

ARMSTRONG'S, calle Jovellanos 5. Tel. 522-42-30.
   Cuisine: AMERICAN/ENGLISH. **Reservations:** Recommended. **Metro:** Banco de España or Seville. **Bus:** 2, 10, 27, or 45.
$ Prices: Appetizers 800–1,500 ptas. ($8–$15); main dishes 1,400–3,500 ptas. ($14–$35); fixed-price menu 1,800 ptas. ($18). AE, DC, MC, V.
   Open: Lunch daily 1–4:30pm; dinner daily 8:30pm–1am; brunch Sat–Sun 10am–4:30pm.

Armstrong's combines excellent cuisine with a sense of lighthearted charm and big-city style. It's a pink-and-white labyrinth of street-level rooms that, until they were altered in 1986 by savvy London attorney Ken Armstrong, served as a furniture showroom owned by a former cohort of Franco. Amid rich planting, Chinese-Chippendale furniture, and the kind of hidden lighting and deep cove molding sometimes shown in *Architectural Digest,* you can enjoy a sophisticated array of dishes. The clientele that has preceded you here has included the King and Queen of Spain and the Prince and Princess of Wales.

Brunch is offered every Saturday and Sunday along with the usual assortment of lunchtime dishes. A brunch special might be eggs Casanova. Other menu offerings, both at brunch and during regular lunch and dinner hours, include an elegant array of salmon and hake dishes, perhaps a luscious version of caviar-topped crêpes concocted from both fresh and smoked salmon, Waldorf salad, grilled breast of duck, beef Wellington, steak-and-kidney pie, a collection of stuffed baked potatoes (some containing caviar), and a full complement of wines, champagnes, and sherries.

EL ESPEJO, paseo de Recoletos 31. Tel. 308-23-47.
   Cuisine: INTERNATIONAL. **Reservations:** Required. **Metro:** Banco de España or Colón. **Bus:** 27.
$ Prices: Appetizers 900–1,600 ptas. ($9–$16); main dishes 2,000–3,200 ptas. ($20–$32). AE, DC, MC, V.
   Open: Lunch daily 1–4pm; dinner daily 9pm–midnight.

Here you'll find good-tasting food and one of the most perfectly crafted art nouveau decors in Madrid. If the weather is good, you can choose one of the establishment's outdoor tables, served by a battery of uniformed waiters who carry food across the busy street to a green area flanked with trees and strolling pedestrians. I personally prefer a table inside, within view of the tile maidens with vines and flowers entwined in their hair. You'll pass through a charming café/bar, where many visitors linger before walking down a hallway toward the spacious and alluring dining room. Dishes include grouper ragoût with clams, steak tartare, guinea fowl with Armagnac, or lean duck meat with pineapple. Profiteroles with cream and chocolate sauce make a delectable dessert.

MODERATE

EDELWEISS, calle Jovellanos 7. Tel. 521-03-26.
> **Cuisine:** GERMAN. **Reservations:** Not accepted. **Metro:** Sevilla. **Bus:** 5.
> **$ Prices:** Appetizers 550–1,900 ptas. ($5.50–$19); main dishes 1,500–3,250 ptas. ($15–$32.50); fixed-price menu 1,600 ptas. ($16). AE, MC, V.
> **Open:** Lunch Mon–Sat 12:30–4pm; dinner Mon–Sat 8:30pm–midnight. **Closed:** Aug.

Edelweiss is a German standby that has provided good-quality food and service at moderate prices since the war. During peak dining hours the bar is likely to be full of clients waiting for tables. You are

---

**Ⓕ FROMMER'S SMART TRAVELER:
RESTAURANTS**

VALUE-CONSCIOUS TRAVELERS
SHOULD CONSIDER THE FOLLOWING:

1. Most budget restaurants offer a *cubierto* or *menu del día*. It's not very adventurous, and limited in selections, but in most cases it's at least 30% cheaper than ordering à la carte.
2. Often, major restaurants will offer a *menu del día* at lunch (the Madrid equivalent of a businessperson's lunch) but will revert to expensive à la carte listings in the evening. Check the menu offerings posted outside the restaurant.
3. Patronize the *tascas* (local taverns), and order two or three *tapas* (hors d'oeuvres). Most portions are generous, and you can dine for a quarter of the price you'd pay in most restaurants.
4. Look for the *platas del día* (daily specials). They're invariably fresh, and usually carry a much lower price tag than regular à la carte listings.
5. Ask for the *vino de la casa* (house wine); it's served in a carafe and is only a fraction of the cost of bottled wine.
6. Anything consumed standing up at a counter or sitting on a bar stool is cheaper than at a table.
7. Patronize the famous budget restaurant streets of Madrid: calle del Barco, Ventura de la Vega, and calle Echegaray.

served hearty portions of food, mugs of draft beer, and fluffy pastries; that's why there's always a wait. *Tip:* To beat the crowds, go for dinner at un-Spanish hours, say around 9pm. But even when it's jammed, service is almost always courteous. You can start with Bismarck herring, then dive into goulash with spätzle, or eisbein (pigs' knuckles) with sauerkraut and mashed potatoes, the most popular dish at the restaurant. Finish with the homemade apple tart. The decor is vaguely German, with travel posters and wood-paneled walls. It's air-conditioned in summer.

INEXPENSIVE

LUARQUÉS, Ventura de la Vega 16. Tel. 429-61-74.
   Cuisine: ASTURIAN/SPANISH. **Reservations:** Recommended. **Metro:** Sevilla.
$ Prices: Appetizers 250–1,900 ptas. ($2.50–$19); main dishes 850–1,600 ptas. ($8.50–$16); fixed-price menu 1,700 ptas. ($17). No credit cards.
   Open: Lunch Tues–Sat 1–4:30pm; dinner Tues–Sat 9–11:30pm.
   Closed: Aug.
Open since 1966, Luarqués dishes up some of the most savory meals on this street. It's not the cheapest place, offering a fixed-price meal of four *platos,* plus bread and wine, for 1,700 ptas. ($17)—but considering what you get, it's a fair buy. The restaurant serves all the standard dishes that are the hallmark of the Spanish cuisine: gazpacho, paella, flan, sopa de pescado (fish soup), and roast chicken.

LA TRUCHA, Manuel Fernández Gonzalez 3. Tel. 492-58-33.
   Cuisine: SEAFOOD. **Reservations:** Recommended. **Metro:** Sevilla.
$ Prices: Appetizers 350–2,000 ptas. ($3.50–$20); main dishes 850–2,500 ptas. ($8.50–$25). No credit cards.
   Open: Lunch Mon–Sat 1–4pm; dinner Mon–Sat 8pm–midnight.
   Closed: Aug.
With its Andalusian tavern ambience, La Trucha boasts a street-level bar and small dining room—the arched ceiling and whitewashed walls festive with hanging braids of garlic, dried peppers, and onions. On the lower level the walls of a second bustling area are covered with eye-catching antiques, bullfight notices, and bric-a-brac. The specialty is fish, and there's a complete à la carte menu including truchas (trout); verbenas de ahumados (literally, a "street party" of smoked delicacies); a stew called fabada ("glorious"; made with beans, Galician ham, black sausage, and smoked bacon); and a comida casera rabo de toro (home-style oxtail). No one should miss nibbling on the tapas variadas in the bar.

2. NEAR THE PLAZA DE ESPAÑA

EXPENSIVE

BAJAMAR, Gran Vía 78. Tel. 248-59-03.

Cuisine: SEAFOOD. **Reservations:** Recommended. **Metro:**
Plaza de España.
$ Prices: Appetizers 700–1,600 ptas. ($7–$16); main dishes
1,600–3,200 ptas. ($16–$32). AE, DC, MC, V.
Open: Lunch daily 1–4pm; dinner daily 8pm–midnight.

Bajamar is one of the best fish houses in Spain, and it's right in the
heart of the city, near the Plaza de España. Both fish and shellfish are
shipped in fresh daily by air from their points of origin. Lobster, king
crab, prawns, soft-shell crabs, and the like are all priced according to
weight. There's a large array of reasonably priced dishes as well. The
setting is contemporary and attractive, and the service is smooth and
professional. The menu is in English. For an appetizer, I'd recommend half a dozen giant oysters or rover crayfish. The special seafood soup is a most satisfying selection, a meal in itself. Try also the
lobster bisque. Some of the more recommendable main courses
include turbot Gallego style, the special seafood paella, even baby
squid cooked in its ink. Desserts are simple, including the chef's
custard.

RESTAURANT JAUN DE ALZATE, calle de la Princesa 18. Tel. 547-00-10.

Cuisine: BASQUE/INTERNATIONAL. **Reservations:** Required. **Metro:** Plaza de España.
$ Prices: Appetizers 1,200–2,200 ptas. ($12–$22); main dishes
1,500–3,500 ptas. ($15–$35); fixed-price menu 6,200 ptas.
($62). AE, DC, MC, V.
Open: Lunch daily 1:30–4pm; dinner daily 9pm–midnight.
Closed: Aug.

This restaurant is in what was originally built as a stable for the
Duchess of Alba's Liria Palace. Although its address is technically on calle Princesa, a sign will direct you to an entrance on
a narrow side street behind the Plaza de España. Inside, most of the
decor's color comes from small vases of seasonal flowers, which
offset an otherwise monochromatic room vaguely influenced by art
deco.

The award-winning chef is Basque-born Iñaki Izaguirre, whom
some observers compare to Salvador Dalí because of his handlebar
mustache and his almost surrealistic combination of unusual ingredients. Although he is ardently committed to the preservation of his
Basque traditions, his culinary style was strongly influenced by the
years he lived in England, Holland, and the U.S.

These specific offerings will almost certainly have changed by the
time of your visit, but examples of Izaguirre's cuisine include a salad
of pine nuts, fresh greens, and poached lobster with an olive-oil
dressing; sushi with chorizos (sausage); rabbit meatballs and mango
balls in cold almond soup; deep-fried crayfish tails marinated in
béchamel sauce; and turbot stuffed with lobster in saffron sauce.

All the fish served in this restaurant comes fresh every day from
the wholesale fish market in the heart of the Basque country, San
Sebastián, where a trusted employee selects the finest fish of the
Cantabrian coast.

Izaguirre believes in food low in fat, cholesterol, and calories, but
loaded with nutrition and bursting with flavor. The cross-cultural
dishes here probably look as good as they taste, arranged on a platter
as an artist would arrange colors on a palette.

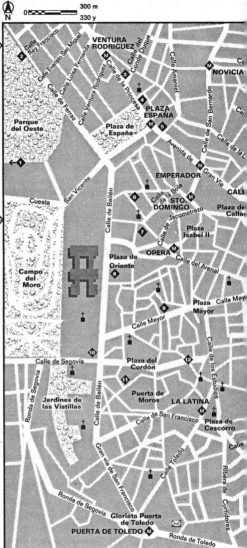
MODERATE

LAS CUEVAS DEL DUQUE, calle de la Princesa 16. Tel. 248-50-37.
    Cuisine: SPANISH. **Reservations:** Required. **Metro:** Ventura Rodríguez. **Bus:** 1, 2, or 42.
$ Prices: Appetizers 800–3,000 ptas. ($8–$30); main dishes 900–2,500 ptas. ($9–$25). AE, DC, MC, V.
    Open: Lunch daily 1–4pm; dinner daily 8pm–midnight.
In front of the Duke of Alba's palace, a short walk from the Plaza de

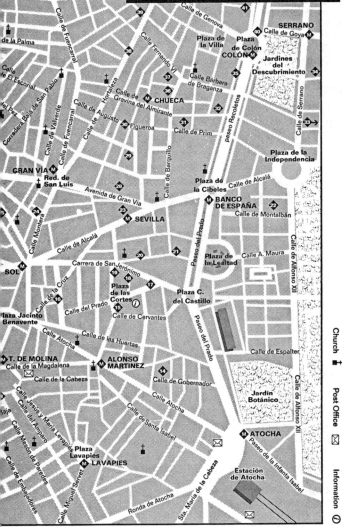

DINING IN CENTRAL MADRID

Church ✝

Post Office ✉

Information ⓘ

España, is Las Cuevas del Duque, with an underground bar and a small, 10-table *mesón* that serves such simple Spanish fare as roast suckling pig, sirloin, lamb cutlets, and a few seafood dishes, including fish cooked in a sheathing of salt. In fair weather a few tables are set outside, beside a tiny triangular garden. Other tables line calle de la Princesa, and make an enjoyable roost for an afternoon drink.

BUDGET

VERA CRUZ, San Leonardo 5. Tel. 247-11-50.

Cuisine: SPANISH. **Reservations:** Not required. **Metro:** Plaza de España.

$ Prices: Appetizers 250–450 ptas. ($2.50–$4.50); main dishes 450–750 ptas. ($4.50–$7.50); fixed-price menu 850 ptas. ($8.50). No credit cards.

Open: Lunch daily 1–5pm; dinner daily 8pm–midnight.

 Behind the Plaza de España, a short walk from the soaring Edificio España, you'll find this old standby for hungry budget-minded diners. It's a simple *económico,* but the food is acceptable and the service polite. The *menu del día* usually includes soup or hors d'oeuvres, followed by a meat or fish dish, then cheese or fruit, plus bread and wine. The Vera Cruz also has daily specials like paella or cocido (a typical Madrid dish of chickpeas, sausage, cabbage, and potatoes).

3. ON OR NEAR THE GRAN VÍA

MODERATE

ARCE, Augusto Figueroa 32. Tel. 522-59-13.

Cuisine: BASQUE. **Reservations:** Required. **Metro:** Colón.

$ Prices: Appetizers 1,090–2,850 ptas. ($10.90–$28.50); main dishes 2,150–2,850 ptas. ($21.50–$28.50). AE, DC, MC, V.

Open: Lunch Mon–Fri 1:30–4pm; dinner Mon–Sat 9pm–midnight. **Closed:** Week before Easter, Aug 15–31.

Arce has brought some of the best modern interpretations of Basque cuisine to the palates of Madrid, thanks to the enthusiasm of owner/chef Inaki Camba and his wife, Theresa. In a comfortably decorated dining room designed for the unabashed enjoyment of food without unnecessary decorative frills, you can enjoy simple preparations of the finest available ingredients, where the natural flavors are designed to dominate your taste buds. Examples include a salad of fresh scallops, an oven-baked casserole of fresh boletus mushrooms with few seasonings other than the woodsy taste of the original ingredients, unusual preparations of hake, and seasonal variations of game dishes such as pheasant and woodcock.

LA BARRACA, Reina 29–31. Tel. 532-71-54.

Cuisine: VALENCIAN. **Reservations:** Recommended. **Metro:** Gran Vía or Sevilla. **Bus:** 1, 2, or 74.

$ Prices: Appetizers 675–4,200 ptas. ($6.75–$42); main dishes 1,600–3,100 ptas. ($16–$31); fixed-price menu 2,850 ptas. ($28.50). AE, DC, MC, V.

Open: Lunch daily 1–4pm; dinner daily 8:30pm–midnight.

La Barraca is like a country inn—right off the Gran Vía. This Valencian-style restaurant is well-managed and recommendable for its tasty provincial cooking. There are four different dining rooms, three of which lie one flight above street level, and they're colorfully cluttered with ceramics, paintings, photographs, Spanish lanterns, flowers, and local artifacts. The house specialty is paella à la valenciana, made with fresh shellfish. The portions are enormous—only the most ravenous will clean out the skillet. Specialties in the appetizer category include desgarrat (a salad made with codfish and red peppers), Barraca mussels, and shrimp Orly. In addition to the paella, you can select at least 16 other rice dishes, including rice with duck and rice with conger eel. Main-dish specialties include angler fish and prawns brochette and rabbit with fines herbes. Lemon-and-vodka sorbet makes a good finish.

CASABLANCA, calle del Berguillo 29. Tel. 521-15-68.

Cuisine: SPANISH/CONTINENTAL/JAPANESE. **Reservations:** Required. **Metro:** Alonso Martínez.

$ Prices: Appetizers 600–1,300 ptas. ($6–$13); main dishes 1,500–2,500 ptas. ($15–$25). AE, DC, MC, V.

Open: Lunch daily 1:30–4pm; dinner daily 9pm–1am.

The theme here, of course, is the famous movie of the "Late Late Show," and memorabilia (such as posters of Bogart and Bergman) are scattered over the two levels of its premises. The cuisine served at the umbrella-covered tables is a combination of northern Spanish, continental, and Japanese. You might begin with Ingrid salad, made with herring, beets, and apple, and named for the co-star of *Casablanca*. The chef's specialties include red peppers with smoked salmon, raw salmon marinated in champagne, raw tuna marinated in soy sauce Japanese style, pineapple-and-seafood cocktail, rice curry Madras, and stuffed hake in crab sauce. The owner is Dick Angstadt, an American. Casablanca also has a tapas bar.

EL MENTIDERO DE LA VILLA, Santo Tomé 6. Tel. 308-12-85.

Cuisine: JAPANESE/SPANISH. **Reservations:** Required. **Metro:** Alonso Martínez, Colón, or Gran Vía. **Bus:** 37.

$ Prices: Appetizers 1,025–1,800 ptas. ($10.25–$18); main dishes 2,000–2,600 ptas. ($20–$26). AE, DC, MC, V.

Open: Lunch Mon–Fri 1:30–4pm; dinner Mon–Sat 9pm–midnight. **Closed:** Last two weeks of Aug.

The success of this restaurant is the result of a collaboration between a Spanish owner, Mario Martínez, and a Japanese chef, each of whom infuses the menu with the best of their respective traditions. The decor is postmodern and includes softly trimmed trompe-l'oeil ceilings, exposed wine racks, ornate columns with unusual lighting techniques, and a handful of antique carved horses from long-defunct merry-go-rounds. Chef Kenjiro Sato prepares such dishes as veal liver in a sage sauce, a version of spring rolls filled with fresh shrimp and leeks, noisettes of veal with tarragon, filet steak with a mustard and brown-sugar sauce, medallions of venison with purées of chestnut and celery, and such desserts as a sherry trifle.

VALENTÍN, San Alberto 3. Tel. 521-16-38.

Cuisine: SPANISH. **Reservations:** Required. **Metro:** Gran Vía or Puerta del Sol.

$ Prices: Appetizers 950–1,500 ptas. ($9.50–$15); main dishes 1,200–2,500 ptas. ($12–$25). AE, DC, MC, V.

Open: Lunch daily 1:30–4pm; dinner daily 8:30pm–midnight.

Founded in 1892, Valentín has drawn its clientele from such widely varied categories as bullfighters, artists, high society, and movie stars, many of whose pictures can be seen on the walls. The restaurant's two rooms have a welcoming atmosphere, and its staff provides excellent service. Especially popular at lunchtime, Valentín serves traditional Spanish food, with a special regional dish offered daily. You might have callos à la madrileña or fabada on a weekday, but if you're there for lunch on Saturday, I recommend the paella. Main dishes also include grilled veal, fresh baked sea bass, Valentín sole, and perhaps the most famous (and most complicated) dish of Madrid, cocido madrileño. A good dessert list and some fine wines add to the pleasure of dining here. The restaurant is air-conditioned.

INEXPENSIVE

PAELLERÍA VALENCIANA, Caballero de Gracia 12. Tel. 531-17-85.
   Cuisine: SPANISH. **Reservations:** Recommended. **Metro:** Gran Vía.
$ Prices: Appetizers 600–700 ptas. ($6–$7); main dishes 900–1,200 ptas. ($9–$12); fixed-price menu 1,200 ptas. ($12). AE, MC, V.
   Open: Lunch only, Mon–Fri 1:30–4:30pm.

This lunch-only restaurant ranks as one of the best in the city for value. The specialty is paella, which you must order by phone in advance. Once you arrive, you might begin with a homemade soup or the house salad, then follow with the paella, served in an iron skillet. At least two diners must order this rib-sticking fare. The choice of desserts includes the chef's special pride, razor-thin orange slices flavored with rum, coconut, sugar, honey, and raspberry sauce. A carafe of house wine comes with the fixed-price menu, and after lunch the owner comes around dispensing free cognac.

4. NEAR THE PUERTA DEL SOL

VERY EXPENSIVE

EL CENADOR DEL PRADO, calle del Prado 4. Tel. 429-15-61.
   Cuisine: INTERNATIONAL. **Reservations:** Required. **Metro:** Puerta del Sol.
$ Prices: Appetizers 1,700–2,800 ptas. ($17–$28); main dishes 1,900–4,500 ptas. ($19–$45); fixed-price menu 6,000 ptas. ($60). AE, DC, MC, V.
   Open: Lunch Mon–Fri 1:45–4pm; dinner Mon–Sat 9pm–midnight. **Closed:** Aug 15–31.

This restaurant is deceptively elegant. In the simple anteroom, an attendant will check your coat and packages in an elaborately carved armoire, and you'll be graciously ushered into one of a trio of rooms. Two of the rooms, done in rich tones of peach and sepia, have thick cove moldings and English furniture in addition to floor-to-ceiling gilded mirrors. A third room, perhaps the most popular, is ringed with lattices and floods of sunlight from a skylight.

You can enjoy such well-flavored specialties as house-style crêpes with salmon and Iranian caviar and many other succulent dishes, including a salad of crimson peppers and salted anchovies, a casserole of snails and oysters with mushrooms, a ceviche of salmon and shellfish, soup studded with tidbits of hake and clams in a potato-and-leek base, and sea bass with candied lemons. A jacket and necktie for men are recommended.

EXPENSIVE

LHARDY, carrera de San Jerónimo 8. Tel. 521-33-85.
  Cuisine: SPANISH. **Reservations:** Recommended. **Metro:**
  Puerta del Sol.
$ Prices: Appetizers 1,200–1,900 ptas. ($12–$19); main dishes
  3,000–3,500 ptas. ($30–$35). AE, DC, MC, V.
  Open: Lunch Mon–Sat 1–3:30pm; dinner Mon–Sat 9–
  11:30pm. **Closed:** Late July to early Sept.

Lhardy opened its doors in 1839. I'm told the food served today isn't
as good as back then, but there's really no one around to verify that
claim. This is a place with a great tradition as a gathering point of
Madrid's literati, its political leaders, and the better-heeled members
of the city's business community. Your consommé is likely to be
presented in cups from a large silver samovar, if you drink it in the
ground-floor tearoom. Lhardy adjoins a deli shop, where you can buy
some of the delicacies you tasted at the bar or in the restaurant
upstairs. There, the decor, known as "Isabella Segundo," gives off a
definite aura of another era. Specialties of the house include an
excellent roast beef and a cocido, the celebrated stew of Madrid.
This might be served with a selection from the extensive wine cellar.

PLATERÍAS COMEDOR, Plaza de Santa Ana 11. Tel. 429-
  70-48.
  Cuisine: SPANISH. **Reservations:** Required. **Metro:** Puerta
  del Sol.
$ Prices: Appetizers 1,200–1,800 ptas. ($12–$18); main dishes
  3,000–4,000 ptas. ($30–$40). AE, DC, MC, V.
  Open: Lunch Mon–Fri 1:30–4pm; dinner Mon–Sat 9pm–
  midnight.

One of the most charming dining rooms in Madrid, Platerías
Comedor has richly brocaded walls evocative of 19th-century Spain.
Despite the busy socializing on the famous plaza outside, this serene
oasis makes few concessions to the new generation in its food, decor,
or formally attired waiters. Specialties include beans with clams,
stuffed partridge with cabbage and sausage, magret of duckling with
pomegranates, duck liver with white grapes, veal stew with snails and
mushrooms, and guinea hen with figs and plums. You might follow
with a passionfruit sorbet.

MODERATE

CASA PACO, Puerta Cerrada 11. Tel. 266-31-66.
  Cuisine: STEAK. **Reservations:** Required. **Metro:** Puerta del
  Sol, Ópera, or La Latina. **Bus:** 3, 21, 35, or 65.
$ Prices: Appetizers 1,000–1,200 ptas. ($10–$12); main dishes
  2,500–3,500 ptas. ($25–$35); fixed-price menu 2,200 ptas.
  ($22). DC.
  Open: Lunch Mon–Sat 1:30–4pm; dinner Mon–Sat 8:30pm–
  midnight. **Closed:** Aug.

Madrileños defiantly name Casa Paco, just beside the Plaza Mayor,
when someone has the "nerve" to put down Spanish steaks. They
know that here you can get the thickest, juiciest, most flavorsome
steaks in Spain. The steaks are priced according to weight. Señor Paco
was the first Madrid restaurant to seal steaks in boiling oil before
serving them on plates so hot that the almost-raw meat continues to
cook, preserving the natural juices.

Located in the old town, this two-story restaurant offers three dining rooms, and reservations are imperative. Otherwise you face a long wait, which you can while away sampling the tapas (hors d'oeuvres) in the tasca in front.

Casa Paco isn't just a steakhouse. You can start with a fish soup and proceed to such dishes as grilled sole, baby lamb, Casa Paco cocido, or callos à la madrileña. You might top it off with one of the luscious desserts, but you can't have coffee here—Paco won't serve it, not necessarily for health reasons but because customers used to be inclined to linger over their cups, keeping tables occupied while people had to be turned away.

LAS CUEVAS DE LUÍS CANDELAS, calle de Cuchilleros 1. Tel. 266-54-28.

Cuisine: SPANISH/INTERNATIONAL. **Reservations:** Required. **Metro:** Puerta del Sol.

$ Prices: Appetizers 550–2,200 ptas. ($5.50–$22); main dishes 1,200–2,800 ptas. ($12–$28). AE, DC, MC, V.

Open: Lunch daily 1–4pm; dinner daily 8pm–midnight.

Right down the steps from the Mesón del Corregidor is the even-better-known Las Cuevas De Luís Candelas which is housed in a building from 1616. The restaurant itself opened its doors in 1900. It's entered through a doorway under an arcade on the steps leading to calle de Cuchilleros, the nighttime street of Madrid, teeming with restaurants, flamenco clubs, and rustic taverns. The restaurant is named after the legendary Luís Candelas, a bandit of the 18th-century—sometimes known as "the Spanish Robin Hood." He is said to have hidden out in this maze of *cuevas* (caves). Although the menu is in English, the cuisine is authentically Spanish. Specialties include hake in the chef's own style. To begin your meal, another house dish is sopa de ajo Candelas (garlic soup). Roast suckling pig and roast lamb, as in the other restaurants on the Plaza Mayor, are the featured specialties.

MESÓN LAS DESCALZAS, Postigo San Martín 3. Tel. 522-72-17.

Cuisine: SPANISH. **Reservations:** Recommended. **Metro:** Callao.

$ Prices: Appetizers 550–700 ptas. ($5.50–$7); main dishes 1,600–1,800 ptas. ($16–$18); fixed-price menu 1,100 ptas. ($11). AE, DC, MC, V.

Open: Lunch daily noon–4pm; dinner daily 8pm–midnight.

Las Descalzas, a tavern-style restaurant, sits behind a red facade accented with a black metal sign. Inside you'll be greeted with a massive tapas bar, often crowded at night. Behind a glass-and-wood screen is the restaurant section, where the specialties include kidneys with sherry, sopa castellana, seafood soup, Basque-style hake, crayfish, shrimp, oysters, clams, and paella with shellfish. For entertainment, there's folk music.

INEXPENSIVE

EL CUCHI, calle de Cuchilleros 3. Tel. 266-44-24.

Cuisine: MEXICAN/SPANISH. **Reservations:** Required. **Metro:** Puerta del Sol.

$ Prices: Appetizers 450–1,000 ptas. ($4.50–$10); main dishes 900–2,700 ptas. ($9–$27). AE, DC, MC, V.

Open: Lunch daily 1–4pm; dinner daily 8pm–midnight.

A few doors down from Hemingway's favorite restaurant (Botín), El Cuchi defiantly claims that "Hemingway never ate here." But about everybody else has, attracted both to its low prices and to its labyrinth of dining rooms. A European link in Mexico's famous Carlos 'n' Charlie's restaurant chain, it stands off a corner of the Plaza Mayor. Ceiling beams and artifacts suggest rusticity. Menu specialties include black-bean soup, ceviche, guacamole, quail Mozambique, "pregnant" trout, and roast suckling pig (much cheaper than that served at Botín).

5. RETIRO/SALAMANCA

VERY EXPENSIVE

EL AMPARO, callejón de Puigcerdá 8, at the corner of Jorge Juan. Tel. 431-64-56.

Cuisine: BASQUE/FRENCH. **Reservations:** Required. **Metro:** Serrano. **Bus:** 21 or 53.

$ Prices: Appetizers 1,700–4,200 ptas. ($17–$42); main courses 3,200–4,500 ptas. ($32–$45). AE, MC, V.

Open: Lunch Mon–Fri 1:30–3:30pm; dinner Mon–Sat 9–11:30pm. **Closed:** Week before Easter, Aug.

El Amparo, behind the cascading vines of its facade, is one of the most elegant gastronomic enclaves of Madrid. It sits beside a quiet alleyway close to a bustling commercial section of the center of the city. Inside, three tiers of roughly hewn wooden beams surround elegantly appointed tables where pink napery and glistening silver add cosmopolitan touches of glamour. A sloping skylight floods the interior with sunlight by day, and at night pinpoints of light from the hi-tech hanging lanterns create intimate shadows. A battalion of uniformed and polite waiters serves well-prepared nouvelle-cuisine versions of cold marinated salmon with a tomato sorbet, cold cream of vegetable and shrimp soup, bisque of shellfish with Armagnac, and ravioli stuffed with seafood.

LA GAMELLA, calle Alfonso XII no. 4. Tel. 541-30-89.

Cuisine: CALIFORNIAN/CASTILIAN. **Reservations:** Required. **Metro:** Retiro. **Bus:** 19.

$ Prices: Appetizers 1,050–2,200 ptas. ($10.50–$22); main dishes 2,300–4,200 ptas. ($23–$42). AE, DC, MC, V.

Open: Lunch Mon–Fri 1:30–4pm; dinner Mon–Sat 9pm–midnight. **Closed:** Aug.

La Gamella established its gastronomic reputation shortly after it opened several years ago in less imposing quarters in another part of town. In 1988 its Illinois-born owner, former choreographer Dick Stephens, moved into the 19th-century building where the Spanish philosopher Ortega y Gasset was born. The prestigious and legendary Horcher (see below) is just across the street, although food at La Gamella is better. The design and decor of La Gamella invite customers to relax in russet-colored, high-ceilinged warmth. Mr. Stephens has prepared his delicate and light-textured specialties for the King and Queen of Spain as well as for many of Madrid's most talked-about artists and merchants, many of whom he knows and greets personally between sessions in his kitchens.

Typical menu items include a ceviche of Mediterranean fish, sliced duck liver in a truffle sauce, Caesar salad with strips of marinated anchovies, a dollop of goat cheese served over caramelized endives, duck breast with peppers, a ragoût of fish and shellfish with Pernod, and an array of sophisticated desserts, among which is an all-American cheesecake. Because of the intimacy and the small dimensions of the restaurant, reservations are important.

HORCHER, calle Alfonso XII no. 6. Tel. 532-35-96.

Cuisine: GERMAN/INTERNATIONAL. **Reservations:** Required. **Metro:** Retiro.

$ Prices: Appetizers 1,100–2,400 ptas. ($11–$24); main dishes 2,200–5,000 ptas. ($22–$50). AE, DC, V.

Open: Lunch Mon–Sat 1:30–4pm; dinner Mon–Sat 8:30pm–midnight.

Horcher originated in Berlin in 1904. In a sudden move—prompted by a tip from a high-ranking German officer that Germany was losing the war—Herr Horcher brought his restaurant to Madrid in 1943. The restaurant has continued its grand European traditions, including excellent service, ever since.

Where to start? You might try the seafood mousse. Wild-duck salad also attains distinction. Both the venison stew in green pepper with orange peel and the crayfish with parsley and cucumber are excellent. For dessert, the house specialty is crêpes Sir Holden, prepared at your table, with fresh raspberries, cream, and nuts, or you may prefer a Sachertorte.

Your best chance of getting a seat is to go early. A jacket and tie are imperative for men.

EXPENSIVE

ALKALDE, Jorge Juan 10. Tel. 576-33-59.

Cuisine: BASQUE. **Reservations:** Required. **Metro:** Retiro or Serrano. **Bus:** 8, 20, 21, or 53.

$ Prices: Appetizers 1,000–2,800 ptas. ($10–$28); main dishes 1,900–4,800 ptas. ($19–$48). AE, DC, MC, V.

Open: Lunch daily 1–4:30pm; dinner Sun–Fri 8:30pm–midnight. **Closed:** Sun July–Aug.

Alkalde has been known for decades for serving top-quality Spanish food in an old tavern setting. It's decorated like a Basque inn, with beamed ceilings and hams hanging from the rafters. Upstairs is a large, *típico* tavern. Downstairs is a maze of stone-sided cellars, pleasantly cool in the summer, although the whole place is air-conditioned.

You might begin with the cream of crabmeat soup, followed by gambas à la plancha (grilled shrimp) or the cigalas (crayfish). Other well-recommended dishes include mero salsa verde (brill in a green sauce), trout Alkalde, stuffed peppers, and chicken steak Alkalde. The dessert specialty is a copa Cardinal.

EL PESCADOR, José Ortega y Gasset 75. Tel. 401-12-90.

Cuisine: SEAFOOD. **Reservations:** Required. **Metro:** Lista.

$ **Prices:** Appetizers 1,200–2,200 ptas. ($12–$22); main dishes 2,200–3,800 ptas. ($22–$38). MC, V.
Open: Lunch Mon–Sat 1:30–4pm; dinner Mon–Sat 8:30pm–midnight. **Closed:** Aug.

El Pescador is a well-patronized fish restaurant that has become a favorite of the Madrileños who appreciate the more than 30 kinds of fish prominently displayed in a glass case. Many of these are unknown in North America, and some originate off the coast of Galicia. Management air-freights them in, and prefers to serve them *à la plancha* (grilled).

You might precede your main course with a spicy fish soup and accompany it with one of the many good wines from northeastern Spain. If you're not sure what to order—even the English translations might sound unfamiliar—try one of the many varieties and sizes of shrimp. These go under the name of langostinos, cigalas, santiaguinos, and carabineros. Many of them are expensive and priced by the gram, so be careful when you order.

INEXPENSIVE

GRAN CAFÉ DE GIJON, paseo de Recoletos 21. Tel. 521-54-25.
   Cuisine: SPANISH. **Reservations:** Required for the restaurant. **Metro:** Banco de España, Colón, or Recoletos.
$ **Prices:** Appetizers 500–650 ptas. ($5–$6.50); main dishes 685–2,500 ptas. ($6.85–$25); fixed-price menu 1,500 ptas. ($15). No credit cards.
   Open: Daily 9am–1am; meals Mon–Sat 1–4pm and 9pm–midnight.

All old European capitals have a coffeehouse that traditionally attracts the literati—in Madrid it's the Gijon, which opened in 1890 during the heyday of the city's Bella Epoca. Artists and writers still patronize this venerated old café, many of them spending hours over one cup of coffee. Hemingway made the place famous for Americans. The place has open street windows looking out onto the wide paseo, as well as a large terrace for sun worshipers and birdwatchers. Along one side of the café is a stand-up bar, and on the lower level is a restaurant. A fixed-price menu consists of two dishes, bread, wine or beer, and dessert, with main dishes varying daily. In summer you can sit in the garden, enjoying a blanco y negro (black coffee with ice cream) or mixed drinks.

6. CHAMBERÍ

VERY EXPENSIVE

LAS CUATRO ESTACIONES, General Ibáñez Ibero 5. Tel. 534-87-34.
   Cuisine: INTERNATIONAL. **Reservations:** Required. **Metro:** Guzmán el Bueno.
$ **Prices:** Appetizers 1,075–2,800 ptas. ($10.75–$28); main

dishes 2,000–4,200 ptas. ($20–$42); fixed-price dinner 6,000 ptas. ($60). AE, DC, MC, V.
Open: Lunch Mon–Fri 1–4pm; dinner Mon–Fri 9pm–midnight.
Closed: Aug.

✪ Las Cuatro Estaciones is placed by gastronomes and horticulturists alike among their favorite dining spots of Madrid. In addition to superb food, the establishment prides itself on the masses of flowers that change with the season, plus a modern and softly inviting decor that has delighted some of the most glamorous diners in Spain. Depending on the time of year, the mirrors surrounding the multilevel bar near the entrance reflect thousands of hydrangeas, chrysanthemums, or poinsettias. Even the napery matches whichever colors the resident botanist has chosen as the seasonal motif. Each person involved in food preparation spends a prolonged apprenticeship at restaurants in France before returning home to try his or her freshly sharpened talents on the taste buds of aristocratic Madrid.

Representative specialties include crab bisque, fresh oysters, a petite marmite of fish and shellfish, imaginative preparations of salmon, fresh asparagus with mushrooms in puff pastry with a parsley-butter sauce, a three-fish platter with fines herbes, brochette of filet of beef in pecadillo, and a nouvelle-cuisine version of blanquette of monkfish so tender it melts in your mouth. A "festival of desserts" includes whichever specials the chef has concocted that day, a selection of which is placed temptingly on your table.

FORTUNY, calle Fortuny 34. Tel. 308-32-58.

Cuisine: SPANISH. **Reservations:** Required. **Metro:** Rubén Darío.
$ Prices: Appetizers 1,700–2,800 ptas. ($17–$28); main dishes 2,800–5,500 ptas. ($28–$55). AE, DC, MC, V.
Open: Lunch Mon–Fri 1–4pm; dinner Mon–Sat 9pm–midnight.
Fortuny is the most elegant restaurant in Madrid, and also one of the best. Lying off paseo de la Castellana, the restaurant opened in 1986 in a 19th-century villa, originally the home of the Marqués Cuevas de Vera. Guests, who include expense-account gourmets and foreign visitors, often arrive by limousine. They are ushered across the courtyard and into the beautifully decorated, luxurious restaurant. Diners can choose to eat in the garden in fair weather. Otherwise they'll be seated in one of several different dining rooms, the most visible of which has a Louis XVI decor.

Imaginative appetizers include codfish ravioli Fortuny, and the menu is likely to feature grilled suckling lamb in its own juice (prepared for two diners), roast duck with fig ravioli, sea bass with shrimp tartare, steamed flatfish served with a sauce based on extract of Ceylon tea, and pork trotters in a hot sauce. The wine list is among the finest in Madrid.

JOCKEY, Amador de los Ríos 6. Tel. 319-24-25.

Cuisine: INTERNATIONAL. **Reservations:** Required. **Metro:** Cuzco.
$ Prices: Appetizers 950–6,500 ptas. ($9.50–$65); main dishes 2,500–6,800 ptas. ($25–$68); fixed-price menu 9,000 ptas. ($90). AE, DC, MC, V.
Open: Lunch Mon–Sat 1–4pm; dinner Mon–Sat 9–11:30pm.
Closed: Aug.

For decades this was considered the premier restaurant of Spain, although competition for that title is now severe today. At any rate, it's the favorite of international celebrities, diplomats, and heads of state, and some of the more faithful patrons look upon it as their own private club. It was, in fact, once known as the "Jockey Club," although the *Club* was eventually dropped because it suggested exclusivity. The restaurant, with tables on two levels, isn't overly large. Wood-paneled walls and colored linen provide warmth. Against the paneling are a dozen prints of horses mounted by jockeys—hence the name of the place.

If you like your decisions made for you, two or more diners can order a *menu dégustation,* which is changed monthly and presumably includes an array of the most sophisticated and creative dishes produced by the chef.

Since Jockey's establishment shortly after World War II, the chef has prided himself on coming up with new and creative dishes. Sheiks from oil kingdoms can still order beluga caviar from Iran, but others might settle happily for Jockey's goose-liver terrine or perhaps slices of Jabugo ham. Cold melon soup with shrimp is soothing on a hot day, followed by such dishes as grill-roasted young pigeon from Talavera cooked in its own juice or sole filets with figs in chardonnay. Stuffed small chicken Jockey style is a specialty, as is tripe madrileña, a local specialty. Desserts are sumptuous, although people may end their meal with the Colombian coffee.

INEXPENSIVE

FOSTER'S HOLLYWOOD, calle Magallanes 1. Tel. 448-91-65.
   Cuisine: AMERICAN. **Reservations:** Not required. **Metro:** Quevedo.
$ Prices: Appetizers 450–600 ptas. ($4.50–$6); main dishes 700–2,200 ptas. ($7–$22). AE, DC, MC, V.
   Open: Daily 1pm–1am.

Foster's is a popular hangout for locals and visiting Yanks. It's a California-style hamburger extravaganza, a fashionable place to eat and be seen, serving, according to many travelers, "the best American food in Europe." This is an establishment that wholeheartedly celebrates the American dream. Outside, you can sit in a director's chair on the terrace, with the name of a movie star on the back. You'll find this one of the most comfortable and best people-watching sites in Madrid, while you enjoy sangría or your back-home favorite beverage. Inside it's nostalgia time, with bentwood chairs and many framed photographs and posters. Some Spaniards have encountered problems in eating the hamburgers, as would anyone not familiar with devouring food five inches high. Hamburgers weigh in at half a pound, and they vary from simple and unadorned to one with cheese, bacon, and Roquefort dressing; they're served with french fries and salad. Other Stateside treats are chili con carne, homemade apple pie, cheesecake, and, as once reported in *The New York Times,* "probably the best onion rings in the world."

The same food is also available at Hollywood's other locations: Apolonia Morales 3 (tel. 457-79-11) in the Castellana area near the Eurobuilding; avenida de Brasil 14 (tel. 597-16-74) for the Meliá Castilla hotels; Velázquez 80 (tel. 435-61-28) in the Serrano shopping area; Tamayo y Baus 1 (tel. 435-61-28), close to the Plaza de Cibeles and the Prado; Guzmán el Bueno 100 (tel. 534-49-23) in the university area; and Plaza Sagrado Corazón de Jesús 2 (tel. 411-41-25), next to the National Music Auditorium.

7. CHAMARTÍN

VERY EXPENSIVE

ZALACAÍN, Alvarez de Baena 4. Tel. 561-48-40.
   Cuisine: BASQUE/FRENCH. **Reservations:** Required.
   Metro: Rubén Darío.
$ **Prices:** Appetizers 1,100–3,500 ptas. ($11–$35); main dishes 2,600–5,000 ptas. ($26–$50). AE, DC, MC, V.
   Open: Lunch Mon–Fri 1:30–3:30pm; dinner Mon–Sat 9–11:30pm. **Closed:** Week before Easter, Aug.

Outstanding both in food and decor, Zalacaín is reached by an illuminated walk from paseo de la Castellana, housed at the garden end of a modern apartment complex. In fact, it's within an easy walk of such deluxe hotels as the Luz Palacio, the Castellana, and the Miguel Angel. It's small, exclusive, and expensive. In an atmosphere of quiet refinement you can peruse the menu, perhaps at the rust-toned bar. Walls are covered with textiles, and some are decorated with Audubon-type paintings. The menu is interesting and varied, often with nouvelle-cuisine touches, along with many Basque and French specialties. It might offer a superb sole in a green sauce, but it also knows the glory of grilled pigs' feet. Among the most recommendable main dishes are a stew of scampi in cider sauce, crêpes stuffed with smoked fish, and ravioli stuffed with mushrooms, foie gras, and truffles. For dessert, I'd suggest a luscious version of praline cream with hot chocolate sauce, or crêpes Zalacaín. Men should wear jackets and neckties.

EXPENSIVE

ASADOR ERROTA-ZAR, Corazón de Maria 32. Tel. 413-52-24.
   Cuisine: BASQUE. **Reservations:** Required. **Metro:** Alfonso XIII. **Bus:** 43.
$ **Prices:** Appetizers 900–2,100 ptas. ($9–$21); main dishes 1,600–3,000 ptas. ($16–$30). AE, DC, MC, V.
   Open: Lunch Mon–Sat 1–4pm; dinner Mon–Sat 9pm–midnight.
   Closed: Aug.

Asador Errota-Zar is one of Madrid's best *asadors,* restaurants that roast meat on racks or spits over an open fire (the technique is said to have been brought to the Basque country by repatriated emigrés who learned it in Argentina and Uruguay a century ago; since then the Basques have claimed it as their own, and presumably do it better than anyone else). It's behind the stucco-and-stone walls of an antique mill, and managed by Basque-born Segundo Olano and his wife, Eugenia.

You might begin your meal with slices of pork loin, grilled spicy sausage, scrambled eggs with boletus mushrooms, a savory soup made from Basque kidney beans, or perhaps red peppers stuffed with codfish. Other dishes include stewed hake with clams in a marinera sauce, but the real specialties of the house are the succulent cuts of beef, fish, and pork that are first gently warmed, then seared, then cooked by the expert hand of Señor Olano himself. The restaurant is at its most interesting when groups of friends arrive, sharing portions of several different appetizers among themselves before concentrating on a main course.

EL BODEGON, calle Pinar 15. Tel. 562-31-37.

Cuisine: INTERNATIONAL. **Reservations:** Required. **Metro:** Rubén Darío.

$ Prices: Appetizers 1,200–2,800 ptas. ($12–$28); main dishes 1,800–3,200 ptas. ($18–$32). AE, MC, V.

Open: Lunch Mon–Fri 1:30–4pm; dinner Mon–Sat 9pm–midnight. **Closed:** Hols., most of August.

El Bodegón is imbued with the atmosphere of a gentleman's club for hunting enthusiasts—in the country-inn style. International globetrotters are attracted here, especially in the evening, as the restaurant is near three deluxe hotels: the Castellana, the Miguel Angel, and the Luz Palacio. King Juan Carlos and Queen Sofia have dined here.

Waiters in black and white, with gold braid and buttons, bring dignity to the food service. Even bottled water is served champagne style, chilled in a silver floor stand. There are two main dining rooms—conservative, oak-beamed.

I recommend cream of crayfish bisque or a cold, velvety vichyssoise to launch your meal. Main-course selections include grilled filet mignon with classic béarnaise sauce or venison à la bourguignonne. Other main-course selections include shellfish au gratin Escoffier, quails Fernand Point, a tartare of raw fish marinated in parsley-enriched vinaigrette, and smoked salmon. For dessert, try homemade apple pie.

EL CABO MAYOR, Juan Ramón Jiménez 37. Tel. 250-87-76.

Cuisine: SEAFOOD. **Reservations:** Recommended. **Metro:** Cuzco.

$ Prices: Appetizers 1,100–2,800 ptas. ($11–$28); main dishes 1,800–4,500 ptas. ($18–$45). AE, DC, MC, V.

Open: Lunch Mon–Sat 1:30–4pm; dinner Mon–Sat 9pm–midnight. **Closed:** Last two weeks of Aug.

In the prosperous northern edges of Madrid, this restaurant is not far from the city-within-a-city of Chamartín station. This is one of the best, most popular, and most stylish restaurants in Spain. The open-air staircase leading to the entranceway descends from a manicured garden on a quiet side street. You'll know you're here by the battalion of uniformed doormen who greet arriving taxis. The restaurant's decor is a nautically inspired mass of hardwood panels, brass trim, old-fashioned pulleys and ropes, a tile floor custom-painted into sea-green and blue replicas of waves, and hand-carved models of fishing boats. In brass replicas of portholes, some dozen bronze statues honoring fishers and their craft are displayed in illuminated positions of honor.

Menu choices include a superb version of paprika-laden peppers stuffed with fish, a salad composed of Jabugo ham and foie gras of duckling, fish soup from Cantabria (a province between the Basque country and Asturias), asparagus mousse, salmon in sherry sauce, and a loin of veal in cassis sauce. Desserts are appropriately sophisticated, among them a mousse of rice with pine-nut sauce.

EL OLIVO RESTAURANT, General Gallegos 1. Tel. 359-15-35.

Cuisine: MEDITERRANEAN. **Reservations:** Recommended.
Metro: Plaza de Castilla.

$ **Prices:** Appetizers 1,000–1,200 ptas. ($10–$12); main dishes 1,050–3,200 ptas. ($10.50–$32); fixed-price meals 3,850–5,800 ptas. ($38.50–$58). AE, DC, MC, V.
Open: Lunch Tues–Sat 1–4pm; dinner Tues–Sat 9pm–midnight.
Closed: Aug and four days around Easter.

Local wits praise the success of a non-Spaniard (in this case, French-born Jean-Pierre Vandelle) in recognizing the international appeal of two of Spain's most valuable culinary resources, olive oil and sherry. His likeable restaurant, located in northern Madrid near the Chamartín station, pays homage to the glories of the Spanish olive. Designed in tones of green and amber that reflect the leaves and oil of the olive tree, it's probably the only restaurant in Spain that wheels a trolley stocked with 38 regional olive oils from table to table. From the trolley, diners select one or another variety, a golden puddle of which is offered for taste testing, soaked up with chunks of rough-textured bread which is—according to your taste—seasoned with a dash of salt.

Menu specialties include grilled filet of monkfish marinated in herbs and olive oil, and served with black-olive sauce over a compote of fresh tomatoes; and four preparations of codfish arranged on a single platter, and served with a pil-pil sauce (named after the sizzling noise it makes as it bubbles on a stove, pil-pil sauce is composed of codfish gelatin and herbs which are whipped into a mayonnaiselike consistency with olive oil). Also popular are thinly sliced roulades of beef stuffed with foie gras of duckling, dredged in flour, and fried in top-quality olive oil. Desserts might be one of several different chocolate pastries, or leche frite served with an orange sauce. A wide array of reasonably priced bordeaux and Spanish wines can accompany your meal.

A final note: Many clients deliberately arrive early as an excuse to linger in El Olivo's one-of-a-kind sherry bar. Although other drinks are offered, the bar features more than 100 brands of vino de Jerez, more than practically any other establishment in Madrid. Priced at 300–800 ptas. ($3–$8) per glass, they make the perfect apéritif before a Spanish meal.

MODERATE

HELEN'S, paseo de la Castellana 204. Tel. 458-63-77.

Cuisine: SPANISH. **Reservations:** Required for lunch.
Metro: Plaza de Castilla. **Bus:** 27.

$ **Prices:** Bar, sandwiches from 550 ptas. ($5.50). Restaurant, appetizers 700–1,000 ptas. ($7–$10); main dishes 1,500–2,200 ptas. ($15–$22). AE, MC, V.
Open: Lunch Mon–Sat 1:30–4pm; dinner Mon–Sat 8:30–11pm.

If you're staying near the Chamartín train station, you'll find Helen's a popular neighborhood bar with a restaurant in the back. In the front café/bar section, you can enjoy drinks, coffee, and a simple selection of sandwiches. If you go on from the bar to the inner room, you can order a delectable fish soup, stuffed pimientos, filet mignon, and a wide array of fish, veal, and steaks. Fresh sardines will be brought to your table as an appetizer.

O'PAZO, Reina Mercedes 20. Tel. 553-23-33.
  Cuisine: GALICIAN/SEAFOOD. **Reservations:** Required.
  Metro: Chamartín or Alvarado. **Bus:** 3 or 5.
$ Prices: Appetizers 900–3,800 ptas. ($9–$38); main courses 2,000–2,800 ptas. ($20–$28). MC, V.
  Open: Lunch Mon–Sat 1–4pm; dinner Mon–Sat 8:30pm–midnight. **Closed:** Aug.

O'Pazo is a deluxe Galician restaurant, considered by the local cognoscenti as one of the top seafood places in the country—the fish is flown in daily from Galicia. It's decorated in a tasteful style for its distinguished clientele. In front is a cocktail lounge and bar, all in polished brass, with low sofas and paintings. The restaurant has carpeted floors, cushioned Castilian furniture, soft lighting, and colored-glass windows. Most diners begin with assorted smoked fish or fresh oysters. The house specialty is hake Galician style, but you may prefer the sea bass, baked in the oven and served with a mustard sauce. O'Pazo sole is also recommended.

INEXPENSIVE

ALFREDO'S BARBACOA, Juan Hurtado de Mendoza 11. Tel. 345-16-39.
  Cuisine: AMERICAN. **Reservations:** Recommended. **Metro:** Cuzco.
$ Prices: Appetizers 425–550 ptas. ($4.25–$5.50); main dishes 750–1,350 ptas. ($7.50–$13.50). AE, DC, MC, V.
  Open: Lunch Mon–Fri 1–4:30pm, Sat 2–5pm; dinner Mon–Fri 8:30pm–midnight, Sat 8:30pm–1am.

 Alfredo's is a popular rendezvous for Americans longing for home-style food other than hamburgers. Al, the owner, directs his bar/restaurant wearing boots, blue jeans, and a 10-gallon hat; his friendly welcome has made the place a center for both his friends and newcomers to Madrid. You *can* have hamburgers here, but they're of the barbecued variety, and you might instead prefer the barbecued spareribs or chicken. The salad bar is an attraction. And it's a rare treat to be able to have corn on the cob. The original Alfred's Barbacoa, at Lagasca 5 (tel. 576-62-71), is still in business, also under Al's auspices.

8. ARGÜELLES/MONCLOA

EXPENSIVE

LOS PORCHES, paseo del Pintor Rosales 1. Tel. 247-70-51.
  Cuisine: INTERNATIONAL. **Reservations:** Required. **Metro:** Ventura Rodríguez. **Bus:** 74.
$ Prices: Appetizers 1,600–2,500 ptas. ($16–$25); main dishes 2,100–3,600 ptas. ($21–$36); fixed-price menu 5,200 ptas. ($52). AE, DC, MC, V.
  Open: Lunch daily 1–4pm; dinner daily 9pm–midnight.

Los Porches is open all year in a garden setting next to an Egyptian temple, the Templo de Debod, which once stood in the Nile Valley. The menu is typically and elaborately gourmet, including lobster salad with avocado vinaigrette or lobster soup, sea bass with aromatic fennel in puff pastry, venison in Rioja wine sauce, partridge prepared in the style of Toledo, ribs of roast baby lamb, or Ávila veal chop. Lemon tart is the perfect dessert finish.

9. CHUECA

INEXPENSIVE

TABERNA CARMENCITA, Libertad 16. Tel. 531-66-12.
   Cuisine: SPANISH. **Reservations:** Recommended. **Metro:** Chueca.
$ Prices: Appetizers 600–900 ptas. ($6–$9); main dishes 1,000–3,000 ptas. ($10–$30); fixed-price menu 1,100 ptas. ($11). AE, DC, MC, V.
   Open: Lunch Mon–Sat noon–5pm; dinner Mon–Sat 8pm–midnight. **Closed:** Aug 15–Sept 15.

Carmencita is a street-corner enclave of old Spanish charm, filled with 19th-century detailing and tilework that witnessed the conversations of a former patron, the poet Federico Garcia Lorca. Meals might include entrecôte with a green-pepper sauce, escalope of veal, braised mollusks with port, filet of pork, codfish with garlic, and Bilbao-style hake. Every Thursday the special dish is a complicated version of the famous cocido (stew) of Madrid.

BUDGET

EL INCA, Gravina 23. Tel. 532-77-45.
   Cuisine: PERUVIAN. **Reservations:** Required on weekends. **Metro:** Chueca.
$ Prices: Appetizers 500–850 ptas. ($5–$8.50); main dishes 1,100–1,400 ptas. ($11–$14). AE, DC, MC, V.
   Open: Lunch Tues–Sat 1:30–4pm; dinner Mon–Sat 9pm–midnight. **Closed:** Aug.

For a taste of South America, try El Inca, decorated with Inca motifs and artifacts. Since it opened a decade ago it has hosted its share of diplomats and celebrities, although on the average night you're more likely to see families and groups of local officeworkers. The house cocktail is a deceptively potent pisco sour—the recipe comes straight from the Andes. Many of the dishes contain potatoes, the national staple of Peru. The potato-and-black-olive salad is given an unusual zest with a white-cheese sauce. Other specialties are the cebiche de merluza (raw hake marinated with onions) and aji de gallina (a chicken-and-rice dish made with peanut sauce), a Peruvian favorite.

LA ARGENTINA, Gravina 18. Tel. 531-91-17.
   Cuisine: INTERNATIONAL. **Reservations:** Not required. **Metro:** Chueca.
$ Prices: Appetizers 350–825 ptas. ($3.50–$8.25); main dishes 500–1,000 ptas. ($5–$10); fixed-priced menu 1,200 ptas. ($12). No credit cards.

🄕 FROMMER'S COOL FOR KIDS: RESTAURANTS

Casa de Campo *(see "Cool for Kids" in Chapter 6)* Children visiting Spain will delight in patronizing any of the restaurants at the Parque de Atracciones in the Casa de Campo.

A Picnic *(see "Picnic Fare and Where to Eat It" in "Specialty Dining" in this chapter).* Another good idea is to go on a picnic.

Fast-Food Chains For a taste of home, there are always the fast-food chains like McDonald's, Burger King, and Kentucky Fried Chicken. Remember, though, that because Spain is a foreign country, everything may have a slightly different taste.

La Dolores *(see page 124)* Try taking the family to a local tasca, where children are bound to find something they like from the wide selection of tapas. This tasca is appropriate for the entire family, and there's an especially good selection of tapas here.

Foster's Hollywood *(see page 115)* This restaurant has the best hamburgers in Madrid, plus lots of fare familiar to American kids.

V.I.P *(see page 127)* This is the most centrally located member of a Madrid chain, serving fast food, hamburgers, and other foodstuffs that kids go for in a big way, especially the ice-cream concoctions.

Open: Lunch Tues–Sun noon–4pm; dinner Tues–Sun 9pm–midnight. **Closed:** July 25–Aug.

 Two blocks away from Nuevo Oliver, La Argentina is run under the watchful eye of its owner, Andrés Rodríguez. The restaurant has only 16 tables, but the food is tops. The best bets are cannelloni Rossini, noodle soup, creamed spinach, and meat dishes, including entrecôte or roast veal. Chicken Villaroy is another special. All dishes are served with mashed or french-fried potatoes. For dessert, have a baked apple or rice pudding. The decor is simple and clean, and you're usually served by one of the two waitresses who have been here for years.

NABUCCO, Hortaleza 108. Tel. 410-06-11.
    Cuisine: ITALIAN. **Reservations:** Recommended. **Metro:** Alonso Martínez. **Bus:** 7 or 36.
$ Prices: Pizzas 500–680 ptas. ($5–$6.80); appetizers 400–700 ptas. ($4–$7); main dishes 725–1,300 ptas. ($7.25–$13). AE, DC, MC, V.
    Open: Lunch Mon–Sat 1:30–4pm; dinner Mon–Thurs 9pm–midnight, Fri–Sat 9pm–1am.

In a neighborhood of Spanish restaurants, the Italian format comes as a welcome change. The decor resembles a postmodern update of an

Italian ruin, complete with trompe-l'oeil walls painted like marble. Roman portrait busts and a prominent bar lend a dignified air. Menu choices include cannelloni, a good selection of veal dishes, and such main courses as osso buco. You might begin your meal with a selection of antipasti, and for dessert try the chocolate mousse.

TIENDA DE VINOS, Augusto Figueroa 35. Tel. 521-70-12.
  Cuisine: SPANISH. **Reservations:** Not accepted. **Metro:** Chueca.
$ Prices: Appetizers 350–450 ptas. ($3.50–$4.50); main dishes 650–950 ptas. ($6.50–$9.50). No credit cards.
  Open: Breakfast/lunch Mon–Sat 9am–4:30pm; dinner Mon–Sat 8:30pm–midnight.

Officially, this restaurant is known as Tienda de Vinos, but in-the-know Madrileños have inexplicably dubbed it "El Communista." This rather rickety old wine shop, with a few tables in the back, is quite fashionable with actors and journalists looking for Spanish fare without frills. There is a menu, but no one ever thinks of asking for it—just ask what's available. Nor do you get a bill—you're just told how much. You sit at wooden tables and on wooden chairs and benches placed around the walls, which are decorated with old posters, calendars, pennants, and clocks. Start with garlic or vegetable soup or lentils, perhaps followed by lamb chops.

10. SOUTH OF THE PLAZA MAYOR

MODERATE

GURE-ETXEA [RESTAURANT VASCO], Plaza de la Paja 12. Tel. 265-61-49.
  Cuisine: BASQUE. **Reservations:** Recommended. **Metro:** La Latina.
$ Prices: Appetizers 1,200–1,800 ptas. ($12–$18); main dishes 1,500–2,500 ptas. ($15–$25). AE, DC, MC, V.
  Open: Lunch Mon–Sat 1:30–4pm; dinner Mon–Sat 9pm–midnight. **Closed:** Aug.

This restaurant is in a stone-walled building that was the convent for the nearby Church of San Andrés before the Renaissance. Today—amid a decor enhanced by Romanesque arches, vaulted tunnels, and dark-grained paneling—you can enjoy selections from a small but choice menu. Specialties include vichyssoise, rape (a whitefish) in green sauce, Gure-Etxea's special filet of sole, and bacalau al pil-pil (codfish in a fiery sauce).

11. SPECIALTY DINING

TASCA HOPPING

If you think you'll starve waiting for Madrid's fashionable 9:30 or 10pm dinner hour, you've been misinformed. Throughout the city you'll find *tascas* (bars) that serve wine, beer, and platters of tempting hot and cold hors d'oeuvres known as *tapas,* which may include mushrooms, salads, baby eels, shrimp, lobster, mussels, sausage, ham—and in one establishment at least, bull testicles. Keep in mind that you can often save pesetas by ordering at the bar.

EL ANCIANO REY DE LOS VINOS, Bailén 19. Tel. 248-50-52.

Cuisine: TAPAS. **Metro:** Ópera.
$ Prices: Tapas 85–400 ptas (85¢–$4). No credit cards.
Open: Thurs–Tues 10am–3pm and 5:30–11pm.

The bar here is jammed during most of the day with crowds of Madrileños out for a glass (or a carafe) of one of the four house wines. These range from dry to sweet and start at 90 ptas. (90¢) per glass. Beer is also served.

ANTONIO SÁNCHEZ, calle Mesón de Parades 13. Tel. 239-78-26.

Cuisine: SPANISH. **Metro:** Tirso de Molina.
$ Prices: Bar, tapas 300–700 ptas. ($3–$7). Restaurant, appetizers 300–650 ptas. ($3–$6.50); main dishes 750–1,500 ptas ($7.50–$15). V.
Open: Mon–Sat noon–4pm and 8pm–midnight, Sun noon–4pm.

Named in 1850 after the founder's son, who was killed in the bullring, Antonio Sánchez is full of bullfighting memorabilia, including the stuffed head of the animal that gored young Sánchez. Also featured on the dark-paneled walls are three works by the Spanish landscape painter and portraitist Ignacio Zuloaga (1870–1945), who held his last public exhibition in this restaurant. A limited array of tapas, including garlic soup, are served with Valdepeñas wine drawn from a barrel. Many guests ignore the edibles, though, in favor of smoking cigarettes and arguing the merits of this or that bullfighter. A restaurant in the back serves Spanish food with a vaguely French influence. The establishment lies close to the Plaza Tirso de Molina.

CERVECERÍA ALEMANIA, Plaza de Santa Ana 6. Tel. 429-70-33.

Cuisine: TAPAS. **Metro:** Alonso Martín or Sevilla.
$ Prices: Beer 95 ptas. (95¢); tapas 100–900 ptas. ($1–$9). No credit cards.
Open: Sun–Mon and Wed–Thurs 10am–12:30pm, Fri–Sat 10am–1:30am.

Hemingway used to frequent this casual spot with the celebrated bullfighter Luís Miguel Domínguín—ask the waiter to point out "Hemingway's table." However, it earned its name because of its long-ago German clients. Opening directly onto one of the liveliest little plazas of Madrid, it clings to its turn-of-the-century traditions. Young Madrileños are fond of stopping in for a mug of draft beer. You can sit at one of the tables, leisurely sipping beer or wine, since the waiters make no attempt to hurry you along. To accompany your beverage, try the fried sardines or a Spanish omelet.

CERVECERÍA SANTA BARBARA, Plaza de Santa Barbara 8. Tel. 419-04-49.

Cuisine: TAPAS. **Metro:** Alonso Martínez.
$ Prices: Beer 150–290 ptas ($1.50–$2.90); tapas 1,000–3,750 ptas. ($10–$37.50). No credit cards.
Open: Daily 11am–11pm.

Unique in Madrid, the Cervecería Santa Barbara is an outlet for a beer factory, and the management has spent a lot to make it modern and inviting. Hanging globe lights and spinning ceiling fans create an attractive ambience, as does the black-and-white marble checkerboard floor. You go here for beer of course: cerveza negra (black beer) or cerveza dorada (golden beer). The local brew is best accompanied by homemade potato chips or by fresh shrimp, lobster, crabmeat, or barnacles. You can either stand at the counter or go directly to one of the wooden tables for waiter service.

LA DOLORES, calle Jesús de Medinaceli 4. Tel. 468-59-30.
Cuisine: TAPAS. **Reservations:** Not required. **Metro:** Atocha.
$ Prices: Glass of house wine 95 ptas. (95¢); tapas 200–450 ptas. ($2–$4.50). No credit cards.
Open: Daily 10am–midnight.

In business since the 1920s, this is one of the best-patronized tascas in the old city. A ceramic tile announces the wine specialty, vinos de Valdepeñas, one so beloved by matadors and their aficionados. As a decor note, beer cans "from all over" are stacked against the walls. However, La Dolores offers only one choice, Mahou, although its wine list is extensive. Many various tapas are served, and frankly, you can make a full meal by sampling two or three of these. Try smoked salmon on bread with cheese.

TABERNA TOSCANA, Ventura de la Vega 22. Tel. 429-60-31.
Cuisine: TAPAS. **Metro:** Puerta del Sol or Sevilla.
$ Prices: Glass of wine 95 ptas. (95¢); tapas 450–2,000 ptas. ($4.50–$20). No credit cards.
Open: Lunch Tues–Sat noon–4pm; dinner Mon–Sat 8pm–midnight. **Closed:** Aug.

Many Madrileños begin their nightly tasca crawl here. The aura is that of a village inn, far removed from 20th-century Madrid. You sit on crude country stools under time-darkened beams from which hang sausages, pimientos, and sheaves of golden wheat. The long tile tapas bar is loaded with tasty tidbits, including the house specialties: lacón y cecina (boiled ham), habas (broad beans) with Spanish ham, and chorizo (a red-pepper and pork sausage)—almost meals in themselves. Especially delectable are the kidneys in sherry sauce and the snails in hot sauce.

DINING WITH A VIEW

CAFÉ DE ORIENTE, Plaza de Oriente 2. Tel. 541-39-74.
Cuisine: FRENCH/SPANISH. **Reservations:** Recommended for the restaurant. **Metro:** Ópera.
$ Prices: Tasca, tapas 850 ptas. ($8.50); coffee 650 ptas. ($6.50). Restaurant, appetizers 1,100–3,000 ptas. ($11–$30); main dishes 2,500–4,500 ptas. ($25–$45). AE, DC, MC, V.
Open: Lunch daily 1–4pm; dinner daily 9pm–midnight.

The Oriente is a café and restaurant complex, the former being one of the most popular in Madrid. From the café tables on its terrace, there's a spectacular view of the Palacio Real (Royal Palace) and the Teatro Real. The dining rooms—Castilian upstairs, French Basque downstairs—are frequented by royalty and diplomats. Typical of the refined cuisine are vichyssoise, fresh vegetable flan, and many savory meat and fresh-fish offerings; the service is excellent. Most visitors, however, patronize the café, trying if possible to get an outdoor table for a "ringside" view of the Royal Palace. The café is decorated in turn-of-the-century style, with banquettes and regal paneling, as befits its location. Pizza, tapas, and drinks (including Irish, Viennese, Russian, and Jamaican coffees) are served.

HEMINGWAY'S ROAST SUCKLING PIG

SOBRINO DE BOTÍN, calle de Cuchilleros 17. Tel. 266-42-17.
   Cuisine: SPANISH. **Reservations:** Required. **Metro:** La Latina or Ópera.
$ **Prices:** Appetizers 450–2,300 ptas. ($4.50–$23); main dishes 750–4,200 ptas. ($7.50–$42); fixed-price menu 3,500 ptas. ($35). AE, DC, MC, V.
   Open: Lunch daily 1–4pm; dinner daily 8pm–midnight.

Ernest Hemingway made Sobrino de Botín famous. In the final two pages of his novel *The Sun Also Rises,* he had Jake invite Brett there for the Segovian specialty, washed down with Rioja Alta.

By merely entering its portals, you step back to 1725, the year the restaurant was founded. You'll see an open kitchen, with a charcoal hearth, hanging copper pots, and an 18th-century tile oven for roasting suckling pig. The aroma from a big pot of regional soup wafts across the tables, which sit under time-aged beams. Your host, Don Antonio, never loses his cool—even when he has 18 guests standing in line waiting for tables.

The two house specialties are roast suckling pig and roast Segovian lamb. From the à la carte menu, you might try the "quarter-of-an-hour" soup, made with fish. Good main dishes include the baked Cantabrian hake and filet mignon with potatoes. The dessert list features strawberries (in season) with whipped cream. You can wash down your meal with Valdepeñas or Aragón wine, although most guests order sangría.

HOTEL DINING

RESTAURANT BELAGUA, in the Hotel Palacio Santo Mauro, calle Zurbano 36. Tel. 319-69-00.
   Cuisine: INTERNATIONAL. **Reservations:** Recommended. **Metro:** Rubén Darío or Alonso Martínez.
$ **Prices:** Appetizers 1,100–3,500 ptas. ($11–$35); main courses 3,600–4,500 ptas. ($36–$45). AE, DC, MC, V.
   Open: Lunch Mon–Sat 1–4pm; dinner Mon–Sat 8:30–11:30pm. **Closed:** National hols.

One of the capital's newest and most fashionable five-star restaurants lies amid the rows of books and the impeccably restored Santo Mauro. The building which contains it was originally constructed in 1894 as a small palace in the French neoclassical style, although in 1991 Catalán designer Josep Joanpere infused the then-dingy villa with new, postmodern life.

Assisted by a well-mannered staff, you'll select from a menu whose inspiration and ingredients change with the seasons. Examples might include a watermelon-and-prawn salad, a light cream of cold ginger soup, haddock baked in a crust of potatoes tinted with squid ink, duck with honey and black cherries, and a dessert specialty which a waiter will define as a palette of seasonal flavors—depending on the efforts of the chef, it might include miniature portions of flan with strawberry sauce plus a sophisticated array of the day's pastries. The restaurant's name, incidentally, derives from a village in Navarre known for its natural beauty.

VEGETARIAN

LA GALETTE, Conde de Aranda 11. Tel. 576-06-41.

Cuisine: VEGETARIAN. **Reservations:** Recommended. **Metro:** Retiro.

$ Prices: Appetizers 300–350 ptas. ($3–$3.50); main dishes 500–700 ptas. ($5–$7); fixed-price menu 2,200 ptas. ($22). AE, DC, MC, V.

Open: Lunch Mon–Sat 2–4pm; dinner Mon–Sat 9pm–midnight.

La Galette was one of Madrid's first vegetarian restaurants, and remains one of the best. Small and charming, it lies in a residential and shopping area in the exclusive Salamanca district, near the Plaza de la Independenca and the northern edge of Retiro Park. There's a limited selection of meat dishes, but the true allure lies in this establishment's imaginative use of vegetarian fare. Examples include baked stuffed peppers, omelets, eggplant croquettes, and even vegetarian "hamburgers." Some of the dishes are macrobiotic. The place is also noted for its mouth-watering pastries.

BREAKFAST/BRUNCH/AFTERNOON TEA

The best place in all of Madrid for Sunday brunch is **Armstrong's** (see "Near the Plaza de las Cortés," above).

The most delightful spot in Madrid for afternoon tea is at a sidewalk table of the **Café de Oriente** (see "Dining With a View," above), overlooking the Royal Palace.

LIGHT & CASUAL FARE

CHEZ LOU CREPERIE, Pedro Munguruza 6. Tel. 250-34-16.

Cuisine: FRENCH. **Reservations:** Required on weekends. **Metro:** Plaza de Castilla. **Bus:** 27 or 147.

$ Prices: Appetizers 450–750 ptas. ($4.50–$7.50); crêpes 550–850 ptas. ($5.50–$8.50); fixed-price menu 1,050 ptas. ($10.50). No credit cards.

Open: Lunch Mon–Fri 1:30–4pm; dinner Mon–Sat 8:30pm–1am.

Near the Eurobuilding Hotel in the northern sector of Madrid, this restaurant stands near the huge mural by Joan Miró, which alone would be worth the trek up here. In this intimate setting you get well-prepared and reasonably priced French food. The restaurant serves pâté as an appetizer, then a large range of crêpes with many different fillings. Folded envelope style, the crêpes are not tearoom size, and they're perfectly adequate as a main course. I've sampled several variations of crêpe, finding the ingredients nicely blended yet distinct enough to retain their identity. A favorite is the large crêpe stuffed with minced onions, cream, and smoked salmon. The ham-and-cheese crêpe is also tasty. The price of your dessert and drink is extra. Come here if you're seeking a light supper when it's too hot for one of those table-groaning Spanish meals.

LA PLAZA, in the Galería del Prado, Plaza de las Cortés 7. Tel. 429-65-37.
Cuisine: SPANISH. **Reservations:** Not required. **Metro:** Sevilla.
$ Prices: Appetizers 500–750 ptas. ($5–$7.50); main dishes 900–1,300 ptas. ($9–$13); fixed-price menu 1,200 ptas. ($12). AE, MC, V.
Open: Mon–Fri 10am–11pm, Sat 10am–1pm.

Its location amid the marble walls of Madrid's most sophisticated shopping complex eliminates the possibility of windows. Nevertheless, this is one of the best choices for light, refreshing meals in an expensive neighborhood. It's also handy for quick meals if you're spending a day at the Prado. Some of its tables spill into the rotunda of the shopping mall; most diners, however, sit in a glossy series of lattices whose rooms form a garden-inspired enclave near a well-stocked salad bar (visits here are priced according to the portions you take). You might begin with Serrano ham or a mountain-fermented goat cheese, perhaps a homemade pâté. Daily specials include such dishes as ragoût of veal. Platters of pasta also provide a zesty way to fill up.

RÍOFRÍO, in the Centro Colón, Plaza de Colón 1. Tel. 319-29-77.
Cuisine: INTERNATIONAL. **Reservations:** Not required. **Metro:** Colón. **Bus:** 5, 6, 14, or 27.
$ Prices: Appetizers 350–750 ptas. ($3.50–$7.50); main dishes 800–2,800 ptas. ($8–$28); fixed-price menu 2,200 ptas. ($22). AE, DC, MC, V.
Open: Daily noon–1:30am.

Ríofrío is an ideal central place for on-the-run snacks and drinks. Its terrace, overlooking the "Columbus Circle of Madrid," is favored on sunny days; otherwise, there's a more formal interior where you can get substantial meals, as well as a self-service section. You can order club sandwiches or perhaps an appetizing combination plate. The Spanish coffee is good here (but different), and you can also drop in just to order a refreshing drink, alcoholic or otherwise.

CAFETERIAS

EL CORTE INGLÉS, calle Preciados 3. Tel. 532-81-00.
Cuisine: SPANISH. **Metro:** Callao.
$ Prices: Buffet 2,000 ptas. ($20). AE, DC, MC, V.
Open: Lunch only, Mon–Sat 12:30–4pm.

El Corte Inglés will be recommended later as one of the most prestigious department stores in Madrid (see Chapter 8). Every in-the-know shopper also knows that it offers some of the best food values around at its buffet on the seventh floor, featuring 70 different plates. Come here if you have a gargantuan appetite.

V.I.P., Gran Vía 41. Tel. 411-60-44.
Cuisine: SPANISH. **Reservations:** Not required. **Metro:** Callao.
$ Prices: Appetizers 450–725 ptas. ($4.50–$7.25); main dishes 650–1,200 ptas. ($6.50–$12). AE, DC, MC, V.
Open: Daily 9am–3am.

This place looks like a bookstore emporium from the outside, but in back is a Formica-sheathed cafeteria serving fast food. You might begin with a cup of soothing gazpacho. There are at least 14 V.I.P.s scattered throughout Madrid, but this is the most central one. Hamburgers are the rage here.

LOCAL FAVORITES

LA BOLA, calle la Bola 7. Tel. 247-69-30.

Cuisine: MADRILEÑA. **Reservations:** Required. **Metro:** Plaza de España or Ópera. **Bus:** 1 or 2.

$ Prices: Appetizers 600–1,800 ptas. ($6–$18); main dishes 1,500–2,600 ptas. ($15–$26). No credit cards.

Open: Lunch Mon–Sat 1–4pm; dinner Mon–Sat 9pm–midnight.
If you'd like to savor the Madrid of the 19th century, then this *taberna,* just north of the Teatro Real, is an inspired choice. It's one of the few restaurants (if not the only one) left in Madrid that's painted with a blood-red facade; once, nearly all fashionable restaurants were so coated. La Bola hangs on to tradition like a tenacious bull. Time has galloped forward, but not inside this restaurant, where the soft, traditional atmosphere, the gentle and polite waiters, the Venetian crystal, the Carmen-red draperies, and the aging velvet preserve the 1870 ambience of the place. Ava Gardner, with her entourage of bullfighters, used to patronize this establishment, but that was long ago, before La Bola became so well known to tourists. Grilled sole is regularly featured, as is filet of veal or roast veal. Basque-style hake is also well recommended, as is grilled salmon. A host of refreshing dishes to begin a meal includes grilled shrimp, red-pepper salad, or a lobster cocktail.

EL CALLEJÓN, Ternera 6. Tel. 522-54-01.

Cuisine: SPANISH. **Reservations:** Recommended. **Metro:** Callao. **Bus:** 147.

$ Prices: Appetizers 500–1,200 ptas. ($5–$12); main dishes 1,500–2,000 ptas. ($15–$20); fixed-price meals 1,600 ptas. ($16) at lunch, 3,200 ptas. ($32) at dinner. AE, MC, V.

Open: Lunch daily 1–4pm; dinner daily 8:15–11:30pm. **Closed:** Sat in summer.
Hemingway's "other favorite" lies on a tiny street in the heart of Madrid, off the Gran Vía near the Galerías Preciados department store. Hemingway, called "Don Ernesto" by the waiters, came here for paella after a bullfight. Opened in 1944, El Callejón still attracts sportsmen, diplomats, and bullfighters. It features regional dishes on set days of the week. On Tuesday and Saturday you can order stewed veal, but you have to go here on Thursday for the Spanish soul-food dish, red beans with rice. Openers might include the classic garlic soup or shrimp Bilbao style. Among the main courses, the special steak and the calves' sweetbreads cost considerably more than the eggs Callejón and the roast half chicken. Roman-style squid is popular, as is Navarre-style trout. For desserts, try the cherries with fresh cream or the fried bananas.

CASA CIRIACO, calle Mayor 84. Tel. 248-50-66.

Cuisine: SPANISH. **Reservations:** Recommended. **Metro:** Puerta del Sol.

$ Prices: Appetizers 450–900 ptas. ($4.50–$9); main dishes 800–3,200 ptas. ($8–$32).

Open: Lunch Thurs–Tues 1–4pm; dinner Thurs–Tues 8:30pm–midnight. **Closed:** Aug.

Since 1906 this has been a special restaurant in one of the most romantic parts of Old Madrid. It enjoys associations with the Spanish painter Ignacio Zuloaga. The casa's definitely not out for the tourist traffic—in fact, foreigners are still regarded with a certain curiosity around here. The chef features dishes from Navarre and Andalusia, but Castilian specialties predominate. Gazpacho makes a fine opener; then you can order Navarre-style trout or tender slices of veal.

CASA MINGO, paseo de la Florida 2. Tel. 247-10-98.

Cuisine: SPANISH. **Reservations:** Not accepted. **Metro:** Norte, then a 15-minute walk.

$ Prices: Main dishes 450–950 ptas. ($4.50–$9.50). No credit cards.

Open: Daily 11am–midnight.

Casa Mingo has been known for decades for its Asturian cider, both still and bubbly. The perfect accompanying tidbit is a piece of the local Asturian cabrales (goat cheese), but the roast chicken is the specialty of the house, with an unbelievable number of helpings served daily. There's no formality here, as customers share big tables under the vaulted ceiling in the dining room. In summer the staff places some tables and wooden chairs outdoors on the sidewalk.

HYLOGUI, Ventura de la Vega 3. Tel. 429-73-57.

Cuisine: CASTILIAN. **Reservations:** Recommended. **Metro:** Sevilla.

$ Prices: Appetizers 350–850 ptas. ($3.50–$8.50); main dishes 750–1,500 ptas. ($7.50–$15). No credit cards.

Open: Lunch daily 1–4:30pm; dinner Mon–Sat 9pm–midnight.

 Hylogui, a local legend, is one of the largest dining rooms along Ventura de la Vega, but there are many arches and nooks for privacy. One globe-trotting American wrote enthusiastically that he took all his meals here in Madrid, finding the soup pleasant and rich, the flan soothing, the regional wine dry. The food is old-fashioned Spanish home-style cooking.

TABERNA DEL ALABARDERO, calle Felipe V no. 6. Tel. 541-51-92.

Cuisine: BASQUE/SPANISH. **Reservations:** Required for the restaurant. **Metro:** Ópera.

$ Prices: Bar, tapas 450–850 ptas. ($4.50–$8.50); glass of house wine 85 ptas. (85¢). Restaurant, appetizers 500–1,075 ptas. ($5–$10.75); main dishes 1,200–2,000 ptas. ($12–$20). AE, DC, V.

Open: Lunch daily 1–4pm; dinner daily 8:30pm–midnight.

Because of its proximity to the Royal Palace, most patrons visit this little Spanish classic for its selection of tasty tapas, ranging from squid cooked in wine to fried potatoes dipped in hot sauce. Photographs of former patrons, including Nelson Rockefeller and race-car driver Jackie Stewart, line the walls. The restaurant in the rear is said to be one of the city's "best-kept secrets." Decorated in typical tavern style, it serves a savory Spanish Basque cuisine with market-fresh ingredients.

PICNIC FARE & WHERE TO EAT IT

On a hot day, do as the Madrileños do. Secure the makings of a picnic lunch and head for the **Casa de Campo** (Metro: El Batán), those once-royal hunting grounds in the west of Madrid across the

Manzanares River. Children delight in this adventure, as they can also visit a boating lake, the Parque de Atracciones, and the Madrid Zoo.

Your best choice for picnic fare is **Mallorca,** Velázquez 59 (tel. 431-99-00; Metro: Velázquez). This place has all the makings for a deluxe picnic.

Another good bet is **Rodilla,** Precíados 25 (tel. 522-57-01; Metro: Callao), where you can find sandwiches, pastries, and takeaway tapas. Sandwiches, including vegetarian, meat, and fish, begin at 75 ptas. (75¢). It's open daily from 8:30am to 10:30pm.

WHAT TO SEE & DO IN MADRID

Tourist officials in Madrid often confide, "We spend so much fuss to get people to visit Madrid. But when we get them here, and they've seen the Prado and a bullfight, we send them off to El Escorial or Toledo." Too true—and regrettably so. As European capitals go, Madrid is hard to know. The city's mainstream attractions—tree-shaded parks, wide paseos, bubbling fountains, the art treasures of the Prado—are obvious. And, of course, it's this Madrid that the routine visitor sees quickly before striking out for the next adventure, usually to one of the satellites such as Segovia. But for the more determined traveler, willing to invest the time and stamina, the Spanish capital tucks away many hidden treasures.

For easy reference, see the Index at the back of this book.

SUGGESTED ITINERARIES

IF YOU HAVE ONE DAY If you have just arrived in Spain after a long flight, don't tackle too much on your first day. Spend the morning at the Prado, one of the world's great art museums, arriving when it opens, at 9am (closed Mon). Have lunch and then visit the Palacio Real (Royal Palace). Have an early dinner near the Plaza Mayor.

IF YOU HAVE TWO DAYS Spend Day 1 as described above. On your second day take a trip to Toledo, where you can visit El Greco's House and Museum, the Santa Cruz Museum, the Church of Santo Tomé, and the Alcázar. Return to Madrid in the evening.

IF YOU HAVE THREE DAYS Follow the suggestions above for Days 1 and 2. On Day 3 take the train (one hour) to the Monastery of San Lorenzo del Escorial, in the foothills of the Sierra de Guadarrama. Return to Madrid in the evening.

IF YOU HAVE FIVE DAYS Follow the suggestions for Days 1–3, above. On your fourth day, be at the Museum of Lázaro Galdiano when it opens (10am). Afterward take one of the walking tours of Madrid (see Chapter 7) and follow it with a late lunch in the old town. In the afternoon, either visit the Goya Pantéon or the Convento de las Descalzas Reales. End the day with another walking tour or revisit the Prado.

On Day 5 take a trip to Segovia in Old Castile. Be sure to see its Alcázar, Roman aqueduct, and cathedral. Sample the region's specialties at lunch and return to Madrid for dinner in the old town.

1. THE TOP ATTRACTIONS

MUSEO DEL PRADO, paseo del Prado. Tel. 420-28-36.

Many Madrileños go once or twice a month all their lives just to gaze upon their particular favorites (the reproductions at home are never adequate). But first-time visitors, with less than a lifetime to spend, will have to limit their viewing—see the walking tour of the Prado in Chapter 7. That task is difficult, as the Prado owns more than 7,000 paintings and is ranked among the top three art museums of the world.

In an 18th-century neoclassic palace designed by Juan de Villanueva, the Prado has been considerably improved in the past few years, especially its lighting. There will be work in progress for some time to come.

The most hurried trekker may want to focus attention on the output of three major artists: the court painters Velázquez and Goya, plus El Greco, who was in fact a Greek (born in Crete in 1541). But don't overlook the exceptional visions of Hieronymus Bosch, the 15th-century Flemish artist who peopled his canvases with fiends and ghouls and conjured up tortures that far surpassed Dante's *Inferno*. In particular, seek out his triptychs, *The Hay Wagon* and *The Garden of Earthly Delights*.

Most of the works of these artists are on the second floor. However, on the ground floor you'll find Goya's "black paintings" and his remarkable drawings. The Prado's single most famous work is *Las Meninas*—the maids in waiting—the masterpiece of Velázquez. In the Goya room is displayed his *Naked Maja*, certainly one of the most recognizable paintings in the West—said to have been posed for by the woman the artist loved, the Duchess of Alba. As a court painter to Charles IV and his adulterous queen, María Luisa, Goya portrayed all their vulgarity of person and mind—and got them to pay for the results.

Other paintings, by Raphael, Botticelli, Correggio, Titian, (Titzano), Pieter Bruegel the Elder, Murillo, Ribera, and Fra Angelico, will make the morning fade quickly into dusk.

The painting stirring up the most excitement in recent years is Picasso's *Guernica* (1937). Long banned in Spain, the painting rested for years in the Museum of Modern Art in New York before it was returned. The Prado houses it in one of its satellites, behind the Ionic columns of the Casón del Buen Retiro, at the edge of nearby Retiro Park. (The casón's main entrance is on calle Felipe IV, and your ticket allows you entrance to both the main body of the Prado and its satellites.) *Guernica* is still considered controversial decades after Picasso painted it to protest Generalíssimo Franco's participation in the Nazi bombing of Guernica (Gernika), an important center of Basque culture. Picasso requested that *Guernica* not be returned to

Spain until the death of Franco and the "reestablishment of public liberties."

Admission: 400 ptas. ($4).

Open: Tues–Sat 9am–7pm, Sun and hols. 9am–2pm. **Closed:** Jan 1, Dec 25. **Metro:** Banco de España or Atocha. **Bus:** 10, 14, 27, 34, 37, or 45.

PALACIO REAL [Royal Palace], on Plaza de Oriente, Bailén 2. Tel. 248-74-04.

Alfonso XIII, grandfather of King Juan Carlos, and his queen, Victoria Eugénie, were the last to use the Palacio Real as a royal abode, in 1931 before they fled into exile. Franco used the Royal Palace (also known as the Palacio de Oriente) for state functions and elaborate banquets for foreign dignitaries, but guides like to point out that he never sat on the king's chair in the Throne Room.

King Juan Carlos and Queen Sofía are more modest in their requirements. They have turned the Royal Palace over to history, choosing not to live there but in their much smaller suburban palace, the Zarzuela, named after the Spanish operetta, or musical comedy.

On the landmark site of the former Alcázar of Madrid (destroyed by fire on Christmas of 1734), the Royal Palace was launched in 1738. Its first tenant was Charles III, the "enlightened despot" of the House of Bourbon. In all, the rooms—many added at a later date—total around 1,800. Not all are open to the public, of course—nor need they be, as the tour would then take a week.

Visitors are conducted on a guided tour of the State Apartments, the Reception Salons, the Royal Armory, and the Royal Pharmacy. If you're rushed—and want just a quick glimpse of the grandeur of the palace—then you'll want to confine your sightseeing to the State Apartments and the Reception Rooms.

After your tour, you can skip across the courtyard to the **Royal Armory,** considered one of the most impressive in Europe. Recalling the days of jousting and equestrian warfare, many of the exhibits date from the reign of Charles V (Charles I of Spain) of the Hapsburg Empire. Roughly, the collection spans about 200 years of the Spanish Empire.

The **Royal Pharmacy** also merits a visit. It was, in its heyday, the "cure-all" source for any ailment that plagued the royal family.

Worth a detour, the **Museo de Carruajes Reales** (Carriage Museum) is also on the palace grounds. Here you can view the horse-drawn vehicles that Spanish aristocrats used in the days when a person was judged solely on appearance.

After your whirlwind tour, you can wind down by strolling through the Campo del Moro, the gardens of the palace.

Admission: 500 ptas. ($5). If you don't want to see everything, you can visit only what you wish.

Open: Mon–Sat 9:30am–12:45pm and 4–5:15pm, Sun 9:30am–12:15pm. **Metro:** Ópera (Ópera, Ventura Rodríguez, or Plaza de España for the Carriage Museum). **Bus:** 1, 25, 33, or 39.

REAL FÁBRICA DE TAPICES [Royal Factory of Tapestries], calle Fuenterrabia 2. Tel. 551-34-00.

The making of tapestries—based on original designs (called cartoons) by Goya, Francisco Bayeu (Goya's brother-in-law), and others—is still a flourishing art in Madrid. You can actually visit the factory where the tapices are turned out and chat with the workers.

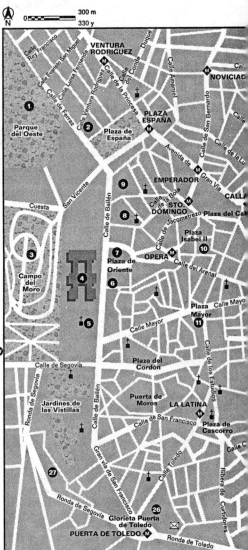

Some of the hand-looms on which they work date back to the days of Goya. The great Spanish artist sketched numerous cartoons that were converted into tapestries to adorn the walls of the Royal Palace not only in Madrid, but also in Aranjuez and La Granja. One of the most famous, reproduced hundreds of times, is *El Cacharrero* (The Pottery Salesman).

Some craftspeople have copied the same design all their lives, so that now they can work on it without thinking. Others, less cavalier, prefer to watch the design carefully through a mirror.

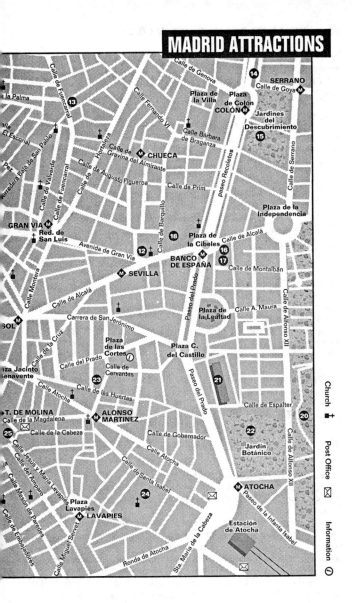

Admission: 50 ptas. (50¢).
Open: Mon–Fri 9am–12:30pm. **Closed:** Aug. **Metro:** Atocha or Pelayo. **Bus:** 14 or 26.

MUSEO LÁZARO GALDIANO, Serrano 122. Tel. 261-60-84.

Deserving of far more visitors than it receives, this remarkable, compact, and art-stuffed museum spans the centuries of artistic development with seeming ease. An elevator takes you to the top floor of what was once one of the great mansions of Madrid. It belonged to José Lázaro Galdiano, a famous 20th-century patron of the arts. You weave your way from room to room (37 in all), descending the stairs as you go.

The collection begins with vestments, some dating from the 15th century. Along the way you can stop and stare at an assemblage of weapons, daggers, and swords, some with elaborate handles dating from the 15th century. Seals, such as one belonging to Napoleon, are displayed; and there's a rare exhibition of Spanish fans, one a possession of Isabella II.

In Room XX are two Flemish paintings by the incomparable Bosch—rats crawling through the eyes of humans, and so on. In the following room (XXI) is a portrait of Saskia signed by her husband, Rembrandt, dating from 1634. In other salons, several of the major artists of Spain are represented: Velázquez, Zurbarán, El Greco, Valdés Leal, Murillo, and Ribera. Room XXV is the salon of English-speaking portraitists: Gainsborough, Sir Joshua Reynolds, Gilbert Stuart, and Constable. Many well-known works by Goya are in his salon (XXX), including some of the "black paintings" and portraits of Charles IV and his voluble spouse.

Other intriguing showcases are filled with 16th-century Limoges crystal, French and Italian ivory carving from the 14th and 15th centuries, and a 15th-century Maltese cross. In Room VI hangs a small portrait of the Savior as an adolescent, encased in green velvet. Although some critics attribute this painting to Leonardo da Vinci, other art historians dispute this claim.

Admission: 300 ptas. ($3).

Open: Tues–Sun 10am–2pm. **Closed:** Hols., Aug. **Metro:** Avenida de América. **Bus:** 9, 16, 19, 51, or 89.

CONVENTO DE LAS DESCALZAS REALES, Plaza de las Descalzas Reales. Tel. 248-74-04.

⭐ What would you do if you were a starving nun surrounded by a vast treasure house of paintings, gold, jewelry, and tapestries? Sell them? Not possible. The order of the Franciscan Clarissas convinced the government to let them open the doors of the convent to the general public—with the pope's permission, of course. The museum is still an operational convent of approximately 30 sisters.

The collection includes tapestries based on Rubens's cartoons, 16th- and 17th-century vestments, a silver forearm said to contain bones of St. Sebastian, and a statue of the Virgin wearing earrings, as is the custom in Andalusia. The most interesting chapel is dedicated to Our Lady of Guadalupe (the statue of the Virgin is made of lead).

The most valuable oil is Titian's *Caesar's Money,* worth millions of pesetas. The Flemish Hall contains other superb canvases—for example, one of a processional by Hans der Berken. You must wait for a guided tour.

Admission: 350 ptas. ($3.50) adults, 250 ptas. ($2.50) children.

Open: Tues–Thurs 10:30am–12:30pm and 4–5:30pm, Fri–Sun 10:30–12:30pm. **Closed:** Jan 1, the week before Easter, May 1, and Dec 24–25. **Directions:** From the Plaza de Callao, a satellite square of the Gran Vía, walk down a narrow street, Postigo de San Martín, to one of the most charming squares in Madrid, the Plaza de las Descalzas Reales. You'll see the convent on your left. **Metro:** Puerta del Sol, Callao, or Ópera.

PANTÉON DE GOYA, Glorieta de San Antonio de la Florida. Tel. 542-07-22.

Emulating Tiepolo, Goya frescoed the Church of San Antonio de la Florida in 1798. Although he depicted in part the miracles of St. Anthony of Padua, his work was nearly secular in its execution. Mirrors are placed that better allow you to capture the beauty of the ceiling. The figure of a woman draped in a cape is one of the most celebrated subjects in Goya's work.

The hermitage is located at the northwestern edge of the city, near the western edge of the Parque Oeste, beyond the Príncipe Pío (north) station. Goya died in exile in Bordeaux, France, in 1828, but his bones were later removed from there and interred here in the memorial that he unknowingly created for himself. In transit his head disappeared, presumably stolen by a souvenir hunter.

Some church officials once considered Goya's frescoes irreverent— hence, the hermitage was not a fit place of worship. A twin of the 18th-century church was erected alongside it, and services are conducted there now. Facing both of them, go into the one on the right to pay your respects to Goya.

Admission: 100 ptas ($1).

Open: Tues–Fri 10am–3pm and 4–8pm, Sat–Sun 10am–2pm. **Metro:** Norte. **Bus:** 41, 46, or 75.

CENTRO DE ARTE REINA SOFIA ("The Sofidou"), Santa Isabel 52, at the corner of calle Atocha. Tel. 467-50-02 or 468-30-02.

"The Sofidou" reigns without challenge as the greatest repository of 20th-century art in Spain. Set in the echoing, futuristically renovated walls of the former General Hospital, originally built between 1776 and 1781, the museum is a sprawling, high-ceilinged showplace named after the Greek-born wife of Spain's present king. Once designated as "the ugliest building in Spain" by Catalán architect Oriol Bohigas, the building is said to be one of the largest, and probably the most security-conscious, museum in Europe. The design hangs in limbo somewhere between the 18th and the 21st century, and incorporates a 50,000-volume art library and database, a café, theater, book-

---

⭐ FROMMER'S FAVORITE MADRID EXPERIENCES

Tasca Hopping The quintessential Madrid experience and the fastest way for a visitor to tap into the local scene. *Tascas* are Spanish pubs serving tantalizing *tapas* (appetizers). You can go from one to the next, sampling the special dishes and wines in each tavern.

Eating "Around Spain" The variety of gastronomic experiences is staggering. You can literally restaurant hop from province to province—without ever leaving Madrid.

Viewing the Works of Your Favorite Artist Spend an afternoon at the Prado, savoring the works of your favorite Spanish artist, devoting all your attention to his work.

Bargain Hunting at El Rastro Madrid has one of the greatest flea markets in Europe, if not the world. Wander through its many offerings, discovering that hidden treasure you've been searching for.

A Night of Flamenco Flamenco folk songs (*cante*) and dances (*baile*) are an integral part of the Spanish experience. Spend at least one night in a flamenco tavern listening to the heartrending laments of gypsy sorrows, tribulations, hopes, and dreams.

Outdoor Café Sitting This is a famous Madrid experience for the summertime, when Madrileños come alive again on their *terrazas*. The drinking and good times can go on until dawn. From glamorous hangouts to lowly street corners, the café scene takes place mainly along an axis shaped by paseo de la Castellana, paseo del Prado, and paseo de Recoletos.

---

store, Plexiglas-sided elevators, and systems which carefully calibrate security, temperature, humidity, and the quality of light surrounding the exhibits.

Special emphasis is paid to the great artists of contemporary Spain: Juan Gris, Dalí, Miró, and the handful of Picassos it has been able to acquire. At press time, plans were being discussed concerning the placement within the museum's walls of Picasso's world-renowned *Guernica*, despite resistance from the curators of the work's present home in the Palace of the Buen Retiro.

As important as is its role as showplace of 20th-century Spanish art, the museum has acted as a huge magnet for the relocation in its neighborhood of several new art galleries and cultural institutions that collectively promise to upgrade both the neighborhood and the cultural quality of life of Spain.

Admission: 400 ptas ($4).

Open: Wed–Mon 10am–9pm. **Metro:** Atocha. **Bus:** 10, 14, 19, 27, 32, 37, or 45.

2. MORE ATTRACTIONS

MUSEUMS

MUSEO DE LA REAL ACADEMIA DE BELLAS ARTES DE SAN FERNANDO [Fine Arts Museum], calle de Alcalá 13. Tel. 522-14-91.

Right on Madrid's busy boulevard, an easy stroll from the Puerta del Sol, the Fine Arts Museum is considered second only to the Prado in importance as a leading Spanish museum. It houses more than 1,500 paintings and 800 sculptures by such masters as Goya, Murillo, and El Greco, plus drawings by Rubens, Ribera, and Velázquez. The collection ranges from the 16th century to the present, and was started in 1752 when the academy was founded during the reign of Fernando VI (1746–59). The emphasis is on works of Spanish, Flemish, and Italian artists, and you can see masterpieces by the artists mentioned above, plus Zurbarán, Sorolla, Cano, and Coello. The museum is in the restored and remodeled palace of Juan de Goyeneche, a banker who had it constructed in 1710 in the baroque style; the building was later redone in the neoclassical style.

Admission: 200 pesetas ($2).

Open: Sun–Mon 9am–2pm, Tues–Sat 9am–7pm. **Metro:** Puerta del Sol or Sevilla.

MUSEO TAURINO [Museum of Bullfighting], calle de Alcalá 237, in the Plaza de Toros de las Ventas (the Patio de Caballos). Tel. 255-18-57.

Ideally, you should visit this museum before you see your first Spanish bullfight, as it serves as a good introduction to "the tragedy" in the arena. It's located beneath the Moorish arcade of the largest bullfight stadium in Madrid. The complete history of the *torero*, as well as a lot of bullfighting trivia, is traced in pictures, historic bullfight posters, and scale models. Works of art include a Goya painting of a matador, plus an exquisite bust, sculpted in bronze, of Manolete.

Admission: Free.

Open: May–Sept, Tues–Fri and Sun 10am–1pm; Oct–Apr, Mon–Fri 10am–1pm. **Metro:** Ventas. **Bus:** 12, 21, 38, 53, or 146.

MUSEO MUNICIPAL, Fuencarral 78. Tel. 522-57-32.

Perhaps more than any other museum in Madrid, the Municipal Museum documents the explosion of Madrid from a sleepy and dusty backwater into a world-class city. It contains exhibits on local history, archeology, art, porcelain, plans, engravings, and photographs, all depicting the history of Madrid. In a churrigueresque baroque structure, the museum displays deal especially with the Bourbon Madrid of the 18th century, whose paseos with strolling couples are shown on huge tapestry cartoons. Paintings from the royal collections are here, plus period models of the best-known city squares and a Goya that was painted for the Town Hall.

Admission: Free.

Open: Tues–Sat 10am–1:45pm and 5–8:45pm, Sun 10am–2:15pm. **Metro:** Tribunal.

MUSEO ARQUEOLÓGICO NACIONAL [Archeological Museum], Serrano 13. Tel. 577-79-12.

For some reason, Iberian archeological museums tend to be dull—surprising, since so many civilizations (prehistoric, Roman, Visigothic, Muslim) have conquered the peninsula. An exception, however, is this stately mansion in Madrid, a storehouse of artifacts from prehistoric times to the heyday of the baroque, which also houses the National Library. One of the prime exhibits here is the Iberian statue *La Dama de Elche,* a piece of primitive carving—probably from the 4th century B.C.—that was discovered on the southeastern coast of Spain, as well as the splendidly polychromed *Dama de Baza* discovered in Granada province, also from the same period.

Treasures from the discovery of some of the finest Punic relics in Europe on the Balearic island of Ibiza—many of them found in a Carthaginian and Roman necropolis—are on display. Excavations from Paestum, Italy, are shown: The statuary of Imperial Rome includes a statue of Tiberius enthroned and one of the controversial Livia, wife of Augustus. The Islamic collection from Spain is outstanding. The collection of Spanish Renaissance lusterware, as well as Talavera pottery and Retiro porcelain, is shown to good advantage, along with some rare 16th- and 17th-century Andalusian glassware.

The "classic" artifacts are impressive, and the contributions from medieval days up through the 16th century are highly laudable. Many of the exhibits were ecclesiastical treasures removed from churches and monasteries. A much-photographed choir stall from Palancia—hand-painted and crude, but remarkable nevertheless—dates from the 14th century.

Worthy of a look are the reproductions of the prehistoric Altamira cave paintings discovered near Santander in northern Spain in 1868. Joseph Dechelette called them "the Sistine Chapel of Quaternary art." The original caves have been closed except to a carefully arranged handful of monthly visitors, so this is your chance to see an excellent copy.

Admission: 250 ptas. ($2.50).

Open: Tues–Sun 9:30am–8:30pm. **Closed:** Hols. **Metro:** Colón or Serrano. **Bus:** 5, 14, 27, or 45.

MUSEO NACIONAL DE ARTES DECORATIVAS [Decorative Arts Museum], Montalbán 12, near the Plaza de la Cibeles. Tel. 532-64-99.

In 62 rooms spread over several floors, this museum displays a rich collection of furniture, ceramics, and decorative pieces from all regions of Spain. It's especially rich in works of the 16th and 17th centuries, but the collection is eclectic, with many surprises—including bronzes from the Ming Dynasty in China. You're greeted by an 18th-century Venetian sedan chair in the vestibule. This bit of whimsy is only a preview of what awaits you: Gothic carvings, tapestries, alabaster figurines, vestments, festival crosses, elaborate dollhouses, Andalusian antique glass, elegant baroque four-poster beds, a chapel covered with leather tapestries, even kitchens from the 17th century. Just keep climbing one flight of steps after another; the surprises continue until you reach the top floor of what must have been one of the grandest mansions in Madrid.

Admission: 200 ptas. ($2).

Open: Tues–Fri 9am–3:30pm, Sat–Sun 10am–2pm. **Closed:** Hols. **Metro:** Banco de España. **Bus:** 14, 19, 27, 34, 37, 45, or M-6.

MUSEO DEL EJÉRCITO [Army Museum], calle Mendez Núñez 1. Tel. 522-06-28.

Behind the Prado, this museum has some outstanding exhibits from military history, including the original sword of El Cid. Isabella carried this same sword when she took Granada from the Moors. In addition, you can see the tent used by Charles V in Tunisia, along with relics from explorers Pizarro and Cortés. The collection of armor is also exceptional. The museum contains a piece of the cross that Columbus carried with him when he discovered the New World, and weapons and memorabilia from the grisly Spanish Civil War. The museum is housed in the Buen Retiro Palace, which dates from 1631 and was destroyed (and subsequently rebuilt in a smaller form) during the Napoleonic Wars.

Admission: 50 ptas. (50¢).

Open: Tues–Sun 10am–2pm. **Metro:** Banco de España. **Bus:** 15, 27, 34, 37, or 45.

MUSEO NAVAL [Naval Museum], paseo del Prado 5. Tel. 521-04-19.

The history of nautical science and the Spanish navy comes alive at this museum. For me, the most fascinating exhibit is the map of the new discoveries of land that the mate of the *Santa Maria* made to show the Spanish monarchs. There are also souvenirs of the Battle of Trafalgar.

Admission: Free.

Open: Tues–Sun 10:30am–1:30pm. **Closed:** Hols. **Metro:** Banco de España. **Bus:** 10, 14, 27, 34, 37, 45, or M-6.

MUSEO SOROLLA, General Martínez Campos 37. Tel. 410-15-84.

Appreciation of the work of painter Joaquín Sorolla (1863–1923) is an acquired taste. In his day he was celebrated, as autographed portraits from King Alfonso XIII and U.S. President Taft reveal. From 1912 he and his family occupied this elegant Madrileño town house off paseo de la Castellana. Two years after his death his widow turned it over to the government—and it is now maintained as a memorial to the artist, inaugurated in 1932. Much of the house remains as Sorolla left it, right down to his stained paint brushes and pipes. In the museum wing, however, a representative collection of the artist's paintings is displayed. All the works owned by the museum can't be exhibited, however, because of the lack of space.

Although Sorolla painted portraits of Spanish aristocrats, he was essentially interested in "the people," often in their native costumes, such as those once worn in Ávila and Salamanca. He was especially fond of painting beach scenes on what is now the Costa Blanca. His favorite subjects are depicted either "before" or "after" their bath, and he was interested in the subtle variations of the Spanish sunlight. One critic wrote that Sorolla "may fail to please certain individuals, contaminated by an unhealthy leaning toward things decadent, pessimistic, and tragic."

Seek out not only the artist's self-portrait, but also the paintings of Madame Sorolla and their handsome son. The house and garden alone are worth the trip. The museum is entered through an Andalusian-style patio.

Admission: 200 ptas. ($2).

Open: Tues–Sun 10am–2:30pm. **Closed:** Hols. **Metro:** Rubén Darío or Iglesia. **Bus:** 5, 16, or 61.

MUSEO ROMANTICO [Romantic Museum], San Mateo 13. Tel. 448-10-45.

Of special interest and limited appeal, this museum attracts those seeking the romanticism of the 19th century. Decorative arts festoon the mansion in which the museum is housed: crystal chandeliers, faded portraits, oils from Goya to Sorolla, opulent furnishings, porcelain, jewelry, ceramics, even *la grande toilette*. Many of the exhibitions date from the days of Isabella II, the high-living, fun-loving queen who was forced into exile and eventual abdication of the throne (she lived in Paris until her death in 1904).

Admission: 200 ptas. ($2).

Open: Tues–Sun 10am–3pm. **Closed:** Hols., Aug. **Metro:** Alonso Martínez. **Bus:** 21, 37, 40, 48, or M-10.

RELIGIOUS SITES

REAL BASILICA DE SAN FRANCISCO EL GRANDE, on the Plaza de San Francisco El Grande, at San Buenaventura 1. Tel. 531-15-46.

In lieu of a great cathedral, Madrid possesses this church, which has a dome larger than that of St. Paul's in London. Constructed on the site of a much earlier church, San Francisco dates from the latter 18th century and owes much of its appearance to Sabatini, a celebrated architect of his day.

Its interior of Doric columns and Corinthian capitals is cold and foreboding, although 19th-century artists labored hard to adorn its series of chapels flanking the nave. The best painting—that of St. Bernardinus of Siena preaching—is by Goya.

You are conducted through the church by a guide, who notes the most outstanding artwork, especially the choir stalls dating from the 16th century.

Admission: 100 ptas. ($1).

Open: Tues–Sat 11am–1pm and 4–7pm. **Metro:** La Latina. **Bus:** 3 or 60.

TEMPLO DE DEBOD, on calle Ferraz, at paseo de Rosales.

This Egyptian temple once stood in the Valley of the Nile, 19 miles from Aswan. When the new dam built there threatened to overrun its site with water, the Egyptian government agreed to have the temple dismantled and presented to the Spanish people. It was taken down stone by stone in 1969 and 1970, then shipped to Valencia. From that Mediterranean port, it was sent by rail to Madrid, where it was reconstructed and opened to the public in 1971. Photos upstairs in the temple depict its long history. The temple stands right off the Plaza de España.

Admission: Free.

Open: Daily 10am–1pm and 4–7pm. **Closed:** National and Catholic hols. **Metro:** Plaza de España or Ventura Rodríguez. **Bus:** 1, 2, 44, or 74.

PARKS & GARDENS

THE RETIRO The most prominent and famous park in Madrid sprawls over 350 acres. A reminder of the large forests that once stood proudly in Castile, the Retiro was originally a royal playground for the exclusive use of the Spanish monarchs and their guests. The huge palaces that stood here were destroyed in the early 19th century.

Only the palace's former dance hall, the Casón del Buen Retiro (housing the modern works of the Prado), and the building containing the army museum remain. The park is filled with numerous fountains (one is dedicated to an artichoke) and statues (one honors Lucifer, strangely heretical in Catholic Spain), and there's a large lake where soldiers meet their girlfriends during the hotter months. There are also a pair of exposition centers, the Velázquez and Crystal Palaces (built to honor the Philippines in 1887), and a lakeside monument, erected in 1922, to Alfonso XII. In summer the rose gardens are worth the visit, and you'll find several places where you can have inexpensive snacks and drinks.

The park is technically open all day and night, but it's at its most popular (and safest) between 7am and 8:30pm. Entrance is free, and hundreds of Madrileños, especially on hot midsummer days, are likely to be here too.

Across calle de Alfonso XII, abutting the southwest corner of the Retiro, are the famous **Botanical Gardens** (Jardín Botánico), Plaza de Murillo 2 (tel. 585-60-00). Founded by Carlos III, and in its present location since the 18th century, it contains more than 104 species of trees and 3,000 types of plants. It also contains a library specializing in botany and an exhibition hall. It's open daily from 10am to 8pm, charging 100 ptas. ($1) per person. Metro: Atocha. Bus: 10, 14, 32, or 45.

THE CASA DE CAMPO   Many visitors to Madrid never make it to the former royal hunting grounds, the Casa de Campo—miles and miles of parkland lying south of the Royal Palace, across the Manzanares. You can see the gate through which the kings rode out of the palace grounds—either on horses or in carriages—and headed for the retiro. Presently, of course, you will have to take less elegant transportation: the Metro to El Lago or El Batán.

The park has a variety of trees and a lake, which is usually filled with rowers. You can have drinks and light refreshments around the lake, or you can go swimming in an excellent municipally operated pool.

Madrileños like to keep the place to themselves; on a hot night or a Sunday morning, the park is thronged with people trying to escape the heat. If you have an automobile you can go for a drive, as the grounds are extensive. The park is open daily until around 11pm. It's cool, pleasant, refreshing—a cheap way to spend an evening.

3. COOL FOR KIDS

The Spanish have always loved children and have created diversions for kids that many Spanish adults remember with great fondness in later years. Here's a sampling of some of them:

MUSEO DE LAS FIGURAS DE CERA (Wax Museum), paseo de Recoletos 41. Tel. 319-26-49.

In this wax museum famous personalities seem to come to life, sometimes in eerily disconcerting ways. Some parents consider it a good way to imbue children with a sense of history. There are scenes depicting Columbus calling on Ferdinand and Isabella, Romans battling with Celts, Arabs fighting with Spaniards, and characters from *Don Quixote*. Twentieth-century international figures aren't neglected either; we see Jacqueline Onassis drinking champagne and Garbo all alone. The heroes and villains of World War II—everyone from Eisenhower to Hitler—are highlighted by the presence of Marlene Dietrich singing "Lili Marlene." The 400 figures that inhabit the 38 tableaux were created by out-of-work filmmakers, who succeeded best with backdrops, falling shortest in their depictions of contemporary celebrities. A film gives a 30-minute recap of Spanish history from the days of the Phoenicians to today.

Admission: 600 ptas. ($6) adults, 400 ptas. ($4) children.
Open: Daily 10:30am–1:30pm and 4–8pm. **Metro:** Colón.
Bus: 27, 45, or 53.

AQUAPOLIS, Villanueva de la Canada, carretera de El Escorial. Tel. 815-69-86.

Just 16 miles northwest of Madrid lies a watery attraction where your kids might happily intermingle with hundreds of other children. Scattered amid shops, a picnic area, and a barbecue restaurant are water slides, wave-making machines, and tall slides that spiral children (and an occasional adult) into the swimming pool below. These water sports are available in summertime only.

Admission: 1,600 ptas. ($16) adults, 1,000 ptas. ($10) children.
Open: Summer, daily 10am–8pm. **Bus:** When the park is open, there's a free bus that runs every hour throughout the day, departing from calle Reyes, next to the Coliseum Cinema, on the eastern edge of the Plaza de España.

PARQUE DE ATRACCIONES, Casa de Campo. Tel. 463-29-00.

At its most popular in July and August, this park was created in 1969 to amuse the young at heart with an array of rides and concessions. The numerous attractions include a tobaggan slide, a carousel, pony rides, an adventure into "outer space," a walk through a transparent maze, a visit to "jungleland," a motor-propelled series of cars disguised as a tail-wagging dachshund puppy, and a gyrating whirligig clutched in the tentacles of an octopus named "El Pulpo." The most popular rides are a pair of roller coasters named "7 Picos" and "Jet Star."

Admission: 175 ptas. ($1.75) adults, 40 ptas. (40¢) children under 9. You can buy an all-inclusive ticket, good for all rides, for around 1,200 ptas. ($12).
Open: July–Aug, Tues–Fri 6pm–1am, Sat 6pm–2am, Sun noon–1am; Sept–Mar, Sat–Sun noon–8 or 9pm (depending on business); Apr–June, Tues–Fri 3 to between 9 and 11pm (depending on business), Sat–Sun noon–8 or 9pm (depending on business). **Transportation:** Take the cable car (teleferico) described below. At the terminus of the cable car, a line of microbuses awaits to complete your journey to the park. An alternative way to get there is to take a suburban train from the Plaza de España, which stops near an entrance to the park (the Entrada del Batán). Of course, the easiest way to get here is by taxi.

ZOO DE LA CASA DE CAMPO, in the Casa de Campo, at the edge of the Parque de Atracciones. Tel. 711-99-50.

Children are invariably delighted by the zoo, which in Madrid lies in the Parque de Atracciones (see above). The zoo was developed in the 1970s using up-to-date theories about layout and planning. Most of the animals are in a simulated natural habitat, with moats separating them from the public. There's an area where small animals may be petted by children. Sprawling over 50 carefully landscaped acres, it contains animals from Spain and throughout the world. It allows you to see, through its division by continents, the wildlife of Africa, Asia, the Americas, and Europe, with about 2,500 animals on display.

Admission: 940 ptas. ($9.40) adults, 695 ptas. ($6.95) children 3–8.

Open: Daily 10am–sunset. **Metro:** Batán. **Bus:** 33 or 65.

TELEFERICO, paseo del Pintor Rosales, at the corner of calle Marqués de Urquijo. Tel. 541-19-97.

An alternative way to reach the zoo is via Madrid's *teleferico* or cable car. It departs from paseo del Pintor Rosales at the eastern edge of the Parque del Oeste (at the corner of calle Marqués de Urquijo) and will carry you high above two parks, railway tracks, and the Manzanares River to a spot near a picnic ground and restaurant in the Casa de Campo park. (Weather permitting, there are good views of the Royal Palace along the way.) The ride takes 11 minutes.

Admission: 360 ptas. ($3.60) round-trip, 250 ptas. ($2.50) one way, free for children under 5.

Open: Mar–Oct, daily noon–9pm; Nov–Feb, Mon and Thurs–Fri noon–2pm and 4–7pm, Sat–Sun and hols. noon–7pm. **Metro:** Plaza de España. **Bus:** 74.

PLANETARIUM, Tierno Galván Park, Méndez Alvaro. Tel. 467-34-61.

This planetarium has a projection room with optical and electronic equipment—including a multivision system—designed to reproduce outer space.

Admission: 300 ptas. ($3) adults, 150 ptas. ($1.50) children.

Open: Shows Tues–Sun at 11:30am and 12:45, 5:30, and 6:45pm. **Closed:** Jan 1–15. **Metro:** Méndez Alvaro. **Bus:** 117.

---

4. SPECIAL-INTEREST SIGHTSEEING

FOR THE LITERARY ENTHUSIAST

CASA DE LOPE DE VEGA, Cervantes 11. Tel. 429-92-16.

Ironically, the House of Lope de Vega stands on a street named after Cervantes, his competitor for the title of the greatest writer of the Golden Age of Spain. The house is considered a *perfecta* reconstruction of the casa in which Lope de Vega lived, and it's furnished with pieces indigenous to his time (1562–1635). The Spanish writer, the major dramatist of Hapsburg Spain, wrote more than 1,000 plays, many of which have been lost to history. You'll be shown through the house, with its volumes upon volumes of manuscript reproductions, and then allowed to roam at random in the garden in back.

Admission: 75 ptas. (75¢).
Open: Tues and Thurs 11am–2pm. **Closed:** Mid-July to mid-Sept. **Metro:** Anton Martín.

HEMINGWAY HAUNTS

CHICOTE, Gran Vía 12. Tel. 532-67-37.
Hemingway used Chicote as a setting for his only play, *The Fifth Column.* He would sit here night after night, gazing at the *putas* (it was a famed hooker bar back then) as he entertained friends with such remarks as "Spain is a country for living and not for dying." The bar still draws a lively crowd. A whisky and soda costs 750 ptas. ($7.50).
Open: Mon–Sat 1:30pm–2:45am. **Metro:** Gran Vía.

MUSEO DEL PRADO, paseo del Prado. Tel. 420-28-36.
Of the Prado, A. E. Hotchner wrote in his *Papa Hemingway:* "Ernest loved the Prado. He entered it as he entered cathedrals." More than any other, one picture held him transfixed, Andrea del Sarto's *Portrait of a Woman.* (For details on the museum, see "The Top Attractions," above.)

SOBRINO DE BOTÍN, Cuchilleros 17. Tel. 266-42-17.
In the final two pages of his novel *The Sun Also Rises,* Jake invites Brett here for the Segovian specialty, roast suckling pig, washed down with Rioja Alta. In another book *Death in the Afternoon,* Hemingway told his mythical "Old Lady": "I would rather dine on suckling pig at Botín's than sit and think of casualties my friends have suffered." Since that time, thousands upon thousands of Americans have visited Botín (see Chapter 5 for details). It's a perennial favorite of all visiting Yankees.

EL CALLEJÓN, Ternera 6. Tel. 522-54-01.
Hemingway's "other favorite" was this restaurant, right in the heart of Madrid, and you can still visit it today (see Chapter 5). The author loved the baby eels, paella, and roast lamb served here, accompanied by some fine Valdapeñas red wine. He'd always arrive smiling from a *corrida.* A round table in the corner of the first dining room, where he always sat, is decorated with photos and clippings as a tribute to his memory.

FOR THE ARCHITECTURE ENTHUSIAST

✪PLAZA MAYOR In the heart of Madrid, this famous square was known as the Plaza de Arrabal in medieval times, when it stood outside the city wall.

The original architect of the Plaza Mayor itself was Juan Gómez de Mora, who worked during the reign of Philip III. Under the Hapsburgs the square rose in importance as the site of public spectacles, including the gruesome autos-da-fé, in which "heretics" were burned. Bullfights, knightly tournaments, and festivals were also staged here.

Three times the buildings on the square burned—in 1631, 1672, and 1790—but each time the Plaza Mayor bounced back. After the last big fire, it was completely redesigned by Juan de Villanueva.

Nowadays a Christmas fair is held around the equestrian statue of Philip III (dating from 1616) in the center of the square. On summer nights the Plaza Mayor becomes the virtual living room of Madrid, as tourists sip sangría at the numerous cafés and listen to music, which is often spontaneous.

PUERTA DE TOLEDO   The Puerta de Toledo is one of the two surviving town gates (the other is the Puerta de Alcalá). Constructed during the brief and unpopular rule of Joseph I Bonaparte, this one marks the spot where citizens used to set out for the former imperial capital of Toledo. On an irregularly shaped square, it stands at the intersection of ronda de Toledo and calle de Toledo. Its original purpose was as a triumphal arch to honor Napoleon Bonaparte. In 1813 it became a symbol of Madrid's fierce independence and the loyalty of its citizens to their Bourbon rulers, who had been restored to the throne in the wake of the Napoleonic invasion. Metro: Puerta de Toledo.

5. ORGANIZED TOURS

A large number of agencies in Madrid book organized tours and excursions to sights and attractions both within and outside the city limits. Although your mobility and freedom might be somewhat hampered, some visitors appreciate the ease, convenience, and efficiency of being able to visit so many sights in a single well-organized day. Also, the hassles of navigating from one sight to the next are almost eliminated as you entrust your itinerary to the bus driver and bilingual guide.

One of Madrid's leading tour operators is **Viajes Marsans,** San Nicolas 15 (tel. 542-55-00). Half-day tours of Madrid include an "artistic tour" priced at 3,700 ptas. ($37) per person (which includes entrance to a selection of the city's museums) and a panoramic half-day tour for 2,700 ptas. ($27). Both these options depart Monday through Saturday at 8:30am from in front of the Pullmantour headquarters at Plaza de Oriente 8.

Southward treks to Toledo are the most popular full-day excursion outside the city limits. They cost 6,200 ptas. ($62). These tours (which include lunch) depart daily at 8:30am from the above-mentioned departure point, last all day, and include ample opportunities for wandering at will through the city's narrow streets. You can, if you wish, take an abbreviated morning tour of Toledo, without stopping for lunch, for 4,000 ptas. ($40).

Another popular tour stops briefly in Toledo, and continues on to visit both the monastery at El Escorial and the Valley of the Fallen (Valle de los Caídos) before returning the same day to Madrid. With lunch included, this all-day excursion costs 8,200 ptas. ($82).

Other worthwhile full-day tours include visits to the walled medieval city of Ávila, with additional stops at El Escorial and the Valle de Los Caídos. With lunch included, the price is 6,500 ptas. ($65). A visit to Segovia and the Bourbon dynasty's 18th-century palace of La Granja costs 5,000 ptas. ($50) without lunch, and 7,500 ptas. ($75) with lunch included. A half-day tour of Aranjuez and Chinchón, without lunch, costs 3,800 ptas. ($38). Full-day visits to the rich cultural troves of either Salamanca or Cuenca, including lunch, cost 9,500 ptas. ($95) each.

6. SPORTS & RECREATION

SPECTATOR SPORTS

The Bullfight

PLAZA MONUMENTAL DE TOROS DE LAS VENTAS, calle de Alcalá 237. Tel. 356-22-00.

Madrid draws the finest matadors in Spain. If a matador hasn't proved his worth in the major ring in Madrid, he just hasn't been recognized as a top-flight artist. The major season begins during the Fiestas de San Isidro, patron saint of Madrid, on May 15. This is the occasion for a series of fights, during which talent scouts help make up the audience. Matadors who distinguish themselves in the ring are signed up for Majorca, Málaga, and other places.

For tickets to this biggest bullfight stadium in Madrid, go to its box office. Many hotels also have good seats that you can buy. Front-row seats are known as *barreras*. Third row seats (*delanteras*) are available in both the *alta* (high) and *baja* (low) sections. The cheapest seats sold, *filas*, afford the worst view and are in the sun (*sol*) during the entire performance. The best seats are in the shade (*sombra*). Bullfights are held on Sunday and holidays at 7pm from Easter to October; in late September and October they often begin at 5pm. Fights by neophyte matadors are sometimes staged on Saturday at 11pm.

On the day of the fight, arrive early to avoid the crowds. You'll want to leave the fight before the very end, again to avoid the crush.

Admission: 300–10,575 ptas. ($3–$105.75).

Open: Box office, Fri–Sun 10am–2pm and 4–8pm. **Metro:** Ventas.

Horse Racing

HIPÓDROMO DE LA ZARZUELA, carretera de la Coruña, Km 7.8. Tel. 207-01-40.

There are two seasons—spring (Feb–June) and fall (mid-Sept to early Dec). Races, often six or seven, are generally held on Sunday and holidays (11am), with a series of night races (11pm) held on weekends in July and August. A restaurant and bar are at the hippodrome, which is 11 miles (18km) from the center of Madrid on the N-VI.

Admission: 500 ptas. ($5).

Directions: Take the free bus, leaving from Moncloa, across from the Air Ministry.

Soccer

Futbol is played with a passion all year in Madrid. League matches, on Saturday or Sunday, run from September to May, culminating in the annual summer tournaments. Madrid has two teams in the top division.

REAL MADRID, Estadio Santiago Bernabéu, Concha Espina 1. Tel. 250-06-00.

Tickets can be obtained at the stadium.

Admission: From 1,500 ptas. ($15).

Metro: Lima.

CLUB ATLÉTICO DE MADRID, Estadio Vicente Calderón, paseo de la Virgen del Puerto 67. Tel. 266-47-07.
Tickets can be obtained at the stadium.
Admission: From 1,500 ptas. ($15).
Metro: Pirámides.

RECREATION

FITNESS CENTERS Although Madrid has scores of gyms, bodybuilding studios, and aerobic-exercise centers, many of them are private. For one open to the public, try **Atenas,** Victor de la Serna 37 (tel. 457-85-85; Metro: Colombia). This facility for men and women has an indoor swimming pool, workout equipment, a sauna, and such personal services as massage. It's open Monday through Saturday from 7:30am to 9:30pm.

JOGGING The **Parque del Retiro** and the **Casa de Campo** both have jogging tracks. For details on how to get there, see "Parks and Gardens" in "More Attractions," above.

SWIMMING & TENNIS The best swimming and tennis facilities are found at the **Casa de Campo,** avenida del Angel (tel. 463-00-50; Metro: Lago), a 4,300-acre former royal hunting preserve that lies on the right bank of the Manzanares River. Today it's a public park, serving as a playground for Madrileños.

CHAPTER 7

STROLLING AROUND MADRID

1. **MEDIEVAL MADRID**
2. **HAPSBURG MADRID**
3. **BOURBON MADRID**
4. **GRANDEUR, PAST & PRESENT**
5. **THE PRADO IN 2 HOURS**

You'll need public transportation to get around New Madrid, as it sprawls for miles in all directions, but walking is the best way to savor the unique charms of Old Madrid.

This chapter is organized into a series of walking tours for those who want to use their own shoe leather to discover the major attractions and districts of the Spanish capital.

Unless you're in Madrid for a long time, it's virtually impossible to see all that's of interest in the city. Much of the dusty environs of Madrid—filled with ugly modern apartment houses and industry—is of little interest to visitors. However, some districts of Madrid are of such architectural interest that every street you wander down holds some fascination.

Chief of these is Medieval Madrid (see Walking Tour 1). After visiting the highlights of the oldest part of the city, you can then explore a section built later: Hapsburg Madrid, whose chief attraction is the Royal Palace (see Chapter 6).

Walking Tour 3 explores Bourbon Madrid, built at a time when Madrid was already an established world-class center. This section is the site of the Prado and the Puerta del Sol. For those who still haven't exhausted their feet, Walking Tour 4 explores some of the major districts and arteries of Madrid, including the Plaza de España and the Gran Vía.

Finally you could wander for weeks in the Prado and still not see everything—but surveys have shown that many visitors have only two hours to devote to this repository of world art. For those rushed individuals, I've recommended only some of the major masterpieces or schools of paintings in Walking Tour 5.

Warning: As you walk around Madrid with your head buried in a map or a guidebook, maintain your usual vigilance against potential muggers, as tourists are frequently victims of robberies.

WALKING TOUR — Medieval Madrid

Start: Plaza de la Villa.
Finish: Plaza de la Puerta Cerrada.
Time: 2½ hours.
Best Times: Any sunny day.
Worst Times: Monday to Saturday 7:30 to 9:30am and 5 to 7:30pm—because of heavy traffic.

The oldest part of the city was a flourishing Muslim area before Madrid became the capital. Begin your tour at the:

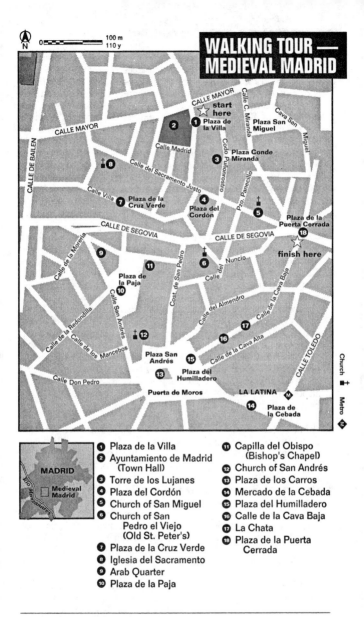

① Plaza de la Villa
② Ayuntamiento de Madrid (Town Hall)
③ Torre de los Lujanes
④ Plaza del Cordón
⑤ Church of San Miguel
⑥ Church of San Pedro el Viejo (Old St. Peter's)
⑦ Plaza de la Cruz Verde
⑧ Iglesia del Sacramento
⑨ Arab Quarter
⑩ Plaza de la Paja

⑪ Capilla del Obispo (Bishop's Chapel)
⑫ Church of San Andrés
⑬ Plaza de los Carros
⑭ Mercado de la Cebada
⑮ Plaza del Humilladero
⑯ Calle de la Cava Baja
⑰ La Chata
⑱ Plaza de la Puerta Cerrada

1. Plaza de la Villa, which stands beside calle Mayor, between the Palacio Real (Royal Palace) and the Puerta del Sol. In the center, note the bronze statue of Don Alvaro de Bazán, an admiral under Philip II, best remembered for defeating the Turks at Lepanto. With your back to calle Mayor, you'll see the red-brick 17th-century facade of the:

2. Ayuntamiento de Madrid (Town Hall) on your right. It was originally built as a prison and today houses the Museo

Municipal (see Chapter 6). On the square's south side rises the depressingly somber stone-and-brick facade of the 15th-century:

3. Torre de los Lujanes, a tower whose simple granite entrance is one of Madrid's few remaining examples of Gothic architecture. Beside the tower, behind a Gothic-Mudéjar archway, lies the tomb of Beatriz Galindo, nicknamed "La Latina" because she taught Latin to the adolescent Isabella I.

With your back to calle Mayor, you'll see two narrow streets stretching parallel to one another to the south. Take the one on the left (calle del Cordón) and walk for about one short block to the:

4. Plaza del Cordón (you won't see any street signs here). You'll find yourself amid a complex of unmarked 16th- and 17th-century municipal buildings, protected and patrolled by uniformed guards.

Turn left at the entrance to the Plaza del Cordón, walk about 50 feet, and notice the convex, semicircular entrance to the baroque:

5. Church of San Miguel, San Justo 4, built by Giacomo Bonavia in the 18th century. A few steps farther, flanking the right side of the church, is a narrow alley, the Pasadizo del Panecillo, where 17th-century priests distributed bread to hungry paupers. Facing the front of the church is one of the oldest houses in Madrid, a grim, rather dingy-looking stone building. Look for the heraldic shields carved into its fortresslike facade. Historical sources report that the legendary Isidro, patron saint of Madrid, worked as a servant in this baronial, now much-faded residence, which today contains private apartments. Its address, although you probably won't see a street sign until you reach the bottom of the hill, is calle del Doctor Letamendi.

Walk down this cobblestone street (you'll have to walk back about 10 feet and enter it from an edge of the Plaza del Cordón). Follow it one block and cross busy calle de Segovia. Then turn right and walk about three blocks (the street will now rise sharply). Look down the Costanilla San Pedro, to your left, and notice the Mudéjar tower of the:

6. Church of San Pedro el Viejo (Old St. Peter's), which marks the border of Madrid's Muslim quarter. The church's mid-14th-century tower is one of the few remnants of medieval architecture in Madrid. The church itself, however, dates from the 17th century; it was severely looted during the Civil War in 1936. Although the houses in this neighborhood look small, they're considered among the most chic and expensive in Madrid.

Walk one more uphill block along calle de Segovia until you reach the Costanilla San Andrés. Before you turn left onto this narrow street, note to the north of calle de Segovia the:

7. Plaza de la Cruz Verde, whose centerpiece is a 19th-century baroque fountain commemorating the end of the Spanish Inquisition. In the background you'll see the back side and the massive brick tower of the:

8. Iglesia del Sacramento, where memorial services for soldiers killed in war or by terrorists are performed. Now, ascend the steep cobblestones of Costanilla San Andrés. Around you is the:

9. **Arab Quarter.** Many buildings that were erected during the past two centuries were built upon foundations of Muslim structures. Very shortly you'll reach the triangular and steeply sloping grounds of the:

10. **Plaza de la Paja,** whose lovely trees and calm give no hint that this was once the most important produce market in the region. Today the neighborhood waits sleepily in the intense sunlight for night to bring business to the several famous restaurants that ring its perimeter. To your left as you climb the square is the:

11. **Capilla del Obispo (Bishop's Chapel),** entered from the Plaza de la Paja. The mortal remains of San Isidro were interred here from 1518 to 1657. Notice its Renaissance doors. The high altar is considered a masterpiece of Plateresque (the late Gothic style of Castile). At the top of the square, follow the continuation of Costanilla San Andrés to the right side of the chapel. You'll discover that it abuts the back of the more imposing:

12. **Church of San Andrés,** Plaza de San Andrés. In one of the most colorful parts of the old town, the church dates from medieval times, but was rebuilt in the 17th century. A fire in 1936 destroyed its greatest treasures. Keep walking and you'll come to the fountains of the:

13. **Plaza de los Carros,** the first of four interconnected squares, each with its own name and allure. Descend the steps at the far edge of the Plaza de los Carros and turn left onto the Plaza de Puerta de Moros. Diagonally across the street, you'll soon notice the modern brick-and-concrete dome of the:

14. **Mercado de la Cebada.** In its echoing interior are open-air markets, open Monday through Saturday from 8am to 2pm and 5 to 8pm. The square has by this time changed its name to the:

15. **Plaza del Humilladero.** Directly in your path are two streets. The one that forks to the left is:

16. **Calle de Cava Baja** (the other is calle la Cava Alta). Some 600 years ago these streets defined the city limits of Madrid. Take calle de Cava Baja, which is filled with some of the most typical cafés, bars, and restaurants in Madrid.

REFUELING STOP   There's a restaurant in back at **17. La Chata,** calle de Cava Baja 24 (tel. 266-14-58), but its stand-up bar up front is more popular. Here, local residents chatter amid hanging Serrano hams and photographs of famous bullfighters. On a hot day, order a glass of beer, or perhaps some tapas. The bar is open Monday and Wednesday through Saturday from noon to 5pm and Wednesday through Monday from 8pm to midnight.

The tour ends at the end of calle de Cava Baja, at the:

18. **Plaza de la Puerta Cerrada,** with its simple white stone cross.

WALKING TOUR — Hapsburg Madrid

Start: Southeastern corner of the Palacio Real.
Finish: Calle del Arenal.
Time: 3 hours.

Best Times: Saturday or Sunday, when you can also visit the flea market of El Rastro.
Worst Times: Monday to Saturday 7:30 to 9:30am and 5 to 7:30pm—because of heavy traffic.

This tour encompasses 16th- and 17th-century Madrid, including the grand plazas and traffic arteries that the Hapsburg families built to transform a quiet town into a world-class capital.
     The tour begins at the:

1. **Palacio Real (Royal Palace),** at the corner of calle de Bailén and calle Mayor. The latter was built by Philip II in the 1560s to provide easy access from the palace to his preferred church, San Jerónimo el Real. Walk east on:
2. **Calle Mayor,** on the south side of the street. Within a block you'll reach a black bronze statue of a kneeling angel, erected in 1906 to commemorate the aborted assassination of King Alfonso XIII (grandfather of the present king, Juan Carlos). Across the street from the kneeling angel is the:
3. **Palacio de Abrantes,** calle Mayor 86, today occupied by the Italian Institute of Culture. On the same side of the street as the kneeling angel, to the statue's left, is the:
4. **Palacio de Uceda,** calle Mayor 79, today the headquarters of Spain's military. Both these palaces are considered among the best examples of 17th-century civil architecture in Madrid.
     Walk half a block east, crossing to the north side of calle Mayor and detouring about 20 yards to the left, down narrow calle de San Nicolás, and you'll come to the somber facade of the oldest church in Madrid, the 12th-century:
5. **Church of St. Nicolás,** Plaza de San Nicolás. Only a brick tower remains from the original building, one of the few examples of the Mudéjar style in the capital. The reredos at the high altar is the work of Juan de Herrera, also the architect of El Escorial.
     Retrace your steps to calle Mayor. Turn left and continue to walk east. You'll pass the Plaza de la Villa on your right, and, one block later, the:
6. **Plaza de San Miguel,** an iron-canopied meat-and-vegetable market. You might stock up on ingredients for a picnic here. (The market is open Monday through Friday from 9am to 2pm and 5 to 8pm, and on Saturday from 9am to 2pm.)
     Leave the Plaza de San Miguel by Ciudad Rodrigo (there might not be a sign), which leads under a soaring granite archway and up a sloping street to the northwestern corner of the:
7. **Plaza Mayor,** the landmark square that's at the heart of Old Madrid.

REFUELING STOP At Plaza Mayor 1, **8. Café Bar Los Galayos** (tel. 165-62-22) has long been one of the best places for *tapas* along this square. If you're taking the walking tour during the day, you may want to return to this café/bar at night, as it's most lively then. In summer you can select one of the outdoor tables for your drinks and *tapas.*

Stroll through the Plaza Mayor, crossing it diagonally, and

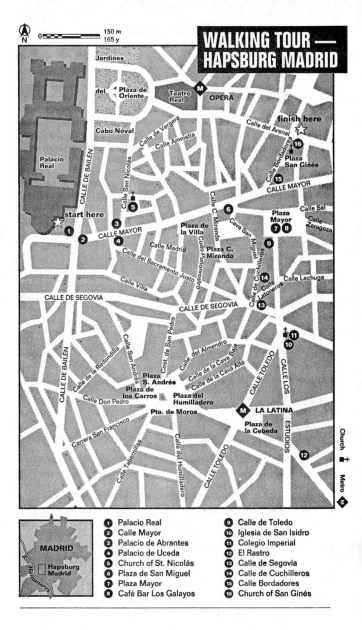

WALKING TOUR — HAPSBURG MADRID

Map labels:

Jardines
del · Plaza de Oriente
Teatro Real
M OPERA
Cabo Noval
Calle de Vergara
Calle Amnistia
Calle del Arenal
finish here
Palacio Real
CALLE DE BAILÉN
Calle San Nicolás
Calle Bordadores
Plaza San Ginés
start here
CALLE MAYOR
Calle C. Miranda
Plaza de la Villa
Codo Puñonrostro
Calle Madrid
Calle del Sacramento Justo
Cava San Miguel
Plaza C. Miranda
CALLE MAYOR
Plaza Mayor
Calle Sal
Calle Zaragoza
Calle de Cuchilleros
Calle Latoneros
Calle Lechuga
Calle Villa
CALLE DE SEGOVIA
CALLE DE SEGOVIA
Cost. de San Pedro
Calle San Pedro
Calle de la Redondilla
Calle San Andrés
Calle del Almendro
Calle de la Cava Baja
Calle de la Cava Alta
CALLE TOLEDO
CALLE LOS
CALLE DE BAILÉN
Plaza S. Andrés
Plaza de los Carros
Calle Don Pedro
Plaza del Humilladero
Pta. de Moros
M LA LATINA
Plaza de la Cebada
ESTUDIOS
Carrera San Francisco
Calle Tabernillas
Calle del Humilladero
CALLE TOLEDO
Church ∎ †
Metro M

0 ___ 150 m / 165 y
N

Legend:

❶ Palacio Real
❷ Calle Mayor
❸ Palacio de Abrantes
❹ Palacio de Uceda
❺ Church of St. Nicolás
❻ Plaza de San Miguel
❼ Plaza Mayor
❽ Café Bar Los Galayos
❾ Calle de Toledo
❿ Iglesia de San Isidro
⓫ Colegio Imperial
⓬ El Rastro
⓭ Calle de Segovia
⓮ Calle de Cuchilleros
⓯ Calle Bordadores
⓰ Church of San Ginés

MADRID
Río ___
□ Hapsburg Madrid

---

exit at the closer of its two southern exits. A dingy, steep flight of stone stairs leads down to the beginning of:

9. Calle de Toledo. Note in the distance the twin domes of the yellow-stucco and granite:

10. Iglesia de San Isidro, legendary burial place of Madrid's patron saint and his wife, Santa María de La Cadeza. The church lost its status as a cathedral in 1992, when the honor went to the larger Church of La Almudena. Adjacent to San Isidro is the baroque facade of the:

11. Colegio Imperial, which was also run by the Jesuits. Lope de Vega, Calderón, and many other famous men studied at this institute.

If your tour takes place on a Saturday or Sunday before 3pm, visit:

12. El Rastro, Madrid's world-famous flea market. Continue along calle de Toledo, then fork left onto calle Estudios and proceed to the Plaza de Cascorro, named after a hero of the Cuban wars. El Rastro begins here.

If your tour takes place Monday through Friday, skip the Rastro neighborhood. Instead, turn right onto:

13. Calle de Segovia, which intersects calle de Toledo just before it passes in front of the Iglesia de San Isidro. Walk one block and turn right onto the first street:

14. Calle de Cuchilleros. Follow it north past 16th- and 17th-century stone-fronted houses. Within a block a flight of granite steps forks to the right. Climb the steps (a sign identifies the new street as calle Arco de Cuchilleros) and you'll pass one of the most famous *mesones* (typical Castilian restaurants) of Madrid, the Cueva de Luís Candelas.

Once again you will have entered the Plaza Mayor, this time on the southwestern corner. Walk beneath the southernmost arcade and promenade counterclockwise beneath the arcades, walking north underneath the square's eastern arcade. Then walk west beneath its northern arcade. At the northwest corner, exit through the archway onto calle 7 de Julio. Fifty feet later, cross calle Mayor and take the right-hand narrow street before you. This is:

15. Calle Bordadores, which during the 17th century housed Madrid's embroidery workshops, staffed exclusively by men. As you proceed, notice the 17th-century brick walls and towers of the:

16. Church of San Ginés, Arenal 15. The church of one of Madrid's oldest parishes owes its present look to the architects who reconstructed it after a devastating fire in 1872. At the end of this tour, you'll find yourself on the traffic-congested calle del Arenal, at the doorstep of many interesting old streets.

WALKING TOUR — Bourbon Madrid

Start: Puerta de Alcalá.
Finish: Plaza de Oriente.
Time: 3 hours.
Best Times: Early morning or late afternoon in summer (or any sunny day in winter).
Worst Times: Monday to Saturday 7:30 to 9:30am and 5 to 7:30pm—because of heavy traffic.

By the time the Bourbons came to power in Spain, Madrid was firmly ensconced as a political and cultural center, proud of its role as head of a centralized government. This tour shows off the broad boulevards, spectacular fountains, and interconnected plazas that put Madrid on a par architecturally with other European capitals. Much

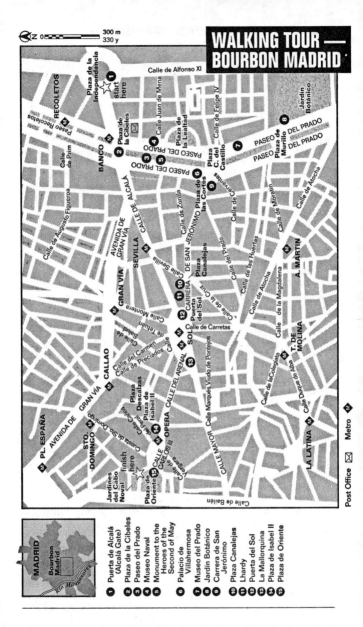

WALKING TOUR — BOURBON MADRID

Directory (map legend):

1. Puerta de Alcalá (Alcalá Gate)
2. Plaza de la Cibeles
3. Paseo del Prado
4. Museo Naval
5. Monument to the Heroes of the Second of May
6. Palacio de Villahermosa
7. Museo del Prado
8. Jardín Botánico
9. Carrera de San Jerónimo
10. Plaza Canalejas
11. Lhardy
12. Puerta del Sol
13. La Mallorquina
14. Plaza de Isabel II
15. Plaza de Oriente

⊠ Post Office   **M** Metro

MADRID — Bourbon Madrid — Río Manzanares

of this tour goes through neighborhoods planned by Charles III in the 18th century.

Begin at the:

1. Puerta de Alcalá (Alcalá Gate), Plaza de la Independencia. One of the grand landmarks of Madrid, the Alcalá Gate was designed by Francesco Sabatini in 1769–78. In neoclassical style, it replaced a baroque arch that used to mark the entry into the city; with its five arched passages, it soon became a symbol of the new Bourbon "enlightenment" that swept over Madrid. Today it guards the approach to the major artery leading to northeastern Spain and on to France.

Walk west, slightly downhill, along calle de Alcalá to the:

2. Plaza de la Cibeles, the most beautiful square in Madrid. In the center of the square is the Fuente de Cibeles, showing the Roman goddess Cybele driving an elaborate chariot pulled by two docile lions, which symbolize elegance and harmony. José Hermosilla and Ventura Rodríguez, architects of paseo del Prado (see below), designed the fountain. To your left, on the corner of calle de Alcalá and Plaza de la Cibeles, is the most magnificent post office in Europe, the Palacio de Comunicaciones. Its lavish embellishments give it the air of an ecclesiastical palace. It dates from 1904.

From the Plaza de la Cibeles you'll see two monuments—the pink-sided Palacio de Buenavista, the army headquarters of Spain, on the right side of the square; and immediately opposite you on the far side of the square, the Banco de España. You're now at the beginning of the most monumental part of Bourbon Madrid. Promenade beneath the leafy canopy of the:

3. Paseo del Prado, which incorporates two busy one-way streets separated by a wide pedestrian promenade. Walk south down the world-famous promenade, passing shrubbery, trees, and benches. Paseo del Prado links the Plaza de la Cibeles with the Plaza del Emperador Carlos V, site of the Atocha train station, the paseo's southern terminus. It's part of the busy north-south axis of the city. This whole section, called the Salon del Prado, incorporates more world-class art masterpieces than any other area of similar size in the world.

On your left, as you head south toward the Plaza del la Lealtad, you'll pass the:

4. Museo Naval, paseo del Prado 5. Adjacent to it, behind a gracefully angled row of neoclassical columns, stands the Madrid stock exchange (La Bolsa), dating from the 19th century. Continue down paseo del Prado to the:

5. Monument to the Heroes of the Second of May. This 19th-century obelisk, on your left behind a barrier of trees, honors the "unknown soldiers" who fell in the Napoleonic wars of independence. To your right, a few paces later, is the:

6. Palacio de Villahermosa, Plaza Cánovas del Castillo. This neoclassical palace holds one of the world's greatest artistic bequests. In the center of the Plaza Cánovas del Castillo (also called the Plaza de Neptuno) is a fountain dedicated to the Roman god Neptune. Continue walking south and you reach:

7. Museo del Prado, paseo del Prado, one of the world's great art museums. The original core of its paintings, which came from royal palaces throughout Spain, was hugely increased in the 19th century by private bequests. Much of the museum's layout results from the efforts of Charles III in the late 1700s. He commissioned the construction of a neoclassical brick-and-stone palace to house a Natural History Museum, named El Prado de San Jerónimo (St. Jerome's Meadow). It had barely been completed before Napoleon's troops sacked and burned it. Under Ferdinand VII the museum was restored and finally opened to the public in 1819.

Continue south along paseo del Prado to the:
8. **Jardín Botánico,** a fine oasis on a hot day.

Head back up paseo del Prado, crossing the street. When you reach the Plaza Cánovas del Castillo, turn left toward the ancient heart of Madrid along calle de las Cortés, which leads into:

9. **Carrera de San Jerónimo** (its name will briefly be the Plaza de las Cortés). Walk along the right side. On your left you'll pass the facade of the deluxe Palace Hotel. Turn around and look behind you for a distant view of the Gothic spire of the Iglesia de San Jerónimo.

Keep walking uphill. On your right you'll pass the Corinthian columns and twin bronze lions flanking the entrance to the Spanish Parliament, built around 1850. Facing it in a small three-sided park is a statue of Cervantes.

At this point, the street will narrow considerably, funneling itself into the:

10. **Plaza Canalejas,** around which sit several charming late 19th- and early 20th-century buildings. On the left side of the square, notice the twin spires of one of the neighborhood's most whimsically appealing structures. Built around 1920, it was designed as an eclectic combination of 17th-century styles, including shells, neoclassical obelisks, and heraldic lions holding shields.

Pass along this square back onto carrera de San Jerónimo, by now a busy, congested, and commercial street lined with stores.

REFUELING STOP At carrera de San Jerónimo 8, **11. Lhardy** (tel. 521-33-85) opened its doors in 1839. It soon became the gathering place of Madrid's literati, political leaders, and executives. Today this place has a decor called "Isabella Segundo," and gives off an aura of another era. Upstairs is a restaurant, but for refueling you can stop downstairs, as have thousands of visitors before you, and enjoy a cup of consommé from a large silver samovar; or in summer, a soothing gazpacho. Each cup costs 170 ptas. ($1.70). It's open Monday through Saturday from 1 to 3:30pm and 9 to 11:30pm.

Continue along carrera de San Jerónimo to the geographical heart of Spain, the:

12. **Puerta del Sol.** Two-thirds of the way along its half-moon-shaped expanse you'll come upon a small brass plaque from which all the distances in Spain are measured, placed immediately in front of a red-brick municipal building called Communidad de Madrid, on the southern edge of the square.

REFUELING STOP The most famous pastry shop in Madrid, **13. La Mallorquina,** Puerta del Sol 8 (tel. 521-12-01), occupies a position at the southwest corner of the Puerta del Sol. It was founded before the turn of the century and became known for one specialty, a Napoletana, filled with cream and studded with almond slices. You can order sandwiches, coffee, and pastries on the ground floor, or head upstairs, where there's sit-down service. It's open daily from 9am to 9:15pm.

At the far end of the Puerta del Sol are two main streets, calle Mayor and calle del Arenal, forking off to the right. Take Arenal, passing the red-brick neoclassical facade of the Iglesia de San Ginés on your left.

Within a short distance, you'll come upon the:

14. Plaza de Isabel II, graced with a bronze statue of the 19th century music-loving queen whose efforts helped construct an opera house for Madrid, the Teatro Real.

Follow calle del Arenal, now called calle Carlos III, around the southern edge of the opera house to the:

15. Plaza de Oriente, with its view of the Palacio Real (Royal Palace).

WALKING TOUR — Grandeur, Past & Present

Start: Gran Vía at Plaza del Callao.
Finish: Plaza de la Encarnación.
Time: 3 hours.
Best Times: Any day except Monday, when collections are closed.
Worst Times: Monday.

The tour begins on the:

1. Gran Vía, the major street of central Madrid, at the Plaza del Callao. The shop-flanked Gran Vía was opened at the end of World War I, and long before deluxe hotels started to sprout up north on paseo de la Castellana, the hotels of Gran Vía were the most expensive and elegant in the Spanish capital. The street runs from calle de Alcalá to the Plaza de España, and is at the heart of the modern city, with banks, department stores, and office blocks, plus an array of cinemas.

Begin your promenade at the Plaza del Callao, dominated by the Palacio de la Prensa (press), dating from 1924, and the Capitol, the most fashionable-looking building, dating from 1931.

From Gran Vía, head west toward the Plaza de España. This section of the Gran Vía is considered the most American in inspiration. The architects of the Gran Vía at that time were much influenced by the 1930s style sweeping New York, especially as reflected by the Roxy and Paramount buildings. The Gran Vía comes to an end at the:

2. Plaza de España, with its two tower blocks from the 1950s, the Edificio de España and the Torre de Madrid. This vast square, overshadowed by these skyscrapers, is at a hub separating Old Madrid from the modern city. Once a military barracks, it's now one of the busiest traffic intersections in Madrid. In the center of the square stands a monument to Cervantes (erected in 1928), with figures of Don Quixote and his faithful Sancho Panza.

From the square, walk up calle de la Princesa, turning to your left (south) as you approach calle de Ventura Rodríguez, where you'll come upon one of the esoteric treasure houses of Madrid, the:

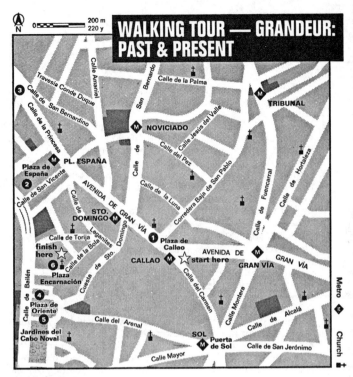

MADRID

1 Gran Vía
2 Plaza de España
3 Museo Cerralbo
4 Plaza de Oriente
5 Café de l'Oriente
6 Convento de la Encarnación

3. Museo Cerralbo, Ventura Rodríguez 17 (tel. 247-36-46). This town house, dripping with the gilt and red-velvet romanticism of the 19th century, was once inhabited by the family of the Marquis of Cerralbo, who filled its every nook and cranny with decorative bric-a-brac and art treasures. Note the crystal chandeliers and the fashionable, opulently colored glass imported from Venice. The Cerralbo clan were art collectors as well, purchasing well-known works by Zurbarán, Ribera, and El Greco. Especially intriguing is the library and study of the late marquis, preserved just as he left it. Admission costs 200 ptas. ($2). It's open Tuesday through Sunday from 10am to 3pm; closed August (Metro: Plaza de España or Ventura Rodríguez).

Returning to the Plaza de España, go to the southeastern corner of the square and head down calle de Bailén to the semicircular:

4. Plaza de Oriente, created in 1840, one of the most famous squares in Spain and the site of the Palacio Real. The square was designed to provide a harmonious panoramic vista between the Royal Palace and the Puerta del Sol. At the overthrow of the Napoleonic dynasty, work ended and the square was not completed until the reign of Isabella II. An equestrian statue of Philip IV stands in the center of the square, the work, based on drawings by Velázquez, of Italian sculptor Pietro Tacca.

REFUELING STOP At Plaza de Oriente 2, the: **5. Café de Oriente** (tel. 541-39-74) gives you a chance to have a drink and *tapas* with a view of the Royal Palace. The café's entrance is a well-marked doorway set behind shaded sidewalk tables and a turn-of-the-century decor.

From the Plaza de Oriente, take a tiny side street to the northeast of the square, calle de Pavia, which will lead to the:

6. Convento de la Encarnación (tel. 247-05-10), on one of the most charming squares in Madrid, the Plaza de la Encarnación. The convent and adjoining church were completed in 1616. A Spanish-speaking guide will show you around, pointing out the most important ecclesiastical paintings and Ribera's *St. John the Baptist.* Other works include a gory Christ with serpentine hair by Gregorio Fernández. The cloisters are filled with richly decorated chapels, one in the Pompeiian style. Admission is 350 ptas. ($3.50). The convent is open Tuesday through Thursday and on Saturday from 10:30am to 1pm and 4 to 5:30pm, on Friday from 10:30am to 1pm, and on Sunday from 11am to 1:15pm (Metro: Ópera).

WALKING TOUR —— The Prado in 2 Hours

Start: Velázquez door (western entrance).
Finish: Room 57A.
Time: 2 hours.
Best Times: At the 9am opening.
Worst Times: 12:30–3pm (too crowded), or Monday (when it's closed).

Considered the most precious cultural institution in all of Spain, and the seat of a deep-seated pride in the country's artistic heritage, the Prado places Madrid firmly on the artistic map of Europe. It's also one of the capital's most consistently reliable tourist attractions, as witnessed by the more than two million visitors who shuffle through its corridors every year.

But because of the Prado's *embarras de richesses* (only a third of the collection can be displayed at any given time), you may need some

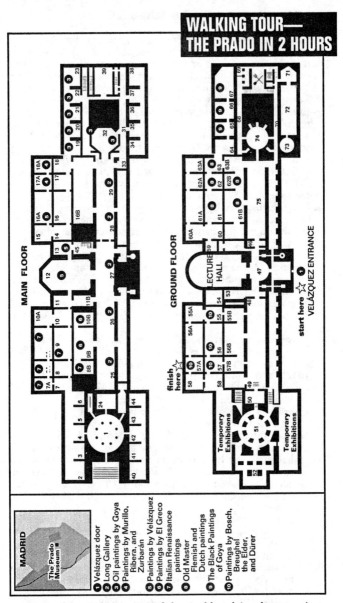

MAIN FLOOR

GROUND FLOOR

LECTURE HALL

Temporary Exhibitions

Temporary Exhibitions

start here ☆
VELÁZQUEZ ENTRANCE

finish here ☆

MADRID

The Prado Museum

❶ Velázquez door
❷ Long Gallery
❸ Oil paintings by Goya
❹ Paintings by Murillo, Ribera, and Zurbarán
❺ Paintings by Velázquez
❻ Paintings by El Greco
❼ Italian Renaissance paintings
❽ Old Master Flemish and Dutch paintings
❾ The Black Paintings of Goya
❿ Paintings by Bosch, Breughel the Elder, and Dürer

guidance to see at least some of the world-acclaimed masterpieces. You could devote weeks to the Prado, but regrettably many visitors have only two hours. Here's how to make the most of that limited time.

Because the lines there tend to be shorter, I usually prefer to enter via the:

1. Velázquez door, the Prado's western (central) entrance, near the larger-than-life bronze statue of the seated artist, Spain's most famous painter. Resolutely ignoring (for the time being) the riches on the museum's street level, climb to the upper floor, using the building's central (western) staircase, which lies a short distance to the right of the entrance turnstile. At the top of the stairs, a short hall will deposit you into the museum's famous:

2. Long Gallery. Though referred to as a gallery, it's more technically the interconnected series of Rooms 24–32. Echoing, marble-sheathed, and often very crowded, these rooms are the main traffic artery of the Prado's second showcase floor. Walk south through Rooms 28 and 29, admiring large-scale works by mainly Italian Renaissance painters as you go. Specific artworks will include representations by Raphael, Titian, Tintoretto, and Fra Angelico. The gallery will eventually funnel into an octagonal room (no. 32), containing:

3. Oil paintings by Goya, including his most famous portraits— the cruel depictions of the family of King Charles IV. You're standing amid the museum's densest concentration of oils by Goya. The best of these lie a few steps to the east. With your back to the Long Gallery, turn left into the long and narrow Room 31. At the end of no. 31, turn left into Room 22. This and four of its neighbors (specifically Rooms 19–23, which lie in a straight uninterrupted line) contain many of Goya's cartoons (sketches for tapestries) which the artist designed for eventual execution by teams of weavers. Walk southward into Room 18 to see:

4. Paintings by Murillo, Ribera, and Zurbarán. Along with its immediate neighbors (Rooms 18A and 17A), you'll find clustered together works by Murillo (1617–82), Ribera (1588–1652), and Zurbarán (1598–1664). Each of these artists is considered a superlative contemporary of the most acclaimed artwork ever to emerge from Spain, the:

5. Paintings by Velázquez. These lie ahead of you, in about half a dozen rooms whose contents are considered the centerpiece of the Prado. Wander through Rooms 16A, 15A, 14, 16, and 13, in any order that appeals to your roving eye. You'll probably intuitively gravitate to the Prado's architectural and artistic centerpiece, Room 12. Though masterpieces await you on all sides, note in particular *Las Meninas* (Ladies of the Court), whose enigmatic grouping has intrigued observers for centuries.

Now, exit from Room 12's northern door into Room 11, turn left into Room 11A, then turn immediately right into Room 10B and 9B. This series of rooms contains one of Europe's most important collections of:

6. Paintings by El Greco. Famous for his nervous depictions of mystical ecstacy, his dramatically lurid colors, and the elongated limbs of his characters (who seem to be physically rising upward to heaven), El Greco was the premier exponent of the late-baroque school of Mannerism.

Time will by now be rushing by. If you choose to prolong your visit, you might want to gaze briefly at the contents of Rooms 8B, 9, 8, 7, 7A, 8A, and 9A, an array of:

7. Italian Renaissance paintings. These interconnected rooms lie within a few steps of one another, and each contains more world-class examples of works by such Italian masters as Tintoretto, Titian, and Paolo Veronese. Know at this point that you have by now seen—albeit briefly—many of the grandest artworks of the Prado's upper floor.

Now, head quickly for the nearest staircase. (You might prefer to ask a guard at this point, but in any event, the museum's most important staircases lie off the Long Gallery, which—as stated earlier, is comprised of Rooms 24–32.) Midway along its length, look for the staircase, and descend to the museum's ground floor. When you reach it, head south through the very long Room 75. Midway down its length, turn left into Room 61B, the beginning of the Prado's superb collection of:

8. Old Master Flemish and Dutch paintings. These are in Room 61B (famous for Rubens's *Martyrdom of St. Andrew*), and continue in a cluster of rooms which include Rooms 62B, 63B, 63, 62, and 61. Room 61 contains some of the most famous paintings in history: Rubens's *The Three Graces* and the somewhat less-well-known *Judgment of Paris*.

Your tour is nearing an end, but if time remains, a final excursion back into the artistic vision of Goya would not be amiss. For views of some of the most depressing paintings in the history of Spain, brilliant for their evocation of neurotic emotional pain and anguish, leave the Flemish section by walking to the ground floor's southeastern corner. There, in Rooms 65, 66, and 67, you'll find:

9. The Black Paintings of Goya. Refresh yourself, if time remains, at the cafeteria, which lies close nearby (signs are prominently posted). Before concluding your tour, however, you might be tempted to view the weird and hallucinogenic paintings of Dutch artist Hieronymus Bosch ("El Bosco," 1450–1516). To reach them, walk briskly to the northeastern corner of the museum's ground floor, where the artist's works lie scattered amid Rooms 55–57A. In these rooms you can also gaze upon:

10. Paintings by Bosch, Breughel the Elder, and Dürer. The most important of these works includes *The Garden of Earthly Delights,* whose convoluted and bizarre images have provided fodder for the nightmares of generations of children.

CHAPTER 8

MADRID SHOPPING

1. THE SHOPPING SCENE

• **FROMMER'S SMART TRAVELER: SHOPPING**

2. SHOPPING A TO Z

Practically everything is available in Madrid, which 17th-century playwright Tirso de Molina called "a shop stocked with every kind of merchandise." Madrid has been one of the major shopping centers of Spain ever since the court moved here. Today its merchandise has expanded and is so diverse in its offerings that it has become a city for people "born to shop." So whatever your travel schedule, try to budget some time for exploring some of the more than 50,000 stores in Madrid, selling everything from its emerging high-fashion clothing (for both men and women) to flamenco guitars to art and ceramics.

If your time is limited and you want a quick overview of Madrid offerings, go to one of the big department stores (see below). Each of them carries a "bit of everything."

1. THE SHOPPING SCENE

BEST BUYS Spain has always been revered for the dedication of its craftspeople, many of whom still work in the time-honored, labor-intensive traditions of their grandparents. It's hard to go wrong if you limit your purchases to the handcrafted objects that the Spanish have always executed so beautifully. These include hand-painted tiles, sturdy ceramics, and fine porcelain. Shipping can be arranged by any reputable dealer, who will send the object to its destination swathed in protective padding.

Hand-woven rugs, handmade sweaters, and intricate embroideries are also good buys. And you'll find some of the best leather in the world.

Jewelry—especially gold set with Majorca pearls, which have been produced in Spain for centuries—represents good value and unquestioned luxury.

Antiques, although no longer the giveaway bargains they were before World War II, are still available in Spain, and are sold in highly sophisticated retail outlets. Better suited to the budgets of many travelers, however, are the flea markets whose weekly bartering and haggling have become a celebrated and elaborate ritual in modern Madrid.

Spain, although hardly the center for haute couture that Milan and Paris are, is still making inroads into fashion. Its young designers are regularly featured in the fashion magazines of Europe. You'll also find some excellent shoes. *Warning:* Shoes and quality clothing are generally more expensive in Madrid than in the United States.

SHOPPING DISTRICTS Drawing on its historical origins as the most interesting part of Madrid, the **center of Madrid** has a dense concentration of all kinds of shops. Their sheer diversity is staggering, interspersing the most old-fashioned mom-and-pop outlets for salt, meat, fish, and staples with hi-tech, high-fashion boutiques. The neighborhood's densest concentration of shops lies immediately north of the Puerta del Sol, radiating out from calle del Carmen, calle Montera, and calle de Preciados.

The **calle Mayor and calle del Arenal district,** although technically in the center (not far from the Puerta del Sol), still seems to exist as a separate shopping entity. Unlike their more stylish neighbors to the north, shops in this district tend toward the small, slightly dusty enclaves of coin and stamp collectors, family-owned souvenir shops, clockmakers, sellers of military paraphernalia, and (thanks to the nearness of the Teatro Real and the Music Conservatory) an abundance of stores selling musical scores for obscure orchestral works.

The **Gran Vía** was conceived, designed, and built in the 1910s and 1920s as a showcase for the city's best shops, hotels, and restaurants. Since those days its allure has been battered by the emergence of other shopping districts, yet the art-nouveau/art-deco glamour of the Gran Vía still survives in the hearts of most Madrileños. The bookshops here are among the best in the city, as are outlets for fashion, shoes, jewelry, furs, and handcrafted accessories from all regions of Spain.

Most visitors are so immediately enamored by the architectural symmetry of the **Plaza Mayor** that they overlook its neighborhood as a shopping opportunity. Within three or four blocks in each direction from the square you'll find more than the predictable concentration of souvenir shops. Under the arcades of the square itself are exhibitions of lithographs and oil paintings, and every Saturday and Sunday there's a loosely organized market of collectible stamps and coins. One of the city's headquarters for the sale of bolts of cloth, threads, and buttons lies amid the stores on calle Marqués Viudo de Pontejos, which runs east from the Plaza Mayor. Also running east of the square, on calle de Zaragoza, are collections of silversmiths and small jewelry shops. On the more practical and of the spectrum, calle Posetas contains shops selling housewares, underwear, soap powders, and almost everything a person would need to create a happy (and clean) home.

Near **carrera de San Jerónimo,** lying several blocks east of the Puerta del Sol, is Madrid's densest concentration of gift shops, craft shops, and antiques dealers—a decorator's delight. Its most interesting streets include calle del Prado, calle de las Huertas, and the Plaza de las Cortés. Because of the nearness of some of Madrid's most expensive and posh hotels and the upscale nature of the neighborhood, don't expect any bargains.

A few blocks east of the Parque del Oeste, the verdant and well-heeled neighborhood of **northwest Madrid** is well stocked with luxury goods and staples for middle-class and upscale homes. Identified by its Metro stop, Argüelles, its main thoroughfare is calle de la Princesa, which contains a bevy of shops selling shoes, handbags, fashions, gifts, and children's clothing. Thanks to the influence and presence of the nearby university, there's also a dense concentration of bookstores, especially on calle Isaac Peral and calle Fernando el Católico (which lie several blocks north and northwest, respectively, from the Argüelles subway stop).

The **Salamanca** district is known throughout Spain as the quintessential upper-bourgeois neighborhood, as uniformly prosperous as anything you're likely to find in Iberia. Its shops are correspondingly exclusive. They include outlets run by interior decorators, furniture shops, fur and jewelry shops, Spanish couture, several department stores, and design headquarters whose output ranges from the solidly conservative to the high-tech *outré* of Europe. The main streets of this district are calle Serrano and calle Velázquez. The district lies northeast of the center of Madrid, a few blocks north of Retiro Park. Its most central Metro stops are Serrano and Velázquez.

HOURS AND SHIPPING   In general, major stores are open Monday through Saturday from 9:30am to 8pm. Many small stores take a siesta between 1:30 and 4:30pm. Of course there's no set formula, and hours can vary greatly from store to store.

Many establishments will crate and ship bulky objects. Any especially large item, such as a piece of furniture, should probably be sent by ship. Every antiques dealer in Spain has lists of reputable maritime shippers; one reliable option is **Emery Queen Freight,** c/o Grupinsa, Goya 115-5, 28009 Madrid (tel. 402-91-49).

For most small and medium-size shipments, air freight isn't much more expensive than ship. **Iberia** offers shipping service from Spain to New York, Miami, Chicago, and Los Angeles. At those gateways, Iberia can arrange to have the cargo transferred to other airlines. A shipment under 99 lbs. (45kg) costs around $4.75 per pound. For an additional fee Iberia will pick up your package. For a truly precious cargo, ask the seller to make a crate for it. For information in Spain about air-cargo shipments, call Iberia's cargo division at Madrid's Barajas Airport (tel. 205-46-50 or 205-40-90, ext. 2671 or 2679).

Remember that your air-cargo shipment will need to clear Customs after it's brought into the United States. This involves some additional paperwork and perhaps a trip to the airport. It's usually easier to hire a commercial Customs broker to do the work for you. **Emery Worldwide** (tel. 800/323-4685 toll free in the U.S.), a division of CF Freightways, can clear your goods for around $100 for most shipments.

TAX AND HOW TO RECOVER IT   If you're a nonresident and make purchases in Spain worth more than 25,000 ptas. ($250), you can get a tax refund. (The internal tax, known as VAT in most of

---

**Ⓕ FROMMER'S SMART TRAVELER:
SHOPPING**

1. Read the section on tax refunds. There's red tape, but refunds can mean substantial savings.
2. Fine-tune your haggling skills in the open-air flea market of Madrid (El Rastro). You can come up with some good buys with strong, steady, firm bargaining.
3. If you pay cash some smaller stores will lower the price.
4. Shop the July and August sales.
5. Don't assume that because a certain product is "made in Spain" that it's cheaper in Spain. It pays to know what something costs at home before you make a substantial purchase.

Europe, is called I.V.A.—pronounced *ee*-bah—in Spain.) Depending on the goods, the rate usually ranges from 6% to 12% of the total worth of your merchandise. Luxury items are taxed at 33%.

To get this refund, you must complete three copies of a form that the store will give you detailing the nature of your purchase and its value. Citizens of non–EC countries show the purchase and the form to the Spanish Customs Office. The shop is supposed to refund the amount due you. Inquire at the time of purchase how they will do so, and discuss in what currency your refund will arrive.

TRADITIONAL SALES The best sales are usually in summer. Called *rebajas*, they start in July and go through August. As a general rule, merchandise is marked down even more in August to make way for the new fall wares.

DUTY-FREE—WORTH IT OR NOT? Before you leave home, check the regular retail price of items that you're most likely to buy. Duty-free prices vary from one country to another and from item to item. Sometimes you're better off purchasing an item in a discount store at home. If you don't remember Stateside prices, you can't tell when you're getting a good deal.

BARGAINING The days of bargaining are, for the most part, long gone. Most stores have what is called *precio de venta al público* (PVP), a firm retail price not subject to negotiation.

With street vendors and in flea markets it's a different story. Here, haggling *à la española* is expected. However, you'll have to be very skilled to get the price reduced a lot, as most of these street-smart vendors know exactly what their merchandise is worth—and they are old hands at getting it.

2. SHOPPING A TO Z

ANTIQUES

In the 19th century, Spain's imperial traditions and status-conscious bourgeoisie created a market for enormous amounts of furniture. Much of these highly desirable antiques are available today.

CENTRE DE ARTE Y ANTIGUEDADES, calle Serrano 5. Tel. 576-96-82.

Other than at the flea market or in the new Mercado de la Puerta de Toledo shopping mall (see below), one of the densest concentration of antiques stores is in the Centre de Arte y Antiguedades. Set in a mid-19th-century building, it has several unusual antiques dealers (and a large carpet emporium as well). Each establishment maintains its own hours, but they tend to be open Monday through Saturday from 10am to 2pm and 4:30 to 8pm. Metro: Retiro. Bus: 1, 2, 9, or 15.

CENTRO DE ANTICUARIOS LAGASCA, calle Lagasca 36.

Another possibility, this contains about a dozen shops specializing in antique furniture. There is no central telephone number. Open Monday through Saturday from 10am to 1:30pm and 5 to 8pm. Metro: Serrano or Velázquez.

KREISLER ANTIGUEDADES, calle Serrano 19. Tel. 576-53-38.

This long-established organization, which originally specialized in porcelain, changed its inventory several years ago to include antique furniture from the 18th and 19th centuries. Especially prominent are Spanish-derived pieces, although a scattering of northern European pieces are also featured. Metro: Serrano. It's open Monday through Friday from 10am to 1:30pm and 4:30 to 8pm, and on Saturday from 10am to 1:30pm.

ART GALLERIES

CALCOGRAFÍA NACIONAL, calle Alcalá 13. Tel. 532-15-43.

This establishment sells Goya prints from the artist's original plates, as well as many other engravings and etchings. Open Tuesday through Friday from 10am to 2pm and on Saturday from 10am to 1:30pm. Metro: Sevilla.

GALERÍA KREISLER, Hermosilla 8. Tel. 431-42-64.

One highly successful entrepreneur on Madrid's art scene is Ohio-born Edward Kreisler, whose gallery specializes in relatively conservative paintings, sculptures, and graphics. The gallery prides itself on occasionally displaying and selling the works of artists who are critically acclaimed in and displayed in museums in Spain. International antiques are also sold. Open Monday through Friday from 10:30am to 2pm and 5 to 8:30pm, and on Saturday from 10:30am to 1pm (closed Aug). Metro: Serrano. Bus: 27, 45, or 150.

JORGE KREISLER GALERÍA, calle Prim 13. Tel. 522-05-34.

Far less conservative than Edward Kreisler's Galería Kreisler is his Jorge Kreisler Galería, which inventories the sculptures, paintings, and graphics of avant-garde artists. This, too, occasionally displays and sells the works of prominent artists in Spain. Open on Monday from 5 to 9pm and Tuesday through Saturday from 10am to 2pm and 5 to 9pm. Metro: Colón.

CAPES

CAPAS SESEÑA, calle Cruz 23. Tel. 531-55-10.

Memories of Zorro have prompted some visitors to Madrid to search out similar attire. If you're looking for the perfect cape, head for Capas Seseña. Founded shortly after the turn of the century, it has been manufacturing and selling the finest wool capes for both men and women for many years. The wool comes from the mountain town of Béjar, near Salamanca. The shop is open Monday through Friday from 9:30am to 1:30pm and 5 to 8pm, and on Saturday from 9:30am to 1:30pm. Metro: Sevilla or Tirso de Molina.

A second outlet is located in the sophisticated new shopping mall at the Puerta de Toledo (see below).

CERAMICS

ANTIGUA CASA TALAVERA, Isabel la Católica 2. Tel. 247-34-17.

Called "the first house of Spanish ceramics," this shop has a sampling of ceramic styles from every major region of Spain. Sangría pitchers, dinnerware, tea sets, plates, vases—all are handmade, and the buyers work hard to find pieces with character. One of the showrooms has an interesting selection of tiles, painted with repro-ductions of everything from scenes from *Don Quijote* to bullfights, dances, and folklore. There's also a series of tiles depicting famous paintings at the Prado. At its present location for more than 80 years, the shop is only a short walk from the Plaza de Santo Domingo. Open Monday through Friday from 10am to 1:30pm and 5 to 8pm, and on Saturday from 10am to 1:30pm. Metro: Santo Domingo. Bus: 1, 2, 46, 70, 75, or 148.

CRAFTS

ARTESPAÑA, calle Hermosilla 14. Tel. 413-62-62.
Handmade objects can be purchased in virtually every neighbor-hood in Madrid, but one of the city's most stylish outlets is sponsored by the Spanish government as a showcase for the best of its national designs. Artespaña exhibits Spanish ceramics, furniture, and household items. Open Monday through Friday from 10am to 1:30pm and 4:30 to 8pm, and on Saturday from 10am to 1:30pm. Metro: Colón.

DEPARTMENT STORES

Despite the presence of innumerable charming boutiques scattered throughout the city, many Madrileños appreciate the congregation of thousands of items under one roof. Department-store shopping is definitely a Spanish *institución*. Many visitors also prefer the conve-nience of making all their purchases in one store, rather than running from boutique to boutique.

EL CORTE INGLÉS, calle Preciados 3. Tel. 232-81-00.
The largest and most glamorous of the department stores, El Corte Inglés is considered by some shopping devotees to be one of Europe's best department-store chains. Despite the throngs of shoppers jamming the corridors and escalators, it manages to retain a cheerfully upper-crust image of a store loaded with desirable and practical goods. Salespeople rarely speak English, but they are so tuned in to the merchandise and to the needs of shoppers that they can often be of great help anyway.

El Corte Inglés sells all kinds of souvenirs and Spanish handcrafts, such as damascene steelwork from Toledo, flamenco dolls, and embroidered shawls. Some astute buyers report that it also sells glamorous fashion articles such as Pierre Balmain for about a third less than elsewhere in Europe.

The chain has a multitude of services that foreign visitors appreciate, including interpreters, currency-exchange facilities, and parcel delivery either to a local hotel or overseas. It will also arrange for all the necessary formalities regarding the I.V.A. (VAT, or Value Added Tax) refund. (For more information on this, see "Tax and How to Recover It" in "The Shopping Scene," above.)

Madrid boasts several different branches of this chain; this is its flagship and is about a block from the Puerta del Sol. Additional branches are at calle Goya 76 (tel. 448-08-04), on the northern end of paseo de la Castellana at the corner of calle Raimunda Fernández Villaverda (tel. 456-50-20); and at calle Princesa 56 (tel. 242-48-00). All branches are open Monday through Saturday from 10am to 9pm (without interruption).

GALERÍAS PRECÍADOS, Plaza de Callao 1. Tel. 522-47-71.

Fiercely competitive with El Corte Inglés is the Galerías Precíados. It's really two stores connected by an underground passageway. It's slightly more downscale than its famous competitor, but with quite presentable ready-made clothing for men, women, and children. There's a top-floor snack bar and restaurant. Some good buys I've noted in the past include guitars, men's suede jackets and Spanish capes, and women's full-length suede coats. There's a tailoring department on the store's second floor where men can have a suit made to order. The selection of fabrics—solids, herringbones, or stripes—can be made into whatever style you prefer. Open Monday through Saturday from 10am to 8pm. Metro: Callao.

EMBROIDERIES

CASA BONET, calle Núñez de Balboa 76. Tel. 575-09-12.

Throughout the 19th and 20th centuries, the intricately detailed embroideries produced in Spain's Balearic Islands (especially Majorca) have been avidly sought out for bridal chests and elegant dinner settings. One outlet that stocks and sells them is Casa Bonet. A few examples are displayed on the walls, but a true concept of the store's inventory comes when tablecloths, sheets, napkins, and pillowcases are unrolled on Spanish tables covered with velvet. You'll find a full range of cottons, linens, and polyesters here, many embroidered into patterns fit for a bride. Open Monday through Friday from 9:45am to 2pm and 5 to 8pm, and on Saturday from 10:15am to 2pm. Metro: Núñez de Balboa.

ESPADRILLES

Espadrilles are those wonderfully lighthearted shoes that no self-respecting Iberian fisher would do without. Although many different styles exist, the tops are usually crafted from canvas and the soles from tightly woven hemp. (The hemp is first woven into ropes, then stitched in oval patterns into what is eventually used as a sole.) Despite these shoes' humble origins, some consumers consider espadrilles perfect for beachwear and occasionally as a kind of casually chic shoe to wear to summer parties.

CASA HERNANZ, calle de Toledo 18. Tel. 266-54-50.

If you want to stock up on this kind of Iberian accessory, head for Casa Hernanz. Located on a busily trafficked street a brisk walk south of the Plaza Mayor, it has been in business for more than 150 years. In addition to espadrilles, the shop sells shoes in other styles and hats. The staff is cordial, but they don't speak English. Open Monday through Friday from 9am to 1:30pm and 4:30 to 8pm, and on Saturday from 10am to 2pm. Metro: Puerta del Sol, Ópera, or La Latina.

FANS & UMBRELLAS

A true mistress of the fan-bearing art can convey a multitude of messages through the way she manipulates her fan, and part of the fun of a trip to Spain is the attempt to figure out the various signals.

Fans and umbrellas have traditionally been sold from the same shops in Spain.

CASA DE DIEGO, Puerta del Sol 12. Tel. 522-66-43.

One well-known shop that can supply you with all the ingredients you'll need for your own Spain-inspired flirtation is Casa de Diego. Fans sold here range from plain to fancy, from plastic to exotic hardwood, from cost-conscious to lavish, in an assortment that will probably tempt you to become (at least during a candlelit evening or two) a bit more *espagnole*. Open: Monday through Friday from 10am to 1:30pm and 5 to 8pm, and on Saturday from 10am to 1pm. Metro: Puerta del Sol.

FASHION

The dowdiness of Franco-era Spain has disappeared as designers typified by Paloma Picasso have transformed the fashion landscape. The array of desirable boutiques is endless, but a representative list might include the following:

For Women

DON CARLOS, calle Serrano 92. Tel. 575-75-07.

Don Carlos strictly maintains its status as a boutique, with a limited but tasteful array of carefully chosen clothing for women, and a somewhat smaller selection for men. Open Monday through Saturady from 10am to 2pm and 5 to 8:30pm. Metro: Núñez de Balboa.

HERRERO, calle Preciados 16. Tel. 521-29-90.

The sheer size and buying power of this popular retail outlet make it a reasonably priced emporium for all kinds of feminine garb. An additional outlet lies on the same street at no. 7 (same phone). Open Monday through Saturday from 10:45am to 2pm and 4:30 to 7pm. Metro: Puerta del Sol or Callao.

JESÚS DE POSO, calle Almirante 28. Tel. 531-66-76.

This shop markets the collections of one of the most fashionable designers for women in Spain. The fabrics are beautiful and the garments expensive. Open Monday through Saturday from 10am to 1:30pm and 5 to 8pm. Metro: Banco de España.

MODAS GONZALO, Gran Vía 43. Tel. 547-12-39.

This boutique's baroque, gilded atmosphere evokes the 1940s, but its fashions are strictly up-to-date, well made, and intended for sophisticated women. No children's garments are sold. Open Monday through Saturday from 10am to 1:30pm and 4:30 to 8pm. Metro: Callao or Puerta del Sol.

Fashions for Men

For the man on a budget who wants to dress reasonably well, the best outlet for off-the-rack men's clothing is one of the branches of the **El Corte Inglés** department-store chain (see above). Most men's boutiques in Madrid are very expensive and may not be worth the investment.

FLEA MARKETS

In addition to the thousands of conventional shops, the Spanish capital has a strong tradition of open-air markets, whose haggling and informality have become part of Madrileño lore. Foremost among these is **El Rastro** (which is translated as either flea market or thieves' market). Located on a meandering network of streets and plazas a few minutes' walk south of the Plaza Mayor, it will warm the heart of anyone attracted to fascinating junk interspersed with bric-a-brac and paintings. (Don't expect to find a Goya.) The neighborhood is also lined with permanent stores that are open, with exceptions, Tuesday through Sunday from 9:30am to 1:30pm and 5 to 8pm. These sell a mixture of dusty junk and antiques, and should be visited during the week if you're seriously interested in buying (or just looking for) antiques. On Sunday between 9am and 2pm, it seems that half of Madrid and many people from the surrounding countryside jostle each other through the narrow streets, searching for real and imagined bargains.

The flea market occupies a roughly triangular district of streets whose center is the Plaza Cascarro and Ribera de Curtidores. As its name implies, thieves are rampant here, so proceed carefully. It's open Tuesday through Sunday from 9:30am to 1:30pm and 5 to 8pm. Metro: La Latina. Bus: 3 or 27.

FOOD & WINE

MALLORCA, calle Velázquez 59. Tel. 431-99-09.

⭐ Each of the capitals of Europe has its own legendary gourmet shop where you can eat, drink, and carry away succulent tidbits for consumption at home or on your picnic. Madrid's Mallorca was originally established in 1931 as an outlet for a pastry called an *ensaimada*. Consumed as part of the coffee-drinking ritual, it's still the store's most famous product. (They emerge ultra-fresh every hour from the ovens.) There are also a tempting array of cheeses, canapés, roasted and marinated meats, sausages, about a dozen kinds of pâtés, and a mind-blowing array of tiny pastries, tarts, and chocolates.

Don't overlook the displays of wine and brandies. There's also a *tapas* bar, where clients stand—three deep sometimes—sampling the wares before buying. Hostesses of chic cocktail parties—and marauding families organizing picnics—sometimes make take-out from Mallorca the gastronomic focal point of their events. *Tapas* cost 200–300 ptas. ($2–$3) per *racion* (portion). Metro: Velázquez.

The five other branches are at calle Serrano 6 (tel. 577-18-59); Metro: Serrano, calle Juan Pérez Zúñiga 39 (tel. 267-18-07); Metro: bulevar Concepción), calle Bravo Murillo 7 (tel. 448-97-49); Metro: Alvarado), calle Comandante Zurita 48 (tel. 253-51-02; Metro: calle Caminos); and calle Alberto Alcocer 48 (tel. 458-75-11); Metro: Cuzco or Colombia). All branches are open daily from 9am to 9pm.

HATS & HEADGEAR

CASA YUSTAS, Plaza Mayor 30. Tel. 266-50-84.

If your sessions with the analyst have revealed a fetish for unusual hats, you can satisfy your inclinations here at this extraordinary emporium established in 1894. Picture yourself as a Congo explorer, a Spanish sailor, an officer in the Kaiser's army, a Rough Rider, a priest, even Napoleon. Open Monday through Friday from 9:45am to 1:30pm and 4:30 to 8pm, and on Saturday from 9:45am to 1:30pm. Metro: Puerta del Sol.

LEATHER

LOEWE, Gran Vía 8. Tel. 577-60-56.

Loewe has been the most elegant leather store in Spain since 1846. Its gold-medal-winning designers have always kept abreast of changing tastes and styles, but there remains a timeless chic to much of their goods. The store sells luggage, handbags, and jackets (leather or suede) for men and women. Much of the inventory is in the supple and soft shade of medium brown for which the store is known. A second outlet is at calle Serrano 26 (tel. 435-30-23; Metro: Serrano). Both branches are open Monday through Saturday from 9:30am to 2pm and 4 to 8:30pm. Metro: Banco de España.

MUSICAL INSTRUMENTS

REAL MUSICAL, Carlos III no. 1. Tel. 541-30-07.

If you're looking to buy a Spanish guitar, a piano, a string or wind instrument, or simply a record, CD, or pieces of sheet music, head for Real Musical. It's open Monday through Friday from 9:30am to 2pm and 5 to 8pm, and on Saturday from 9:30am to 2pm. Metro: Ópera.

PERFUMES

PERFUMERÍA PADILLA, calle Precíados 17. Tel. 522-66-83.

This store sells a large and competitively priced assortment of Spanish and international scents for women. They also maintain a branch at calle del Carmen 78 (same phone). Both branches are open Monday through Saturday from 9:45am to 8:30pm. Metro: Puerta del Sol.

URGUIOLA, calle Mayor 1. Tel. 521-59-05.

Located at the western edge of the Puerta del Sol, this time-tested shop carries one of the most complete stocks of perfume in Madrid—both national and international brands. It also sells gifts, souvenirs, and costume jewelry. Open Monday through Saturday from 10am to 2pm and 5 to 8:30pm. Metro: Puerta del Sol.

PORCELAIN

Some visitors prefer the thick and rustic pottery and stoneware that Spanish artisans churn out by the thousands at potters' wheels throughout the country. Others search out only the delicately realistic porcelain sculptures whose elongated limbs and whimsically yearning expressions were probably inspired by the Mannerist paintings of El Greco. Foremost among the manufacturers of this style of porcelain sculpture is Lladró. Many different shops have concessions to sell Lladró porcelain.

LASARTE, Gran Vía 44. Tel. 521-49-22.

An imposing outlet for Lladró porcelain, this store is devoted almost exclusively to its distribution. The staff can usually tell you about new designs and releases the Lladró company is planning for the near future. Open Monday through Friday from 9:30am to 2pm and 5 to 8pm, and on Saturday from 10am to 2pm. Metro: Callao.

SHOPPING MALLS

GALERÍA DEL PRADO, Plaza de las Cortés 7.

Spain's top designers are represented in this marble-sheathed concourse below the Palace Hotel. It opened in 1989 with 47 different shops, many featuring *moda joven* (fashions for the young). Merchandise changes with the season, but you'll always find a good assortment of fashion, Spanish leather goods, cosmetics, perfumes, and jewelry. You can also eat and drink here. The entrance is in front of the hotel, facing the broad tree-lined paseo del Prado across from the Prado itself. Open Monday through Saturday from 10am to 9pm. Metro: Banco de España or Atocha.

MERCADO PUERTA DE TOLEDO, Puerta de Toledo. Tel. 266-46-02.

⭐ This is one of Spain's most upscale, ambitious, and architec-turally unusual shopping malls. More than 150 of the most glamorous names in Spainish retail are collected into the slightly run-down neighborhood just southwest of the historic center. Fashion and antiques are featured—an unusual contrast for a building that served until very recently as Madrid's central fish market. Today, thanks to many pesetas invested by the municipal government, the complex is perceived as a showcase, and some observers have compared it to London's revitalized Covent Garden marketplace. Interspersed among the stores are museum-quality temporary expositions devoted to such subjects as the pottery of Talaverde or the Toledo-based art of metalworking.

Highly stylized and futuristic, the market rises five floors above a sun-flooded courtyard that contains an artistic rendering of a lunar clock and sun dial. You won't go hungry between shopping binges because of the many restaurants, *tapas* bars, and cafés on the premises.

Each of the individual shops maintains hours of its own choosing, but most of them do business Monday through Saturday from 10am to 8:30pm. Metro: Puerta de Toledo.

MADRID NIGHTS

The Madrileños are called *gatos* (cats) because of their excessive fondness for prowling around at night. If you're going to a club, the later you go, the better. If you arrive too early, you'll probably have the place to yourself.

In recent years nightlife in Madrid has changed more dramatically than in any other capital of Europe. There's something going on at night to interest virtually everyone. The young people of Madrid rarely seem to stay home watching television. They're out exploring the many nocturnal facets of their city.

Nightlife is so plentiful in Madrid that the city can be roughly divided into "night zones." The most popular district—both traditionally and from the standpoint of tourist interest—is the **Plaza Mayor/Puerta del Sol** district. These areas can also be dangerous (muggings, for example), so explore them with caution, especially late at night. The area is filled with *tapas* bars and *cuevas* (drinking "caves"). Here it's customary to begin a tasca crawl, going from tavern to tavern, sampling the wine in each, along with a selection of tapas. The major streets for such a crawl are Cava de San Miguel, Cava Alta, and Cava Baja. You can order *pinchos y raciones* (tasty snacks and tidbits).

Nightlife along the **Gran Vía** is confined mainly to cinemas and theaters. Most of the after-dark action takes place on little streets branching off the Gran Vía.

Another area much frequented by tourists is the section around **Plaza de Isabel II** and **Plaza de Oriente,** site of the Royal Palace. Both are in the center of Madrid. Many restaurants and cafés flourish in this area, including the famous Café de Orient.

Chueca—embracing such streets as Hortaleza, Infantas, Barquillo, and San Lucas—is the gay nightlife district, with many clubs. Cheap restaurants, along with a few striptease joints, are also found here. Again, this area can be dangerous at night; be alert for pickpockets and muggers.

For university students, the area of **Argüelles-Moncloa** sees most of the action. However, if it's a weeknight and there are classes tomorrow, most students head home by 11pm. Many discos are found in the area, along with ale houses and fast-food joints. The area is bounded by Pintor Rosales, Cea Bermúdez, Bravo Murillo, San Bernardo, and Conde Duque.

FREE EVENTS & DISCOUNTS In summer Madrid becomes a virtual free festival, as the city sponsors a series of plays, concerts, and films—all gratis. Pick up a copy of the **Guía del Ocio** (available at most newsstands) for listings of these events. This guide also provides information about occasional discounts for commercial events, such as concerts staged in Madrid's parks. Also check the program of the **Fundación Juan March,** calle Castelló 77 (tel. 435-42-40; Metro: Nuñez de Balboa), which frequently gives free concerts.

FLAMENCO & DISCOS   Flamenco in Madrid is geared mainly to tourists with fat wallets, and nightclubs are expensive. But since Madrid is preeminently a city of song and dance, you can often be entertained at very little cost—in fact, for the price of a glass of wine or beer, if you sit at a bar with live entertainment.

Discos also tend to be expensive, but they often open for what is called "afternoon" sessions (from 7 to 10pm). Although discos charge entry fees, at an "afternoon" session the cost might be as low as 300 ptas. ($3), rising to 2,000 ptas. ($20) and beyond for a "night" session—that is, one beginning at 11:30pm and lasting until the early-morning hours. Therefore, go early, dance till 10pm, then go on to dinner (you'll be eating at the fashionable hour).

1. THE PERFORMING ARTS

Madrid is home to a wide variety of large-scale theaters, opera companies, and ballet groups. To discover the specific cultural events occurring during your visit, pick up a copy of the *Guía del Ocio* for 85 ptas. (85¢) at a city newsstand.

TICKETS   Admission to dramatic and musical events usually ranges in price from 700 to 1,800 ptas. ($7 to $18), with discounts of up to 50% on certain days of the week (usually Wednesday and early performances on Sunday). The concierge at most major hotels can usually get you tickets to specific concerts; however, he or she will charge a considerable markup. You'll save money if you go directly to the box office. If the event of your choice is sold out, you may be able to get tickets (with a considerable markup attached to them) at the **Galicia Localidades** at the Plaza del Carmen (tel. 531-27-32; Metro: Puerta del Sol). This agency also markets tickets to bullfights and sports events. It's open Tuesday through Sunday (except holidays) from 10am to 1pm and 4:30 to 7:30pm.

MAJOR PERFORMING ARTS COMPANIES

Madrid offers many different theater performances, which may be enjoyable for you only if your Spanish is fluent. If it isn't, check out *Guía del Ocio* for performances by English-speaking companies on tour from Britain, or select a concert or subtitled movie instead.

For those who speak Spanish, the **Companía Nacional de Nuevas Tendencias Escénicas** is an avant-garde troupe that performs new—often controversial—works by undiscovered writers. On the other hand, the **Companía Nacional de Teatro Clásico,** as its name suggests, is devoted to the Spanish classics, including works by the ever-popular Lope de Vega or Tirso de Molina.

Among dance companies, the national ballet of Spain—devoted exclusively to Spanish dance—is the **Ballet Nacional de España.** Their performances are always well attended. The national lyrical ballet company of the country is the **Ballet Lírico Nacional.**

Madrid's opera company is **Teatro de La Ópera,** and its

MAJOR CONCERT/PERFORMANCE HALLS

Auditorio Nacional de Música (tel. 337-01-00)
Auditorio del Real Conservatorio de Música (tel. 337-01-00)
Centro Cultural de la Villa (tel. 573-57-62)
Teatro Calderón (tel. 239-13-33)
Teatro de la Comedia (tel. 521-49-31)
Teatro Español (tel. 429-03-18)
Teatro María Guerrero (tel. 419-29-49)

---

symphony orchestra is the outstanding **Orquesta Sinfónica de Madrid.** The national orchestra of Spain—widely acclaimed on the continent—is the **Orquesta Nacional de España,** which pays homage to Spanish composers in particular.

MAJOR CONCERT HALLS & AUDITORIUMS

In addition to those listed below, there are another 30 formally designated concert halls in Madrid. Dozens of impromptu concerts—sometimes in churches—are given throughout the capital. And as part of their regular program, bars often feature music.

AUDITORIO NACIONAL DE MÚSICA, calle Príncipe de Vergara 136. Tel. 337-01-00.

The ultramodern home (1988) of both the National Orchestra and the National Chorus is considered a major addition to the competitive circles of classical music in Europe; it's sheathed in slabs of Spanish granite, marble, and limestone and capped with Iberian tiles. Standing just north of Madrid's Salamanca district, it's devoted exclusively to the performance of symphonic, choral, and chamber music. In addition to the *auditorio principal* (Hall A), whose capacity is almost 2,300, there's a hall for chamber music (Hall B) and a small auditorium for intimate concerts seating 250 spectators or fewer. The lofty space of the main hall is noteworthy for having absolutely no sound-absorbing materials of any kind (such as carpeting or curtains). This, and a smooth-finished wooden ceiling, give it a sound that experts say is distinctive. Metro: Cruz del Rayo.

Admission: Tickets, 1,300–3,200 ptas. ($13–$32).

AUDITORIO DEL REAL CONSERVATORIO DE MÚSICA, Plaza Isabel II. Tel. 337-01-00.

This is one of the home bases of the Spanish Philharmonic Orchestra, which presents its concerts between September and May. The space is sometimes lent to relatively unknown musical newcomers, who perform at admission-free concerts. Also presented are concerts by chamber-music ensembles visiting from abroad. Containing only about 400 seats, the hall is sometimes sold out long in advance, especially for such famous names as Plácido Domingo. Metro: Ópera.

Admission: Tickets, 1,100–5,000 ptas. ($11–$50).

FUNDACIÓN JUAN MARCH, calle Castelló 77. Tel. 435-42-40.

There are free weekly concerts at lunchtime here, although the advance schedule is notoriously difficult to predict. Metro: Núñez de Balboa.

Admission: Free.

AUDITORIO DEL PARQUE DE ATRACCIONES, Casa de Campo.

This theater's schedule might include everything from rock to the more highbrow warm-weather performances of visiting symphonic orchestras. It can hold 3,500 spectators and is in the most complete amusement park in Spain. Consult Galicia Localidades (see "Tickets" above) for information on events at the time of your visit.

Admission: Ticket prices depend on the event.

BALLET

CENTRO CULTURAL DE LA VILLA, Plaza de Colón. Tel. 573-57-62 or 275-60-80.

Ballet, Spanish style, is presented at this cultural center. Tickets go on sale five days before each event, and performances are usually presented at two different evening shows (8 and 10:30pm). Metro: Serrano or Colón.

Admission: Tickets, 900–3,500 ptas. ($9–$35), depending on the event.

THEATER

In addition to those listed below, there are at least 30 other theaters in Madrid—including one devoted almost entirely to performances of children's plays, the **Sala La Bicicleta,** in the Ciudad de los Niños in the Casa de Campo. Dozens of other plays are staged by nonprofessional groups in such places as churches. All that are open to the public will be listed in *Guía del Ocio.*

TEATRO CALDERÓN, calle Atocha 18. Tel. 239-13-33.

The largest theater in Madrid, the Calderón has a seating capacity for 1,700 spectators. It's known for its popular reviews, performances of popular Spanish plays, and flamenco. Metro: Tirso de Molina.

Admission: Tickets, 600–2,600 ptas. ($6–$26).

TEATRO DE LA COMEDIA, calle Príncipe 14. Tel. 521-49-31.

More prestigious is the home of the Compañía Nacional de Teatro Clásico. Here, more than anywhere else in Madrid, you're likely to see performances from the classic repertoire of great Spanish drama. Metro: Seville. Bus: 15, 20, or 150. Closed: Thurs and July to August.

Admission: Tickets, 800–1,200 ptas. ($8–$12).

TEATRO ESPAÑOL, calle Príncipe 25. Tel. 429-03-18.

This theater is funded by Madrid's municipal government. Its repertoire is a time-tested assortment of great and/or favorite Spanish plays. Metro: Sevilla.

Admission: Tickets, from 1,300 ptas. ($13).

TEATRO MARÍA GUERRERO, Tamayo y Baus 4. Tel. 410-29-49.

Also funded by the government, this theater works in cooperation with its sister theater, the Teatro Español (see above) to stage performances of works by such classic Spanish playwrights as García Lorca and Lope de Vega. The theater was named after a much-loved Spanish actress. Metro: Banco de España or Colón.

Admission: Tickets, 800–1,200 ptas. ($8–$12).

LOCAL CULTURAL ENTERTAINMENT
Flamenco

The strum of a guitar, the sound of hands clapping rhythmically, and you know that flamenco is about to start. Soon, colorfully dressed women, and occasionally men, flounce onto the stage to swirl in time with the music. The staccato beat of castanets and the tapping of heels make the rafters ring. Flamenco—the incomparable Spanish performing art.

Flamenco personifies the blood and guts of Andalusia, where it originated. Nowadays, gypsies have virtually taken over the art form, making flamenco part of their own folklore. Their fire and flair add another dimension to an already-passionate dance.

The songs are chanted in a passionate, tense tone, almost Arabic in origin. Age doesn't keep an artist off the center stage. Flamenco singers *(cantores)* seem to perform forever.

Many of the major flamenco clubs in Madrid are patronized almost exclusively by foreigners searching for a glimpse of an earlier era. For that privilege you'll pay dearly, but some visitors still consider it worth the expense.

CAFÉ DE CHINITAS, calle Torija 7. Tel. 248-51-35.

Here you'll find one of the swankiest and most expensive flamenco spots in town. In the old part of Madrid, between the Ópera and the Gran Vía, it features the dancer La Chunga and the guitarist Serranito. They join with about 40 other artists to make up the *cuadro* (an ensemble of flamenco singers and dancers). The show starts at about 11pm and runs until 2:30am. You can go for dinner and then stay for the show; a fixed-price dinner costs 9,000 ptas. ($90) and is served from 9:15pm to 12:30am. You sit in an elongated room at tables with fair visibility. The decor is amorphously elegant, sometimes in questionable taste, and doesn't quite live up to the promise of the building's exterior. Reservations in advance are recommended. Open Monday through Saturday throughout the year. Metro: Santo Domingo.

Admission (including first drink): 4,000 ptas. ($40).

CORRAL DE LA MORERÍA, calle de la Morería 17. Tel. 265-84-46.

This club is in the old town, the Morería—meaning a quarter where Moors reside. It sizzles more in its flamenco than in its skillet. Strolling performers, colorfully costumed, get the proceedings under way around 11pm, but they're there only to warm up the audience. A flamenco showcase follows, with at least 10 dancers who initiate the stage for the star, who always appears late and with an almost hyperbolic drama.

The management has devised ways of putting tables in the most unlikely places; reserve near the front and go early if you really want a ringside table. The show and an à la carte dinner, which is served any time after 9:30pm, costs 7,000 ptas. ($70). Open daily from 9pm to at least 3am. Metro: La Latina or Puerta del Sol.

Admission (including first drink): 2,900 ptas. ($29).

ZAMBRA, in the Hotel Wellington, Velázquez 8. Tel. 435-51-64.

Zambra is a subterranean supper club in the Hotel Wellington's premises. Some of the best flamenco singers and dancers of Spain appear here before enthusiastic audiences. The doors open Monday through Saturday at 9:30pm for dinner. The show is scheduled to begin at 10:15pm, although it's occasionally delayed, perhaps for dramatic effect. It ends around 3am. With dinner included, the show costs 7,000 ptas. ($70) per person. Reservations are a good idea. Metro: Velázquez.

Admission (including first drink): 3,000 ptas. ($30).

ARCO DE CUCHILLEROS, calle Cuchilleros 7. Tel. 266-58-67.

Lots of single men and women come here. All in all, it's fun to be here, if you don't take the proceedings too seriously. Open daily from 10:30pm to 2:30am. Metro: Puerta del Sol.

Admission (including first drink): 2,800 ptas. ($28).

Zarzuela

For an authentic Spanish experience, you can attend a *zarzuela,* a Spanish operetta with turn-of-the-century music, lots of Iberian panache, bright costumes, and what usually turns out to be a predictably sentimental plot with plenty of schmaltz. Sometimes the theaters sandwich flamenco numbers and musical revues between excerpts from the time-tested librettos.

TEATRO NUEVO APOLO, Plaza Tirso de Molina 1. Tel. 527-38-16.

This is one of the best places to view this type of musical theater. Housed within its imperially ornate walls is the headquarters of the renowned Antologia de la Zarzuela company. Metro: Tirso de Molina.

Admission: Tickets, usually 2,500 ptas. ($25), but varies.

TEATRO LÍRICO NACIONAL DE LA ZARZUELA, calle Jovellanos 4. Tel. 429-82-25.

Near the Plaza de la Cibeles, zarzuela is performed at this theater along with ballets and an occasional opera. Metro: Banco de España.

Admission: Ticket prices depend on the attraction.

2. THE CLUB & MUSIC SCENE

CABARET & SPECTACLES

Madrid's nightlife is no longer steeped in prudishness, as it was (at least officially) during the Franco era. You can now see glossy cabarets and shows with lots of nudity.

SCALA MELÍA CASTILLA, calle Capitán Haya 43 (entrance at Rosario Pino 7). Tel. 450-44-00.

Madrid's most visible manifestation of glossy cabaret serves dinners, but few of its patrons show up only for the food. The allure is the show—women, glitter, and the gloss of ballet, a gaggle of musicians, and a graceful duo of ice skaters. Sunday through Thursday there are shows at 9pm (for guests who want dinner) and at

10:30pm (for spectators who want only to drink and see the show). The show with dinner costs 8,000 ptas. ($80) per person; the late show costs 3,900 ptas. ($39) with a first drink included. Reservations are needed. Metro: Cuzco.

Admission (including first drink): 3,900 ptas. ($39).

LAS NOCHES DE CUPLE, calle de la Palma 51. Tel. 532-71-15.

More subtle, and sometimes vastly more poignant, is this nostalgic cabaret of a type that's fading fast. Its entrance is on a crowded street barely wide enough for the pedestrians and cars that compete for space. Like everything else in Madrid, the show begins very late and ends when dawn begins to trickle through the alleyways. Inside, a long room with a vaulted ceiling and a tiny stage are the forum for the still-charming former beauty Señora Olga Ramos, who conducts an evening of Iberian song. The charm of her all-Spanish act is increased by the discreet humor of an octogenarian accompanist with an ostrich-feather tiara and a fuchsia-colored boa. If you want dinner, it will cost 6,000 ptas. ($60). After your first drink (see below), each additional drink will cost around 1,000 ptas. ($10). Dinner is served between 9:30pm and midnight (don't go too early), and the show usually begins around midnight. Even if you don't speak Spanish, the kitsch, the unabashed camp, and the sometimes lavish sentimentality of the evening will give you something to remember. Open Monday through Saturday until 2:30am. Metro: Noviciado.

Admission: One-drink minimum at 2,800 ptas. ($28).

JAZZ CLUBS

CLAMORES, calle Alburquerque 14. Tel. 445-79-38.

Clamores is the largest jazz club in Madrid, accommodating some 450 people. With dozens of small tables and a huge bar in its somewhat dark interior, the club serves beer, whisky, wine, and the best Catalán champagne to go with the music of bands from Spain and the rest of Europe. The best jazz usually begins after 11:30pm. When music is playing, there's a 350-pta. ($3.50) surcharge on the price of each drink. Without the surcharge, beer costs 400 ptas. ($4); whisky with soda, around 800 ptas. ($8). Monday night is salsa night, and the place is transformed into something akin to what you'd see in Brazil. Open Sunday through Thursday from 3pm to 3am and on Friday and Saturday from 3pm to 4am. Metro: Bilbao.

Admission: Free.

WHISKY JAZZ, Diego de León 7. Tel. 561-11-65.

Whisky Jazz is a hideaway for jazz enthusiasts just a block away from the U.S. Embassy. If you arrive at the right time, you'll be presented with one of the best showcases of jazz in all of Spain. In the interior of the two-story brick building is a stairway leading to an open mezzanine that projects out over a downstairs bar. The walls and a glass case contain intriguing jazz memorabilia, including autographs and photos from its heyday in Chicago and New Orleans. The entrance price depends on which group is performing. Open Monday through Saturday from 9pm to 3:30am.

Admission: From 1,000 ptas. ($10). Metro: Núñez de Balboa.

CAFÉ CENTRAL, Plaza del Angel 10. Tel. 468-08-44.

Off the Plaza de Santa Ana, beside the famed Gran Hotel Victoria, the Café Central has a vaguely art deco interior with an unusual series of stained-glass windows. Many of the customers read newspapers and talk at the marble-top tables during the day, but the ambience is far more animated during the nightly jazz sessions. Open Monday through Thursday from 1pm to 1:30am and Friday through Sunday from 1pm to 2:30am; live jazz, daily from 10pm to 2am. Drinks begin at 350 ptas. ($3.50). Metro: Antón Martín.

Admission: Cover charge 450 ptas. ($4.50) Mon–Thurs, 550 ptas. ($5.50) Fri–Sun, but prices vary depending on the show.

CAFÉ BERLIN/OBA-OBA, calle Jacometrezo 4. Tel. 531-08-10 (for Café Berlin) or 531-06-40 (for Oba-Oba).

This establishment carries a double whammy thanks to its dual nature. In its basement lies Oba-Oba, whose specialty is Caribbean- and Brazilian-inspired jazz, to which an animated clientele dances the lambada, the salsa, and an occasional paso doble. If you haven't yet mastered these steps, don't be shy—there will almost certainly be someone there to teach you. Upstairs, the Café Berlin has live jazz concerts that pack spectators tightly inside whenever the music is playing. You'll pay around 700 ptas. ($7) for each drink. They're both open nightly from 6pm until 4 or 5am, sometimes even later. Here, like everywhere else, it's most crowded after 11pm. Metro: Callao.

Admission: Free.

CAFÉ POPULART, calle Huertas 22. Tel. 429-84-07.

This café is known in town for hiring exciting jazz groups that encourage the audience to dance. Run by an engaging entrepreneur named Arturo, it specializes in Brazilian, Afro-bass, reggae, and "new African wave" music. Patrons are charged 350 ptas. ($3.50) for a beer and 600 ptas. ($6) for a whisky with soda when live music isn't playing (when the music starts, prices of drinks nearly double). Open daily from 6pm to 4 or 5am. Metro: Antón Martín or Sevilla. Bus: 6 or 60.

Admission: Free.

DANCE CLUBS/DISCOS

Some discos are spectacular, complete with the latest sound systems and lasers. Others are little cellar dives where the owner plays records to special but fickle late-night claques who desert him the next day for a newer club. Be assured of one thing: It's a matter of *gato* pride that no club worth its entrance charge will be crowded and hot until at least 11pm.

BOCACCIO, Marqués de la Ensenada 16. Tel. 419-10-08.

Bocaccio is considered one of the most elegant discos in the Spanish capital, known for a clientele of show-biz entrepreneurs and an occasional mogul. This is no rock-and-roll palace, but rather a stylish triumph of art nouveau design. Tufted red velvet crescent-shaped banquettes seat attractive young and older people. The regally attired bartenders, who become part of the show, charge 900 ptas. ($9) and up for a whisky and soda. Open Sunday through Thursday from 7 to 10pm and 11:30pm to 4:30am, and on Friday and Saturday from 7 to 10pm and 11:30pm to 5am.

Admission: 1,800 ptas. ($18).

JOY ESLAVA, calle de Arenal 11. Tel. 266-37-33.

Joy Eslava is housed in an old theater whose walls have been painted almost entirely black. It's filled with up-to-date lighting and sound equipment and a prominent array of bars, with imitation lasers that shoot bursts of light into almost every corner. If you don't feel like dancing, comfortable chaises longues are scattered throughout the establishment. Libations begin at 1,200 ptas. ($12) each. Open daily from 11:30pm to 7am (unless it happens to be closed for a private party). Metro: Puerta del Sol or Ópera.

Admission: 2,000 ptas. ($20).

MAU-MAU, Padre Damian 23. Tel. 457-94-23.

Mau-Mau is in the Eurobuilding complex, an appropriately glamorous location for one of the most glamorous clienteles of Madrid. You can order a whisky and soda for 1,800–2,300 ptas. ($18–$23), but the preferred drink on many nights is a bottle of champagne. Anyone with hopes of being included in the *tout Madrid* category will eventually make his or her appearance in Mau-Mau's gloriously luxurious interior. Management requires that men wear jackets, except on Sunday and between July 1 and late September. Open Monday through Saturday from midnight to 5am. Metro: Colombia.

Admission: One-drink minimum.

3. THE BAR SCENE

PUBS & BARS

MR. PICKWICK'S, Marqués de Urquijo 48, at the corner of paseo del Pintor Rosales. Tel. 559-51-85.

For homesick English expatriates, no other establishment in Madrid better captures the pub atmosphere than Mr. Pickwick's, a 10-minute walk from the Plaza de España. Although only a few of the staff speak fluent English, the decor includes everything you might have expected in London: framed prints of Dickens characters, brass hunting horns, and pewter and ceramic beer mugs. Loners can drink at the bar, or you can sit at one of the small tables, sinking into the soft sofas and armchairs. The pub is open daily from 6pm to 1am. Beer begins at 350 ptas. ($3.50); whisky, at 700 ptas. ($7). Metro: Argüelles.

OLIVER PIANO BAR, calle Almirante 12. Tel. 521-73-79.

This bar attracts a youthful, sophisticated crowd in an atmosphere that resembles a private drawing room or a members-only club. The street-floor room evokes a stage setting by one of London's gifted designers. There's a pastoral mural on the ceiling, a formal fireplace, and recessed alcoves containing shelves of books. On the walls hang old paintings and engravings. The color scheme is aged Mediterranean: faded red, sienna, bronze, and gold. At the bottom of a winding staircase is a lower level ringed with couches. Often someone plays the piano softly in the background. You pay 750 ptas. ($7.50) for a whisky with soda and 450 ptas. ($4.50) for a beer at a table; it's slightly less at the stand-up bar. Music begins most evenings about 30 minutes after midnight. Open daily from 4pm to 6am. Metro: Chueca.

BAR COCK, calle de la Reina 16. Tel. 532-28-26.

The name comes from the word *cocktail*. Cock attracts some of the most visible artists, actors, models, and filmmakers in Madrid, including award-winning Spanish director Almodovar, who is rumored to be here frequently. The decoration is elaborately antique, perhaps in deliberate contrast to its clientele. Drinks start at 650 ptas. ($6.50). Open Monday through Saturday from 9pm to 3am; closed December 24–31. Metro: Gran Vía.

VIVA MADRID, calle Manuel Fernández y Gonzalez 7. Tel. 410-55-35.

With its lushly ornate tiled facade and the animated crowd that sometimes spills out onto the sidewalk during peak hours, Viva Madrid is hard to resist. It sits near the Plaza Santa Ana in a neighborhood of narrow streets loaded with marauding *gatos* searching for friendship, love, and fulfillment (sometimes successfully). A congenial mixture of students, artists, foreign tourists, and visiting Yanks crams into its turn-of-the-century interior, where tilework murals and carved animals contribute an undeniable charm. Beer begins at 400 ptas. ($4); drinks, at 800 ptas. ($8). Open Sunday through Friday from noon to 1am and on Saturday from noon to 2am. Metro: Antón Martín.

BALNEARIO, Juan Ramón Jiménez, 37. Tel. 458-24-20.

Balneario serves gratifyingly potent drinks in an enclave of fresh flowers, white marble, and the kind of stone bathtub that might have been used by Josephine Bonaparte. Near the Chamartín station in one of the capital's northern edges, it's one of the most stylish and upmarket bars in Madrid. Many guests precede a meal at the restaurant El Cabo Mayor (see Chapter 5) with a drink here; the two establishments share a well-tended garden a few steps away. Tapas such as endive with smoked salmon, asparagus mousse, and anchovies with avocadoes cost 500–1,500 ptas. ($5–$15). Drinks run 500–900 ptas. ($5–$9). Open Monday through Friday from noon to 2:30am and on Saturday from noon to 3am. Metro: Cuzco.

MARAVILLAS NEW AGE CENTER, calle San Vicente Ferrer 33. Tel. 532-79-87.

In this new-wave bar, youthful clients in costumes bordering on punk style listen to occasional live concerts of folk music, pop music, or jazz. The schedule is unpredictable. Drinks cost around 650 ptas. ($6.50). Open daily from 10pm to 5:30am. Metro: Tribunal.

BALMORAL, calle Hermosilla 10. Tel. 431-41-33.

Balmoral is unashamedly Anglo-Saxon. Its exposed wood and comfortable chairs evoke something you'd expect to find in London. Its clientele tends toward journalists, politicians, army brass, owners of large estates, bankers, diplomats, and an occasional literary star. *Newsweek* once dubbed it "one of the best bars in the world." Beer costs around 400 ptas. ($4); whisky with soda, around 800 ptas. ($8). No food, other than tapas, is served. Open daily from 7:30pm to 2am. Metro: Serrano.

HISPANO, paseo de la Castellana 78. Tel. 411-48-76.

Hispano is a popular place. Every day, especially at the end of a workday, its crowded clientele includes everyone from officeworkers to entrepreneurs. Open daily from 7:30pm to 3am. Drinks run 800 ptas. ($8). Metro: Nuevos Ministerios.

LOS GABRIELES, calle Echegaray 17. Tel. 429-62-61.

Located in the heart of one of Madrid's most visible warrens of narrow streets, in a district which pulsates with after-dark nightlife options, this historic bar served throughout most of the 19th century as a sales outlet for a Spanish wine merchant. In the 1980s its two rooms were transformed into a bar and café, where you can admire lavishly tiled walls with detailed scenes of courtiers, dancers, and Andalusian maidens peering from behind *mantillas* and fans. Open daily from 1pm to 2:30am. Drinks go for 250–600 ptas. ($2.50–$6). Metro: Tirso de Molina.

GAY BARS

Spain has witnessed an explosion of gay life since the 1970s, perhaps as a reaction against the omnipresent pressures of machismo and traditional models of femininity. Many gay Spaniards agree, however, that the ghetto-style segregation of gay men from gay women simply doesn't apply with the rigid boundaries you might have expected. In the most sophisticated clubs, people of all sexual orientations mix comfortably together.

HANOI, calle Hortaleza 81. Tel. 319-66-72.

Hanoi is a stylish and minimalist assemblage of stainless steel, curving lines, and space-age angles. Its clientele is fun, young, attractive, and articulate. The mood is amusedly permissive, and the crowd blends comfortably with both heterosexual and homosexual expressions. There's a small restaurant in the rear, a bevy of male and female models who seem to be in constant attendance, eight video screens showing adventure shows from some long-defunct TV series, and up-to-date music. No matter who you are, you'll probably have fun in Hanoi. Open daily from 9:30pm to 3:30am, but it becomes more densely populated with gay men and women after 1am. Drinks begin at 800 ptas. ($8). Metro: Alonso Martínez.

NO SÉ LOS DIGAS A NADIE, calle Ventura de la Vega 7. Tel. 420-29-80.

This establishment defines itself as a women's entertainment center, although it seems to attract an almost equal number of men to its two floors hidden behind a black garage door on this street of budget restaurants. Inside there's an art gallery, a bar/café, a staff with information on women's activities in Madrid, and live or recorded music every evening after 11pm. Open Sunday through Wednesday from 7pm to 1:30am and Thursday through Saturday from 7pm to 2:30am. Drinks cost about 700 ptas. ($7). Metro: Puerta del Sol.

BLACK & WHITE, calle Gravina at the corner of Libertad. Tel. 532-71-63.

Black & White lies on a not-very-safe street in the center of town. A guard will open the door to a large room painted, as its name implies, in black and white. There's a disco in the basement. The street-level bar, however, is the premier gathering spot for gay men in Madrid. Old movies are shown against one wall, and all kinds of men, from many different worlds of Madrid, are likely to come in. Open daily from 8pm to 2 or 4am. Drinks run 450 ptas. ($4.50). Metro: Chueca.

CAFÉ FIGUEROA, Augusto Figueroa 17, at the corner of Hortaleza. Tel. 521-16-73.

This turn-of-the-century café attracts a diverse clientele, including a large number of gay men and women. It's one of the city's most popular gathering spots for drinks and conversations. Open Monday through Thursday from 3pm to 1:30am, on Friday and Saturday from 3pm to 2:30am, and on Sunday from 4pm to 1:30am. Drinks cost 475 ptas. ($4.75); beer, 300 ptas. ($3). Metro: Chueca.

CRUISING, Perez Galdos 5. Tel. 521-51-43.

This major gay bar has a vaguely permissive atmosphere, as its name suggests. In the heart of Chueca, it doesn't get lively until late at night. Open daily from 7:30pm to 3:30am. Drinks go for 500 ptas. ($5). Metro: Chueca.

DUPLEX, calle Hortaleza 64. Tel. 531-37-92.

Duplex attracts a young crowd of disco-loving gays, both men and women. It has a modern decor, a disco with recent and very danceable music, and an amply stocked bar. There's no cover charge, and beer costs 400 ptas. ($4); drinks, 800 ptas. ($8). Open daily from 10pm to 5am. Metro: Chueca.

CAVE CRAWLING

To capture a peculiar Madrid *joie de vivre* of the 18th century, visit some *mesones* and *cuevas,* many found in the so-called *barrios bajos*. From the Plaza Mayor, walk down calle Arco de Cuchilleros until you find a gypsylike café that fits your fancy. Young people love to meet in the taverns and caves of Old Madrid for communal drinking and songfests. The sangría flows freely, the atmosphere is charged, the room usually packed; the sound of guitars wafts into the night air. Sometimes you'll see a strolling band of singing students (*tuna*) go from bar to bar, colorfully attired, with ribbons fluttering from their outfits.

MESÓN DE LA GUITARRA, Cava de San Miguel 13. Tel. 248-95-31.

My favorite *cueva* in the area, Mesón de la Guitarra is loud and exciting any night of the week, and as warmly earthy as anything you'll find in Madrid. The decor combines terra-cotta floors, antique brick walls, hundreds of sangría pitchers clustered above the bar, murals of gluttons, old rifles, and faded bullfighting posters. Like most things in Madrid, the place doesn't get rolling until around 10:30pm, although you can stop in for a drink and tapas earlier. Don't be afraid to start singing an American song if it has a fast rhythm—60 people will join in, even if they don't know the words. Open daily from 6:30pm to 1:30am. Beer goes for 275 ptas. ($2.75); wine, 100 ptas. ($1); tapas, 500–700 ptas. ($5–$7). Metro: Puerta del Sol or Ópera.

MESÓN AUSTRIAS, Cava de San Miguel 11.

One of several tapas bars just behind the Plaza Mayor, Mesón Austrias has a number of sit-down cells stretching off toward a second bar in the rear. Most customers prefer to stand near the front entrance. In winter the favorite spot is by the open fireplace in the front room, when a pitcher of sangría is the thing to order. There's often accordion music at night. Open daily from 6:30pm to 1:30am. Beer costs 275 ptas. ($2.75); a pitcher of sangría, 1,000 ptas. ($10); tapas, from 500 ptas. ($5). Metro: Puerta del Sol or Ópera.

MESÓN DEL CHAMPIÑON, Cava de San Miguel 17. Tel. 248-67-90.

The barmen keep a brimming bucket of sangría behind the long stand-up bar as a thirst-quencher for the many people who crowd in. The name of the establishment translates as "mushroom," and that's what you see delineated in various sizes along sections of the vaulted ceilings. A more appetizing way to experience a *champiñon* is to order a *ración* of grilled, stuffed, and salted mushrooms, served with toothpicks. A portion costs 450 ptas. ($4.50) at the bar, and 500 ptas. ($5) at a table. The pair of tiny, slightly dank rooms in the back is where Spanish families jam in for the organ music played by a stalwart musician performing in one corner. Sangría runs 1,000 ptas. ($10). Open daily from 1:30pm to 6am. Metro: Puerta del Sol, Ópera, or La Latina.

SESAMO, calle Príncipe 7. Tel. 429-65-24.

Despite its rustic and bohemian appearance (or perhaps because of it), "Sesame" has hosted Truman Capote and many other celebrated people. Styles and cultural heroes rise and fall, but Sesamo seems to go on forever. Its two cellar rooms are reached via a long flight of steps. Downstairs, you'll find seats gathered around tiny tables. Guests have been known to bring their guitars or banjos, spontaneously singing folk songs, laments of love, or political protests. When no one in the audience is particularly musical, management provides a piano player. Like virtually everything else in Madrid, the action here doesn't get going until around 11pm. If you're with a group, it's customary to order a pitcher of sangría for 1,000 ptas. ($10). Open daily from 6pm to 2am. Metro: Sevilla or Puerta del Sol.

---

4. MORE ENTERTAINMENT

MOVIES & FILMS Spanish film director José Luís Garci has written that no other city in the world treats films and the pronouncements of publicity agents with greater respect than Madrid. Recent cinematic releases from Paris, New York, Rome, and Hollywood come quickly to Madrid, where an avid audience often waits in long lines for tickets. Most foreign films are dubbed into Spanish, unless they're indicated as *V.O.* (original version).

The premier theaters of the city are the enormous, slightly faded movie palaces of the Gran Vía, whose huge movie marquees announce in lurid colors whichever romantic or adventure *espectáculo* happens to be playing at the moment.

Madrid boasts at least 90 legitimate movie houses (many of which have several theaters under one roof), and many others running pictures for adults only. All listings are in the *Guía del Ocio*, in the *Guía de Diario 16* (also available at newsstands), or in the film listings of Madrileño newspapers.

If you want to see a film while in Madrid, one of the best places is **Alphaville,** with four different theaters at calle Martín de los Héroes 14 (tel. 248-72-33). It shows English-language films with Spanish subtitles. Metro: Plaza de España.

The movie houses on the Gran Vía, dear to the heart of thousands of Madrileños simply because of their endurance power and their enormous marquees, include the **Rex,** Gran Vía 45 (tel. 247-12-37);

the **Palacio de la Música,** Gran Vía 35 (tel. 521-62-09); and the **Coliseum,** Gran Vía 78 (tel. 217-66-12). All are reached by taking the Metro to Gran Vía.

For classic revivals and foreign films, check out the listings at Filmoteca in the **Cine Doré,** calle Santa Isabel 3 (tel. 369-11-25). Movies here tend to be shown in their original language. Tickets cost around 250 ptas. ($2.50). There's a bar and a simple restaurant. Metro: Antón Martín.

GAMBLING CASINOS The **Casino Gran Madrid** is in Torrelodones at Km 28.3 on the N-VI heading toward La Coruña (tel. 856-11-00). Even nongamblers sometimes make the trek here from the capital; the casino's many entertainment facilities are considered by some to be the most exciting thing around. Its scattered attractions include two restaurants, four bars, and a nightclub. The casino is open Sunday through Thursday from 5pm to 4am, and on Friday, Saturday, and holiday evenings from 5pm to 5am. For an entrance fee of 700 ptas. ($7), you can sample the action in the gaming rooms, including French and American roulette, blackjack, punto y banco, baccarat, and chemin de fer.

An à la carte restaurant in the French Gaming Room offers an international cuisine, with dinners beginning at 8,000 ptas. ($80). A buffet in the American Gaming Room will cost around 2,800 ptas. ($28). The restaurants are open from 9:30pm to 2am.

The casino is about 17 miles northwest of Madrid, along the Madrid–La Coruña N-VI highway. If you don't feel like driving, the casino has buses that depart from Plaza de España 6 every afternoon and evening at 4:30, 6, 7:30, 9, and 11:30pm. Note that between October and June men must wear jackets and ties; jeans and tennis shoes are forbidden in any season. To enter, European visitors must present an identity card, and non-European visitors must present a passport.

EASY EXCURSIONS FROM MADRID

1. TOLEDO
2. ARANJUEZ
3. SAN LORENZO DE EL ESCORIAL
4. SEGOVIA

Some of the most interesting and varied scenery and attractions in Europe lie in the satellite cities and towns ringing Madrid. These include Toledo with its El Greco masterpieces, a monastery considered the eighth wonder of the world (El Escorial), castles that "float" in the clouds (Segovia), and palaces of the Bourbon dynasty at La Granja.

If your time is short, go at least to Toledo, which captures the ages of Spain in miniature. Many tourists combine a tour of Toledo with a stopover at the royal palace of Aranjuez.

1. TOLEDO

42 miles SW of Madrid, 85 miles SE of Ávila

GETTING THERE By Train RENFE trains run frequently every day. Those departing Madrid's Atocha railway station for Toledo run from 8:15am to 8:55pm; those leaving Toledo for Madrid run daily from 6:25am to 9:50pm. Travel time is approximately 90 minutes. For train information in Madrid, call 522-05-18; in Toledo, call 22-12-71.

By Bus Buses are faster and more direct than trains. Galiano Continental (tel. 22-29-61) runs about 12 different buses daily. They depart every half hour from 6:30am to 10pm from the lower level of Estación Sur de Autobuses, Canarías 17 (Metro: Palos de Moguer). Buses take about 75 minutes to complete the trip between Madrid and Toledo, and are usually marked "Santa Barbara" or "Poligano." They'll deposit you in Toledo's central square, the Plaza de Zocodover.

By Car Exit Madrid via the Puerta del Toledo on the N-401 south.

ESSENTIALS Toledo's **telephone area code** is 925. The **Tourist Information Office** is at Puerta Nueva de Bisagra (tel. 925/22-08-43).

The ancient capital of Spain looms on the horizon like an El Greco painting, seemingly undisturbed by the ages. The See of the

Primate of Spain, the ecclesiastical center of the country, Toledo is medieval but well preserved. The Tagus River loops around the granite promontory on which Toledo rests, surrounding the Imperial City on three sides like a snake.

Toledan steel, known as early as the 1st century B.C., has sliced its name down through the ages. Many a Mexican or Peruvian—if he had lived—could attest to the deadly accuracy of a Toledan sword. But except for its steel and damascene work, the lack of major industrial activity has kept Toledo a virtual museum. Many of its buildings are intact, having survived countless battles, the most recent being the bloody fighting the city witnessed in the Spanish Civil War. It's not uncommon for mansions to preserve their original coats-of-arms in their facades.

The natural fortress that is Toledo is a labyrinth of narrow and precipitous streets, decaying palaces, towers, and squares—all of them tourist-trodden. The Spanish government has seen fit to preserve all of Toledo as a "national monument." One critic labeled the entire city "a gallery of art," with every style represented from Romanesque to Moorish to Gothic (best exemplified by the cathedral) to Renaissance.

Essentially, Toledo is a blending of the widely diverse cultures that made Spain what it is today: Roman, Visigothic, Moorish, Jewish, and Christian. Perhaps for that reason, Tirso de Molina, the 17th-century dramatist, called Toledo "the heart of Spain." He named three of his dramas *Los Cigarrales de Toledo,* which brings us to a most important suggestion: Before you leave the Imperial City, you should—preferably in the late afternoon—traverse the **carretera de Circunvalación,** that most scenic of roads across the left bank of the Tagus. Along the slopes of the hills, you'll find the *cigarrales,* the rustic houses. From this side of the river, you can obtain the best panorama, and see the city in perspective as El Greco did. With luck, you'll be perched on some belvedere as the sun goes down. Then you'll know why Toledo's sunsets are called violet.

WHAT TO SEE & DO

You can see all the major sightseeing attractions in one day, provided you arrive early and stay late.

CATHEDRAL OF TOLEDO, Arco de Palacio. Tel. 22-22-41.

Built at the flowering peak of the Gothic era of architecture, the cathedral, which stands directly east of the Plaza del Ayuntamiento in the heart of Toledo, is one of the greatest in Europe. It was erected principally between the years 1226 and 1493, although there have been later additions. The monument is a bastion of Christian architecture, but a great deal of the actual construction work was carried out by the Moors, master builders themselves.

The cathedral witnessed many prime moments in Spanish history—such as a proclamation naming "Juana la Loca" (the insane daughter of Isabella I) and her husband, Philip the Handsome, heirs to the throne of Spain.

Inside, the Transparente—the altar completed in 1732 by Narciso Tome—is a landmark in European architecture. Lit by a "hole" cut through the ceiling, this production includes angels on fluffy clouds, a polychrome *Last Supper,* and a Madonna winging her way to heaven.

Dating from the 16th century, the iron gate of the cathedral is in

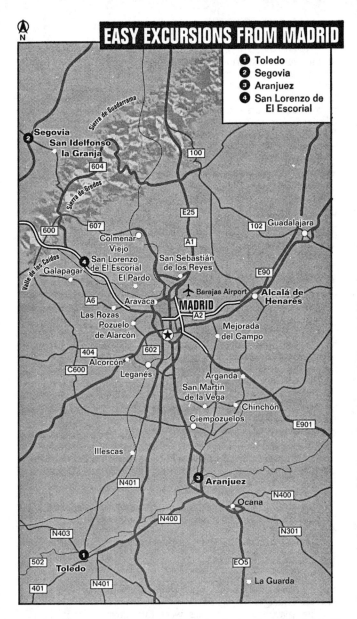

the plateresque style. Works of art include *The Twelve Apostles* by El Greco and paintings by Velázquez, Goya, Morales, and van Dyck. El Greco's first painting in Toledo was commissioned by the cathedral. Called *El Expolio*, it created a furor when the devout saw the vivid coloring of Christ's garments. The artist was even hauled into the courts. Many elaborately sculpted tombs of both the nobility and ecclesiastical hierarchy are sheltered inside.

Don't fail to visit the Gothic cloister, the Capilla Mayor, and the

Renaissance-style Choir Room (elaborate wood carvings), and you should see the rose windows, preferably near sunset. In the Treasure Room is a 500-pound monstrance, dating from the 16th century and said to have been made, in part, from gold that Columbus brought back from the New World. To celebrate Corpus festivities, the monstrance is carried through the streets of Toledo. The Mozarabic Chapel dates from the 16th century and contains paintings by Juan de Borgoña (a mass using Mozarabic liturgy is still conducted here).

Admission: Cathedral, free; Treasure Room, 350 ptas. ($3.50).
Open: Daily 10:30am–1pm and 4–6pm. **Bus:** 5 or 6.

MUSEO DE SANTA CRUZ, calle de Miguel Cervantes. Tel. 22-14-02.

Dating from the 16th century and built in the form of a Greek cross, the plateresque hospice has been turned into a museum of fine arts and archeology. As a hospital, it was originally founded by Cardinal Mendoza. It's of such beautiful construction—especially its paneled ceilings—that it's a question of the "frame" competing with the pictures inside.

In the Fine Arts Museum are 18 paintings by El Greco (*The Burial of Count Orgaz* is a copy of his masterpiece). *The Assumption of the Virgin* is his most important canvas here. Other works are by Ribera and Goya. Flemish tapestries, antique furnishings, and jewelry round out the exhibit.

In the Archeological Museum the past ages of Toledo are peeled away: prehistoric, Iberian, Roman (note the mosaics), Moorish, Visigothic, and Gothic. The museum is an easy walk from the Plaza de Zocodover in the very heart of Toledo.

Admission: 200 ptas. ($2).
Open: Tues–Sat 10am–6:30pm, Sun–Mon 10am–2pm. **Bus:** 5 or 6. **Directions:** Pass beneath granite archways piercing eastern edge of the Plaza de Zocodover and walk about one block.

CASA Y MUSEO DEL GRECO, calle de Samuel Leví. Tel. 22-40-46.

The famous painter Domenicos Theotocópoulos, called El Greco because he was born in Crete, arrived in Toledo in 1577 and lived here with Doña Jerónima, a noted beauty (either his wife or mistress) until his death in 1614. His living quarters stood in the *antiguo barrio judío,* or the old Jewish quarter, on calle de Samuel Leví in the heart of Toledo. It is believed that the painter moved to this site in 1585.

Samuel Ha-Leví, chancellor of the exchequer to Pedro the Cruel, is said to have built a series of houses here, forming a complex in the 14th century. These little interconnected houses were often called "apartments." Ha-Leví had subterranean passages dug to hide his treasury; and a Don Enrique de Villena, it is said, practiced alchemy in these underground cellars.

The apartments or houses were torn down in the late 19th century, but many people in Toledo say El Greco's house or apartment was rescued. Perhaps it was, but critics aren't sure. What emerged, nevertheless, was identified for visitors as "Casa del Greco." Eventually a neighboring house was incorporated to shelter a museum with 19 pictures by El Greco.

Visitors are admitted into the studio of El Greco, which contains a painting by the artist. Especially interesting are the garden and kitchen.

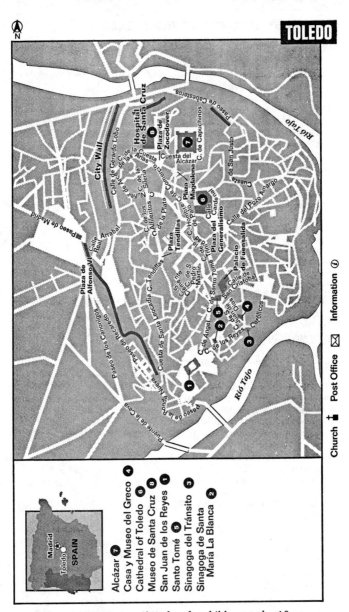

TOLEDO

Church ✝ Post Office ☒ Information ⊙

Alcázar ❼
Casa y Museo del Greco ❹
Cathedral of Toledo ❻
Museo de Santa Cruz ❽
San Juan de los Reyes ❶
Santo Tomé ❺
Sinagoga del Tránsito ❸
Sinagoga de Santa María La Blanca ❷

Admission: 200 ptas. ($2), free for children under 10.
Open: Tues–Sat 10am–2pm and 4–6pm, Sun 10am–2pm. **Bus:** 5 or 6.

SAN JUAN DE LOS REYES, calle de los Reyes Católicos 17. Tel. 22-38-02.

This church was founded by King Ferdinand and Queen Isabella to commemorate their triumph over the Portuguese at Toro in 1476. Its construction was started in 1477, according to the plans of architect Juan Guas. It was finished, together with the splendid cloisters, in 1504, dedicated to St. John the Evangelist, and used, from the very beginning, by the Franciscan Friars. It's a perfect example of Gothic-Spanish-Flemish style.

San Juan de los Reyes was restored after being damaged in the invasion of Napoleon and abandoned in 1835. Actually, the national monument has been entrusted again to the Franciscans since 1954.

Admission: 100 ptas. ($1), free for children under 9.
Open: Daily 10am–1:45pm and 3:30–6pm. **Bus:** 5 or 6.

SANTO TOMÉ—EXPOSICIÓN ANEXA, Plaza del Conde 2, calle de Santo Tomé. Tel. 21-02-09.

Except for its mudéjar tower, this little 14th-century chapel is rather unprepossessing. But by some strange twist it was given the honor of exhibiting El Greco's masterpiece, *The Burial of Count Orgaz.* Long acclaimed for its composition, the painting is a curious work in its blending of realism with mysticism.

Admission: 100 ptas. ($1).
Open: Daily 10am–1:45pm and 3:30–6:45pm. **Closed:** Jan 1, Dec 25.

ALCÁZAR, Plaza de Zocodover. Tel. 21-39-61.

The characteristic landmark dominating the skyline of Toledo is the Alcázar, in the very center of the city. It attracted worldwide attention during the siege of the city in 1936, when Nationalists held the fortress for 70 days until relief troops could respond to their plea for help, arriving on September 27, 1936.

The most famous event surrounding that battle was a telephone call the Republicans placed to the Nationalist leader inside. He was informed that his son was being held captive and would be executed if the Alcázar were not surrendered. He refused to comply with their demands and his son was sacrificed.

The Alcázar was destroyed. The one standing in its place today is a reconstruction that houses an Army Museum. A monument out front is dedicated to the heroes of that 1936 siege.

Admission: 125 ptas. ($1.25), free for children under 9.
Open: Tues–Sun 9:30am–1:30pm and 4–6:30pm. **Bus:** 5 or 6.

SINAGOGA DEL TRÁNSITO, calle de Samuel Leví. Tel. 22-36-65.

Down the street from El Greco's museum is the once-important place of worship for the large Jewish population that used to inhabit the city, living peacefully with both Christians and Arabs. This 14th-century building is noted for its superb stucco and its Hebrew inscriptions. There are some psalms along the top of the walls and on the east wall a poetic description of the temple. The construction of the synagogue was ordered by Don Samuel Ha-Leví, the chancellor of the exchequer to King Pedro el Cruel (Peter the Cruel). The name of the king appears clearly in a frame in the Hebrew inscription.

The synagogue is the most important part of the **Museo Sefardi,** which was inaugurated in 1971 and contains tombstones with Hebrew epigraphy dating from before 1492 and other art works.

Admission: 200 ptas. ($2).
Open: Tues–Sat 10am–2pm and 4–6pm, Sun 10am–2pm. **Bus:** 5 or 6.

SINAGOGA DE SANTA MARÍA LA BLANCA, calle de los Reyes Católicos. Tel. 22-84-29.

In the late 12th century, the Jews of Toledo erected an important synagogue in the *almohade* style, which employs graceful horseshoe arches and ornamental horizontal moldings. Although by the early 15th century it had been converted into a Christian church, much of the original remains, including the five naves and elaborate Mudéjar decorations—mosquelike in their effect. The synagogue lies on the western edge of the city, midway between the El Greco museum and San Juan de los Reyes.

Admission: 75 ptas. (75¢).

Open: Apr–Sept, daily 10am–2pm and 3:30–7pm; Oct–Mar, daily 10am–2pm and 3:30–6pm. **Bus:** 5 or 6.

HOSPITAL DE TAVERA, paseo de Madrid. Tel. 22-04-51.

This 16th-century Greco-Roman palace north of the medieval ramparts of Toledo was originally built by Cardinal Tavera; it now houses a spectacular art collection. Titian's portrait of Charles V hangs in the banqueting hall, and the museum owns five paintings by El Greco: *The Holy Family, The Baptism of Christ,* and portraits of St. Francis, St. Peter, and Cardinal Tavera. Ribera's *The Bearded Woman* also attracts many. The collection of books in the library is priceless. In the nearby church is the mausoleum of Cardinal Tavera, designed by Alonso Berruguete.

Admission: 250 ptas. ($2.50).

Open: Daily 10:30am–1:30pm and 3:30–6pm.

WHERE TO STAY

Very Expensive

PARADOR DE TURISMO DE TOLEDO, Cerro del Emperador, 45000 Toledo. Tel. 925/22-18-50. Fax 925/22-51-66. 76 rms. MINIBAR TV TEL **Directions:** Drive across Puente San Martín and head south for 2½ miles (4km).

$ Rates: 10,300 ptas. ($103) single; 15,000 ptas. ($150) double. Breakfast 1,200 ptas. ($12) extra. AE, DC, MC, V. **Parking:** Free.

Make reservations well in advance for this parador, built on the ridge of a rugged hill where El Greco is said to have painted the *View of Toledo*. The main living room/lounge has fine furniture—old chests, brown-leather chairs, heavy tables—and leads to a sunny terrace overlooking the city. On chilly nights you can sit by the fireplace. A stairway and balcony lead to dark oak-paneled doors opening onto the bedrooms, the most luxurious in all of Toledo. Spacious and beautifully furnished, they contain reproductions of regional antique pieces.

Dining/Entertainment: See restaurant recommendation in "Where to Dine," below.

Services: Room service, laundry/valet.

Facilities: Outdoor swimming pool.

Expensive

HOSTAL DEL CARDENAL, paseo de Recaredo 24, 45005 Toledo. Tel. 925/22-49-00. Fax 925/22-29-91. 27 rms, 2 suites. A/C TEL **Bus:** 2 from the rail station.

$ Rates: 6,000 ptas. ($60) single; 9,000 ptas. ($90) double; from

13,000 ptas. ($130) suite. Breakfast 500 ptas. ($5) extra. AE, DC, MC, V.

The entrance to this unusual hotel is set into the stone fortifications of the ancient city walls, a few steps from the Bisagra Gate. Inside you'll find flagstone walkways, Moorish fountains, rose gardens, and cascading vines. To reach the hotel you must climb a series of terraces to the top of the crenellated walls of the ancient fortress. There, grandly symmetrical and very imposing, is the former residence of the 18th-century cardinal of Toledo, Señor Lorenzana. The establishment has tiled walls, long, narrow salons, dignified Spanish furniture, and a smattering of antiques.

HOTEL MARIA CRISTINA, Marqués de Mendigorría 1, 45003 Toledo. Tel. 925/21-32-02. Fax 925/21-69-54. 60 rms, 3 suites. A/C TV TEL
$ Rates: 6,680 ptas. ($66.80) single; 9,650 ptas. ($96.50) double; from 13,800 ptas. ($138) suite. Breakfast 600 ptas. ($6) extra. AE, DC, MC, V. **Parking:** 600 ptas. ($6).

Located adjacent to the historic Hospital de Tavera, near the northern perimeter of the old town, this stone-sided, awning-fronted hotel resembles a palatial home in the country. Originally built as a convent, and later used as a hospital, it was transformed into this comfortably stable hotel in the early 1980s. Sprawling, historic, and generously proportioned, it contains clean and amply sized bedrooms, each attractively but simply furnished.

Dining/Entertainment: On site is the very large and well-recommended restaurant El Abside, where fixed-price lunches and dinners begin at 2,800 ptas. ($28). There's also a bar.

Services: 24-hour room service, laundry, concierge, babysitting.
Facilities: Tennis courts.

Moderate

HOTEL CARLOS V, Trastamara 1, 45001 Toledo. Tel. 925/ 22-21-00. Fax 095/22-21-05. 69 rms (all with bath). A/C TEL **Bus:** 5 or 6.
$ Rates: 5,200 ptas. ($52) single; 8,500 ptas. ($85) double. Breakfast 700 ptas. ($7) extra. AE, DC, MC, V.

This old favorite midway between the Alcázar and the cathedral has a handsome, albeit somber, exterior. It looks more expensive than it is. The rooms are well appointed and the service is fine. Dining is available; lunch or dinner costs 2,200 ptas. ($22).

HOTEL RESIDENCIA ALFONSO VI, General Moscardó, 45001 Toledo. Tel. 925/22-26-00. Fax 925/21-44-58. 88 rms (all with bath). A/C TV TEL **Bus:** 5 or 6.
$ Rates: 5,500 ptas. ($55) single; 8,500 ptas. ($85) double. Breakfast 600 ptas. ($6) extra. AE, DC, MC, V.

Although built in the early 1970s, this hotel has been kept up-to-date. It sits near a great concentration of souvenir shops in the center of the old city, at the southern perimeter of the Alcázar. Inside you'll discover a high-ceilinged, marble-trimmed decor with a scattering of Iberian artifacts, copies of Spanish provincial furniture, and dozens of leather armchairs. You can dine in the stone-floored dining room, where fixed-price meals are 2,200 ptas. ($22).

Inexpensive

HOTEL IMPERIO, Cadenea 5, 45001 Toledo. Tel. 925/22-76-50. Fax 925/25-31-83. 21 rms (all with bath). A/C TEL
$ Rates: 3,500 ptas. ($35) single; 5,500 ptas. ($55) double; Breakfast 350 ptas. ($3.50) extra. MC, V.

Just off calle de la Plata, one block west of the Plaza de Zocodover, the Imperio is the best bet for those on a tight budget. The rooms are clean and comfortable, but small. Eleven units contain a TV. Most overlook a little church with a wall overgrown with wisteria.

HOTEL LOS CIGARRALES, carretera Circunvalación 32, 45001 Toledo. Tel. 925/22-00-53. Fax 925/21-55-46. 36 rms (all with bath). A/C TEL **Bus:** Chamartín from the rail station.
$ Rates: 3,500 ptas. ($35) single; 5,500 ptas. ($55) double. Breakfast 400 ptas. ($4) extra. MC, V. **Parking:** Free.
About a mile south of the city center, this hotel offers quiet seclusion. Built in the 1960s in traditional red brick, it looks like a private villa with a garden; the friendliness of the family owners adds to this feeling. Most of the interior is covered with blue and green tiles. The rooms are clean and sunny, and decorated with heavy Spanish furniture. The dining room offers meals for 1,600 ptas. ($16). From the flower-filled terrace of the cozy bar you can see the towers of medieval Toledo.

HOTEL MARAVILLA, Plaza de Barrio Rey 7, 45001 Toledo. Tel. 925/22-33-00. 18 rms (all with bath). A/C TEL **Bus:** 5 or 6.
$ Rates: 3,800 ptas. ($38) single; 6,600 ptas. ($66) double. No credit cards.
If you enjoy hotels with lots of local color, then this little place will please you. It's only one block south of the Plaza de Zocodover, and opens directly onto its own cobblestone plaza. Semi-modernized in 1971, the building has many bay windows; the bedrooms are modest but adequate, the furnishings so-so. You can hang your laundry on the roof and use an iron in the downstairs laundry room.

Nearby Places to Stay

For readers who have a car or who don't mind one or two taxi rides a day, there are some excellent accommodations across the Tagus.

LA ALMAZARA, carretera de Piedrabuena 47 (C-781), 48080 Toledo. Tel. 925/22-38-66. 21 rms (all with bath). TEL **Directions:** Follow the road to the Parador of Ciudad Real; then take the C-781 to Cuerva.
$ Rates: 3,500 ptas. ($35) single; 6,000 ptas. ($60) double. Breakfast 450 ptas. ($4.50) extra. AE, MC, V. **Closed:** Nov–Mar 15.
Taking its name from an olive-oil mill that used to stand here, La Almazara offers some of the most offbeat accommodations around. Hidden away in the hills, this old-fashioned country villa, with its own courtyards and vineyards, offers a rare opportunity to soak up the atmosphere of Old Spain, far removed from the pace of city life. It

has an exceptional view of Toledo. You may be assigned either a spacious chamber in the main house or a bedroom in the annex. A continental breakfast is served.

WHERE TO DINE

Very Expensive

ASADOR ADOLFO, calle La Granada 6. Tel. 22-73-31.
   Cuisine: SPANISH. **Reservations:** Recommended. **Bus:** 5 or 6.
$ Prices: Appetizers 650–1,200 ptas. ($6.50–$12); main dishes 1,850–2,500 ptas. ($18.50–$25); fixed-price menus 4,500 ptas. ($45). AE, DC, V.
   Open: Lunch daily 1–4pm; dinner Mon–Sat 8pm–midnight.

⭐ Located less than a minute's walk north of the cathedral, in a warren of narrow medieval streets, this is considered by many residents as the finest and most renowned restaurant in Toledo. Sections of the building were originally built during the 1400s, although recent renovations in the kitchens have enabled its chefs to prepare many modern variations of traditional Toledo-derived dishes. The ceilings of the several dining rooms are supported by massive beams, and occasionally contain faded frescoes dating from the year of the building's original construction.

The house specialties include different preparations of game dishes, which are said to be among the best anywhere. These might include partridge with white beans, venison, or any of the wild game birds that the region produces in such abundance. Nongame dishes include hake flavored with local saffron, and any of a wide array of beef, veal, or lamb dishes. To begin, try the pimientos rellenos (red peppers stuffed with pulverized shellfish). The house dessert is marzipan; it's prepared in a wood-fired oven and is noted for its lightness.

The restaurant lies at the corner of calle Hombre de Palo, behind an understated and discreet sign.

PARADOR DE TURISMO DE TOLEDO, Cerro del Emperador. Tel. 22-18-50.
   Cuisine: CASTILIAN. **Reservations:** Not accepted. **Directions:** Drive across Puente San Martín and head south for 2½ miles (4km).
$ Prices: Appetizers 1,200–1,500 ptas. ($12–$15); main dishes 2,000–2,600 ptas. ($20–$26); fixed-priced menu 3,600 ptas. ($36). AE, DC, MC, V.
   Open: Lunch daily 1–4pm; dinner daily 8:30–11pm.

Some of the best Castilian regional cuisine is combined here with one of the most spectacular views from any restaurant in Europe. Located in a fine parador, the restaurant is on the crest of a hill—said to be the spot that El Greco selected for his *View of Toledo*. The fixed-price meal might include tasty Spanish hors d'oeuvres, hake, then perhaps either veal or beef grilled on an open fire, plus dessert. If you're dining lightly, try a local specialty, tortilla española con magra (potato omelet with ham or bacon). There's a bar on the upper level.

Expensive

HOSTAL DEL CARDENAL, paseo Recaredo 24. Tel. 22-08-62.

Cuisine: SPANISH. **Reservations:** Required. **Bus:** 2 from the train station.

$ **Prices:** Appetizers 500–2,000 ptas. ($5–$20); main dishes 900–2,300 ptas. ($9–$23); fixed-price menu 2,200 ptas. ($22). AE, DC, MC, V.

Open: Lunch daily 1–4pm; dinner daily 8:30–11:30pm.

You may want to treat yourself to Toledo's best and most expensive restaurant, owned by the same people who run Madrid's Casa Botín, so beloved by Hemingway. The menu is very similar. You might begin with "quarter of an hour" (fish) soup or white asparagus, then move on to curried prawns, baked hake, filet mignon, or smoked salmon. Roast suckling pig is a specialty, as is partridge in casserole. Arrive early and enjoy a sherry in the bar or in the courtyard.

Moderate

CASA AURELIO, calle de la Sinagoga 6. Tel. 22-77-16.

Cuisine: CASTILIAN. **Reservations:** Recommended. **Bus:** 5 or 6.

$ **Prices:** Appetizers 550–900 ptas. ($5.50–$9); main dishes 1,300–2,000 ptas. ($13–$20); fixed-price menu 2,700 ptas. ($27). AE, DC, MC, V.

Open: Lunch Thurs–Tues 1–4pm; dinner Thurs–Tues 8–11:30pm.

Centrally located by the northern edge of the cathedral, the Aurelio is one of the best-value restaurants in Toledo, offering good food and efficient service. Begin with sopa castellana, then follow with grilled hake, lubina à la sol (white fish cooked in salt), fresh salmon, roast lamb, or, if you're feeling up to it, Toledo partridge or roast suckling pig.

LA PARILLA, Horno de los Bizcochos 8. Tel. 21-22-45.

Cuisine: SPANISH. **Reservations:** Not accepted. **Bus:** 5 or 6.

$ **Prices:** Appetizers 450–600 ptas. ($4.50–$6); main dishes 1,200–2,000 ptas. ($12–$20); fixed-price menu 2,200 ptas. ($22). AE, DC, MC, V.

Open: Lunch daily 1–4pm; dinner daily 8–11pm.

This classic Spanish restaurant, given a two-fork rating, stands on a cobblestone street near the Alfonso VI Hotel, just east of the cathedral. The menu offers no surprises, but it's reliable. Likely inclusions on the bill of fare: roast suckling pig, spider crabs, Castilian baked trout, stewed quail, baked kidneys, and La Mancha rabbit.

VENTA DE AIRES, Circo Romano 35. Tel. 22-05-45.

Cuisine: SPANISH. **Reservations:** Recommended.

$ **Prices:** Appetizers 750–1,200 ptas. ($7.50–$12); main dishes 1,200–2,000 ptas. ($12–$20); fixed-price menu 2,400 ptas. ($24). AE, DC, MC, V.

Open: Lunch daily 1–4pm; dinner daily 8–11pm.

Just outside the city gates, directly southwest of the Circo Romano (Roman Circus), this restaurant has served Toledo's pièce de résistance—*perdiz* (partridge)—since 1891, when the place was only a little roadside inn. On the à la carte menu, this dish is best eaten with the red wine of Méntrida, but if you want to keep your tab low, you'd better stick to the fixed-price menu. For dessert, try the marzipan, an institution in Toledo. On your way out, take note of former President Nixon's entry in the guest book (he dined here in 1963).

Inexpensive

EL EMPERADOR, carretera del Valle 1. Tel. 22-46-91.
   Cuisine: SPANISH. **Reservations:** Recommended. **Bus:** Carretera del Valle.
$ **Prices:** Appetizers 600–950 ptas. ($6–$9.50); main dishes 1,000–1,800 ptas. ($10–$18); fixed-price menu 1,500 ptas. ($15). MC, V.
   Open: Lunch Tues–Sat 1–4pm; dinner Tues–Sat 8–11pm.
   Closed: Sept 1–15.

 A modern restaurant on the outskirts of Toledo, southwest of the historic core, El Emperador is reached via an arched bridge. Its terraces overlook the river and the towers of Toledo, while the tavern-style interior has leather-and-wooden chairs, heavy beams, and wrought-iron chandeliers. Service is attentive. The fixed-price menu might include a choice of soup (beef, vegetable, or noodle), followed by a small steak with french fries, then fresh fruit, plus wine.

MARAVILLA, Plaza de Barrio Rey 5. Tel. 22-33-00.
   Cuisine: SPANISH. **Reservations:** Not accepted. **Bus:** 5 or 6.
$ **Prices:** Appetizers 650–1,200 ptas. ($6.50–$12); main dishes 1,300–1,750 ptas. ($13–$17.50); fixed-price menu 1,200 ptas. ($12). No credit cards.
   Open: Lunch Tues–Sun 1–4pm; dinner Tues–Sun 8–11pm.

Located in the Barrio Rey, this restaurant is on a small square off the historic Plaza de Zocodover. The square is filled with budget restaurants and cafés that change their names so often it's virtually impossible to keep track. Maravilla offers the best all-round dining bargain.

A Tapas Bar

BAR LUDEÑA, Plaza de la Horn Madelena 13, Corral de Don Diego 10. Tel. 22-33-84.
   Cuisine: TAPAS. **Reservations:** Not accepted.
$ **Prices:** Tapas 200–650 ptas. ($2–$6.50). No credit cards.
   Open: Thurs–Tues 10am–midnight.

Delectable combinations of tapas are served here to a loyal clientele. Sometimes glasses of wine are passed through a small window to clients who are standing outside enjoying the view of the square. The bar is little more than a narrow corridor, serving *raciones* of tapas that are so generous they make little meals, especially when served with bread. The roasted red peppers in olive oil are especially tasty, along with the stuffed crabs. Huge dishes of pickled cucumbers, onions, and olives are available. A tiny dining room behind a curtain at the end of the bar serves inexpensive fare.

2. ARANJUEZ

29 miles S of Madrid, 30 miles NE of Toledo

GETTING THERE By Train Trains run about every 20 minutes, to and from Madrid's Atocha railway station (50 minutes).

Trains run less often along the east-west route to and from Toledo (40 minutes). The Aranjuez station lies about a mile outside town. You can walk it in about 15 minutes, but taxis and buses line up on calle Stuart (two blocks from the city tourist office). The bus that makes the run from the center of Aranjuez to the railway station is marked "N-Z."

By Bus   Autominibus Interurbaños, paseo de las Delicias 18 (tel. 230-46-070), operates buses that depart from Madrid's Estación Sur de Autobuses, Canarías 17. Buses run about seven times a day between Aranjuez and Madrid. They arrive and depart from the City Bus Terminal, calle Infantas 8 (tel. 891-01-83), in Aranjuez.

By Car   Driving is easy and takes about 30 minutes once you reach the southern city limits of Madrid. To reach Aranjuez, follow the signs to Aranjuez and Granada, taking the N-IV highway.

ESSENTIALS   The **telephone area code** of Aranjuez is 91. The **Tourist Information Office** is on Plaza Santiago Rusiñol (tel. 91/891-04-27).

On the Tagus River, Aranjuez strikes visitors as a virtual garden. It was mapped out by the royal architects and landscapers of Ferdinand VI in the 18th century. The natural setting has been blended with wide boulevards and fountain- and statuary-filled gardens.

Surrounded in late spring by beds of asparagus and heavily laden strawberry vines, Aranjuez exudes the spirit of May. But for some visitors, autumn best reveals the royal town. It's then that the golden cypress trees cast lingering shadows in countless ponds, evoking a painting by Santiago Rusiñol Prats.

WHAT TO SEE & DO

PALACIO REAL, Plaza del Palacio. Tel. 891-07-40.

Since the beginning of a united Spain, the climate and natural beauty of Aranjuez have attracted Spanish monarchs, notably Ferdinand and Isabella and Philip II, who managed to tear himself away from El Escorial. But the Palacio Real, lying immediately west of the center, in its present form dates primarily from the days of the Bourbons, who used to come here mainly in the autumn and spring, reserving La Granja, near Segovia, for their summer romps. The palace was also favored by Philip V and Charles III.

Fires have swept over the structure numerous times, but most of the present building dates from 1778. William Lyon, writing in the Madrid weekly, the *Guidepost,* called its dominant note one of "deception: in almost each of its widely varying rooms there is at least one thing that isn't what it first appears." Mr. Lyon cites assemblages of mosaics that look like oil paintings, a trompe-l'oeil ceiling that seems three-dimensional although it's flat, and a copy of a salon at the Alhambra Palace at Granada.

In spite of these eye-fooling tricks, the palace is lavishly and elegantly decorated. Especially notable are the dancing salon, the throne room, the ceremonial dining hall, the bedrooms of the king and queen, and a remarkable Salon de Porcelana (Porcelain Room). Paintings include works by Lucas Jordan and José Ribera.

Admission: 300 ptas. ($3).
Open: Apr–Sept, daily 10am–12:30pm and 3:30–7pm; Oct–Mar, daily 10am–1pm and 3:30–6pm. **Bus:** Routes from the rail station converge at square and gardens at westernmost edge of palace.

JARDÍN DE LA ISLA, Palacio Real. Tel. 891-07-40.

These gardens appear somehow forgotten, their mood melancholic. They lie to the east of the Palacio Real, adjoining a royal ornamental garden, called Parterre. From the Parterre, two bridges lead to the "garden of the island." The "Non Plus Ultra" fountain is dazzling. Under linden trees, the fountain of Apollo is romantic, and others honor the king of the sea and Cybele, goddess of agriculture. The most delightful stroll is along an avenue of trees, called Salón de los Reyes Católicos, which lies along the river.

Admission: 300 ptas. ($3).
Open: Apr–Oct, daily 10am–12:30pm and 3:30–7pm; Oct–Mar, daily 10am–1pm and 3:30–6pm.

CASITA DEL LABRADOR, calle de la Reina. Tel. 891-07-40.

"The little house of the worker" is a classic example of understatement. Actually, it was modeled after the Petit Trianon at Versailles. If you visit the Royal Palace in the morning, you can spend the afternoon here in the northeastern part of town. Those with a car can motor to it through the tranquil **Jardín del Príncipe,** with its black poplars.

The little palace was built in 1803 by Charles IV, who later abdicated in Aranjuez. The queen came here with her youthful lover, Godoy (whom she had elevated to the position of prime minister), and the feebleminded Charles didn't seem to mind a bit. Surrounded by beautiful gardens, the "bedless" palace is lavishly furnished in the grand style of the 18th and 19th centuries. The marble floors represent some of the finest workmanship of that day. The brocaded walls emphasize luxurious living—and the royal bathroom is a sight to behold (in those days, royalty preferred an audience). The clock here is one of the treasures of the house.

Admission: 150 ptas. ($1.50).
Open: Wed–Mon 10am–1:30pm and 3:30–6:30pm.

WHERE TO STAY

HOSTAL CASTILLA, carretera Andalucía 98, 28300 Aranjuez. Tel. 91/891-26-27. 17 rms (all with bath). MINIBAR TV TEL
$ Rates: 3,500 ptas. ($35) single; 4,500 ptas. ($45) double. Breakfast 350 ptas. ($3.50) extra. AE, DC, V.

On one of the town's main streets north of the Royal Palace and gardens, the Castilla consists of the ground floor and part of the first floor of a well-preserved early 18th-century house. Most of the accommodations overlook a courtyard with a fountain and flowers. The owner, Joaquin Suárez, speaks English fluently. There are excellent restaurants nearby, and the hostal has an arrangement with a neighboring bar for an inexpensive lunch. This is a good location from which to explore either Madrid or Toledo on a day trip.

WHERE TO DINE

CASA PABLO, Almibar 42. Tel. 891-14-51.
Cuisine: SPANISH. **Reservations:** Recommended.

$ Prices: Appetizers 700–900 ptas. ($7–$9); main dishes 1,500–2,000 ptas. ($15–$20); fixed-price menu (four courses) 3,200 ptas. ($32). V.

Open: Lunch daily 1–4:30pm; dinner daily 8pm–midnight.

Closed: Aug.

A two-fork restaurant near the bus station in the town center, Casa Pablo offers good values. At tables set outside under a canopy, you can dine while enjoying the tree-lined street and the red and pink geraniums; in cooler weather you can eat either upstairs or in the cozy dining room in the rear. The fixed-price menu includes several courses, a carafe of wine, bread, and service. If it's hot and you don't want a heavy dinner, try a shrimp omelet or half a roast chicken; once I ordered just a plate of asparagus in season, accompanied by white wine. If you want a superb dish, try a fish called mero (Mediterranean pollack of delicate flavor), grilled over an open fire.

LA RANA VERDE, calle de la Reina 1. Tel. 891-32-38.

Cuisine: SPANISH. **Reservations:** Recommended.

$ Prices: Appetizers 550–700 ptas. ($5.50–$7); main dishes 950–1,800 ptas. ($9.50–$18); fixed-price menu 2,200 ptas. ($22). No credit cards.

Open: Daily noon–midnight.

The Green Frog, just east of the Royal Palace and next to a small bridge spanning the Tagus, is still the traditional choice for many. The restaurant looks like a summer house with its high-beamed ceiling and soft ferns drooping from hanging baskets. The preferred tables are in the nooks overlooking the river. As in all the restaurants of Aranjuez, asparagus is a special feature. Game, particularly partridge, quail, and pigeon, can be recommended in season; fish, too, including fried hake and fried sole, makes a good choice. Strawberries are served with sugar, orange juice, or ice cream.

3. SAN LORENZO DE EL ESCORIAL

30 miles W of Madrid, 32 miles SE of Segovia

GETTING THERE **By Train** More than two dozen trains depart daily from Madrid's Atocha and Chamartín train stations. During the summer extra coaches are added. The railway station for San Lorenzo de El Escorial is located about a mile outside town. The Herranz bus company meets all arriving trains with a shuttle bus that ferries passengers to and from the Plaza Virgen de Gracia, about a block east of the entrance to the monastery.

By Bus Madrid's Empresa Herranz, calle Isaac Peral 8 (tel. 243-36-45), runs about 15 buses daily to El Escorial from the capital. It leaves passengers at the Plaza Virgen de Gracia, about a block east of the entrance to the monastery. This same company also sells tickets for the single trip per day it makes between El Escorial's Plaza Virgen de Gracia and the Valley of the Fallen (see below). A round-trip ticket from El Escorial to this sight costs 425 ptas. ($4.25). Departure is at 3:15pm; return to El Escorial is at 6:15pm. Travel time is 20 minutes each way.

By Car Follow the N-VI highway (on some maps marked as the

A-6) from the northwestern perimeter of Madrid, in the direction of Lugo, La Coruña, and San Lorenzo de El Escorial. After about half an hour, fork left onto the C-505 toward San Lorenzo de El Escorial. Driving time is about an hour.

ESSENTIALS San Lorenzo de El Escorial's **telephone area code** is 91. The **Tourist Information Office** is at Floridablanca 10 (tel. 91/890-15-54).

Next to Toledo, the most important excursion from Madrid is the austere Royal Monastery of San Lorenzo de El Escorial. Philip II ordered the construction of this granite-and-slate rectangular monster in 1563, two years after he moved his capital to Madrid. Once the haunt of aristocratic Spaniards, El Escorial is now a summer resort where hotels and restaurants flourish in summer, as hundreds flock here to escape the heat of the capital. Despite the appeal of its climate, the town of San Lorenzo itself is not very noteworthy. But because of the monastery's size, you might decide to spend a night or two at San Lorenzo—or more if you have the time.

San Lorenzo makes an ideal base for visiting the cities and towns of nearby Segovia and Ávila, the royal palace of La Granja, the Valley of the Fallen, and even the more distant university city of Salamanca.

WHAT TO SEE & DO

ROYAL MONASTERY OF SAN LORENZO DE EL ESCORIAL, calle San Lorenzo de El Escorial 1. Tel. 890-58-88.

In the Guadarrama mountain resort of El Escorial stands the imposing Monastery of San Lorenzo el Real del Escorial. Many refer to its as the eighth wonder of the world. Both a palace and a monastery, it was ordered built south of the town by Philip II to commemorate the triumph of his forces at the Battle of San Quentin in 1557. Escorial was dedicated to St. Lawrence, the martyred saint burned to death.

The original architect of El Escorial in 1563 was Juan Bautista de Toledo. After his death the monumental task was assumed by the greatest architect of Renaissance Spain, Juan de Herrera, who completed it in the shape of a gridiron in 1584.

The severe lines of the great pile of granite strike many as being as austere as the pious Philip himself. Architectural critic Nikolaus Pevsner called it "overwhelming, moving no doubt, but frightening."

In the **Charter Hall** is one of the greatest art collections in Spain outside of the Prado, the canvases dating primarily from the 15th to the 17th centuries. Among the most outstanding works are El Greco's *The Martyrdom of St. Maurice,* Titian's *Last Supper,* Velázquez's *The Tunic of Joseph,* van der Weyden's *Crucifixion,* and another version of Bosch's *The Hay Wagon* (see also a remarkable tapestry based on a painting by "El Bosco" as the Spanish call this artist); there are also works by Ribera, Tintoretto, and Veronese.

The **Biblioteca**—one of the most important libraries in the world—has an estimated number of volumes in excess of 50,000. The collection, started by Philip II, ranges far and wide: Muslim codices; a Gothic "Cántigas" of the 13th century from the reign of Alfonso X (known as "The Wise King"); and signatures from the Carmelite nun, St. Teresa de Jesús, who conjured up visions of the devil and of angels sticking burning-hot lances into her heart.

For many sightseers, the highlight of the tour is a visit to the **Apartments of Philip II,** which contain many of the original furnishings of the monarch. He died in 1598, in the "cell for my humble self" that he ordered built. He desired quarters that were spartan, and so they remain today—graced by a painting by Bosch, a copy he made of his *The Seven Capital Sins,* now at the Prado.

The **Apartments of the Bourbons** reflect a different style—a complete break from the asceticism imposed by the Hapsburg king. They are richly decorated, with a special emphasis on tapestries (many resembling paintings) based on Goya and Bayeu cartoons at the Royal Factory in Madrid.

From a window in his bedroom, a weak and dying Philip II could look down on the services being conducted in the **basilica.** As the dome clearly indicates, the church was modeled after Michelangelo's drawings of St. Peter's in Rome. Works of art include a crucifix by Benvenuto Cellini, choir stalls by Herrera, and sculpted groups of father and son (Charles V and Philip II), along with their wives, flanking the altar.

The **Royal Pantheon,** burial place of Spanish kings from Charles V to Alfonso XII, is under the altar. (The Bourbon king, Philip V, is interred at La Granja, and the body of Ferdinand VI was placed in a tomb in a Madrid church). In the octagonal mausoleum you'll see the tombs of queens who were mothers of kings.

On the lower level rests one of the curiosities of El Escorial: a "wedding cake" tomb for royal children. The Whispering Hall, with its odd sound effects, is also intriguing.

Admission: Comprehensive ticket, 550 ptas. ($5.50) for adults, 325 ptas. ($3.25) for children.

Open: Tues–Sun 10am–1pm and 3:15–6pm. **Directions:** Walk uphill from virtually any point in town.

CASA DE PRÍNCIPE (Prince's Cottage), calle de la Reina. Tel. 891-03-05.

This small but elaborately decorated 18th-century palace near the railway station was originally a hunting lodge built for Charles III by Juan de Villanueva. Most visitors stay in El Escorial for lunch, visiting the cottage when it reopens in the afternoon.

Admission: Included in the comprehensive ticket, above.

Open: Tues–Sat 10am–1pm and 3:30–6:30pm.

VALLE DE LOS CAÍDOS (Valley of the Fallen). Tel. 890-56-11.

This architectural marvel took two decades to complete, and is dedicated to those who died in the Spanish Civil War. Its detractors say that it represents the worst of Neo-Fascist design; its admirers say that they have found renewed inspiration by coming here.

A gargantuan cross, nearly 500 feet high, dominates the Rock of Nava, a peak of the Guadarrama Mountains. Directly under the cross is a basilica in mosaic, completed in 1959. Here José Antonio Primo de Rivera, the founder of the Falange party, is buried. When this Nationalist hero was buried at El Escorial, many, especially influential monarchists, protested that he was not a royal. Infuriated, Franco decided to erect another monument. Originally it was slated to honor the dead on the Nationalist side only, but the intervention of several parties led to a decision to include all the *caídos* (fallen). In time the mausoleum claimed Franco as well; his body was interred behind the high altar.

On the other side of the mountain is a Benedictine monastery that has sometimes been dubbed "the Hilton of monasteries" because of its seeming luxury.

Admission: 400 ptas. ($4).

Open: Tues–Sun 10am–7pm. **Directions:** Drive to the valley entrance, about 5 miles (8km) north of El Escorial in the heart of the Guadarrama Mountains. Once there, drive 3½ miles (6km) along a dusty road west to the underground basilica. **Bus:** Autocares Herranz in El Escorial runs a bus here at 3:15pm, returning at 6:15pm; the trip takes 15 minutes. Tour buses from Madrid usually include an excursion to the Valley of the Fallen on their one-day trips to El Escorial. **Funicular:** It extends from near the entrance to the basilica to the base of the gigantic cross erected on the mountaintop above, with a superb view at the top. Price: 250 ptas. ($2.50). Open: 10:30am–1:15pm and 4–6pm.

WHERE TO STAY

HOSTAL CRISTINA, Juan de Toledo 6, 28200 San Lorenzo de El Escorial. Tel. 91/890-19-61. 16 rms (all with bath).

$ Rates: 5,000 ptas. ($50) double. Breakfast 400 ptas. ($4) extra. MC, V.

 The best low-budget accommodation in the center of town offers clean, comfortable rooms and a helpful staff. No singles are available. With the food both good and plentiful, many Spanish visitors prefer to book in here for a summer holiday. Meals begin at 1,550 ptas. ($15.50). There's also a small garden.

HOTEL VICTORIA PALACE, calle Juan de Toledo 4, 28200 San Lorenzo de El Escorial. Tel. 91/890-15-11. Fax 91/890-12-48. 87 rms (all with bath), 4 suites. TV TEL

$ Rates: 10,000 ptas. ($100) single; 13,500 ptas. ($135) double; from 23,500 ptas. ($235) suite. Breakfast 950 ptas. ($9.50) extra. AE, DC, MC, V. **Parking:** Free.

The Victoria Palace, with its view of El Escorial, is the finest hotel in town—a traditional establishment that has been modernized without losing its special aura of style and comfort. It's surrounded by beautiful gardens and has an outdoor swimming pool. The rooms, some with private terrace, are well furnished and maintained. The rate—reasonable enough, and a bargain for a four-star hotel—also includes admission to El Escorial. The dining room serves some of the best food in town, with a meal averaging around 3,500 ptas. ($35). Laundry and room service are provided.

MIRANDA & SUIZO, Floridablanca 18, 28200 San Lorenzo de El Escorial. Tel. 91/890-47-11. Fax 91/890-43-58. 48 rms (all with bath).

$ Rates: 6,000 ptas. ($60) single; 8,500 ptas. ($85) double. Breakfast 500 ptas. ($5) extra. AE, DC, MC, V.

On a tree-lined street in the heart of town, within easy walking distance of the monastery, this excellent middle-class establishment ranks as a leading two-star hotel. The Victorian-style building has good rooms, some with terraces. Ten rooms contain TV. The furnishings are comfortable, the beds often have brass frames, and sometimes you'll find fresh flowers on the table. In summer there's outside dining.

WHERE TO DINE

CHAROLÉS, Floridablanca 24. Tel. 890-59-75.
   Cuisine: SPANISH/INTERNATIONAL. **Reservations:** Required.
$ Prices: Appetizers 1,050–1,900 ptas. ($10.50–$19); main dishes 2,200–3,900 ptas. ($22–$39); fixed-price menu 4,800 ptas. ($48). AE, DC, MC, V.
   Open: Lunch daily 1–4pm; dinner daily 9pm–midnight.

Its sunny terrace, air-conditioned interior, and impeccable service are reasons to seek this place out, but the best reason of all is the fresh meat and fish that owner Manolo Miguez imports daily from Madrid. The specials change daily depending on what's available, but outstanding past dishes have included shellfish soup, a pastel of fresh vegetables with crayfish, pepper steak, and herb-flavored baby lamb chops. Kiwi tart is a good choice for dessert.

MESÓN LA CUEVA (The Cave), San Antón 4. Tel. 890-15-16.
   Cuisine: SPANISH. **Reservations:** Recommended.
$ Prices: Appetizers 750–850 ptas. ($7.50–$8.50); main dishes 1,050–1,500 ptas. ($10.50–$15). No credit cards.
   Open: Lunch Tues–Sat 1–4pm; dinner Tues–Sat 8:30–11pm.

Founded in 1768, this restaurant recaptures the world of Old Castile. A *mesón típico,* built around an enclosed courtyard, it boasts such nostalgic accents as stained-glass windows, antique chests, faded engravings, paneled doors, and iron balconies. The cooking is on target, the portions generous. Regional specialties include Valencian paella and fabada asturiana (pork sausage and beans), but fresh trout broiled in butter may be best of all. The menu's most expensive items are Segovian roast suckling pig and roast lamb (tender inside, crisp outside). Off the courtyard through a separate doorway is La Cueva's *tasca,* filled with Castilians quaffing their favorite before-dinner drinks.

Near the Valley of the Fallen

HOSTELERIE VALLE DE LOS CAÍDOS, Valle de los Caídos. Tel. 890-55-11.
   Cuisine: SPANISH. **Reservations:** Not accepted.
$ Prices: Appetizers 550–600 ptas. ($5.50–$6); main dishes 850–1,200 ptas. ($8.50–$12); fixed-price menu 1,200 ptas. ($12). No credit cards.
   Open: Lunch daily 1–4pm.

This three-fork restaurant occupies a dramatic location halfway up to the Valley of the Fallen. Reachable only by car, it's a mammoth modern structure with wide terraces and floor-to-ceiling windows. The *menu del día* can include cannelloni Rossini as an opener, pork chops with potatoes, dessert, and wine.

4. SEGOVIA

54–63 miles NW of Madrid, 42 miles NE of Avila

GETTING THERE By Train About a dozen trains leave Madrid's Atocha railway station every day and arrive 2½ hours later in Segovia, where you can board bus no. 3, which departs every quarter hour for the Plaza Mayor. (Note that some maps and some residents still refer to the Plaza Mayor as the Plaza Franco.) The station is on paseo Obispo Quesada (tel. 42-07-74), a 20-minute walk southeast of the town center.

By Bus Buses arrive and depart from the Estacionamiento Municipal de Autobuses, paseo de Equezuile González 10 (tel. 42-77-25), near the corner of avenida Fernández Ladreda and the steeply sloping paseo Conde de Sepulveda. There are eight or nine buses a day to/from Madrid (which depart from paseo de la Florida 11; Metro: Norte), and about four a day traveling between Ávila, Segovia, and Valladolid. One-way tickets from Madrid cost around 570 ptas. ($5.70).

By Car Take the N-VI (on some maps it's known as the A-6) or the Autopista del Nordeste northwest from Madrid, toward León and Lugo. At the junction with Route 110 (signposted Segovia), turn northeast.

ESSENTIALS Segovia's **telephone area code** is 911. The **Tourist Information Office** is at Plaza Mayor 10 (tel. 911/43-03-28).

In Old Castile, Segovia is one of the most romantic of Spanish cities, its glory of another day. Isabella I was proclaimed Queen of Castile here in 1474. Segovians live with the memory of the time when their star was in the ascendancy.

The capital of a province of the same name, it lies on a slope of the snow-capped Sierra de Guadarrama mountains, between two ravine-studded valleys and the Eresma and Clamores Rivers (actually streams). As it appears on the horizon, dominated by its Alcázar and its Gothic cathedral, Segovia is decidedly of the Middle Ages.

The city was of strategic importance to the Roman troops, and one of its greatest monuments, the Aqueduct, dates from those times. The skyline is characterized by the Romanesque belfries of the churches and the towers of its old and decaying palaces.

The Upper Town is mainly encased by its old walls; but the part outside the walls is of interest too, especially for views of the Alcázar.

WHAT TO SEE & DO

EL ALCÁZAR, Plaza de la Reina Eugenia. Tel. 43-01-76.

If you've ever dreamed of castles in the air, then all the fairy-tale romance of childhood will return when you view the Alcázar. Many have waxed poetic about it, comparing it to a giant boat sailing through the clouds. See it first from down below, at the junction of the Clamores and Eresma Rivers. It's on the west side of Segovia, and you may not spot it when you first enter the city, but that's part of the surprise.

The castle dates back many hundreds of years—perhaps to the 12th century. But a large segment of it—notably its Moorish ceilings—was destroyed by fire in 1862. Over the years, under an ambitious plan, the Alcázar has been restored.

Inside you'll discover a facsimile of Isabella's dank bedroom. It was at the Alcázar that she first met Ferdinand, preferring him to the

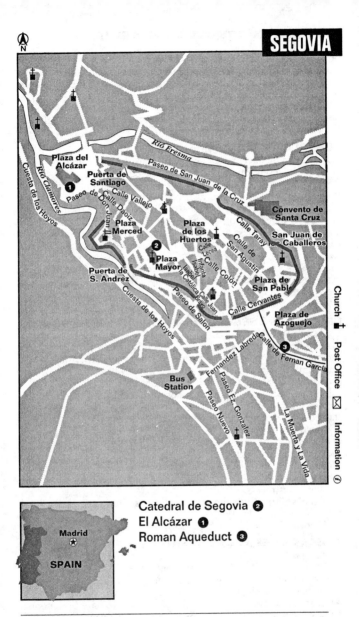

SEGOVIA

Plaza del Alcázar

Puerta de Santiago

Paseo de San Juan de la Cruz

Río Eresma

Río Clamores

Cuesta de los Hoyos

Paseo de Don Juan

Calle Vallejo

Calle Daoíz

Plaza Merced

Plaza de los Huertos

Convento de Santa Cruz

Calle Taray

Calle de San Agustín

San Juan de los Caballeros

Calle Lecea

Calle Infanta

Plaza Mayor

Puerta de S. Andrés

Calle Juan Bravo

Calle Colón

Cuesta de los Hoyos

Isabel la Católica

Plaza de San Pablo

Paseo de Salón

Calle Cervantes

Plaza de Azoguejo

Fernández Labrede

Calle de Fernán García

Bus Station

Paseo Ez. González

Paseo Nuevo

La Muerte y La Vida

Church ✝ Post Office ⊠ Information ⓘ

Catedral de Segovia ❷
El Alcázar ❶
Roman Aqueduct ❸

Madrid ⊛

SPAIN

---

more "fatherly" King of Portugal. But she wasn't foolish enough to surrender her "equal rights" after marriage. In the Throne Room, with its replica chairs, you'll note that both seats are equally proportioned. Royal romance continued to flower at the Alcázar. Philip II married his fourth wife, Anne of Austria, here.

After you inspect the polish on some medieval armor inside, you may want to walk the battlements of this once-impregnable castle, whose former occupants poured boiling oil over the ramparts onto their uninvited guests below. Or you can climb the tower, originally built by Isabella's father as a prison, for a supreme view of Segovia. (In particular, note the so-called pregnant-woman mountain.)

Admission: 300 ptas. ($3) adults, 125 ptas. ($1.25) children 8–14.

Open: Apr–Sept, daily 10am–7pm; Oct–Mar, daily 10am–6pm.
Directions: Take either calle Vallejo, calle de Velarde, calle de Daoiz, or paseo de Ronda. **Bus:** 3.

ROMAN AQUEDUCT, Plaza del Azoguejo.

⭐ The aqueduct, an architectural marvel, is still used to carry water, even though it was constructed by the Romans almost 2,000 years ago. It's not only the most colossal reminder of Roman glory in Spain, but also one of the best-preserved Roman architectural achievements in the world. It consists of 118 arches, and in one two-tiered section—its highest point—it soars 95 feet. You'll find no mortar in these granite blocks brought from the Guadarrama Mountains. The Spanish call it El Puente, and it spans the Plaza del Azoguejo, the old market square, stretching out to a distance of nearly 800 yards. When the Moors took Segovia in 1072, they destroyed 36 arches. However, Ferdinand and Isabella ordered that they be rebuilt in 1484. You can see it anytime night or day as it's an integral landmark of Segovia.

CATEDRAL DE SEGOVIA, Plaza Mayor, calle Marqués del Arco. Tel. 43-53-25.

This 16th-century structure lays claim to being the last Gothic cathedral built in Spain. Fronting the historic Plaza Mayor, the Cathedral of Segovia stands on the spot where Isabella I was proclaimed Queen of Castile. It's affectionately called "la dama de las catedrales." Inside, it contains numerous treasures, such as the Blessed Sacrament Chapel (created by the flamboyant Churriguera), stained-glass windows, elaborately carved choir stalls, and 16th- and 17th-century paintings, including a reredos portraying the deposition of Christ from the cross by Juan de Juni. Older than the cathedral are the cloisters, which belong to a former church destroyed in the War of the Communeros. The cathedral's museum exhibits jewelry, paintings, and a rare collection of antique manuscripts, along with the inevitable vestments.

Admission: Cathedral, free; cloisters, museum, and chapel room, 150 ptas. ($1.50).

Open: Daily 9:30am–7pm. **Bus:** 3.

CHURCH OF VERA CRUZ, carretera de Zamarramala. Tel. 43-14-75.

Built in either the 11th or 12th century by the Knights Templars, this is the most fascinating Romanesque church in Segovia. It stands in isolation outside the walls of the old town, overlooking the Alcázar. Its unusual 12-sided design is believed to have been copied from the Church of the Holy Sepulchre in Jerusalem. Inside you'll find an inner temple, rising two floors, where the knights conducted nightlong vigils as part of their initiation rites.

Admission: 100 ptas. ($1).

Open: Apr–Sept, Tues–Sun 10:30am–1:30pm and 3:30–7pm; Oct–Mar, Tues–Sun 10:30am–1:30pm and 3:30–6pm.

MONASTERY OF EL PARRAL, calle del Marqués de Villena (across the Ersema River). Tel. 43-12-98.

The recently restored Monastery of the Grape was established for the Hironymites by Henry IV, a Castilian king (1425–74) known as "The Impotent." The monastery's major art treasure is a large retable (1528) by Juan Rodríguez. A robed monk guides you through.

Admission: Free.

Open: Mon–Sat 10am–12:30pm and 4–6pm, Sun and hols., 10am–noon and 4–6pm. **Directions:** Take Ronda de Sant Lucia, cross the Ersema River, and head down calle del Marqués de Villena.

CHURCH OF ST. MARTIN, Plaza de las Sirenas.

Located in the center of Segovia, this church was once the most outstanding in Old Castile. The porticoes of the 12th-century Romanesque structure are especially striking, but except for the rare altar, the interior is less interesting. The square on which the church stands, the Plaza de las Sirenas, was modeled after the Piazza di Spagna in Rome. A fountain commemorates the legend of Juan Bravo, the hero of the War of the Communeros against Charles V. Nearby is the 15th-century **Mansion of Arias Davila,** one of the old houses of the Segovian aristocracy.

Admission: Free.

Open: Apr–Sept, daily 10:30am–1:30pm and 3:30–7pm; Oct–Mar, daily 10:30am–1:30pm and 3:30–6pm.

WHERE TO STAY

GRAN HOTEL LAS SIRENAS, Juan Bravo 30, 40001 Segovia. Tel. 911/43-40-11. Fax 911/43-06-33. 39 rms (all with bath). A/C TEL

$ Rates: 5,500 ptas. ($55) single; 8,000 ptas. ($80) double. Breakfast 500 ptas. ($5) extra. AE, DC, MC, V.

Standing on the most charming old plaza in Segovia, opposite the Church of St. Martin, this modest establishment ranks as one of the town's leading hotels. It attracts those with traditional tastes. Each room is well kept. No meals other than breakfast are served, but there are several cafés nearby.

HOTEL LAS LINAJES, Dr. Velasco 9, 40003 Segovia. Tel. 911/43-17-12. Fax 911/43-15-01. 55 rms (all with bath), 10 suites. TV TEL **Bus:** 1.

$ Rates: 6,900 ptas. ($69) single; 10,500 ptas. ($105) double; from 13,200 ptas. ($132) suite. Breakfast 750 ptas. ($7.50) extra. AE, DC, MC, V. **Parking:** 700 ptas. ($7).

In the historic district of St. Stephen, at the northern edge of the old town, stands this hotel, the former home of a Segovian noble family. While the outside facade dates from the 11th century, the interior is modern except for some Castilian decorations. One of the best hotels in town, Los Linajes offers gardens and patios where guests can enjoy a panoramic view over the city. The hotel also has a bar/lounge, coffee shop, disco, and garage.

PARADOR DE SEGOVIA, carretera Valladolid (N-601), 40003 Segovia. Tel. 911/44-37-37. Fax 911/44-73-62. 113 rms (all with bath), 7 suites. A/C MINIBAR TV TEL

$ Rates: 12,600 ptas. ($126) single; 15,500 ptas. ($155) double; from 20,575 ptas. ($205.75) suite. Breakfast 1,300 ptas. ($13) extra. AE, DC, MC, V. **Parking:** 925 ptas. ($9.25).

This 20th-century tile-roofed parador sits on a hill two miles northeast of Segovia (take the N-601). The rooms are deluxe. The vast lawns and gardens contain two lakeside swimming pools, and there's also an indoor pool. Other facilities include saunas and tennis courts. You can eat in the dining room for 3,600 ptas. ($36) and up.

WHERE TO DINE

EL BERNARDINO, calle Cervantes 2. Tel. 43-32-25.
Cuisine: CASTILIAN. **Reservations:** Recommended.
$ Prices: Appetizers 375–850 ptas. ($3.75–$8.50); main dishes 1,050–2,000 ptas. ($10.50–$20); fixed-price menus 2,000–2,200 ptas. ($20–$22). AE, DC, MC, V.
Open: Lunch daily 1–4:15pm; dinner daily 8–11:15pm.

El Bernardino, a three-minute walk west of the Roman aqueduct, is built like an old tavern. Lanterns hang from beamed ceilings, and the view over the red-tile rooftops of the city is delightful. The menu del día might include a huge paella, roast veal with potatoes, flan or ice cream, plus bread and wine. You might begin your meal with sopa castellana (made with ham, sausage, bread, egg, and garlic).

CASA DUQUE, calle Cervantes 12. Tel. 43-05-37.
Cuisine: CASTILIAN. **Reservations:** Recommended.
$ Prices: Appetizers 700–900 ptas. ($7–$9); main dishes 1,600–2,200 ptas. ($16–$22); fixed-price menu 2,200 ptas. ($22). AE, DC, MC, V.
Open: Lunch daily 12:30–5pm; dinner daily 8–11:30pm.

Duque—the *maestro asador,* as he calls himself—supervises the roasting of the pig, the house specialty. Waitresses, wearing the traditional garb of the mayoress of Zamarramala, will serve you other Segovian gastronomic specialties such as sopa castellana or a cake known as ponche alcázar. There's a tavern below so that you may enjoy a before-dinner drink.

MESÓN DE CANDIDO, Plaza del Azoguejo 5. Tel. 42-59-11.
Cuisine: CASTILIAN. **Reservations:** Recommended.
$ Prices: Appetizers 700–900 ptas. ($7–$9); main dishes 1,800–2,600 ptas. ($18–$26); fixed-price menu 2,800 ptas. ($28). AE, DC, MC, V.
Open: Lunch daily 12:30–4:30pm; dinner daily 8–11:30pm or midnight.

For years this beautiful old Spanish inn, standing on the eastern edge of the old town, has maintained a monopoly on the tourist trade. The proprietor of the House of Candido is known as *mesonero mayor de Castilla* (the major innkeeper of Castile). He has been decorated with more medals and honors than paella has grains of rice, and has entertained everyone from King Hussein to Hemingway. The restaurant's popularity can be judged by the flocks of hungry diners who fill every seat in the six dining rooms. It offers an à la carte menu that includes cordero asado (roast baby lamb) or cochinillo asado (roast suckling pig).

MESÓN EL CORDERO, Carmen 4. Tel. 43-51-96.
Cuisine: CASTILIAN. **Reservations:** Recommended.
$ Prices: Appetizers 400–600 ptas. ($4–$6); main dishes 1,800–3,500 ptas. ($18–$35). AE, DC, MC, V.
Open: Lunch daily 12:30–4:30pm; dinner daily 8–11:30pm.

Aficionados say this is *the* best place to sample cordero lechal (milk-fed baby lamb). An entire leg of tender lamb is served, bone included, seasoned with fresh herbs such as thyme. Many dishes are reasonably priced, but the meat dishes, especially the lamb, carry a high tariff. The service is good, and if you get a table near the corner window, you'll view the aqueduct, in whose shadow the restaurant stands.

RESTAURANTE JOSÉ MARÍA, Cronista Lecea 11. Tel. 43-44-84.

Cuisine: CASTILIAN. **Reservations:** Recommended.

\$ Prices: Appetizers 400–1,800 ptas. ($4–$18); main dishes 1,000–2,500 ptas. ($10–$25); fixed-price menu 3,800 ptas. ($38). AE, DC, MC, V.

Open: Lunch daily 1–4pm; dinner daily 8–11:30pm.

This centrally located bar and restaurant, a block east of the Plaza Mayor, serves quality regional cuisine in a rustic stucco-and-brick dining room. Before dinner, locals crowd in for tapas at the bar, then move into the dining room for such Castilian specialties as roast suckling pig or some nouvelle cuisine dishes. Try the cream of crabmeat soup, roasted peppers, salmon with scrambled eggs, or house-style hake. For dessert, try the ice-cream tart with whisky sauce.

AN EXCURSION TO LA GRANJA

To reach La Granja, seven miles southeast of Segovia, you can take a 15-minute bus ride from the center of the city. About 12 buses a day leave from paseo Conde de Sepulveda at avenida Fernández Ladreda (tel. 42-77-25).

PALACIO REAL DE LA GRANJA, Plaza de España 17, San Ildefonso (Segovia). Tel. 911/47-00-19.

San Ildefonso de la Granja was the summer palace of the Bourbon kings of Spain, who imitated the grandeur of Versailles here in this Segovia province. Set against the snow-capped Sierra de Guadarrama, the slate-roofed palace dominates the village (nowadays a summer resort) that grew up around it.

The founder of La Granja was Philip V, grandson of Louis XIV and the first Bourbon king of Spain (his body, along with that of his second queen, Isabel de Fernesio, is interred in a mauseoleum in the Collegiate Church). Philip V was born at Versailles in 1683, which partially explains why he wanted to re-create that atmosphere at Segovia.

Before the palace was built in the early 18th century, a farm stood here—hence the totally inappropriate name *granja,* meaning farm in Spanish. Inside you'll find valuable antiques (many in the Empire style), paintings, and a remarkable collection of tapestries of Flemish design and others based on Goya cartoons from the Royal Factory in Madrid.

Most visitors, however, seem to find a stroll through the gardens more to their liking, so allow adequate time for it. The fountain statuary is a riot of gods and nymphs cavorting with abandon, hiding indiscretions behind jets of water. The gardens are studded with chestnuts and elms.

The royal palace charges an admission fee of 350 ptas. ($3.50) for adults, 125 ptas. ($1.25) for children 5–14. It can be visited Tuesday through Saturday from 10am to 1:30pm and 3 to 5pm, and on Sunday 10am to 2pm. A spectacular display comes when the water jets are turned on.

CHAPTER 11

THE COSTA DEL SOL

The most popular beach strip in Spain—and Europe's most spectacular real-estate boom—begins at the port of Algeciras and stretches eastward all the way to Almería. Against the backdrop of once-pagan Andalusia, the Sun Coast curves gently along the Mediterranean, studded with beaches, sandy coves, lime-washed houses, high-rise apartments, tennis courts, golf courses, swimming pools, and hotels of every type and description.

Sun-seekers from all over Europe and North America are drawn to the mild climate and virtually guaranteed sunshine. You can bathe in the sun year round, but in January and February only northern Europeans dare the sea. The less hardy splash in sheltered, heated pools. The mean temperature in January, the coldest month of the year, is 56° Fahrenheit. In August, the hottest month, the mean temperature is about 75°F, as prevailing sea breezes mercifully keep the heat down.

Once the Sun Coast was only a spring-to-autumn affair. Now, so many shivering refugees have descended from the cold cities of northern Europe that the strip is alive year round. From June through October, however, "alive" isn't the half of it. Bullfights, flamenco, and fiestas crowd its calendar all year. Holy Week in Málaga, for example, is among the most stunning celebrations in Spain—it rivals that of Seville. And then there's Málaga's winter festival, packed with cultural and sporting events ranging from horse racing to folk songs and dances. On August fiesta days, Málaga's bullfights are second to none. There are hundreds of good restaurants along the Sun Coast for those desiring to escape from their hotel dining rooms. I'll review only a sampling of the many, many possibilities.

First, a word about the food specialties of the area. In this part of the Mediterranean, fish (such as whitebait), chopitos, and anchovies are the major part of the banquet. Particular specialties include fish soup (*sopa de pescade*), a fisher's rice dish of crayfish and clams (*arroz à la marinera*), and grilled sardines (*espetones de sardinas*). In all of Andalusia, soothing gazpacho is a refreshing opener to many a meal. Of course, everything's better when washed down with the renowned wines of Málaga, including Pedor Ximénez and Muscatel.

SEEING THE COSTA DEL SOL

GETTING THERE   By Plane   None of the airlines that fly into Spain from North America touches down in Málaga. Transfers are required in either Madrid or Barcelona, although some airlines (such

☑ **WHAT'S SPECIAL ABOUT THE COSTA DEL SOL**

Beaches

☐ Marbella, 17 miles of sandy beaches.

☐ Torremolinos, sandy but crowded beaches—try Bajondillo or El Lido.

☐ Fuengirola, 3½ miles of beaches. Best bets: Las Gaviotas, Carrajal, Santa Amalja.

Great Resorts

☐ Marbella, where glitter and hype reach their pinnacle; visit the "Golden Mile" strip of the super-wealthy.

☐ Torremolinos, the "eye" of the Costa del Sol hurricane.

Great Villages

☐ Mijas, an Andalusian pueblo.

☐ Nerja, fishing village transformed into a resort.

Historic Cities

☐ Málaga, former harbor for the Moorish kingdom of Granada.

Architectural Highlights

☐ Marbella's old quarter, around the Plaza de los Naranjos.

☐ Alcazaba at Málaga, an 11th-century fortress with an Hispano-Muslim garden.

Pocket of Posh

☐ Puerto Banús, a yacht-clogged harbor for the rich.

Festivals/Special Events

☐ Málaga's major festivals on religious occasions; a big annual *feria* (fair) in August.

☐ Marbella's flamenco festival in the second half of June.

---

as the well-recommended British Airways, for example) offer flights to Málaga nonstop from such other European cities as London.

For passengers who opt for a transfer through Madrid, the largest operator, with the greatest number of connections, is **Iberia** (tel. toll free 800/772-4642), the national airline of Spain. Iberia offers daily nonstop service to Madrid from New York, Miami, Los Angeles, Montréal, and Toronto. Iberia offers an even greater selection of itineraries into Málaga through its affiliate airlines, which include Binter, Viva, and Aviaco. Flights on any of these airlines can be booked via Iberia's toll-free reservations line.

By Train and Bus   Málaga maintains good rail connections with Madrid: at least five trains a day, and the trip takes 8–10 hours. Many visitors arrive by train after having explored the Andalusian city of Seville. There are at least three trains a day connecting Seville with Málaga, a 4-hour run. It's also possible to go from Madrid to Málaga by bus. Three major coaches make the 9-hour run from Madrid to Málaga daily. For rail information in Málaga, call RENFE (tel. 952/21-31-22), and for bus information call Málaga's new central bus station (tel. 952/35-00-61).

GETTING AROUND THE COAST   Once at Málaga, you can go

by train along the coast as far west as the resort of Fuengirola. There is rail service every 50 minutes between Málaga and Fuengirola. The run to Torremolinos takes only 30 minutes by train. For train information, there's a RENFE office in Málaga at calle Strachan 2 (tel. 952/21-31-22). Here you can not only get information but also purchase tickets. It's open Monday through Friday from 9am to 1:30pm and 4:30 to 7:30pm.

If you're in Málaga and plan to go to Marbella, you'll need to take a bus. Buses leave about every 30 minutes in either direction and the ride takes about 1½ hours. It's also possible to get to Nerja by bus from Málaga in about 1½ hours. The Málaga bus depot lies just behind the RENFE offices, opening onto Paseo de los Tilos (tel. 952/35-00-61).

If you're planning to rent a car and drive along the coast, exercise extreme caution. The impossibly overcrowded highway running along the Costa del Sol is considered one of the most dangerous in the world in terms of accidents: Many of the drivers (some, such as the British, unfamiliar with driving on the right-hand side) are drunk on Spanish wine. However, the road isn't quite as notorious as it once was, as it has been turned into a major highway, with only one-way (two-lane) traffic going each way. A series of traffic circles allows for directional changes. However, if you want to chance it, you may want to arrange your car rental in advance with one of the major companies with toll-free numbers in the United States. For more details about rentals, and the financial advantages of reserving a car in advance, see "Getting Around," Chapter 3.

1. MÁLAGA

340 miles S of Madrid, 82 miles E of Algeciras

GETTING THERE   See "Getting There," earlier in this chapter.

By Car   From the resorts in the west (such as Torremolinos or Marbella), head east along the N-340 to Málaga. If you're in the east at the end of the Costa del Sol (Almería), take the N-340 west to Málaga, with a recommended stopover at Nerja.

ESSENTIALS   The **telephone area code** for Málaga is 952. The **Tourist Information Office** is at pasaje de Chinitas 4 (tel. 952/21-34-45).

Warning: Málaga has one of the highest crime rates in Spain. The most common complaint is purse-snatching, with an estimated 75% of the crimes committed by juveniles. Stolen passports are also a problem—if it happens to you, contact the U.S. Consulate, Edificio El Ancla, calle Ramón y Cajal, Apt. 502, in nearby Fuengirola (tel. 952/47-48-91).

❶ne of the most important seaports on the Mediterranean, Málaga is the major city of the Costa del Sol and the second-largest city of Andalusia, after Seville. At the foot of Mount Gibralfaro, it's marked by orange trees, flower markets, and fishing boats. The best way to

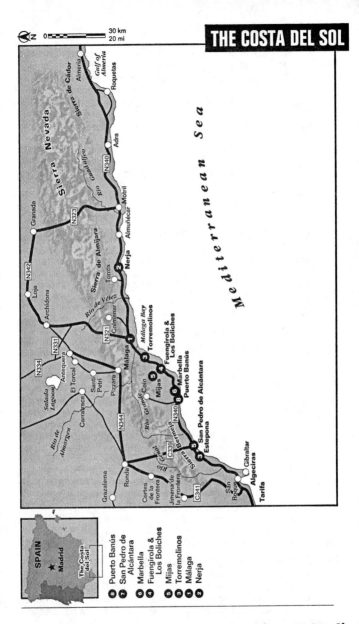

THE COSTA DEL SOL

0 — 30 km
— 20 mi

Gulf of Almería

Mediterranean Sea

Sierra Nevada

Almería
Roquetas
Adra
Motril
Almuñécar
Nerja
Torrox
Málaga Bay
Torremolinos
Fuengirola & Los Boliches
Marbella
Puerto Banús
San Pedro de Alcántara
Estepona
Gibraltar
Algeciras
Tarifa
San Roque
Granada
Loja
Archidona
Antequera
El Torcal
Ronda
Grazalema
Cortes de la Frontera
Jimena de la Frontera

Sierra de Cádor
Sierra de Almijara
Río Guadalfeo
Río de Vélez
Río Grande
Río Verde
Río de Almanzora
Salada Lagoon
Santi Petri
Pizarra
Colmenar
Coín
Mijas
Carratraca

N340
N323
N342
N321
N331
N34
N344
C339
C341

SPAIN
Madrid ★
The Costa del Sol

8 Puerto Banús
7 San Pedro de Alcántara
6 Marbella
4 Fuengirola & Los Boliches
5 Mijas
3 Torremolinos
1 Málaga
2 Nerja

see the city in true 19th-century style is in a horse-drawn carriage. If possible, visit the vegetable and fish markets.

Málaga's winter climate ranks as one of Europe's most idyllic—perhaps sufficient explanation for the luxuriant vegetation in the city's parks and gardens. Truly, El Parque, which dates from the 19th century and is filled with many botanic species, ranks among the most handsome parks in Spain.

The most festive time in Málaga is the first week in August, when the city celebrates its reconquest by Ferdinand and Isabella in 1487. The big *feria* (fair) is the occasion for parades and bullfights. A major tree-shaded boulevard of the city, paseo del Parque, is transformed into a fairground featuring amusements and restaurants.

Málaga's most famous citizen is Pablo Picasso, born here in 1881 at the Plaza de la Merced, in the center of the city. The co-founder of cubism, who would one-day paint his *Guernica* to express his horror of war, unfortunately left little of his spirit in his birthplace, and only a small selection of his work.

WHAT TO SEE & DO

After sightseeing, head back to town and do some shopping on calle Larios and its satellite alleys, all of which contain stores brimming with Spanish handcrafts.

BELLES ARTES [Fine Arts Museum], San Agustín 6. Tel. 21-83-82.

Málaga is not especially known for its art treasures, even though Pablo Picasso was born here. This museum owns two of his works, an oil painting and a watercolor, both done when he was a teenager. The museum is located behind the cathedral.

Admission: 250 ptas. ($2.50).

Open: Mon–Fri 10:30am–1:30pm and 5–8pm, Sat–Sun 10:30am–1:30pm. **Bus:** 4, 18, 19, or 24.

THE ALCAZABA AND ARCHEOLOGICAL MUSEUM, Plaza de la Aduana, Alcazabilla. Tel. 21-60-05.

The Alcazaba forms the remains of the ancient palace of Málaga's former Moorish rulers. Towers encircle two walled precincts. In ruins, it's considered an outstanding example of Moorish-Spanish architecture. Troops loyal to Isabella and Ferdinand fought a savage battle with the Arabs to take it. When the Catholic monarchs conquered Málaga, they lodged at the castle. Right in the center of town, it offers spectacular views. Wander at your leisure through the open patios, tile-lined pools, and flower gardens.

Inside is an archeological museum that contains artifacts found in prehistoric caves in Málaga province. Other exhibits document cultures ranging from Greek to Phoenician to Carthaginian.

Admission: Museum, 30 ptas. (30¢).

Open: Museum, summer, Mon–Sat 10am–1pm and 5–8pm, Sun 10am–2pm; winter, Mon–Fri 10am–1pm and 5–7pm, Sat 10am–1pm and 5–8pm, Sun 10am–2pm. **Bus:** 4, 18, 19, or 24.

CATHEDRAL OF MÁLAGA, Plaza Obsipo. Tel. 21-59-17.

The Cathedral of Málaga was begun in 1528. Its 300-foot tower stands as a lone sentinal, without a mate. Although never finished, the cathedral took so long to build that it's a melange of styles, roughly classified as "Spanish Renaissance." Inside, seek out in particular its ornate choir stalls.

Admission: Free.

Open: Mon–Sat 10am–1pm and 4–7pm. **Bus:** 14, 81, 19, or 24.

CASTILLO DE GIBRALFARO, Cerro de Gibralfaro.

On a hill overlooking Málaga and the Mediterranean are the ruins of an ancient Moorish castle-fortress of unknown origin. It's near the government-run parador and might easily be tied in with a luncheon visit.

Warning: Don't walk to Gibralfaro Castle from town. Readers have reported muggings along the way, and the area around the castle is dangerous. Take the bus (see below).

Admission: Free.

Open: Daily dawn–dusk. **Microbus:** H, leaving hourly from the cathedral.

WHERE TO STAY

For such a large city in a resort area, Málaga has a surprising lack of hotels. The best ones in all price ranges are documented below. *Note:* Book well in advance for all paradores.

Expensive

HOTEL GUADALMAR, Urbanización Guadalmar, carretera de Cádiz, Km 238, 29080 Málaga. Tel. 952/23-17-03. 196 rms. A/C MINIBAR TV TEL

$ Rates: 10,650 ptas. ($106.50) single; 15,850 ptas. ($158.50) double. Children under 12 stay free in parents' room. MC, V. **Parking:** Free.

The Hotel Guadalmar is a nine-story resort hotel located five miles from the center of the city and about a mile from the airport. The hotel has its own private beach, and all rooms open onto the swimming pool and garden. Each well-furnished accommodation is spacious, with a private sea-view balcony and a private bath. For those traveling with children, there are cribs, babysitters, and special menus available, as well as a playground. Take your meals in the dining room, La Bodega, which opens onto the sea and is decorated in a rustic theme. For a live combo to listen and dance to, go straight to La Corrida.

MÁLAGA PALACIO, Cortina del Muelle 1, 29015 Málaga. Tel. 952/21-51-85. Fax 952/21-51-85. 223 rms. A/C MINIBAR TV TEL **Bus:** 4, 18, 19, or 24.

$ Rates: 15,000 ptas. ($150) single; 16,000 ptas. ($160) double. Breakfast 1,050 ptas. ($10.50) extra. AE, DC, MC, V. **Parking:** 1,000 ptas. ($10).

This is the leading three-star hotel in a city that, frankly, lags behind in its innkeeping. The hotel is thrust right in the core of the city and opens directly on a tree-lined esplanade, near the cathedral and harbor. The building is built flat-iron style, rising 15 stories and crowned by an open-air swimming pool and refreshment bar. Most of the balconies open onto views of the port, and down below you can see graceful turn-of-the-century carriages pulled by horses. The bedrooms are traditionally furnished and have private baths. The street-floor lounges mix antiques with more modern furnishings. There's a cafeteria and boutiques.

PARADOR NACIONAL DEL GOLF, carretera de Málaga (Apdo. 324, 29080 Torremolinos), Málaga. Tel. 952/38-12-55. Fax 952/38-21-41. 60 rms. A/C MINIBAR TV TEL

$ Rates: 15,000 ptas. ($150) double. Breakfast 1,200 ptas. ($12) extra. AE, DC, MC, V. **Parking:** Free.

This is another tasteful resort hotel created by the Spanish government. Surrounded by an 18-hole golf course on one side, the Mediterranean on another, it is arranged hacienda style, with several low tile buildings. You're greeted by chirping birds and grounds planted with flowers. All bedrooms have a private balcony, with a view of the green, the circular swimming pool, or the water. The furnishings are attractive. There are no single rooms. Long tile corridors lead to the public rooms, graciously furnished lounges, and a bar and restaurants. The parador is less than 2 miles from the airport, 6½ miles west of Málaga, and 2½ miles east of Torremolinos.

Moderate

HOTEL LOS NARANJOS, paseo de Sancha 35, 29016 Málaga. Tel. 952/22-43-16. Fax 952/22-59-75. 41 rms (all with bath), 1 suite. A/C MINIBAR TV TEL **Bus:** 11.

$ Rates: 8,900 ptas. ($89) single; 11,900 ptas. ($119) double; from 19,200 ptas. ($192) suite. AE, DC, MC, V. **Parking:** 750 ptas. ($7.50).

The Hotel Los Naranjos is one of the more reasonably priced (and safer) choices in the city. This is a well-run and maintained hotel lying just outside the heart of town on the eastern side of Málaga past the Plaza de Toros (bullring). It's in the vicinity of the best beach in Málaga, Baños del Carmen. The rooms are contemporary with private baths or showers. The public rooms are decorated in the typical Andalusian style, with colorful tiles and ornate wood carving. Breakfast is the only meal served and costs extra.

PARADOR DE MÁLAGA-GIBRALFARO, Monte Gibralfaro, 29016 Málaga. Tel. 952/22-43-16. Fax 952/22-59-75. 12 rms (all with bath). A/C MINIBAR TV TEL **Directions:** Take the coast road, paseo de Reding, which becomes avenida Casa de Pries and finally paseo de Sancha; turn left onto Camino Nuevo and follow the small signs the rest of the way.

$ Rates: 11,000 ptas. ($110) single; 12,500 ptas. ($125) double. Breakfast 1,200 ptas. ($12) extra. AE, DC, MC, V. **Parking:** Free.

A government-owned hotel/restaurant perched high on a hill near the ancient castle, this parador has a view of the sea, the city, the mountains, and beaches. It's an unusual combination of taste, beauty, and comfort. Imagine a building of rugged stone with long arched open corridors and bedrooms furnished with hand-loomed fabrics. Each of the bedrooms comes with a private bath, a sitting area, and a terrace bedecked with garden furniture. However, don't attempt to walk down to the heart of Málaga—it's not safe: Many readers have been mugged. The location is 1½ miles north of the center.

Inexpensive

EL CENACHERO, Barroso 5, 29001 Málaga. Tel. 952/22-40-88. 14 rms (8 with bath). **Bus:** 15.

$ Rates: 3,700 ptas. ($37) single without bath; 5,000 ptas. ($50) double with bath. No credit cards.

Opened in 1969, this modest little hotel is five blocks from the park (near the harbor). Each of the nicely carpeted rooms is different; half of them have showers. Everything is kept clean. No meals are served.

HOSTAL RESIDENCIA CARLOS V, Cister 6, 29015 Málaga. Tel. 952/21-51-20. 50 rms (all with bath). TEL **Bus:** 15 from the rail station.

$ Rates: 3,200 ptas. ($32) single; 5,500 ptas. ($55) double.

Breakfast 450 ptas. ($4.50) extra. AE, DC, MC, V. **Parking:** 1,000 ptas. ($10).

This might serve as an emergency stopover if nothing else is available in the old city. It has a good central location near the cathedral, as well as an interesting facade decorated with wrought-iron balconies and *miradores* (bay windows). The lobby is fairly dark, but this remains an old, safe haven. An elevator will take you to your room, furnished in a no-frills style.

HOSTAL RESIDENCIA DERBY, San Juan de Dios 1, 29015 Málaga. Tel. 952/21-13-01. 16 rms (all with bath). TEL **Bus:** 15.

$ Rates: 3,500 ptas. ($35) single; 5,000 ptas. ($50) double. No credit cards.

 The Derby is a real find. This fourth-floor boarding house right in the heart of Málaga, on a main square directly north of the train station, has some rooms with excellent views of the Mediterranean and the port of Málaga. The hostal is quite clean, and all rooms have hot and cold running water. No breakfast is served.

A Nearby Retreat

LA BOBADILLA, Finca La Bobadilla (Apdo. 53), 18300 Loja (Granada). Tel. 958/32-18-61. Fax 958/32-18-10. 60 rms (all with bath), 8 suites. A/C MINIBAR TV TEL **Directions:** From the airport at Málaga, follow the signs toward Granada, but at Km 502 continue through the village of Salinas; take the road marked "Salinas/Rute" but after 2 miles (3km) follow the signposts for the hotel to the entrance.

$ Rates (including breakfast): 26,700 ptas. ($267) single; 35,700 ptas. ($357) double, 42,700 ptas. ($427) double with a salon; from 52,000 ptas. ($520) suite. AE, DC, MC, V. **Parking:** Free.

An hour's drive northeast of Málaga, La Bobadilla is the most luxurious retreat in the south of Spain. A secluded oasis, it lies in the foothills of the Sierra Nevada near the town of Loja, which is 44 miles north of Málaga. La Bobadilla is a 13-mile drive from Loja.

The hotel complex is built like an Andalusian village, a cluster of whitewashed *casas* (cottages) constructed around a tower and a white church. Every casa in this re-created village is complete with a roof terrace and balcony overlooking the olive-grove-studded district. Each accommodation is individually designed, from the least expensive doubles to the most expensive King's Suite, the latter with plenty of room for bodyguards. The hotel service is perhaps the finest in all of Spain.

Superb craftsmanship is reflected at every turn, from the wrought-iron gates to the Andalusian fountains. The hotel breeds its own domestic animals, and grows much of its own food, including fruit and vegetables.

If you get bored in this lap of luxury, you can always drive to Granada in only an hour. Should you decide to marry your companion at this resort, you'll find a chapel with an organ 30 feet high with 1,595 pipes.

Dining/Entertainment: Even the King of Spain has dined at La Finca, which serves both a Spanish national and an international cuisine. Meals begin at 6,000 ptas. ($60). El Cortijo, on the other hand, specializes in a regional cuisine. Concerts, featuring flamenco, are presented on Friday and Saturday nights.

Services: Room service, laundry/valet, massage, babysitting.

Facilities: Two tennis courts, horseback riding, archery, outdoor swimming pool, heated indoor swimming pool, Jacuzzis, Finnish sauna, Turkish steam bath, fitness club.

WHERE TO DINE
Very Expensive

CAFÉ DE PARIS, Vélez Málaga 8. Tel. 22-50-43.

Cuisine: FRENCH. **Reservations:** Required. **Bus:** 13.

$ Prices: Appetizers 900–2,900 ptas. ($9–$29); main dishes 1,400–3,500 ptas. ($14–$35). AE, DC, MC, V.

Open: Lunch Mon–Sat 1:30–4pm; dinner Mon–Sat 8:30pm–midnight. **Closed:** June 21–July 21.

The Café de Paris brings elegance and a refined French cuisine to Málaga. The location is in La Malagueta, the district surrounding the Plaza de Toros (bullring) of Málaga. This is the domain of the proprietor and chef de cuisine, José García Cortés, who has worked at many important dining rooms before carving out his own niche. Some critics have suggested that the chef's cuisine is pitched too high for the taste of the average Malagueño patronizing this establishment—at least too high for the pocketbook. By that, reference is made to such costly items as caviar, game (including partridge), or foie gras often featured on the menu.

Much of his cuisine has been adapted from classic French dishes to please the Andalusian palate. Menus are changed frequently, reflecting both the chef's imagination and the availability of produce in the Málaga markets. You might on any given night be served crêpes gratinées (filled with baby eels) or local white fish baked in salt (it doesn't sound good but is excellent). Meat Stroganoff is made here not with the usual cuts of beef but with ox meat. Save room for the creative desserts. Try, for example, a citrus-flavored sorbet made with champagne. One pleased diner pronounced the custard apple mousse "divine."

Moderate

ANTONIO MARTÍN, paseo Marítimo 4. Tel. 22-21-13.

Cuisine: SPANISH. **Reservations:** Required. **Bus:** 13.

$ Prices: Appetizers 600–1,650 ptas. ($6–$16.50); main dishes 1,200–2,200 ptas. ($12–$22). AE, DC, MC, V.

Open: Lunch Tues–Sun 1–4pm; dinner Tues–Sun 8pm–midnight.

Although this tastefully designed brick building is close to a busy intersection near the Plaza de Toros, you'll hardly be aware of the traffic outside. Three dining rooms with natural brick walls are clustered under a peaked wooden ceiling. The most rustic of them, the Rincón de Ordóñez, honors one of Spain's top matadors. On the wall is the head of the last bull Ordóñez killed before retiring, and the suit he wore. In summer the shaded harborfront terrace makes an ideal place to dine. Menu items include grilled sirloin, leg of baby lamb, grilled salmon, mixed fried fish, fresh fried anchovies, shrimp cocktail, and shellfish soup. Service is both fast and attentive.

EL CORTE INGLÉS, avenida de Andalucía 4. Tel. 30-00-00.

Cuisine: SPANISH. **Reservations:** Not required. **Bus:** 15.

$ Prices: Appetizers 650–850 ptas. ($6.50–$8.50); main dishes 1,300–1,900 ptas. ($13–$19); fixed-price menu 1,800 ptas. ($18). AE, DC, MC, V.

Open: Mon–Sat 10am–9pm.

There are two restaurants on the top floor of the Corte Inglés department store in the center of Málaga. The more formal of the two is the Steak House, which offers comfortable seating and a formally dressed staff that serves such specialties as green peppers stuffed with shellfish, filet of pork in a pepper-cream sauce, and an array of temptingly seasoned brochettes, along with a complete wine list.

Immediately adjacent to the Steak House is a popular buffet, with over 70 dishes available for a fixed price of 1,800 ptas. ($18), half price for children under 6. Wine is extra.

PARADOR DE MÁLAGA-GIBRALFARO, Monte Gibralfaro. Tel. 22-19-02.

Cuisine: SPANISH. **Reservations:** Not required. **Microbus:** H, leaving hourly from the cathedral.

$ Prices: Appetizers 550–850 ptas ($5.50–$8.50); main dishes 1,600–2,000 ptas. ($16–$20). AE, DC, MC, V.

Open: Lunch daily 1–4pm; dinner daily 8:30–11pm.

Government owned, this restaurant sits on a mountainside high above the city, and is preferred for its view. You can look down into the heart of the Málaga bullring, among other things. Meals are served in the attractive dining room or under the arches of two wide terraces, which provide views of the coast. Featured are hors d'oeuvres parador—your entire table literally covered with tiny dishes of tasty tidbits. Another specialty is an omelet of chanquetes—tiny whitefish popular in this part of the country—or chicken Villaroi.

PARADOR NACIONAL DEL GOLF, carretta de Málaga. Tel. 38-12-55.

Cuisine: SPANISH. **Reservations:** Not required.

$ Prices: Appetizers 550–850 ptas. ($5.50–$8.50); main dishes 1,600–2,000 ptas. ($16–$20). AE, DC, MC, V.

Open: Lunch daily 1:30–4pm; dinner daily 8:30–11pm.

Another government-owned restaurant, this has an indoor/outdoor dining room that opens onto a circular swimming pool, golf course, and private beach. The interior dining room, furnished with reproductions of antiques, has a refined country-club atmosphere. Before-lunch drinks at the sleek modern bar tempt golfers, among others, who then proceed to the covered terrace for their Spanish meals.

REFECTORIUM, avenida Juan Sebastián Elcano 146. Tel. 29-45-93.

Cuisine: SPANISH. **Reservations:** Recommended on week-ends.

$ Prices: Appetizers 750–1,100 ptas. ($7.50–$11); main dishes 1,500–2,000 ptas. ($15–$20). MC, V.

Open: Lunch Tues–Sun 1–4pm; dinner Tues–Sun 8pm–midnight.

The Refectorium is removed from the typical tourist hustle and bustle of the coast. Located outside town near the Playa de El Palo beachfront, about three miles east of the bullring, the Refectorium stands on the east side of the bridge spanning Arroyo Jaboneros.

Although finding it may involve a bit of a search, the result is worth it. It offers dining with the flair of old Spanish tradition, in an atmosphere of brick-red terra-cotta floors, old wooden beams, and white stucco walls. The cuisine has a certain old-fashioned flair, and the servings are more than generous, so take that into consideration when ordering.

You might begin with a typical soup of the Málaga district, called ajo blanco con uvas (cold almond soup flavored with garlic and garnished with big muscatel grapes). A classic opener—also popular in the north of Spain—is garlic-flavored mushrooms seasoned with bits of sweet-tasting ham. The fresh seafood is generally a delight, including rape or angler fish. Lamb might be served with a savory saffron-flavored tomato sauce, and you might finish with a homemade dessert, such as rice pudding.

Inexpensive

FOSTER'S HOLLYWOOD, Plaza de la Malagueta 2. Tel. 22-05-05.
   Cuisine: AMERICAN. **Reservations:** Recommended Sat-Sun. **Bus:** 15.
$ Prices: Appetizers 450–600 ptas. ($4.50–$6); main dishes 750–2,200 ptas. ($7.50–$22); fixed-price menu 1,200 ptas. ($12). AE, DC, MC, V.
   Open: Daily 1pm–1am.
This fashionable California-style hamburger joint is one of the central zone's most popular hangouts for locals and visiting Yanks. A member of a 16-restaurant chain that was praised by a recent U.S. ambassador for its good-natured promotions of popular American culture, it serves a choice of 13 half-pound hamburgers, steaks, chicken dishes, and platters inspired by the Hispano-American traditions of Tex-Mex. Any of these might be accompanied by what *The New York Times* reports as "probably the best onion rings in the world."

LA MANCHEGA, Marín García 4. Tel. 22-21-80.
   Cuisine: SPANISH. **Reservations:** Not required. **Bus:** 7 or 9.
$ Prices: Appetizers 350–500 ptas. ($3.50–$5); main dishes 600–850 ptas. ($6–$8.50); fixed-price menu 1,000 ptas. ($10). No credit cards.
   Open: Lunch daily 11:30am–4:30pm; dinner daily 7:30–11:30pm.
La Manchega is representative of the local bars and eateries on this popular pedestrians-only street in a downtown commercial area. Outside are sidewalk tables for drinking or dining; inside, a ground-floor bar with tile walls and a decorator's attempt to create an indoor Andalusian courtyard. A Salon Comedor offers additional space for dining on an upper floor. Specialties include shrimp omelets, Málaga-style soup, beans with Andalusian ham, snails, eels, and a full array of shellfish, including grilled shrimp, clams, and mussels. Try the fish soup.

MESÓN DANES [FAARUP], Barroso 7. Tel. 22-74-42.
   Cuisine: DANISH/SPANISH. **Reservations:** Not accepted. **Bus:** 15.
$ Prices: Appetizers 475–600 ptas. ($4.75–$6); main dishes 1,095–1,850 ptas. ($10.95–$18.50); fixed-price menu 1,350 ptas. ($13.50). V.

Open: Lunch Mon–Sat noon–4pm; dinner Mon–Sat 8–11:30pm. **Closed:** Aug.

S Here you can enjoy Danish and Spanish snacks at low prices, with choices including Danish or Spanish soup, fish, and meat. Also available is a special Faarup plate with assorted food. The cheaper *menu del día* represents one of the best food values in Málaga. Mesón Danes is located near the bus station.

EVENING ENTERTAINMENT

Drinks and Tapas

EL BOQUERÓN DE PLATA, Bolsa 8. Tel. 22-20-20.

El Boquerón de Plata has long been one of the most frequented bars of Málaga. You come here for good Spanish wine and tapas. If you're a local, the latest gossip will be the order of the day. Most guests have a beer and a helping of the prawns. The fish depends on the catch of the day—it's invariably fresh—a plate of the day ranges from 400 ptas. ($4); beer, from 100 ptas. ($1). Open daily from 10am to 3pm and 6 to 10pm. Bus: 15.

Warning: There are two other places in the region using the same name.

LA TASCA, calle de Marín García 1. Tel. 22-20-82.

La Tasca is not the place to go if you're looking for a quiet and mellow tasca where no one ever raises his or her voice. The most famous bar in Málaga, this is really a hole in the wall, but it has style, conviviality, and a large staff crowded behind the bar to serve the sometimes-strident demands of practically everyone in Málaga—many of whom bring their children with them. You can have a choice of beer from the tap, wine, and an array of tapas. Try the croquettes (croquetas) and pungent shish kebabs laced with garlic and cumin. If you see an empty seat, try to commandeer it politely—otherwise you'll stand in what might be awestruck observation of the social scene around you. Tapas begin at 400 ptas. ($4); beer, at 100 ptas. ($1). The bar lies between calle Larios and calle Nueva. Open daily from noon to 1:30pm and 7 to 10:30pm. Bus: 15.

BAR LOQÜENO, calle de Marín García 12. Tel. 22-30-48.

This place offers basically the same tapas as its neighbor, La Tasca. The entrance is behind a wrought-iron and glass door that leads into a stucco-lined room decorated in a "local tavern style" with a vengeance. There are enough hams, bouquets of garlic, beer kegs, fish nets, and sausages to feed an entire village for a week. There's hardly enough room to stand, and you'll invariably be jostled by a busy waiter shouting "calamari" to the cooks in the back kitchens. Tapas start at 400 ptas. ($4); wine by the glass, at 125 ptas. ($1.25). Open daily from noon to 4pm and 7pm to midnight. Bus: 15.

---

2. NERJA

33 miles E of Málaga, 341 miles S of Madrid,
104 miles W of Almería

GETTING THERE By Bus Nerja is well serviced by buses from Málaga, at least 10 per day (1½ hours). If you're coming from Almería in the east, there are two buses a day (3 hours).

By Car   Head along the N-340 east from Málaga, or take the N-340 west from Almería.

ESSENTIALS   Nerja's **telephone area code** is 952. The **Tourist Information Office** is at calle Puerta del Mar 2 (tel. 952/52-15-31).

Nerja is known for its good beaches and small coves, its seclusion, its narrow streets and courtyards, and its whitewashed flat-roofed houses. Nearby is one of Spain's greatest attractions, the Cave of Nerja (see below).

At the mouth of the Chillar River, Nerja gets its name from an Arabic word, *narixa,* meaning "bountiful spring." Its most dramatic spot is the **Balcón de Europa,** a palm-shaded promenade that juts out into the Mediterranean. The sea-bordering walk was constructed in 1885 and named to honor Alfonso XIII, and it commands a panoramic coastline view. To reach the best beaches, go west from the Balcón and follow the shoreline.

A NEARBY ATTRACTION

The most popular outing from Málaga or Nerja is to the ✪ **Cueva de Nerja,** carretera de Maro (tel. 52-00-76), which scientists believe was inhabited from 100,000 to 40,000 B.C. This prehistoric stalactite-and-stalagmite cave lay undiscovered until 1959, when it was found by a handful of men on a routine exploring mission. When fully opened, it revealed a wealth of treasures left from the days of the cave dwellers, including Paleolithic paintings believed to be 15,000 years old. These depict horses and deer, but as of this writing they are not open to public view. The archeological museum in the cave contains a number of prehistoric artifacts; don't miss walking through its stupendous galleries. In the Hall of the Cataclysm, the ceiling soars to a height of 200 feet.

From May 1 to September 1, the cave is open daily from 9:30am to 9pm; during other months, from 10am to 1:30pm and 4 to 7pm. Admission is 300 ptas. ($3) for adults, 150 ptas. ($1.50) for children 6–12.

Nerja-bound buses leave from the Plaza Queipo de Llano in Málaga at 10am and again at noon, returning at 3 and 4:45pm. The trip takes two hours each way, since the bus makes frequent stops. Cave-bound buses leave from the center of Nerja hourly during the day, costing 65 ptas. (65¢).

WHERE TO STAY

Expensive

HOTEL MÓNICA, Playa de la Torrecilla, 29780 Nerja. Tel. 952/52-11-00. Fax 952/52-11-62. 234 rms, 1 suite. A/C TV TEL

$ Rates: 8,200 ptas. ($82) single; 12,500 ptas. ($125) double; from 14,500 ptas. ($145) suite. Breakfast 800 ptas. ($8) extra. AE, MC, V.

The Hotel Mónica looks something like a three-pronged propeller if you view it from the air. At ground level as you approach the entrance, you see that it has North African arches and green-and-white panels.

This is the newest and the most luxurious hotel in Nerja. You'll find this four-star establishment in an isolated position about a 10-minute walk from the Balcony of Europe, on a low-lying curve of beachfront.

The glistening white marble in its lobby is highlighted with such neobaroque touches as elaborately detailed cast-iron balustrades, curved marble staircases, and bas-reliefs, paintings, and sculptures. Some of the stairwells even contain oversize copies, set in tiles, of the beach scenes of Claude Monet. A nautical theme is carried out in the bar with brass navigational instruments, models of clipper ships, and comfortable sofas. Both the hotel's restaurants have outdoor terraces or patios for indoor/outdoor dining. A curved swimming pool was built into a terrace a few feet above the beach. The comfortable bedrooms offer private balconies.

PARADOR NACIONAL DE NERJA, Playa de Burriana-Tablazo, 29780 Nerja. Tel. 952/52-00-50. Fax 952/52-19-97. 73 rms. A/C MINIBAR TV TEL
$ Rates: 12,000 ptas. ($120) single; 14,500 ptas. ($145) double. Breakfast 1,200 ptas. ($12) extra. AE, DC, MC, V. **Parking:** Free.

On the outskirts of town, this government-owned hotel takes the best of modern motel designs and blends them with a classic Spanish ambience of beamed ceilings, tile floors, and hand-loomed draperies. It's built on the edge of a cliff, around a flower-filled courtyard with a splashing fountain, and its social life centers around a large swimming pool. There is a sandy beach below, reached by an elevator, and lawns and gardens. The bedrooms are spacious and furnished in an understated but tasteful style, and each has a private bath. International and Spanish meals are served in the hotel restaurant, where a complete dinner costs 3,500 ptas. ($35).

Moderate

HOTEL BALCÓN DE EUROPA, paseo Balcón de Europa 1, 29780 Nerja. Tel. 952/52-08-00. Fax 952/52-44-90. 101 rms (all with bath), 20 suites. A/C TV TEL
$ Rates: 7,200 ptas. ($72) single; 9,500 ptas. ($95) double; from 12,000 ptas. ($120) suite. Breakfast 600 ptas. ($6) extra. DC, MC, V. **Parking:** 750 ptas. ($7.50).

Occupying the best position in town at the edge of the Balcón de Europa, the hotel offers rooms with private balconies overlooking the water and the rocks. At a private beach nearby, parasol-shielded tables offer a place to gaze upon the peaceful vista. The comfortable bedrooms are decorated with modern furniture and terra-cotta floors. There's a private garage a few steps away.

Guests can dine at the fourth-floor Restaurant Azul, which offers a panoramic view, or at the beach restaurant, Nautico. An international menu is served. Facilities include a sauna, health club, and solarium, and services include babysitting, laundry, and room service.

Budget

CALA-BELA, Puerta del Mar 8, 29780 Nerja. Tel. 952/52-07-00. 10 rms (all with bath). TEL
$ Rates: 3,500 ptas. ($35) single; 4,800 ptas. ($48) double. Breakfast 400 ptas. ($4) extra. AE, DC, MC, V.

A recently improved miniature hotel just a one-minute walk from the

Balcón de Europa, the Cala-Bela has bedrooms opening onto the sea. They may be small, but they're clean—and what a view! The lounge is charming. In the seafront dining room, seated in a bone-white Valencian chair, you are served a fixed-price meal for 1,500 ptas. ($15). The food is good, so even if you're not staying at the hotel, you may want to give it a try. Enjoy the filet of pork in a sherry sauce, the chef's paella, grilled crayfish, or trout with cream.

HOSTAL MENA, Alemania 15, 29780 Nerja. Tel. 952/52-05-41. 14 rms (8 with bath). TV TEL

$ Rates: 3,000 ptas. ($30) single without bath; 4,200 ptas. ($42) double with bath. No credit cards.

This modest little residencia near the Balcón de Europa has a lot of charm about the place, including the central hallway whose back walls are lined with hundreds of blue and white Andalusian tiles. The family running the hostal are very helpful. Bedrooms are plain and functional, but clean. No meals are served.

HOSTAL MIGUEL, calle Almirante Ferrándiz 31, 29780 Nerja. Tel. 952/52-15-23. Fax 952/52-34-85. 9 rms (all with bath).

$ Rates: 3,000 ptas. ($30) single; 4,000 ptas. ($40) double. Breakfast 300 ptas. ($3) extra. MC, V.

The Miguel is a pleasant, unpretentious inn with only nine simply furnished rooms. Housed in a 19th-century building with iron-rimmed balconies, it's situated on a quiet back street about a three-minute walk from the Balcón de Europa, and across from the well-known Pepe Rico Restaurant. Breakfast is the only meal served.

WHERE TO DINE

CASA LUQUE, Plaza Cavana 2. Tel. 52-10-04.
Cuisine: ANDALUSIAN. **Reservations:** Required.
$ Prices: Appetizers 475–1,550 ptas. ($4.75–$15.50); main dishes 950–1,650 ptas. ($9.50–$16.50). AE, MC, V.
Open: Lunch Mon–Sat 1–4pm; dinner Mon–Sat 7:30pm–midnight.

With its impressive canopied and balconied facade, the Casa Luque looks like a dignified private villa. The interior has an Andalusian courtyard. Meals might include pâté maison with raspberry sauce, shoulder of ham, osso buco, pork filet, hot-pepper chicken Casanova, grilled meats, or a limited selection of fish, including grilled Mediterranean grouper.

CASA PACO Y EVA, Barrio 50. Tel. 52-15-27.
Cuisine: SEAFOOD. **Reservations:** Required.
$ Prices: Appetizers 650–850 ptas. ($6.50–$8.50); main dishes 1,600–2,000 ptas. ($16–$20). MC, V.
Open: Lunch Thurs–Tues noon–4pm; dinner Thurs–Tues 7pm–midnight.

The first things you'll notice in this air-conditioned tavern restaurant—on the ground floor of an apartment building five minutes from the Balcón de Europa—are the fresh flowers on the wooden tables. Many of the featured menu items are seafood and include a fish soup, crayfish, and a house salad. In autumn you can order pheasant with grapes. For dessert, try one of the house pastries.

EL COLONO, calle Granada 6. Tel. 52-18-26.

Cuisine: ANDALUSIAN/INTERNATIONAL. **Reservations:** Required.

$ Prices: Appetizers 595–1,395 ptas. ($5.95–$13.95); main dishes 1,095–2,000 ptas. ($10.95–$20); fixed-price menu 1,950 ptas. ($19.50). No credit cards.

Open: Lunch Tues–Sun 12:30–3:30pm; dinner Tues–Sun 8pm–midnight. **Closed:** Nov 15–Dec 20.

A family place for a night of Spanish fun—that's El Colono, near the Balcón de Europa, a three-minute walk from the main bus stop at Nerja. Guitar music and flamenco dancing account for the entertainment highlights, and you can also dine here in a tavern atmosphere, either à la carte or from fixed-price menus featuring local specialties. If you just want a glass of wine, you can still enjoy the shows (three an evening, from 8pm until "the wee hours").

PEPE RICO RESTAURANT, Almirante Ferrándiz 28. Tel. 52-02-47.

Cuisine: INTERNATIONAL. **Reservations:** Recommended.

$ Prices: Appetizers 650–1,050 ptas. ($6.50–$10.50); main dishes 1,300–2,100 ptas. ($13–$21); fixed-price menu 2,800 ptas. ($28). DC, MC, V.

Open: Dinner only, Wed–Mon 7:30–10pm. **Closed:** Nov and Feb.

Established in 1966, Pepe Rico is today one of the finest places for food in Nerja. It's housed in a white building with grill windows and little balconies. The rooms open onto a large rear balcony, which overlooks a flower-filled courtyard. Dining is in a tavern room, half wood paneled, with handmade wooden chairs, plaster walls, and ivy vines—the vines creep in from the patio, where you can also order meals al fresco.

The specialty of the day, which might be a Spanish, German, Swedish, or French dish, ranges from almond-and-garlic soup to Andalusian gazpacho, available only in the summertime. The list of hors d'oeuvres is impressive—including Pepe Rico salad, smoked swordfish, and prawns pil-pil (with hot chili peppers). Main dishes include filet of sole Don Pepe, rosada Oriental style, prawns Café de Paris, and steak dishes. Considering the quality of the food, the prices are reasonable.

PORTOFINO, Puerta del Mar 4. Tel. 52-01-60.

Cuisine: FRENCH. **Reservations:** Required.

$ Prices: Appetizers 450–850 ptas. ($4.50–$8.50); main dishes 1,200–1,800 ptas. ($12–$18); menu del día 1,800 ptas. ($18). MC, V.

Open: Dinner only, daily 7–10:30pm. **Closed:** Dec–Feb.

Portofino may offer just the ambience you're looking for, particularly if you crave well-prepared food, a sweeping view of the sea, and a tasteful but whimsical decor stressing sunlight and different shades of pink and white. The open hearth greets you near the front entrance. Dinner can be eaten either behind the shelter of large sheets of glass or on the open terrace at the edge of the bay. Specialties include salade de chèvre chaud (a salad garnished with goat cheese and baked in an apple); red mullet with tomatoes, black olives, and anchovies; pork simmered in mustard sauce; and filet of sole à l'Orientale; plus such tempting desserts as tarte Tatin (apple crumble enriched with butter and caramel) and gratin de fruits in a sweet sauce.

RESTAURANTE DE MIGUEL, calle Pintada 2. Tel. 52-29-96.

Cuisine: INTERNATIONAL. **Reservations:** Recommended.
$ Prices: Appetizers 900–1,500 ptas. ($9–$15); main dishes 1,700–2,400 ptas. ($17–$24). MC, V.
Open: Lunch Mon–Sat 1–3pm; dinner Mon–Sat 7–11pm.
Closed: Feb–Mar 20.

This restaurant was established several years ago by the son of a Nerja resident. At first it was patronized only by local families hoping for their friend to succeed. Since then, however, mostly because of the excellent food, the place has attracted a devoted coterie of foreign visitors and expatriate residents of the Costa del Sol. It sits in the center of town near the busiest traffic intersection, behind a plate-glass aquarium loaded with fresh lobsters, fish, and shellfish. Its not-very-large air-conditioned interior is one of the most decidedly upscale places in Nerja, with white marble floors, elegant crystal and porcelain, and crisply ironed white napery. The menu lists a full array of international dishes, including cream of shrimp soup flavored with cognac, tournedos with a sauce made from goat-milk cheese, sea bass with Pernod and fennel, a wide selection of beef and steak dishes, and imaginative concoctions composed from the cornucopia of fish from the aquarium.

RESTAURANTE REY ALFONSO, paseo Balcón de Europa. Tel. 52-01-95.

Cuisine: SPANISH/INTERNATIONAL. **Reservations:** Recommended.
$ Prices: Appetizers 450–800 ptas. ($4.50–$8); main courses 850–2,100 ptas. ($8.50–$21). MC, V.
Open: Lunch Thurs–Tues 1–4pm; dinner Thurs–Tues 7–11pm.
Closed: Nov–Dec.

Set at the most distant (and most panoramic) tip of the Balcón de Europa, the Rey Alfonso lies at the bottom of a flight of concrete stairs which skirt some of the most dramatic rock formations along the coast. Host to such personalities as the President of Spain and the Queen of Denmark, it's one of the best-reputed and most popular restaurants in town. The menu doesn't hold many surprises, but the view, the ambience, and the polite staff make it worthwhile.

The establishment welcomes customers into the bar area if they don't want a full meal. If they do, menu specialties include paella valenciana, several kinds of soup, including a succulent version made with local crabmeat, wienerschnitzels, five different preparations of sole, fondue bourguignonne, crayfish in whisky sauce, and for dessert, crêpes Suzette.

3. TORREMOLINOS

9 miles W of Málaga, 76 miles E of Algeciras,
353 miles S of Madrid

GETTING THERE By Plane Málaga airport is nearby.

By Train There are frequent departures from the terminal at Málaga.

By Bus   Buses run frequently between Málaga and Torremolinos.

By Car   Take the N-340 west from Málaga or the N-340 east from Marbella.

ESSENTIALS   The **telephone area code** for Torremolinos is 952. The **Tourist Information Office** is at La Nogalera 517 (tel. 952/38-15-78). In winter the weather can get chilly, so pack accordingly.

On a rocky promontory in the heart of the Costa del Sol, this resort dominates a magnificent bay at the foot of the Sierra Mijas. This international tourist center achieved prominence because of its five-mile-long beach, one of the finest along the Mediterranean, although its level of pollution has long been under attack by the media.

If you get up at daybreak and go to the beach, you'll see the fishers bringing in their nets; but by 10am the sun worshippers have taken over. Many stay on the beach all day, depending on vendors who come around selling snacks and drinks. The once-sleepy fishing village pulsates with life in its high-rise apartments, hotels of every hue, discos, flamenco clubs, wine *bodegas,* boutiques, restaurants, and numerous bars—some with such unlikely names as "Fat Black Pussycat."

The original village runs along **calle de San Miguel,** still distinctively Andalusian despite its boutiques and restaurants. Reached past a zigzag of buildings leading down to the beach, **La Carihuela** was the old fishers' village—it still is, if you ignore the hotels and apartments. Opposite is **Montemar,** a smart residential quarter of villas and gardens. For a slice of old Andalusia, see the **El Calvario** area, with its whitewashed houses, donkeys, and street vendors.

In the evening, the sidewalk café life flourishes. You can spend an entire evening along the traffic-free **calle del Cauce,** with its open-air restaurants and bars (sample before-dinner *tapas* here).

If you want to do some shopping, you won't be disappointed: the best stores of Barcelona and Madrid operate branches in Torremolinos.

WHERE TO STAY

At first, everything in town looks like a hotel, a restaurant, a bar, or a souvenir shop—and that's about it. Actually, considering the number of visitors, Torremolinos doesn't have as many hotels as you'd expect. That's because many European visitors rent apartments on short-term leases during their vacation stays. Hotels are clustered not only in Torremolinos but in nearby Benalmádena Costa (see below). Many of the hotels in Torremolinos are filled with package-tour groups. The quality of accommodations is wide ranging, everything from expensive choices (but nothing to equal the luxury of some of the Marbella hostelries) to cheap *hostales* (some of the latter seem popular with revelers who like to party until dawn on cheap wine). The best advice if you're planning to make Torremolinos your center in the Costa del Sol is to pick and choose carefully among the hotels, looking for one compatible with your interests and, most definitely, your pocketbook.

Expensive

ALOHA PUERTO SOL, via Imperial 55, 29620 Torremolinos. Tel. 952/38-70-66. Fax 952/38-57-01. 418 rms. A/C MINIBAR TV TEL

$ Rates: 10,200 ptas. ($102) single; 13,900 ptas. ($139) double. AE, DC, MC, V.

The Aloha Puerto Sol, one of the most modern hotels along the Costa del Sol, stands on the seashore in the residential area of El Saltillo. Away from the noise in the center of Torremolinos, it offers spacious rooms facing the sea and beach, protected by the Benalmádena Marina. Each unit has a sitting room. In this resort setting, guests are given a choice of two restaurants and four bars. During the day you can lounge around two swimming pools (one heated). Spanish evenings at El Comodoro, one of the bars on the premises, last well into the early morning.

CASTILLO DE SANTA CLARA, calle Castillo del Inglés 1, 29620 Torremolinos. Tel. 952/38-31-55. Fax 952/38-95-79. 213 rms, 30 suites. A/C TV TEL

$ Rates (including breakfast): 11,450–14,200 ptas. ($114.50–$142) single; 14,500–16,500 ptas. ($145–$165) double; from 20,000 ptas. ($200) suite. AE, DC, MC, V. **Parking:** Free.

This angular modern palace was built in 1975 above the cliffs that separate Torremolinos from its satellite village of La Carihuela. It was designed so that about half the accommodations lie below the terraced gardens. Into these gardens were sunk a pair of curvaceous swimming pools, whose waters are shaded with exotic cacti, palms, and well-maintained flower beds. The public rooms are sheathed almost entirely in russet-colored marble, the expanses of which are relieved with sculpted terra-cotta bas-reliefs, scattered copies of Chippendale antiques, and nautical accessories. Each bedroom has a private bath and a wood-trimmed balcony. On the premises are a sauna, a gymnasium, a nightclub, a tennis court, and an elevator that takes you down the cliffs to the beach.

DON PABLO, paseo Marítimo, 29620 Torremolinos. Tel. 952/38-38-88. Fax 952/38-37-83. 443 rms. A/C MINIBAR TV TEL

$ Rates (including buffet breakfast): 9,100 ptas. ($91) single; 12,700 ptas. ($127) double. AE, DC, MC, V.

One of the most desirable hotels in Torremolinos is housed in a modern building, located a minute from the beach, and surrounded by its own garden and playground areas. There are two unusually shaped open-air swimming pools, with terraces for sunbathing and refreshments, and a large indoor pool as well. The surprise is the glamorous interior, which borrows heavily from Moorish palaces and medieval castle themes. Arched tile arcades have splashing fountains, and life-size stone statues of nude figures in niches line the grand staircase. The bedrooms have sea-view terraces.

The hotel has a full day-and-night entertainment program, including keep-fit classes, dancing at night to a live band, and a disco. Piano music is also played in a wood-paneled English lounge, and the hotel has video movies shown on a giant screen every night. At lunch, a buffet is spread before you.

HOTEL CERVANTES, calle de las Mercedes, 29620 Torre-

molinos. Tel. 952/38-40-33. Fax 952/38-48-57. 397 rms. A/C TV TEL
$ Rates: 9,200 ptas. ($92) single; 14,000 ptas. ($140) double. AE, DC, MC, V.

The Cervantes is a four-star hotel—about a seven-minute walk to the beach. It has its own garden and is adjacent to a maze of patios and narrow streets of boutiques and open-air cafés. The Cervantes is self-contained, with a sun terrace, sauna, massage, two pools (one covered and heated), hairdressers, gift shop, TV and video lounge, and a game room. The bedrooms have streamlined modern furniture, baths, music, safes, TVs, and spacious terraces; many have sea-view balconies.

A restaurant, a bar with an orchestra and entertainment programs, and a coffee shop are among the attractions. You can enjoy lunch or dinner for 2,500 ptas. ($25) and up. Los Molinos Grill on the top floor offers excellent grill meals.

MELÍA COSTA DEL SOL, paseo Marítimo 19, 29620 Torremolinos. Tel. 952/38-66-77, or toll free 800/336-3542 in the U.S. Fax 952/38-64-17. 540 rms, 18 suites. A/C TV TEL
$ Rates: 7,500–10,600 ptas. ($75–$106) single; 11,000–13,000 ptas. ($110–$130) double; from 27,500 ptas. ($275) suite. AE, DC, MC, V. **Parking:** Free.

There are two Melía hotels in Torremolinos, both operated by a popular hotel chain in Spain, but this one is preferred by many clients because of its more central location. It's practically twice the size of the smaller hotel and offers modern and well-maintained bedrooms. However, the hotel is popular with package-tour groups, and you may not feel a part of things if you're here alone. There's a garden, swimming pool, Thalassotherapy center, disco, and shopping arcade.

MELÍA TORREMOLINOS, avenida de Carlotta Alessandri 109, 29620 Torremolinos. Tel. 952/38-05-00, or toll free 800/336-3542 in the U.S. Fax 952/38-05-38. 281 rms, 7 suites. A/C TV TEL
$ Rates: 10,200 ptas. ($102) single; 15,000–22,000 ptas. ($150–$220) double; from 26,800 ptas. ($268) suite. Breakfast 1,000 ptas. ($10) extra. AE, DC, MC, V. **Closed:** Nov–Mar.

This is the more luxurious of the two Melía hotels, and it has better service, too. The rooms in this five-star hotel have private baths or showers and are well furnished and maintained. The hotel, which has its own garden, stands on the western outskirts of Torremolinos on the road to Cádiz. There's a good restaurant, offering meals for 3,200 ptas. ($32), a swimming pool, and tennis courts. Flamenco shows are occasionally presented.

Moderate

AMARAGUA, Los Nidos 23, 29620 Torremolinos. Tel. 952/38-47-00. Fax 952/38-49-45. 198 rms (all with bath), 12 suites. TEL **Bus:** 10.
$ Rates: 5,500 ptas. ($55) single; 8,000 ptas. ($80) double; from 11,800 ptas. ($118) suite. Breakfast 700 ptas. ($7) extra. AE, DC, MC, V.

The Amaragua is right on the beach in the middle of the residential area of Torremolinos-Montemar. All units have a terrace and sea view. The hotel has lounges, a bar, three large swimming pools (one heated), gardens, water sports, a children's playground, a sauna, parking facilities, and a tennis court. Rooms have baths or showers, but no air conditioning.

HOTEL LOS ARCOS, avenida de Carlotta Alessandri 192, 29620 Torremolinos. Tel. 952/38-08-22. 51 rms (all with bath). A/C TV TEL

$ Rates (including breakfast): 7,500 ptas. ($75) single; 9,500 ptas. ($95) double. AE, DC, MC, V.

Once a grand old villa, the Hotel Los Arcos is reminiscent of the Spanish-style houses built for movie stars in Beverly Hills in the 1920s. Eclectic furnishings are placed throughout, and the bedrooms are pleasant, each with a balcony and a garden view. A complete lunch or dinner is available for 1,500 ptas. ($15). The hotel stands 225 yards from the beach and three-quarters of a mile from the town center.

LAS PALOMAS, Carmen Montes 1, 29620 Torremolinos. Tel. 952/38-50-00. Fax 952/38-64-66. 345 rms (all with bath). TEL

$ Rates: 7,500 ptas. ($75) single; 11,000 ptas. ($110) double. Breakfast 600 ptas. ($6) extra. AE, DC, MC, V. **Parking:** Free.

Originally built during the heyday of Torremolinos's construction boom (1968), this well-managed hotel is one of the town's most attractive, surrounded as it is with carefully tended gardens. Located near the coastal road, a 1-minute walk from the beach and a 10-minute walk south of the center of town, it has an Andalusian decor that extends into the bedrooms, a formal entrance, and a devoted clientele of repeat visitors who hail mostly from France, Belgium, and Holland. Each of the bedrooms contains a private balcony, tiled bathroom, and furniture inspired by southern Spain. None contains air conditioning, although many clients compensate by opening windows and balcony doors to let in the sea breezes. The hotel contains a sauna, three swimming pools (one reserved for children), some form of entertainment going on throughout the day and early evening, a handful of shops, and an unending series of lunchtime and dinner buffets priced at 1,400 ptas. ($14) per person.

SIDI LAGO ROJO, Miami 1, 29620 Torremolinos. Tel. 952/38-76-66. Fax 952/38-08-91. 144 rms (all with bath). A/C TEL

$ Rates: 6,300 ptas. ($63) single; 8,850 ptas. ($88.50) double. Breakfast 625 ptas. ($6.25) extra. AE, DC, MC, V.

In the heart of the still-preserved fishing village of La Carihuela, this hotel is only 150 feet from the beach and the waterside fish restaurants and bars. It's the finest place to stay in the fishing village, with its own surrounding gardens and swimming pool, along with terraces for sunbathing and a refreshment bar. The modern hotel offers studio-style doubles, tastefully appointed with contemporary Spanish furnishings, tile baths, and terraces with views. The bar, with a sophisticated decor, is a popular gathering point. In the late evening there's disco dancing. The hotel also has a good restaurant, with meals costing 2,000 ptas. ($20).

Inexpensive

ALTA VISTA, Ma Barrabino, 29620 Torremolinos. Tel. 952/38-76-00. Fax 952/38-78-34. 107 rms (all with bath). TEL

$ Rates: 5,500 ptas. ($55) single; 7,500 ptas. ($75) double. Breakfast 450 ptas. ($4.50) extra. No credit cards.

A few minutes' walk from the beach, the Alta Vista is situated in the old marketplace, right in the heart of Torremolinos, surrounded by little lanes of boutiques and patios with coffee shops. The entire roof of the hotel is a tiled solarium with umbrella tables, lounge chairs, and a bar. Each of the bedrooms—furnished with ornate wrought-iron beds, reed-seated chairs, phones, and bedside reading lamps—has a balcony. Guests gather in the lounge or the bar. Lunch and dinner are served in a stylish dining room, with meals from 1,600 ptas. ($16).

HOSTAL LOS JAZMINES, avenida del Lido, 29620 Torremolinos. Tel. 952/38-50-33. Fax 952/37-27-02. 85 rms (all with bath). TEL

$ Rates: 6,000 ptas. ($60) double. Breakfast 350 ptas. ($3.50) extra. AE, MC, V.

On one of the best beaches in Torremolinos—facing a plaza at the foot of the shady avenida del Lido—this paradise for sun-seekers is replete with terraces, lawns, and an odd-shaped swimming pool. Meals are served al fresco or inside the appealing dining room, furnished with Spanish reproductions. The bedrooms, all doubles, seem a bit impersonal, but they have their own little balconies, coordinated colors, and compact baths. From here it's a good hike up the hill to the town center.

HOTEL BLASÓN, avenida de los Manantiales 1, 29620 Torremolinos. Tel. 952/38-67-67. 48 rms (all with bath). TEL **Bus:** 4.

$ Rates: 4,800 ptas. ($48) single; 5,500 ptas. ($55) double. Breakfast 350 ptas. ($3.50) extra. AE, DC, MC, V.

Those who want a simple, centrally located place to stay should try the Hotel Blasón. But beware of the noise: The hotel opens directly onto the Plaza de Costa del Sol, where there are outdoor tables for drinks and snacks. The bedrooms are furnished with reproductions of Spanish provincial pieces.

HOTEL PLATA, pasaja Pizarro 1, 29620 Torremolinos. Tel. 952/37-57-34. 39 rms (all with bath). TEL **Bus:** 4.

$ Rates: 3,300 ptas. ($33) single; 5,500 ptas. ($55) double. Breakfast 350 ptas. ($3.50) extra. MC, V.

A centrally located hotel, right on the coastal road to Málaga, the Plata is surrounded by private terraces with chairs and tables set out for breakfast or drinks. The oddly shaped rooms are large; there's enough space to add extra beds if required. The air-conditioned dining room—which serves reasonably good meals—captures the Andalusian spirit with its beamed ceiling, crude yet comfortable chairs, and lots of bric-a-brac.

HOTEL EL POZO, Casablanca 4, 29620 Torremolinos. Tel. 952/38-06-22. 28 rms (all with bath). TV TEL

$ Rates: 3,200 ptas. ($32) single; 5,500 ptas. ($55) double. Breakfast 375 ptas. ($3.75) extra. DC, MC, V.

This hotel isn't for light sleepers. It's in one of the liveliest sections of town, a short walk from the train station. The lobby-level bar has an open fireplace, heavy Spanish furniture, cool white tiles, and a view of a small courtyard. From your window or terrace you can view the promenades below. Rooms are furnished in a simple, functional style. The double rooms have TV, and some are air-conditioned.

MIAMI, Calle Aladino 14, 29620 Torremolinos. Tel. 952/ 38-52-55. Fax 952/38-52-55. 27 rms (all with bath). TEL
$ Rates: 3,200 ptas. ($32) single; 5,500 ptas. ($55) double. Breakfast 325 ptas. ($3.25) extra. No credit cards.

 Near the Carihuela section, the Miami is like one of those Hollywood movie-star homes of the 1920s. It may even bring back silent-screen memories of Vilma Banky and Rod La Rocque. Its swimming pool is isolated by high walls and private gardens. In the rear patio fuchsia bougainvillea climbs over arches. A tile terrace is used for sunbathing and refreshments. The country-style living room contains a walk-in fireplace, plus lots of brass and copper. The bedrooms are furnished with style, each traditional and comfortable with a balcony. Breakfast is the only meal served.

Nearby Places to Stay

Where Torremolinos ends and Benalmádena-Costa in the west begins is hard to say. Benalmádena-Costa has long since become a resort extension on the western frontier of Torremolinos, and it's packed with hotels, restaurants, and tourist facilities.

HOTEL TORREQUEBRADA, carretera de Cádiz, Km 220, 29630 Benalmádena. Tel. 952/44-60-00. Fax 952/44-57-02. 350 rms (all with bath). A/C MINIBAR TV TEL
$ Rates: 20,000 ptas. ($200) single; 24,000 ptas. ($240) double. Breakfast 1,800 ptas. ($18) extra. AE, DC, MC, V. **Parking:** Free.

One of the newest five-star luxury hotels along the Costa del Sol opens onto the beach and offers a wide range of facilities and attractions, including one of the largest casinos in Europe and a world-class golf course. In addition, it has an array of restaurants, bars, pools, gardens, nightclub, health club, beach club, and tennis courts. You'll almost need a floor plan to navigate your way around the complex. Nine levels of underground parking accommodate motorists. The hotel is furnished in muted Mediterranean colors, and both antique and modern furniture is used.

The hotel offers handsomely furnished and coordinated bedrooms in two 11-story towers. All accommodations have large terraces with sea views and private safes.

A specialty restaurant, Café Royal, overlooks the gardens and the sea, enjoying a five-fork rating for its international cuisine. Meals begin at 5,000 ptas. ($50). At garden level, the Pavillion provides buffet and cafeteria service throughout the day.

TRITÓN, avenida António Machado 29, 29491 Benalmádena-Costa. Tel. 952/44-32-40. Fax 952/44-26-49. 196 rms (all with bath), 10 suites. A/C MINIBAR TV TEL
$ Rates (including breakfast): 14,100–15,000 ptas. ($141–$150) single; 18,200–20,200 ptas. ($182–$202) double; from 41,000 ptas. ($410) suite. AE, DC, MC, V. **Parking:** Free.
Less than two miles north of Torremolinos, the Tritón is a Miami Beach–style beachfront resort colony in front of the marina of Benalmádena-Costa. It features a high-rise stack of bedrooms as well

as an impressive pool and garden area. Surrounding the pool are subtropical trees and vegetation, plus thatched sun-shade umbrellas. The bedrooms have roomwide windows opening onto sun balconies.

Among the public rooms are multilevel lounges and two bars with wood paneling and handmade rustic furniture (one has impressive stained-glass windows). For food, there's the main dining room with its three-tiered, mouth-watering display of hors d'oeuvres, fruits, and desserts; a barbecue grill; plus a luncheon terrace where ferns and banana trees form the backdrop. The Tritón also offers tennis courts, a Swedish sauna, and a piano player in the bar.

WHERE TO DINE

The cuisine in Torremolinos is more American and continental than Andalusian. The hotels often serve elaborate four-course meals. If you're on a budget you may want to seek out the food court called **La Nogalera,** the major gathering place in Torremolinos, located between the coast road and the beach. Head down calle del Cauce to this compound of modern whitewashed Andalusian buildings. Open to pedestrian traffic only, it features a maze of passageways, courtyards, and patios for eating and drinking. If you're seeking anything from sandwiches to Belgian waffles to scrambled eggs to pizzas, you'll find it here.

At La Nogalera

EL CABALLO VASCO, calle Casablanca, La Nogalera. Tel. 38-23-36.
   Cuisine: BASQUE. **Reservations:** Accepted, but not usually required.
$ Prices: Appetizers 750–1,200 ptas. ($7.50–$12); main dishes 1,500–2,200 ptas. ($15–$22). AE, DC, MC, V. **Closed:** Nov–Dec.
   Open: Lunch Tues–Sun 1–4pm; dinner Tues–Sun 8pm–midnight.

Right in the heart of Torremolinos, El Caballo Vasco is the best place to dine among the independent restaurants. It serves the deservedly popular Basque cuisine from the top floor of a modern building complex reached by an elevator. Picture windows lead to a terrace. As a prelude to your repast, you might try melon with ham or fish soup. Generous portions of tasty, well-prepared seafood are served, including prawns in garlic sauce and codfish Basque style. The meat dishes are of uniformly good quality, and you get some imaginative interpretations not usually found on menus along the Costa del Sol—pork shanks Basque style and oxtail in a savory sauce. For timid diners, one of the safest bets is chicken in sherry sauce (it's also one of the least expensive main courses).

EL GATO VIUDO, La Nogalera 8. Tel. 38-51-29.
   Cuisine: SPANISH. **Reservations:** Not required.
$ Prices: Appetizers 400–800 ptas. ($4–$8); main dishes 750–1,200 ptas. ($7.50–$12). AE, DC, MC, V.
   Open: Lunch Thurs–Tues noon–3pm; dinner Thurs–Tues 6–11:30pm.

This two-fork tavern-style restaurant, off calle San Miguel, offers sidewalk tables with tartan tablecloths and Kelly-green Spanish chairs. The chef specializes in Spanish cuisine, and the small but interesting à la carte menu (in English) includes shellfish soup, paella, and roast chicken. Fresh fruit is your best bet for dessert. The atmosphere is informal, and the international clientele shows up in all kinds of attire.

RESTAURANT FLORIDA, calle Casablanca 15, La Nogalera. Tel. 38-50-85.

Cuisine: DANISH. **Reservations:** Required.

$ Prices: Appetizers 295–950 ptas. ($2.95–$9.50); main dishes 850–2,000 ptas. ($8.50–$20); buffet 1,100 ptas. ($11) at lunch, 1,600 ptas. ($16) at dinner. AE, DC, MC, V.

Open: Lunch Tues–Sun 1–4pm; dinner Tues–Sun 7pm–midnight.

This is an international Danish restaurant on the lower level of a modern shopping complex near calle del Cauce. The decor is South Seas, and the spread is gargantuan—one of the best food values in Torremolinos. For a fixed price you can enjoy a vast array of dishes from the smörgåsbord; many diners linger late, making occasional forays to the table for fine herring, tasty salads, cold meats, and hot dishes. A spread of cheeses and fruits is offered along with desserts.

In the Center

RESTAURANTE CANTON, Plaza de la Gamba Alegre 22. Tel. 38-21-17.

Cuisine: CHINESE. **Reservations:** Recommended. **Bus:** 4 to the town center.

$ Prices: Appetizers 465–890 ptas. ($4.65–$8.90); main dishes 655–2,000 ptas. ($6.55–$20); fixed-price menu 950 ptas. ($9.50). AE, MC, V.

Open: Lunch Wed–Mon 1–4pm; dinner Wed–Mon 7pm–midnight.

Near the main shopping center of Torremolinos, this is one of the resort's most reasonably priced restaurants. Its very popular fixed-price menu includes a spring roll, sweet-and-sour pork, beef with onions, steamed white rice, dessert, and a drink. You can also order à la carte, partaking of such specialties as Cantonese roast duck and grilled king prawns Chinese style. The staff is efficient and cordial.

At La Carihuela

If you want to get away from the brash high-rises and honky-tonks, head to nearby Carihuela, the old fishing village on the western outskirts of Torremolinos, where some of the best bargain restaurants are found. You can walk down a hill toward the sea to reach it.

CASA PRUDENCIO, Carmen 41, at La Carihuela. Tel. 38-14-52.

Cuisine: SEAFOOD. **Reservations:** Recommended.

$ Prices: Appetizers 550–750 ptas. ($5.50–$7.50); main dishes 850–1,800 ptas. ($8.50–$18); fixed-price menu 1,500 ptas. ($15). AE, MC, V.

Open: Lunch Tues–Sun 1–5pm; dinner Tues–Sun 7:30pm–midnight. **Closed:** Dec 25–Feb 15.

 The leading seafood restaurant on the beach at Carihuela packs in diners like sardines, but its devotees don't seem to mind the wait. The decor inside is rustic. In summer the favored place is a reed-canopy-covered open-air terrace where you dine elbow to elbow. The owner choreographs the waiters at a fast and nervous pace. Service is haphazard but friendly. For an appetizer, a soothing gazpacho is ideal. Most diners are fascinated by the specialty of the house, lubina à la sal (salted fish). Cooked in an oblong pan, the fish is completely covered with white salt, which is then scraped away in front of the diner to get to the well-flavored, tender white flesh inside. Other main courses are swordfish, shish kebab, and a special paella. For dessert, try the fresh strawberries.

EL ROQUEO, Carmen 35, at La Carihuela. Tel. 38-49-46.
   Cuisine: SEAFOOD. **Reservations:** Recommended.
$ Prices: Appetizers 550–850 ptas. ($5.50–$8.50); main dishes 1,400–2,200 ptas. ($14–$22). AE, MC, V.
   Open: Lunch Wed–Mon 1–4pm; dinner Wed–Mon 7pm–midnight. **Closed:** Nov.

Right near the beach, El Roqueo is the perfect place for a seafood dinner—one of the best restaurants in this fishing village. Spanish families often fill up some of the tables and gorge themselves on an array of fresh fish. Diners may begin with a savory sopa de mariscos (fish soup). Some dishes are priced by the gram and can be expensive, so order carefully. A special is fish baked in rock salt. Grilled sea bass and grilled shrimp are favorites. For dessert, why not that Spanish standard, a carmelized flan (custard)?

At Playamar

EL VIETNAM DEL SUR, Bloque 9 at Playamar. Tel. 38-67-37.
   Cuisine: VIETNAMESE. **Reservations:** Required.
$ Prices: Appetizers 475–600 ptas. ($4.75–$6); main dishes 650–1,200 ptas. ($6.50–$12). V.
   Open: Lunch Sun 1–4pm; dinner Thurs–Tues 7pm–midnight. **Closed:** Jan–Feb.

Vietnam Sur will wake up your taste buds after you've had a lazy day on the beach. The food here is inexpensive and best shared, so bring as many friends as possible. Chopsticks are the norm as you begin with spring rolls served with mint and a spicy sauce for dipping. The Vietnamese use a lot of vegetables in their food. Two chef's specials are fried stuffed chicken wings and beef with rice noodles. The wine list is short and moderately priced. The restaurant has a terrace for dining.

At Los Alamos

FRUTOS, carretera de Cádiz, Km 235, Urbanización Los Alamos. Tel. 38-14-50.
   Cuisine: SPANISH. **Reservations:** Recommended.
$ Prices: Appetizers 600–1,200 ptas. ($6–$12); main dishes 1,400–2,200 ptas. ($14–$22); fixed-price menu 1,550 ptas. ($15.50). MC, V.
   Open: Lunch daily 1–4:30pm; dinner daily 8pm–midnight. **Closed:** Sun dinner July–Sept.

Frutos stands next to the Los Alamos service station about a mile and a quarter from the center of Torremolinos. Malagueños frequent the place in droves, as they like its old-style cooking. Here the food is Spanish with a vengeance; nothing is made fancy for the occasional tourist who might wander in. The portions are large, and the food good—if you don't mind a bit of a wait on crowded days. Service can be hectic at times, but chances are you'll be pleased.

Many diners like to begin with ham and melon, followed by fresh seafood, likely to be something from the day's catch. Perhaps rape (angler fish) will be served, or mero (grouper), which rarely appears fresh on any menu along the coast. Maybe you'll be in for a garlic-studded leg of lamb or oxtail prepared with a savory ragoût. It's wise to reserve a table and hope that it will be available upon your arrival.

At Benalmádena

MAR DE ALBORAN, avenida de Alay 5. Tel. 44-64-27.

   Cuisine: BASQUE/ANDALUSIAN. **Reservations:** Recommended.

$ **Prices:** Appetizers 900–1,900 ptas. ($9–$19); main dishes 2,000–3,200 ptas. ($20–$32); five-course menu degustación 4,000–5,000 ptas. ($40–$50). AE, DC, MC, V.

   Open: Lunch Sun and Tues–Fri 1:30–3:30pm; dinner Tues–Sun 8:30–11:30pm. **Closed:** Dec 23 to late Jan.

   Stylishly decorated in themes of citron, white, and green, this restaurant offers an elegantly airy decor which seems appropriate for its open-windowed location near the sea. Located a short walk from the resort's Puerto Marina, it offers a tempting combination of the regional specialties of both Andalusia and the Basque region of northern Spain. Menu items change with the seasons, but might include a cold terrine of leeks; crabmeat salads; Basque piperadda in puff pastry; piquillos rellenos (red peppers stuffed with pulverized fish in a sweet-pepper sauce); bacalao (salted cod) "Club Ranero," served with garlic and a red-pepper cream sauce; kokotxas, the Basque national dish of hake cheeks in a green sauce with clams; anglerfish with prawns; pork filet with béarnaise sauce; duck with apples; and foie gras served with sweet Málaga wine and raisins. In season, the restaurant's game dishes are renowned. Dessert might be a frothy version of peach mousse served with a purée of fruit and a dark-chocolate sauce.

MARRAKECH, carretera de Benalmádena 7. Tel. 38-21-69.

   Cuisine: MOROCCAN. **Reservations:** Recommended.

$ **Prices:** Appetizers 650–850 ptas. ($6.50–$8.50); main dishes 1,200–1,800 ptas. ($12–$18). No credit cards.

   Open: Lunch Wed–Sat 12:30–4:30pm; dinner Mon and Wed–Sat 7:30pm–midnight.

Marrakech offers an excellent Moroccan cuisine in the midst of a rather garish decor. Some of the more famous dishes of the Maghreb are served here, including couscous, tagine (meat pies), and various kebabs, usually made with lamb. The stuffed pastries make a fitting dessert if you like them on the sweet side.

MESÓN CANTARRANAS, avenida de Benalmádena. Tel. 38-15-77.

   Cuisine: ANDALUSIAN. **Reservations:** Recommended. **Directions:** Head out the road to Arroyo de la Miel and Benalmádena, to the western end of the Torremolinos bypass; the restaurant is set back from the Arroyo de la Miel–El Pinillo highway.

$ **Prices:** Appetizers 700–1,200 ptas. ($7–$12); main dishes 1,200–1,700 ptas. ($12–$17). MC, V.

   Open: Lunch daily noon–4pm; dinner daily 8pm–midnight.

In this former olive mill dating from 1840 you feel like you're dining in a country inn. Perhaps you'll arrange for a table on the terrace in the rear, overlooking the olive grove. At this restaurant "of the singing frogs," you can, naturally, order frogs' legs, but you might prefer a hefty portion of roast suckling pig or roast baby lamb. Daily specials are featured, and they're often from the sea, including bream. Squid is cooked in its own ink, and the hake prepared Cantabrian style is invariably good. For dessert, the poached pears in red wine is always tempting, but there are many other selections as well.

EVENING ENTERTAINMENT

Torremolinos has more nightlife activity than any other spot along the Costa del Sol. The earliest action is always at the bars, which are lively most of the night, serving drinks and *tapas* (Spanish hors d'oeuvres). Sometimes it seems there are more bars in Torremolinos than people, so you shouldn't have trouble finding one you like. *Note:* Some of the bars are open during the day as well.

Drinks and Tapas

BAR EL TORO, calle San Miguel 32. Tel. 38-65-04.

Bar El Toro, in the very center of Torremolinos, is for bullfight aficionados. Kegs of beer, stools, and the terrace in the main shopping street make it perfect for drinking a before-dinner sherry or an after-dinner beer. As a special attraction, the staff prepares a bullfight poster, with your name between those of two famous matadors, for 500 ptas. ($5). Drinks at your table begin at 175 ptas. ($1.75) for beer or 380 ptas. ($3.80) for a pitcher of sangría. Open daily from 8am to midnight.

BAR CENTRAL, Plaza Andalucía, Bloque 1. Tel. 38-27-60.

Bar Central offers coffee, brandy, beer, cocktails, limited sandwiches, and pastries, served on a large, French-style covered terrace if you prefer. It's a good spot to meet congenial people. Drinks begin at 100 ptas. ($1) for a beer or 350 ptas. ($3.50) for a hard drink. Open Monday through Saturday from 9am to 1am.

LA BODEGA, calle San Miguel 38. Tel. 38-73-37.

La Bodega relies on its colorful clientele and the quality of its *tapas* to draw customers, who seem to seek this place out above the dozens of other tascas in this very popular tourist zone. You'll be fortunate to find space at one of the small tables, since many clients consider the bar food plentiful enough for a satisfying lunch or dinner. Once you begin to order one of the platters of fried squid, pungent tuna, grilled shrimp, or tiny brochettes of sole, you might not be able to stop. Most *tapas* cost 175–650 ptas. ($1.75–$6.50). A beer costs 110 ptas. ($1.10). Open daily from noon to midnight.

Dance Clubs/Discos

NEW PIPER'S CLUB, Plaza Costa del Sol. Tel. 38-29-94.

The leading disco in town resembles a subterranean world; the decor is tongue-in-cheek and suggests the caves at Nerja. Spread over many levels, with connecting ramps and tunnels, it has several dance floors, splashing water in reflecting pools, strobe lightning, and an aggressive set of international records to amuse its packed audience. It's very much the 1960s in aura and ambience. After your first drink, a beer costs 300 ptas. ($3). Open daily from 6 to 10:30pm and 11pm to 4:30am.

Admission (including first drink): Before 11pm, 800 ptas. ($8); after 11pm, 1,100 ptas. ($11) Sun–Thurs, 1,300 ptas. ($13) Fri–Sat.

CAPRICE, paseo Marítimo, Playa Mar. Tel. 238-18-38.

Located about a mile west of the town center, in a modern building set beside the sea, this is one of Torremolinos's newest nightclubs. Popular with a wide spectrum of both local residents and visiting vacationers from northern Europe, it offers danceable music, a gregarious ambience, and nightly floor shows which begin spontaneously whenever the mood seems right. Featuring flamenco dancers with traditional guitarists, or live performances by local musical hopefuls, they vary widely from night to night and might include just about anything. Open nightly from 9pm to 4am.

Admission (including first drink): 2,000 ptas. ($20).

EL PALLADIUM, avenida Montemar 68. Tel. 238-42-89.

Set close to the Hotel Las Palomas, within a 10-minute walk south of the town center, this well-designed nightclub is one of the most convivial in Torremolinos. The illumination contains strobes and spotlights which accompany a sound system described as loud and distortion-free. Drinks begin at 350 ptas ($3.50). Open daily from 6pm to 4am, with disco music beginning around 10pm.

Admission: 700 ptas. ($7) (after 10pm only).

Piano Bars

INTERMEZZO PIANO CLUB, Plaza del Remo 2. Tel. 38-32-67.

This is by far the most sophisticated bar in Carihuela, the little fishing village at the foot of Torremolinos. The sea is visible from the front door, and the interior opens generously into a large, almost square room whose focus is a shiny black piano. Its curves are repeated in the upholstered bar area, which is skillfully lit with a series of dramatically placed spotlights. The decor might be called a combination of Victorian and ultramodern. There's a small dance floor for those who want to follow the live music. Drinks range upward from 450 ptas. ($4.50). Open daily from 10pm–3am.

The Gay Life

Torremolinos has the largest cluster of gay life, including bars and restaurants, of any resort along the coast of southern Spain. Gay men (and to a lesser degree, women) flock here from England, Germany, and Scandinavia. Gay bars seem to huddle together in clusters. The most outstanding of these is in **Pueblo Blanco,** which is like a little village of its own. Young men bar-hop here with gay abandon.

Much gay life sprawls across the development of **La Nogalera,** which is like a village within a village, with a wide scattering of restaurants, bars, souvenir shops, and apartment complexes. The restaurants here—even those that draw a large gay clientele—tend to be mixed.

BRONX, Edificio Centro Jardín. Tel. 38-73-60.

The leading gay disco is called Bronx, with beer going for 350 ptas. ($3.50). Open daily from 10pm to 6am.

Admission: 1,000 ptas. ($10).

MEN'S BAR, La Nogalera 714. Tel. 38-42-05.

One of the most popular gay bars in La Nogalera is called simply

"Men's Bar." Crowded most nights, it charges 275 ptas. ($2.75) for beer. Open daily from 9pm to 5am.

LA GORILA, Pueblo Blanco 33.

The best bar, in the opinion of some of its patrons, is La Gorila, which has good music and a usually congenial crowd. Beer goes for 275 ptas. ($2.75). Open daily from 9pm to 3am.

Gambling Casinos

CASINO TORREQUEBRADA, carretera de Cádiz 266, Benalmádena-Costa. Tel. 44-25-45.

Considered one of the major casinos along the Costa del Sol, and located on the lobby level of the previously recommended Hotel Torrequebrada, this establishment combines a nightclub/cabaret with a restaurant, and an impressive array of tables devoted to blackjack, chemin de fer, punto y banco, and two kinds of roulette. The cabaret offers two different shows every night. The first features Spanish flamenco and Spanish guitar; the second presents a Las Vegas–inspired revue replete with magicians and damsels dressed in feathers with lots of glitter. Between acts, a band provides music for dancing. The casino is open daily from 8am to 4am, nightclub acts begin at 10:30pm (Spanish revue) and midnight (Las Vegas revue) and the restaurant is open nightly from 9:30pm to 2am.

Admission: Casino, 600 ptas. ($6); cabaret/nightclub, 3,500 ptas. ($35), which includes two drinks, admission to both shows, and admission to the casino.

---

4. FUENGIROLA & LOS BOLICHES

20 miles W of Málaga, 64½ miles E of Algeciras, 356 miles S of Madrid.

GETTING THERE By Train From Torremolinos, take the Metro at the Nogalera station (under the RENFE sign). Trains depart every 30 minutes.

By Bus Fuengirola is on the main Costa del Sol bus route between Algeciras in the west and Málaga in the east.

By Car Take the N-340 east from Marbella.

ESSENTIALS The **telephone area code** for Fuengirola and Los Boliches is 952. The **Tourist Information Office** is on the Plaza de España (tel. 952/46-74-57).

The twin fishing towns of Fuengirola and Los Boliches lie halfway between the more famous resorts of Marbella and Torremolinos. The promenade along the water stretches some 2½ miles, with the less developed Los Boliches just half a mile from Fuengirola.

The towns don't have the facilities or drama of Torremolinos and Marbella. Except for two major luxury hotels, Furengirola and Los Boliches are cheaper, though, and that has attracted a horde of budget-conscious European tourists.

On a promontory overlooking the sea are the ruins of **San Isidro**

Castle. The Santa Amalja, Carvajal, and Las Gaviotas **beaches** are broad, clean, and sandy. Everybody goes to the big **flea market** at Fuengirola on Tuesday.

WHERE TO STAY

BYBLOS ANDALUZ, Urbanización Mijas Golf, 29640 Fuengirola. Tel. 952/47-30-50. Fax 952/47-67-83. 144 rms (all with bath), 36 suites. A/C MINIBAR TV TEL

$ Rates: 26,000–32,000 ptas. ($260–$320) single; 34,000–42,000 ptas. ($340–$420) double; from 55,000 ptas. ($550) suite. Buffet breakfast 2,000 ptas. ($20) extra. AE, DC, MC, V. **Parking:** Free.

This luxurious resort, which has a health spa and lavish rooms, is in a magnificent setting. It's three miles from Fuengirola and six miles from the beach. The grounds contain shrubbery, a white minaret, Moorish arches, tile-adorned walls, and an orange-tree patio inspired by the Alhambra grounds, 97 miles away. Two 18-hole golf courses designed by Robert Trent Jones, tennis courts, spa facilities, a gymnasium, and swimming pools bask in the Andalusian sunshine. The spa is a handsome classic structure, Mijas Thalasso Palace.

The rooms and suites are elegantly and individually designed and furnished in the Roman, Arabic, Andalusian, and rustic styles. Private sun terraces and lavish bathrooms add to the comfort.

Dining/Entertainment: Dining choices include Le Nailhac, with its French gastronomic offerings; El Andaluz, with its regional and Spanish specialties, and La Fuente, with its dietetic cuisine. The San Tropez Bar opens onto a poolside terrace, and live entertainment is often presented. The Discothèque Europa is open on Friday and Saturday night.

Services: Room service, laundry/valet, babysitting.

Facilities: Health club, sauna, solarium, two outdoor pools, three indoor pools, golf courses, tennis.

FLORIDA, paseo Marítimo, 29640 Fuengirola. Tel. 952/47-61-00. Fax 952/58-15-29. 116 rms (all with bath). TV TEL

$ Rates: 5,000 ptas. ($50) single; 8,000 ptas. ($80) double. Breakfast 550 ptas. ($5.50) extra. AE, DC, MC, V.

There's a semitropical garden in front of the Florida, and guests can enjoy refreshments under a wide, vine-covered pergola. Most of the comfortable rooms have balconies overlooking the sea or mountains. The floors are of tile, and the furnishings, particularly in the lounge, have been renewed. It's a 10-minute walk from the train station.

HOSTAL SEDEÑO, Don Jacinto 1, 29640 Fuengirola. Tel. 952/47-47-88. 30 rms (all with bath).

$ Rates: 2,500 ptas. ($25) single; 4,200 ptas. ($42) double. No credit cards.

The Sedeño is three minutes from the beach, in the heart of town. Its modest lobby leads to a larger lounge furnished with antiques and reproductions. You pass a small open courtyard where stairs go up to the second- and third-floor balconied bedrooms. These overlook a small garden with fig and palm trees, plus a glassed-in room with terrace. No breakfast is served, but there are cafés nearby.

LAS PIRÁMIDES, paseo Marítimo, 29640 Fuengirola. Tel.

952/47-06-00. Fax 952/58-32-97. 320 rms (all with bath), 40 suites. A/C MINIBAR TV TEL

$ Rates: 9,500 ptas. ($95) single; 12,500 ptas. ($125) double; from 15,000 ptas. ($150) suite. Breakfast 675 ptas. ($6.75) extra. AE, MC, V. **Parking:** 800 ptas. ($8).

A complex under pyramidal roofs, Las Pirámides is favored by travel groups from northern Europe. It's a citylike resort 50 yards from the beach, with seemingly every kind of divertissement: flamenco shows on the large patio, a cozy bar and lounge, traditionally furnished sitting rooms, a coffee shop, a poolside bar, and a gallery of boutiques and tourist facilities, such as car-rental agencies. All rooms have slick modern styling, as well as private bath and terrace. Room service is provided, as are laundry/valet services and babysitting.

WHERE TO DINE

CASA VIEJA, avenida Los Boliches 27, Los Boliches. Tel. 58-38-30.
  Cuisine: FRENCH. **Reservations:** Recommended.
$ Prices: Appetizers 600–1,800 ptas. ($6–$18); main courses 1,000–2,800 ptas. ($10–$28); fixed-price three-course lunch (Sat–Sun only) 1,750 ptas. ($17.50). AE, MC, V.
  Open: Lunch Sat–Sun 12:30–3pm; dinner Tues–Sun 7:30–11pm.

Set inside the thick stone walls of a cottage that was originally built in the 1870s for a local fisherman, this sophisticated restaurant lies on the main street of Los Boliches, a short walk east of the center of Fuengirola. Owned and managed by London-born Jon Adams, with a cuisine which is prepared by French-trained, Spain-born Carlos Durán, the establishment is a favorite of the British expatriate community living among the nearby hills. A flowering patio is available, weather permitting, for outdoor dining, and there's a cozy bar available for dialogues with the owner as well. Menu items include a subtly flavored terrine of oxtail, fresh vegetable soup, king prawns, tournedos with béarnaise sauce, suprême of salmon, a gratin of sole in puff pastry, guinea fowl with cumin and honey-glazed turnips, duck breast with a creamy foie-gras sauce, and turbot in a white wine sauce. Desserts are elegantly caloric, and might include caramelized apple slices on a pistachio-cream sauce with a raspberry coulis.

DON PE', calle de la Cruz 19, Fuengirola. Tel. 47-83-51.
  Cuisine: CONTINENTAL. **Reservations:** Recommended for dinner.
$ Prices: Appetizers 450–1,475 ptas. ($4.50–$14.75); main dishes 750–2,100 ptas. ($7.50–$21). AE, DC, MC, V.
  Open: Lunch Mon–Sat 1–3:30pm; dinner Mon–Sat 7–11:30pm.
  Closed: Lunch July–Sept.

Don Pe' lies amid a cluster of less desirable restaurants in the center of Fuengirola. Because of its quality, it seems to get more repeat business than most of its competitors. During hot weather many visitors prefer to dine in the courtyard, whose roof can be mechanically retracted to allow in the air and light. During cold weather, the staff builds a fire in a hearth.

The menu lists specialties in three different languages and includes a selection of game dishes, such as medallion of venison in wine sauce accompanied with red cabbage, roast filet of wild boar, and duck with orange sauce. The ingredients are imported especially for the restaurant from the forests and plains of nearby Andalusia. Less powerful dishes include peppers stuffed with prawns, fresh salmon covered with a herb sauce, and even an alpine version of fondue bourguignonne.

MONOPOL, calle los Palangreros 7. Tel. 47-44-48.

Cuisine: INTERNATIONAL. **Reservations:** Recommended.

$ Prices: Appetizers 600–1,300 ptas ($6–$13); main courses 1,100–2,600 ptas ($11–$26). AE, MC, V.

Open: Dinner only, Mon–Sat 6:30pm–midnight. **Closed:** Aug.

Set in the heart of town, near both the beach and Fuengirola's new post office, this cozy restaurant is the domain of German-born Paul Wartman and his wife, Barbal. Since 1981 the restaurant has catered to a varied clientele from many corners of Europe, many of whom appreciate the culinary specialties of their respective homelands. The building was constructed about a century ago, and although not graced with an open-air courtyard, it offers a quartet of rustically decorated dining rooms and a wine list that includes a fine assortment of Riojas. Specialties include a gratin of scallops, a ragoût of seafood in a saffron-flavored cream sauce, lamb filets in provençal sauce, and filet of beef in a morel-studded cream sauce.

EL PASO, Francisco Cano 39, at Los Boliches. Tel. 47-50-94.

Cuisine: MEXICAN. **Reservations:** Recommended.

$ Prices: Appetizers 550–750 ptas. ($5.50–$7.50); main courses 700–1,600 ptas. ($7–$16). No credit cards.

Open: Dinner only, daily 7pm–midnight.

The building was originally built a century ago as a canning factory for sardines, with a row of fishermen's cottages set close nearby. Today this is one of the neighborhood's busiest Mexican restaurants, where a splashing fountain enlivens an outdoor patio rich with blooming flowers. (There are additional tables set up inside.) By far the most popular drink here is a frothy Margarita, which might be followed by your choice of tacos, burritos, frijoles, fajitas, and guacamoles. Be alert to the numbers of drinks you consume, however, since the bill, once you begin, seems to mount quickly.

RESTAURANT CEFERINO, Rotonda de la Luna 1, Pueblo López. Tel. 46-45-93.

Cuisine: SPANISH. **Reservations:** Required.

$ Prices: Appetizers 760–3,300 ptas. ($7.60–$33); main dishes 1,900–2,800 ptas. ($19–$28). AE, MC, V.

Open: Lunch Mon–Sat 1–4pm; dinner Mon–Sat 8pm–midnight. **Closed:** Jan.

When you enter this restaurant, your first view will be of a small bar area (where you might want to linger) and an open kitchen whose pots and bubbling stocks are visible for anyone to see. The air-conditioned dining room is small enough to accommodate only about two dozen diners, who sit amid a straightforward Iberian decor of stucco, brick, and a scattering of tiles. The chef is Sr. Ceferino Garcia Jiménez, who claims that his fascination with cuisine began when he helped prepare meals as a child in his family home in Guadalajara. Since then, he has prepared dinners for royalty, statespeople, and glamorous resort guests in both Spain and South America. Meals might include an avocado-based gazpacho; stuffed crêpe Ceferino filled with spinach, pine kernels, and smoked salmon; venison with muscatel sauce; grilled turbot with roe; Norwegian salmon in shrimp sauce; and braised duck with spinach pudding and pears. Service is excellent.

RESTAURANT TOMATE, calle el Troncon 19. Tel. 46-35-59.
   Cuisine: INTERNATIONAL. **Reservations:** Recommended.
$ **Prices:** Appetizers 500–1,100 ptas. ($5–$11); main courses 1,050–2,600 ptas. ($10.50–$26). AE, MC, V.
   Open: Dinner only, daily 7pm–midnight.

One of the most gastronomically sophisticated restaurants in town presents the best culinary traditions of northern and southern Europe. Set in the heart of Fuengirola, in a century-old town house whose dining space was recently added on in back, the restaurant is the creative statement of German-born Michael Lienhoop. Meals might include dishes from Spain (gazpacho, filet of hake floating on a lake of mustard-flavored cream-and-herb sauce), France (langoustines provençales), Germany (sauerkraut with an assortment of smoked meats, or pork in a red wine and mushroom sauce), and Scandinavia (a selection of marinated herring and marinated salmon with dill sauce).

5. MIJAS

18½ miles W of Málaga, 363 miles S of Madrid

GETTING THERE   **By Bus**   There's frequent bus service from the terminal at Fuengirola.

By Car   At Fuengirola, take the Mijas road north.

ESSENTIALS   The **telephone area code** for Mijas is 952.

It's called "White Mijas" because of its bone-white Andalusian houses. Just five miles from Fuengirola above the Costa del Sol, the village is a gem, standing at the foot of a sierra. From its lofty perches 1,400 feet above sea level, a panoramic vista of the Mediterranean unfolds. Along its narrow, cobblestone streets have walked Celts, Phoenicians, and Moors. You'll do better hiring a "burro-taxi." In a park at the top of Cuesta de la Villa, you see remnants of a Moorish citadel dating from 833. Shops threaten to inundate the village and sell everything from original art to olive-wood jewelry. Incidentally, Mijas possesses the only square bullring in Spain.

WHERE TO STAY

HOTEL MIJAS, Urbanización Tamisa, 29650 Mijas. Tel. 952/48-58-00. Fax 952/48-58-25. 100 rms (all with bath), 3 suites. TV TEL
$ **Rates:** 10,600 ptas. ($106) single; 13,350 ptas. ($133.50) double; from 25,000 ptas. ($250) suite. Buffet breakfast 1,100 ptas. ($11) extra. AE, DC, MC, V. **Parking:** Free.

The Hotel Mijas, in the center of the village about five miles from the nearest beach, is one of the special places along the coast, with a view of the sea and surrounding mountains.

Designed hacienda style, it's perched on the side of a hill, with a semi-enclosed flower patio, a terrace with white wicker furniture and a view, a swimming pool, a tennis court, and a lounge that's Castilian in decor. The living room is furnished with fine antiques and inlaid chests, even a framed fan collection. All excellently furnished bedrooms contain a private tile bath. Other facilities include a sauna, gymnasium, and beauty parlor. Barbecues are held in the open air. Entertainment is provided in season in the evening, and during the day guests can enjoy the 18-hole Mijas golf course.

WHERE TO DINE

CLUB EL PADRASTRO, paseo del Compás. Tel. 48-50-00.
   Cuisine: INTERNATIONAL. **Reservations:** Recommended.
$ Prices: Appetizers 600–1,000 ptas. ($6–$10); main dishes 1,050–2,000 ptas. ($10.50–$20); fixed-price menu 1,500 ptas. ($15). AE, DC, MC, V.
   Open: Lunch daily 12:30–4pm; dinner daily 7–11pm.

In Spanish, *padrastro* is a curious word, for it means both "stepfather" and "hangnail." However, it also suggests height, a commanding position—which you'll appreciate after climbing the 77 steps to reach the restaurant, although it's more sensible to take the elevator from the town parking lot. The restaurant is in the center of Mijas. After you've scaled the heights, a swimming pool and an artfully decorated restaurant await you. Before dinner, order a drink under pine trees by the pool and enjoy the view. Inside, picture windows on two levels also open onto the panorama, and soft music plays. The food is quite good. Specialties include fish soup Padrastro, bass with fennel, and a special flambé Padrastro.

RESTAURANT EL CAPRICHO, calle los Caños 5. Tel. 48-51-11.
   Cuisine: INTERNATIONAL. **Reservations:** Recommended.
$ Prices: Appetizers 625–950 ptas. ($6.25–$9.50); main dishes 1,075–2,000 ptas. ($10.75–$20); fixed-price menus 1,050–1,400 ptas. ($10.50–$14). AE, DC, MC, V.
   Open: Lunch Thurs–Tues 12:30–4pm; dinner Thurs–Tues 7–11:30pm. **Closed:** Feb.

El Capricho, located in what was once a private home in the town center, draws a large English-speaking clientele, and the varied menu is geared to their tastes. Appetizers include prawn cocktail, Serrano ham, omelets, corn on the cob, soups, and salads. Among the main dishes are sole and trout, grilled swordfish, chicken Kiev, shish kebab, steak Diane, chicken Hawaii, and pheasant Capricho. You might prefer the paella Mijena, which is excellent. Desserts range from flambéed concoctions to baked Alaska. The wine list offers good choices, including the house Valdepeñas.

6. MARBELLA

37 miles W of Málaga, 28 miles W of Torremolinos,
47 miles E of Algeciras, 373 miles S of Madrid

GETTING THERE   By Bus   Nine buses run from Málaga to Marbella daily, and two depart from Madrid daily.

By Car   Marbella is the first major resort as you head east on the N-340 from Algeciras.

ESSENTIALS   The **telephone area code** for Marbella is 952. The **Tourist Information Office** is at Miguel Cano 1 (tel. 952/77-14-42).

I n the shadow of what was once an Arab fortress, Marbella is definitely chic and attracts a fashionable crowd of movie people and socialites. Many mansions and villas are found hereabouts.

About halfway between Málaga and Gibraltar, Marbella is at the foot of the Sierra Blanca, which keeps the climate mild. Its best beaches are the 600-yard-long El Fuerte and the 800-yard-long Fontanilla. But actually Marbella is one long beach, taking in about 17 miles of sand from Guadalmina to Cabopino. Some 60 beachfront complexes and hotel clusters line this stretch. The beach resorts have elaborate swimming pools and all the trappings; the beachfronts are open to the public. From national highway N-340, you'll see different roads signposted leading to the various beaches.

You don't need to get dressed to go to lunch either, as many of these beaches have bar-restaurants called *chiringuitos*. Right on the beach, these places sell cold beer throughout the day and often grill freshly caught fish for your lunch. Women often go topless on these beaches, but total nudity is prohibited. However, nudists still disrobe at some of the more isolated places at the eastern stretch of beach. Sports, such as waterskiing, shark fishing, and tennis, are popular. The even more athletically inclined dance until dawn.

Traces of Marbella's past are found in its palatial town hall, its medieval ruins, and its ancient Moorish walls. Marbella's most charming area is the **old quarter,** with narrow cobblestone streets and Arab houses, centering around the Plaza de los Naranjos.

WHERE TO STAY

Since the setting is so ideal—pure Mediterranean sun, sea, and sky, plus the scent of Andalusian orange blossoms in the air—some of the best hotels along the Costa del Sol are found in Marbella.

Expensive

ANDALUCÍA PLAZA, Urbanización Nueva Andalucía (Apdo. 21), 29660 Nueva Andalucía Marbella. Tel. 952/81-20-00. Fax 952/81-09-96. 393 rms, 22 suites. A/C MINIBAR TV TEL

$ Rates: 13,000 ptas. ($130) single; 16,000 ptas. ($160) double; from 23,000 ptas. ($230) suite. Breakfast 1,100 ptas ($11) extra. AE, DC, MC, V. **Parking:** Free.

Originally built in 1972, the Andalucía Plaza is a resort complex on a grand scale. On the mountain side of the coastal road between Marbella and Torremolinos, twin five-story buildings are linked by a reception lounge and formal gardens. On the sea side is the hotel's beach club. The public rooms in the hotel buildings are spacious and lavishly decorated. Equally luxurious are the bedrooms furnished with reproductions in the classic Castilian manner. The hotel is on more than a 300-foot strip of sand, four miles west of the center of Marbella.

Dining/Entertainment: The restaurant Córdova serves upscale international meals. The Bar Toledo, primarily a watering hole, offers light snacks and suppers. There's an in-house casino recommended separately.

Services: 24-hour room service, concierge, babysitting, laundry.

Facilities: The hotel's beach club includes a 300-foot strip of sand, with adjacent sunbathing terraces, tennis courts, two saunas, a gymnasium, an open-air swimming pool, and an enclosed all-weather pool. About half a mile away there's a 1,000-berth marina, where the hotel will arrange the rental of a vessel for deep-sea fishing.

HOTEL DON CARLOS, Jardines de las Goldondrinas, carretera de Cádiz, Km 192, 29600 Marbella. Tel. 952/83-11-40. Fax 952/83-34-29. 234 rms, 15 suites. A/C MINIBAR TV TEL

$ Rates: 20,300–22,000 ptas. ($203–$220) single; 25,600–27,000 ptas. ($256–$270) double; from 45,000 ptas. ($450) suite. Breakfast 1,400 ptas. ($14) extra. AE, MC, V. **Parking:** Free.

One of the most dramatically alluring hotels along the coastline, the Don Carlos rises on a set of angled stilts above a forest of pines. Between it and its manicured beach, considered the best in Marbella, are 130 acres of award-winning gardens replete with cascades of water, a full-time staff of 22 gardeners, and thousands of subtropical plants. There's far more to this hotel than the modern tower that rises above the eastern edge of Marbella. Its low-lying terraces and elegant eating and drinking facilities attract high-powered conferences from throughout Europe, as well as individual nonresident diners from along the Mediterranean coast.

Each of the accommodations has its own panoramic balcony, lacquered furniture, a private bath done in honey-colored marble, and satellite TV.

Dining/Entertainment: You can dine amid splashes of bougainvillea beside an oversize swimming pool bordered with begonias and geraniums, or in La Pergola, where ficus and potted palms decorate the hundreds of lattices. A hideaway, Los Naranjos, has a sun-flooded atrium with mosses and orange trees. A grand piano on the marble dais provides diverting music. Fixed-price meals here go for 4,800 ptas. ($48) each. Meals in the other restaurants, including grills or elaborate buffets in the semi-outdoor beachfront cabaña, cost about half as much.

Among the bars scattered around the various terraces and marble-lined hideaways of the public rooms, the most popular offers an English-inspired decor of exposed hardwoods, a panoramic view of the sea, plenty of sofas, a dance floor, and a musical trio.

Services: 24-hour room service, laundry, babysitting.

Facilities: Three swimming pools, golf course, saunas, gym, tennis courts; water sports cost extra.

HOTEL PUENTE ROMANO, carretera de Cádiz, Km 167, 29600 Marbella. Tel. 952/77-01-00. Fax 952/77-57-66. 185 rms, 15 suites. A/C MINIBAR TV TEL

$ Rates: 28,000 ptas. ($280) single; 33,000 ptas. ($330) double; from 60,000 ptas. ($600) suite. Breakfast 1,600 ptas. ($16) extra. AE, DC, MC, V. **Parking:** Free.

⭐ This hotel was originally built as a cluster of vacation apartments, a fact that influenced the attention to detail and the landscaping that surrounds it. In the early 1970s a group of entrepreneurs transformed it into one of the most unusual hotels in the south of Spain, sitting close to the frenetic coastal highway, 2½ miles west of Marbella midway between Marbella and Puerto Banús.

If you're wondering who your fellow guests might be, the King of Spain, Barbara Striesand, Björn Borg, Stevie Wonder, Julio Iglesias, the Kennedys, and the President of Ireland have all enjoyed the pleasures of this establishment.

Once inside the complex, guests wander through a maze of arbor-covered walkways. Along the route, they pass cascades of water, masses of vines, and a subtropical garden. The Moorish-style accommodations are a showcase of fabrics, accessories, and furniture. Each of the rooms has a semi-sheltered balcony with flowers, private bath, and electronic safe.

Dining/Entertainment: Nestled amid the lushness are well-upholstered indoor/outdoor bars and restaurants. Three of these overlook a terra-cotta patio, bordered at one end by the stones of a reconstructed Roman bridge, the only one of its kind in southern Spain. There's also a nightclub.

Services: 24-hour room service, laundry/valet, babysitting.

Facilities: The edges of the free-form swimming pool are bordered by trees and vines and a drain-away waterfall, which makes it look something like a Tahitian lagoon. There's also a sandy beach with water sports, tennis courts, and a cluster of boutiques; health club, sauna, solarium.

MARBELLA CLUB, carretera de Cádiz, Km 178, 29600 Marbella. Tel. 952/77-13-00. Fax 952/82-98-84. 76 rms, 24 suites, 10 bungalows. A/C MINIBAR TV TEL

$ Rates: 27,000 ptas. ($270) single; 33,000–36,000 ptas. ($330–$360) double; from 45,000 ptas. ($450) suite; from 100,000 ptas. ($1,000) bungalows. Breakfast 1,600 ptas. ($16) extra. AE, DC, MC, V. **Parking:** Free.

⭐ Until a handful of equally chic hotels were built along the Costa del Sol to compete with it, the Marbella Club reigned almost without equal as the ultimately exclusive hangout of the world's commercial and genealogical aristocracy. Among its first guests when it opened in 1953 were actress Merle Oberon and novelist Leon Uris, and since then the names and titles on its roster of famous guests could keep a society columnist busy for months. Established on land originally owned by the father of Prince Alfonso von Hohenlohe, the resort sprawls gracefully over a lushly landscaped property which slopes from its roadside reception area down to the beach. Composed of small, ecologically conscious clusters of garden pavilions, bungalows, and surprisingly small-scale annexes (none of which is taller than two stories), it basks amid some of the most well-conceived gardens along the coast. Today its clientele is discreet, international, elegant, and appreciative of the resort's small scale and superb service.

Dining/Entertainment: The Marbella Club Restaurant moves from indoor shelter to an outdoor terrace according to the season. (For more information, see "Where to Dine," below.) A bar is located in the garden nearby.

Services: 24-hour room service, babysitting, laundry/valet, massage, and a concierge well-versed in the arrangement of almost anything.

Facilities: Two swimming pools, and a beach whose sunbathing and lunchtime restaurant are famous for their glamour. Golf can be arranged nearby. Tennis courts are available within a two-minute walk at the Marbella Club's twin resort, Puente Romano.

MELÍA DON PEPE, Finca Las Merinas, 29600 Marbella. Tel. 952/77-03-00, or toll free 800/336-3542 in the U.S. Fax 952/77-03-00. 204 rms, 18 suites. A/C MINIBAR TV TEL

$ Rates: 22,000–25,900 ptas. ($220–$259) single; 25,900–32,000 ptas. ($259–$320) double; from 55,000 ptas. ($550) suite. Breakfast 1,500 ptas. ($15) extra. AE, DC, MC, V. **Parking:** Free.

The Melía Don Pepe occupies six acres of tropical gardens and lawns between the coastal road and the sea. Its well-furnished bedrooms, with private baths and wall-to-wall carpeting, face either the sea or the Sierra Blanca mountains. The facilities are so vast you could spend a week here and not use them all.

Dining/Entertainment: The hotel has lounges, bars, and restaurants. La Farola grill provides international à la carte cuisine, with meals costing from 5,500 ptas. ($55).

Services: 24-hour room service, laundry/valet, babysitting.

Facilities: Four swimming pools, tennis courts, Swedish sauna, bridge clubroom, boutiques, yacht harbor along the beach, golf course.

LOS MONTEROS, carretera de Cádiz, Km 187, 29600 Marbella. Tel. 952/77-17-00. Fax 952/82-58-46. 169 rms, 10 suites. A/C MINIBAR TV TEL

$ Rates (including breakfast): 24,100–32,000 ptas. ($241–$320) single; 35,000–40,000 ptas. ($350–$400) double; from 53,000 ptas. ($530) suite. AE, DC, MC, V. **Parking:** Free.

Los Monteros, 400 yards from a beach and four miles east of Marbella, is one of the most tasteful and imaginative resort complexes along the Costa del Sol. Between the coastal road and its own private beach, it attracts those seeking intimacy and luxury. No cavernous lounges exist here; instead, many small tasteful rooms, Andalusian/Japanese in concept, are the style. The hotel offers various salons with open fireplaces, a library, and terraces. The bedrooms are brightly decorated, with lightly colored lacquered furniture, private baths, and terraces.

Dining/Entertainment: The hotel has a bar and four restaurants on different levels that open onto flower-filled patios, gardens, and fountains. Within the precincts, Grill El Corzo is one of the finest grill rooms along the coast. The grill, done up in Toledo red, is on the first floor. Wall-size scenic murals are in the background, and tables are bedecked with bright cloths and silver candlesticks. Soft, romantic music is played nightly. Meals begin at 6,000 ptas. ($60). The cuisine is a pleasing combination of French and Spanish.

Services: 24-hour room service, babysitting, laundry/valet.

Facilities: Guests can use the nearby 18-hole golf course, Río Real, for free. Other facilities include several swimming pools, a beach club with a heated indoor swimming pool, 10 tennis courts, five squash courts, a riding club and school, plus a fully equipped gymnasium with sauna, massage, and Jacuzzi.

Moderate

ESTRELLA DEL MAR, carretera de Cádiz, Km 190.5, 29600 Marbella. Tel. 952/83-12-75. Fax 952/83-35-40. 83 rms (all with bath), 15 suites. TEL

$ Rates: 6,100 ptas. ($61) single; 9,500 ptas. ($95) double; 13,800 ptas. ($138) suite. Breakfast 800 ptas. ($8) extra. V. **Parking:** Free. **Closed:** Dec–Feb.

One of the most tranquil and isolated resorts in the region, the four-story Estrella del Mar lies within a sprawling private park, only part of which is devoted to gardens. The pines, mimosas, and sandy soil of the remainder afford plenty of privacy to families with young children, and to quiet couples looking for calm and seclusion. Located about 5½ miles east of Marbella, the hotel was originally built in the 1950s and renovated in 1971. It's proud of its role as the hotel whose staff has been employed longer than at virtually any other hotel around (an average of around 20 years work history per employee). Rows of trees shield all but a few of the bedrooms from views of the nearby beach, but rooms are attractively furnished and contain balconies. None offers air conditioning.

Informal meals are served in the beachfront La Pescaderia, while more formal ones are featured in the establishment's main restaurant, the Estrella del Mar. The multilingual staff will happily call a taxi for the ride into Marbella, the cost of which averages about 1,000 ptas. ($10) each way.

HOTEL EL FUERTE, avenida el Fuerte, 29600 Marbella. Tel. 952/77-15-00. Fax 952/82-44-11. 261 rms (all with bath), 2 suites. A/C MINIBAR TV TEL

$ Rates: 9,500 ptas. ($95) single; 13,500–17,500 ptas. ($135–$175) double; 33,000 ptas. ($330) suite. Breakfast 1,000 ptas. ($10) extra. AE, DC, MC, V. **Parking:** Free.

The largest and most recommendable hotel in the center of Marbella, with a balconied and angular facade divided into two separate six-story towers, El Fuerte is set directly on the waterfront. Catering to a sedate clientele of conservative northern Europeans, it offers a palm-fringed swimming pool set across the street from a sheltered lagoon and a wide-open beach. Originally built in 1957, and expanded and renovated many times since, the hotel offers a handful of terraces, some shaded by flowering arbors, which provide hideaways for quiet drinks. Inside, the public rooms contain a wide variety of tilework, certain sections of which were culled from much older buildings. Bedrooms are contemporary, with piped-in music and terraces.

The hotel has a coffee shop, two restaurants, two bars, and easy access to the many commercial allures in the center of Marbella. Facilities for leisure activities include the above-mentioned swimming pool, a floodlit tennis court, and two squash courts.

HOTEL GUADALPÍN, carretera 340 Cadiz–Málaga, Km 186, 29600 Marbella. Tel. 952/77-11-00. 110 rms (all with bath). TEL

$ Rates: 6,700 ptas. ($67) single; 9,400 ptas. ($94) double. Breakfast 525 ptas. ($5.25) extra. AE, DC, MC, V. **Parking:** Free.

The Hotel Guadalpín is right on the rugged coast, only 50 yards from the beach (one mile from the center of Marbella). Guests spend hours relaxing around two swimming pools, or they walk along a private pathway lined with fir trees to the Mediterranean. The dining room has large windows overlooking the patio and pool, and the main lounge has been designed in a ranch style with round marble tables and occasional leather armchairs arranged for conversational groups. The bar area of the spacious lounge is brick and natural wood, which makes it warm and attractive.

Each room has not only two terraces, but also a living room and bedroom combined. All have a private bath. Most of the rooms are furnished in "new ranch" style. Only 10 single rooms are available.

Inexpensive

RESIDENCIA FINLANDIA, Finlandia 12, 29600 Marbella. Tel. 952/77-07-00. 11 rms (all with bath). TEL
$ Rates: 4,500 ptas. ($45) single; 7,000 ptas. ($70) double. Breakfast 450 ptas. ($4.50) extra. DC, V.

Situated in the Huerta Grande, a peaceful residential section, the Finlandia is only a five-minute walk from the center of the old quarter, and a two-minute walk from the Mediterranean. It's clean, modern, and well run, with spacious rooms and contemporary furnishings. Your bed will be turned down at night.

RESIDENCIA LIMA, avenida Antonio Belón 2, 29600 Marbella. Tel. 952/77-05-00. Fax 952/86-30-91. 64 rms (all with bath). TEL
$ Rates: 5,500 ptas. ($55) single; 6,800 ptas. ($68) double. Breakfast 450 ptas. ($4.50) extra. AE, DC, MC, V.

Tucked away in a residential section of Marbella, right off the N-340 and near the sea, this hotel is more secluded than the others nearby. The modern eight-story structure features bedrooms with Spanish provincial furnishings and private balconies.

RESIDENCIA SAN CRISTÓBAL, Ramón y Cajal 3, 29600 Marbella. Tel. 952/77-12-50. Fax 952/86-20-44. 96 rms (all with bath). TEL
$ Rates: 5,500 ptas. ($55) single; 8,000 ptas. ($80) double. Breakfast 450 ptas. ($4.50) extra. DC, MC, V.

In the heart of Marbella, 200 yards from the beach, this modern five-story hotel has long, wide terraces and flower-filled windowboxes. The bedrooms have walnut headboards, individual overhead reading lamps, and room dividers separating the comfortable beds from the small living-room areas. An added plus is the private terrace attached to each room—just right for a continental breakfast, the only meal served here.

EL RODEO, Victor de la Serna, 29600 Marbella. Tel. 952/77-51-00. Fax 952/82-33-20. 100 rms (all with bath). TEL
$ Rates: 6,900 ptas. ($69) single; 8,500 ptas. ($85) double. Breakfast 500 ptas. ($5) extra. AE, DC, MC, V.

Even though this modern hotel stands just off the main coastal road of Marbella—within walking distance of the bus station, the beach, and the old quarter—it's quiet and secluded. Facilities in the seven-story structure include a swimming pool, terrace, sunbathing area, solarium, and piano bar. Two elevators whisk you to the sunny, spacious second-floor lounges with country furnishings, there's also a bar with tropical bamboo chairs and tables. Continental breakfast is the only meal served in the cheerful breakfast room. The bedrooms are functional, with several shuttered closets, lounge chairs, and white desks.

Budget

EL CASTILLO, Plaza San Bernabé 2, 29600 Marbella. Tel. 952/77-17-39. 44 rms (all with bath).

$ Rates: 3,500 ptas. ($35) single; 4,500 ptas. ($45) double. No credit cards.

 At the foot of the castle in the narrow streets of the old town, this small but choice budget hotel opens onto a minuscule triangular square used by the adjoining convent and school as a playground. There's a small covered courtyard, and the second-floor bedrooms have only inner windows. The spartan rooms are scrubbed clean, and contain white-tile baths. No morning meal is served, and not one word of English is spoken.

HOSTAL MUNICH, Virgen del Pilar 5, 29600 Marbella. Tel. 952/77-24-61. 18 rms (all with bath). TEL

$ Rates: 3,500 ptas. ($35) single; 4,500 ptas. ($45) double. No credit cards.

Set back from the street and shielded by banana and palm trees, this unassuming three-story hostal is just a short walk from the water and the bus station. Some rooms have balconies; all are simply furnished and well kept. No breakfast is served, but a café opposite the hostal serves breakfast. The homey lounge is cluttered with knickknacks and a mixture of old and new furniture.

WHERE TO DINE

Expensive

LA FONDA, Plaza Santo Cristo 9-10. Tel. 77-25-12.
  Cuisine: INTERNATIONAL. **Reservations:** Required.
$ Prices: Appetizers 1,000–2,000 ptas. ($10–$20); main dishes 1,200–2,800 ptas. ($12–$28). AE, DC, MC, V.
  Open: Dinner only, Tues–Sat 8–11:30pm.

Considered both a gem of 18th-century Andalusian architecture and a gastronomic citadel of renown, La Fonda is the Costa del Sol extension of one of the most famous restaurants in Europe, the Madrid-based Horcher's (for more information, see Chapter 5). The restaurant was the outgrowth of a simple inn, which had been originally created by interconnecting a trio of town houses in Old Marbella. Today a central patio with a murmuring fountain, a series of colonnaded loggias, carefully chosen Andalusian *azulejos* (glazed tiles), beamed ceilings, open fireplaces, grill-covered windows, and checkerboard-patterned marble floors have been respectfully maintained. What's new, however, is the professionalism and sophistication that exudes from virtually everything here.

Some of the most beautiful faces (and some of the richest) come here regularly for long and languid dinners. The cuisine is international, and so is the crowd. Menu specialties change every four months or so, but might include fish terrine with herb sauce, avocado pancakes with prawns, guineau fowl or partridge, coq au vin, blanquette de veau, and chicken Kiev.

LA HACIENDA, Urbanización Hacienda Las Chapas, carretera de Cádiz, Km 193. Tel. 83-11-16.

Cuisine: INTERNATIONAL. **Reservations:** Recommended,
$ Prices: Appetizers 1,200–1,800 ptas. ($12–$18); main dishes 2,100–2,800 ptas. ($21–$28); fixed-price menu 6,500 ptas. ($65). AE, DC, MC, V.
Open: Summer, dinner only, Wed–Sun (plus Mon in Aug) 8:30–11:30pm. Winter, lunch Wed–Sun 1–3:30pm, dinner Wed–Sun 8:30–11:30pm. **Closed:** Nov 15–Dec 20.

⊛ La Hacienda, a tranquil choice eight miles east of Marbella, enjoys a reputation for serving some of the best food along the Costa del Sol. In cooler months you can dine inside in the rustic tavern before an open fireplace. However, in fair weather, meals are al fresco, served on a patio partially encircled by open Romanesque arches. The chef is likely to offer calves' liver with truffled butter, lobster croquettes (as an appetizer), and roast guinea hen with cream, minced raisins, and port. A baked Alaska finishes the repast quite nicely, although you may prefer an iced soufflé. Even for such good food, the bill is high.

MARBELLA CLUB RESTAURANT, in the Marbella Club, carretera de Cádiz, Km 178. Tel. 77-13-00.
Cuisine: INTERNATIONAL. **Reservations:** Recommended.
$ Prices: Lunch buffet 5,300 ptas. ($53) per person; evening three-course fixed-price menu 5,300 ptas. ($53). AE, DC, MC, V.
Open: Lunch daily 1–3:30pm; dinner 9pm–12:30am in summer, 7:30–11:30pm in winter.

Much of this establishment's charm derives from the willingness of the staff to move its venue outdoors onto a flowering terrace whenever the weather justifies it. Lunch is traditionally a buffet served under an open-sided pavilion. Teams of formally dressed waiters frequently replenish a groaning table best described as tastefully elaborate for a clientele which has often been a *Who's Who* of the discreetly rich and famous. Dinners are served amid blooming flowers, flickering candles, and the strains of live music which might include a Spanish classical guitarist, a small chamber orchestra playing 19th-century classics, or perhaps the soothing tones of a South American vocalist. Menu items change with the season, but include an international array of foods inspired by the cuisines of the European continent.

VILLA TIBERIO, carretera de Cádiz, Km 178.4. Tel. 77-17-99.
Cuisine: ITALIAN. **Reservations:** Recommended.
$ Prices: Appetizers 1,300–2,500 ptas. ($13–$25); main courses 1,800–2,450 ptas. ($18–$24.50). AE, MC, V.
Open: Dinner only, Mon–Sat 7:30pm–midnight.

The Villa Tiberio's nearness to the upscale Marbella Club, about a five-minute walk away, ensures a flow of visitors from that hotel's elite confines. Set in what was originally built as a private villa during the 1960s, it serves what might be the most innovative Italian food in the region. Owned by the Morelli brothers, gregarious proprietors of restaurants as far away as London, it was established in 1990 and today is considered a venue for important events in the lives of the many northern European expatriates living nearby.

Appetizers include grilled eggplant stuffed with onions, mushrooms, and tomatoes; slices of thinly sliced smoked beef with fresh avocadoes and an oil-and-lemon dressing; prawn crêpes au gratin; and a "funghi fantasia," composed of a large wild mushroom stuffed with seafood-and-lobster sauce, and any of a sophisticated array of pastas. Especially tempting is the pappardelle alla Sandro, large flat noodles studded with chunks of lobster, tomato, and garlic. Other versions come with cream, caviar, and smoked salmon. Main dishes include grilled monkfish with prawns and garlic butter, grilled filets of pork or veal with mushroom-cream sauce, and osso buco. Live music sometimes accompanies a meal here.

Moderate

CALYCANTO, avenida Cánovas del Castillo 9. Tel. 77-19-59.

Cuisine: SPANISH. **Reservations:** Not required.
$ Prices: Appetizers 700–950 ptas. ($7–$9); main courses 1,650–2,075 ptas. ($16.50–$20.75); fixed-price menu 2,200 ptas. ($22). MC, V.
Open: Lunch daily 1–3:30pm; dinner daily 7:30pm–midnight.
Closed: Lunch July–Aug.

At the west end of the bypass road is a restaurant built in *cortijo* style that stands in its own grounds. The garden is the setting for meals in summer, while winter service is in a large room with a log fire. The menu offers a number of good dishes, and the wine list is extensive, with good table wines as well as vintage products. Vegetarians can be happy here, with such main dishes as vegetable-mousse pudding and, of course, crisp salads. Try the tagliatelle, asparagus mousse, and endives Roquefort. For your main course, you might choose guinea fowl or an interesting fish dish with grapes.

HOSTERÍA DEL MAR, avenida Cánovas del Castillo 1. Tel. 77-02-18.

Cuisine: MEDITERRANEAN. **Reservations:** Recommended.
$ Prices: Appetizers 600–800 ptas. ($6–$8); main dishes 1,500–2,200 ptas. ($15–$22). AE, MC, V.
Open: Dinner only, Mon–Sat 7:30pm–midnight.

The Hostería del Mar lies at the beginning of the bypass road that runs beside the Hotel Meliá Don Pepe. Its cuisine is known throughout the region as being both delicious and highly unusual. It has been called the most consistently good restaurant in the region—a judgment that many loyal clients agree with. Part of its excellence stems from the many years that the Spanish co-owners, Rafael Aguero and Roberto Pecino, worked as restaurateurs in Toronto, Canada, where they acquired a vivid concept of what international diners would enjoy.

You'll be seated in a dining room decorated in shades of fern green and cream, accented with wooden columns, a blue and terra-cotta floor, decorative ceiling beams, and hand-painted porcelain. In summer, a tree-shaded patio is set with tables for additional seating. Meals might include calves' sweetbreads in a mustard sauce, clams stuffed with ratatouille, roast duck with a sauce made from roasted figs and cassis, Catalán-style shrimp with chicken, and quail stuffed with spinach, mushrooms, and pâté. Desserts are appropriately sumptuous, and include a selection of cold soufflés.

MARBELLA HILL CLUB RESTAURANT, Urbanización Jardines Colgantes. Tel. 82-40-85.

Cuisine: MEDITERRANEAN. **Reservations:** Required on weekends.

$ Prices: Appetizers 600–1,050 ptas. ($6–$10.50); main courses 1,600–2,400 ptas. ($16–$24). AE, MC, V.

Open: Lunch Tues–Sun 1–4pm; dinner Tues–Sun 8:30pm–midnight.

In this restaurant located in the hills north of Marbella, you'll appreciate the sweeping views down to the sea. The ambience is sophisticated, airy, and polite, centered within a simple but stylish decor of green and white accessories. Partners Fabio Mezzasalna and Benito Palacio feature dishes from a Mediterranean repertoire of French, Spanish, and Italian cuisines. The menu changes with the availability of the ingredients, and might include vichyssoise, a salad of avocado and duckling, quenelles of fish with lobster sauce, a ragoût of crayfish with tarragon, and John Dory in puff pastry with spinach and hollandaise sauce.

SANTIAGO, avenida Duque de Ahumada 5. Tel. 77-43-39.

Cuisine: SEAFOOD. **Reservations:** Required.

$ Prices: Appetizers 700–3,000 ptas. ($7–$30); main dishes 1,000–3,200 ptas. ($10–$32). AE, DC, MC, V.

Open: Lunch daily 12:30–5pm; dinner daily 7pm–midnight.

As soon as you enter Santiago, the bubbling lobster tanks give you an idea of the kinds of dishes available. The decor, the stand-up *tapas* bar near the entrance, and the summertime patio join together with fresh fish dishes to make this one of the most popular eating places in town. On my most recent visit I arrived so early for lunch that the mussels for my mussels marinara were just being delivered. The fish soup is well prepared, well spiced, and savory. The sole in champagne comes in a large serving, and the turbot can be grilled or sautéed. On a hot day, the seafood salad—garnished with lobster, shrimp, and crabmeat, and served with a sharp sauce—is especially recommended. For dessert I suggest a serving of Manchego cheese.

Inexpensive

LA GITANA, calle Buitrago 2. Tel. 77-66-74.

Cuisine: INTERNATIONAL. **Reservations:** Recommended.

$ Prices: Appetizers 500–900 ptas. ($5–$9); main dishes 1,100–2,000 ptas. ($11–$20). AE, MC, V.

Open: Dinner only, daily 8–11:45pm.

La Gitana offers popular rooftop dining on a narrow street in the old pueblo off the Plaza de los Naranjos. It specializes in barbecued meats, including honey-glazed chicken, spareribs, sirloin steak, and even lamb. Other dishes, such as fresh fish, are also available.

MESÓN DEL PASAJE, Pasaje 5. Tel. 77-12-61.

Cuisine: CONTINENTAL. **Reservations:** Required.

$ Prices: Appetizers 550–650 ptas. ($5.50–$6.50); main dishes 1,050–1,800 ptas. ($10.50–$18). No credit cards.

Open: Lunch Wed–Sun 1–3pm; dinner Tues–Sun 7:30–11:30pm. **Closed:** Nov to mid-Dec.

 A well-run restaurant in an old house in the ancient quarter, just off the Plaza de los Naranjos, this *mesón* is a maze of little dining rooms. Since word is out that the food is the best in the old town—for the price—the place invariably fills up. You can fill up on one of the excellent pastas, which are most reasonable, or try the well-prepared, but more expensive, seafood and meat selections. The place has charm and good value.

LA TRICYCLETTE, calle Buitrago 14. Tel. 77-78-00.

Cuisine: INTERNATIONAL. **Reservations:** Not required.

$ Prices: Appetizers 750–1,750 ptas. ($7.50–$17.50); main dishes 350–1,350 ptas. ($3.50–$13.50). AE, MC, V.

Open: Lunch (Nov–Mar only) Mon–Sat 12:30–3pm; dinner Mon–Sat 8pm–midnight in summer, 7:30–11pm in winter.

⑤ One of the more popular dining spots in Marbella, this restaurant is in a converted home—courtyard and all—located on a narrow street in the old quarter near the Plaza de los Naranjos. Sofas in the bar area provide a living-room ambience, and a stairway leads to an intimate dining room with an open patio that's delightful in the warmer months. Start with crêpes with a soft cream-cheese filling or grilled giant prawns, then move on to a delectable main dish such as roast duck in beer, filet steak with a green-pepper sauce, or calves' liver cooked in sage and white wine. The wine list is extensive and reasonable.

Nearby Dining

EL REFUGIO, carretera de Ojén (C-337). Tel. 88-10-00.

Cuisine: FRENCH. **Reservations:** Not required.

$ Prices: Appetizers 550–750 ptas. ($5.50–$7.50); main dishes 1,300–1,800 ptas. ($13–$18). AE, DC, MC, V.

Open: Lunch Tues–Sun 1–4pm; dinner Tues–Sat 8–11pm.

If the summer heat has you down, retreat to the Sierra Blanca, just outside Ojén, where motorists come to enjoy both the mountain scenery and the French cuisine at El Refugio. Meals are served in a rustic dining room, with an open terrace for drinks. The lounge has an open fireplace and comfortable armchairs, along with a few antiques and Oriental rugs.

EVENING ENTERTAINMENT

No doubt about it—the best way to keep food costs low in Marbella is to do what the Spaniards do: Eat your meals in the *tapas* bars. You get plenty of atmosphere, lots of fun, good food, and low costs. On a **Marbella *tasca* crawl** you can order a first course in one bar with a glass of wine or beer, a second course in another, and on and on as your stamina and appetite dictate. You can eat well in most places for around 600 ptas. ($6)—and *tascas* are found all over town.

A Dance Club

ANA MARÍA, Plaza del Santo Cristo 4-5. Tel. 86-07-04.

The elongated *tapas* bar here is often crowded with locals, and a frequently changing collection of singers, dancers, and musicians performs everything from flamenco to popular songs. Open daily from 11pm to 4am; closed November and Monday from December to March. Drinks cost 1,000 ptas. ($10).

Admission: 2,200 ptas. ($22).

A Casino

CASINO NUEVA ANDALUCÍA MARBELLA, Urbanización Nueva Andalucía. Tel. 81-40-00.

Set six miles west of Marbella, close to Puerto Banús, this casino lies on the lobby level of the Andalucía Plaza Hotel (see "Where to Stay," above). The designers carefully incorporated graceful traffic flows between the facilities of the hotel and the jangle and clatter of the casino it contains. Unlike the region's competing casino at the Hotel Torrequebrada, the Nueva Andalucía does not offer cabaret or nightclub shows. The focus instead is on gambling, which the mobs of visitors from northern Europe perform with abandon. Individual games include French and American roulette, blackjack, punto y banco, craps, and chemin de fer. You can dine before or after gambling in the Casino Restaurant, which is raised a few steps above the gaming floor, for about 3,500 ptas. ($35) per person, excluding wine. Jackets are not required for men, but shorts and T-shirts will probably be frowned upon. Live music for dancing the *sevillana* is sometimes presented in the La Caseta Bar, at which time a minimum bar tab of 1,500 ptas. ($15) per person is enforced.

Admission: Casino, 600 ptas. ($6) and the presentation of a valid passport.

7. SAN PEDRO DE ALCÁNTARA

43 miles W of Málaga, 42½ miles E of Algeciras

GETTING THERE By Bus Service is every 30 minutes from Marbella.

By Car Take the N-340 west from Marbella.

ESSENTIALS The **telephone area code** for San Pedro de Alcántara is 952.

Between Marbella and Estepona, this interesting village contains **Roman remains** that have been officially classified as a national monument. In recent years it has been extensively developed as a resort suburb of Marbella, and now offers some good hotel selections.

WHERE TO STAY

CORTIJO BLANCO, carretera de Cádiz, Km 172, 29670 San Pedro de Alcántara. Tel. 952/78-09-16. Fax 952/78-09-16. 327 rms (all with bath). A/C TEL

$ Rates: 7,500 ptas. ($75) single; 11,000 ptas. ($110) double. Breakfast 700 ptas. ($7) extra. MC, V. **Parking:** Free.

The design of this carefully landscaped hotel emulates that of an extended Andalusian village. Accommodations are contained in a sprawling compound of white-sided *pueblos,* groups of which are clustered around courtyards with splashing fountains and banks of flowers. Linking them into a coherent unit are views of a soaring bell tower, and tangled masses of subtropical vines and vegetation which entwine themselves through wrought-iron balustrades. Many bedrooms face the main garden, which is dominated by a generously sized swimming pool.

Originally built during the early 1960s, the hotel was renovated and doubled in size in 1991. The hotel dining room has a decor inspired by Old Spain, with copies of Valencian antiques and attentive service. Lunch is usually served around the garden's covered pergola which, like the rest of the hotel, lies 600 yards from the beach.

GOLF HOTEL GUADALMINA, Hacienda Guadalmina, carretera N-340, 29670 San Pedro de Alcántara. Tel. 952/78-14-00. Fax 952/88-22-91. 92 rms (all with bath). A/C MINIBAR TV TEL

$ Rates: 16,400 ptas. ($164) single; 20,800 ptas. ($208) double. Breakfast 1,200 ptas. ($12) extra. **Parking:** Free.

At this moderately priced, large, country club–type resort, the first tee and 18th green are right next to the hotel. The golf course is open to both residents and nonresidents. An informal place, it's really a private world on the shores of the Mediterranean. You reach it by a long driveway from the coastal road; the location is 50 yards from the beach, 8 miles east of Marbella, and 1¼ miles from the center of San Pedro de Alcántara. Three seawater swimming pools attract those seeking the lazy life; the tennis courts appeal to the athletic. The bedrooms—most of them opening onto the pool/recreation area and the sea—are attractive in their traditional Spanish style and have private baths.

The hotel offers two excellent dining choices—one a luncheon-only reed-covered poolside terrace overlooking the golf course and the sea; the other an interior room in the main building, with a sedate clubhouse aura. Informality and good food reign.

8. PUERTO BANÚS

5 miles E of Marbella, 486 miles S of Madrid

GETTING THERE By Bus Fifteen buses a day connect Marbello to Puerto Banús.

By Car Drive east from Marbella along the 340.

ESSENTIALS The **telephone area code** for Puerto Banús is 952.

This marine village is a favorite resort of celebrities from all over the world. Almost overnight the village was created in the traditional Mediterranean style. There is no sameness here—each building appears different in design—yet everything blends into a harmonious whole. Yachts can be moored at your doorstep. Along the harborfront is an array of sophisticated bars and restaurants, all expensive.

Try, if you can, to wander through the back streets as well, past elegant archways and grilled patios. The rich and elegant rent apartments in this village for the winter season. In all, Puerto Banús is like a Disney World concoction of what a Costa del Sol fishing village should look like.

WHERE TO STAY

HOTEL MARBELLA-DINAMAR, Urbanización Nueva Andalucía, carretera de Cádiz, Km 175, 29660 Puerto Banús. Tel. 952/81-05-00. Fax 952/81-23-46. 112 rms (all with bath), 5 suites. A/C TV TEL

$ Rates: 12,000 ptas. ($120) single; 17,000 ptas. ($170) double; 56,500 ptas. ($565) suite. Breakfast 1,100 ptas. ($11) extra. AE, DC, MC, V. **Parking:** Free.

Distinctly Moorish in flavor and feeling, this striking and exotic resort celebrates the Arab domination of what is today Spanish Andalusia. Set on the seafront, just 400 yards from both the beach and the borders of Puerto Banús's congested center, it was built around 1980 with stark-white walls, soaring arches, and a central courtyard which contains a large abstractly shaped swimming pool. Bedrooms offer views of the palm trees beside the pool or of the sea, and each contains two large beds and a simple and airy collection of furniture. The resort offers tennis courts (floodlit at night), easy access to both the casino at the neighboring Hotel Plaza Andalucía, and one of the best all-around golf courses along the Costa del Sol. There's also an additional indoor swimming pool which is suitable for year-round use. Perhaps best of all, the diversions and facilities of Puerto Banús lie within a three-minute walk.

WHERE TO DINE

DALLI'S PASTA FACTORY, Muelle de Rivera. Tel. 81-24-90.

Cuisine: PASTA. **Reservations:** Not accepted.

$ Prices: Pasta 550–1,100 ptas. ($5.50–$11); garlic bread 200 ptas. ($2); carafe of house wine 525 ptas. ($5.25) for a half liter, 850 ptas. ($8.50) for a liter. No credit cards.

Open: Dinner only, daily 7pm–1am.

Its lighthearted, California-inspired philosophy has added a new way to save pesetas in high-priced Puerto Banús. Its specialty is pasta, pasta, and more pasta, which, served with a portion of garlic bread and a carafe of house wine, is amply adequate for the gastronomic needs of many budget travelers. In a setting inspired either by hi-tech or art deco (even the owners aren't absolutely certain of how to define it), you can order nutmeg-flavored ravioli with spinach filling, penne all arrabiata, lasagne, and several kinds of spaghetti. More filling are the chicken cacciatore, and the scaloppine of chicken and veal, each priced at around 1,200 ptas. ($12) per platter. These are served with—guess what?—pasta as a side dish. The establishment maintains another branch in Marbella, at calle Fontanilla 3. The establishment's owners, incidentally are a trio of Roman-born brothers who were raised in England and educated in California.

DON LEONE, Muelle Ribera 45. Tel. 81-17-16.

Cuisine: ITALIAN. **Reservations:** Recommended.

$ Prices: Appetizers 700–1,500 ptas. ($7–$15); main courses 1,800–2,900 ptas. ($18–$29). AE, DC, MC, V.

Open: Lunch daily 1–4pm; dinner daily 8pm–1am. **Closed:** Nov 21–Dec 21 and lunch mid-June to mid-Sept.

Consistently popular, with a hard-working and polite staff, Don Leone has built up a loyal clientele scattered along the Costa del Sol. Featuring Italian specialties based on seasonal ingredients, it sits in Puerto Banús's center, at the edge of the dock. Tables are scattered along the wharfside, in emulation perhaps of a chic restaurant on Italy's Amalfi peninsula. A broad-based array of wines can accompany your meal, which might include consistently popular versions of spinach salad and Caesar salad, minestrone, osso buco, veal or chicken parmigiana, fish, and roast baby lamb. Pasta addicts will appreciate the choice of homemade pastas, made on the premises and served in an array of savory sauces.

RED PEPPER, Muelle Ribera. Tel. 81-21-48.

Cuisine: GREEK/CYPRIOT. **Reservations:** Recommended.

$ Prices: Appetizers 550–750 ptas. ($5.50–$7.50); main dishes 1,500–2,500 ptas. ($15–$25). AE, DC, MC, V.

Open: Daily 11:30am–1am.

Run by an exuberant band of Cypriot expatriates, Red Pepper offers an array of Greek and Cypriot food in a sunny and sparsely furnished dining room. Selections include Hellenic chicken soup, moussaka, a variety of well-seasoned grilled meats, and honey-flavored Greek pastries. Full meals are usually accompanied by a selection of Greek and Spanish wines. You'll find the place in the center on the paseo Marítimo.

LA TABERNA DEL ALABARDERO, Muelle Benabola A2. Tel. 87-27-94.

Cuisine: INTERNATIONAL. **Reservations:** Required.

$ Prices: Appetizers 1,050–4,500 ptas. ($10.50–$45); main dishes 850–3,200 ptas. ($8.50–$32). AE, DC, MC, V.

Open: Lunch daily 1–4pm; dinner daily 8pm–midnight. **Closed:** Sun in winter, lunch mid-July to mid-Sept.

This restaurant lies directly on the harborfront, within full view of the hundreds of strolling pedestrians whose numbers seem to ebb and flow like the tides. You can dine inside its big-windowed interior, but you might have more fun at one of the dozens of outdoor tables, where the only clues to the upper-crust status are the immaculate napery, well-disciplined waiters, and discreet twinkle of some very expensive jewelry among the blue jeans or formal attire of the prosperous and fashionable clientele. An armada of private yachts bobs at anchor a few feet away. Meals might include crêpes stuffed with chunks of lobster and crayfish, hake and small clams served in a Basque-inspired green sauce, filet of duck's breast with green peppercorns or with orange sauce, and a sophisticated array of desserts.

EVENING ENTERTAINMENT

SINATRA BAR, Muelle Ribera 2. Tel. 81-48-25.

The Sinatra Bar is a center for people-watching. Residents of the nearby apartments meet here for drinks late in the evening. The preferred spot, if the weather is right, is on one of the chairs set out on the sidewalk. Only a few feet away, rows of luxury yachts await your inspection. Tables are usually shared, and piped-in music lets you hear Sinatra's voice. Snacks such as the "Mama-burger" are served throughout the night. Hard drinks begin at 650 ptas. ($6.50); burgers, at 550 ptas. ($5.50). Open daily from 9pm to 4am.

HOLLYWOOD BAR, Muelle Ribera 14. Tel. 81-68-12.

The Hollywood Bar offers a place to sit and examine the yachts bobbing a few feet away and the pedestrians who may be admiring the boats as much as you are. The establishment contains a green-and-white decor of arched awnings and terra-cotta tiles focused around a series of collages of the best shots of the Hollywood stars of yesteryear. Monroe and Chaplin mark the entrance to the toilets. Beer starts at 250 ptas. ($2.50), with hard drinks going for 550 ptas. ($5.50) and up. Open daily from 9:30am to 2am.

APPENDIX

A. BASIC PHRASES & VOCABULARY

ENGLISH	SPANISH	PRONUNCIATION
Hello	**Buenos días**	*bway*-noss *dee*-ahss
How are you?	**Como está usted?**	koh-moh ess-*tah* oo-*steth*
Very well	**Muy bien**	mwee byen
Thank you	**Gracias**	*gra*-thee-ahss
Good-bye	**Adiós**	ad-*dyohss*
Please	**Por favór**	pohr fah-*bohr*
Yes	**Sí**	see
No	**No**	noh
Excuse me	**Perdóneme**	pehr-*doh*-neh-may
Give me	**Deme**	*day*-may
Where is . . . ?	**Donde está . . . ?**	*dohn*-day ess-*tah*
the station	**la estación**	la ess-tah-*thyohn*
a hotel	**un hotel**	oon-oh-*tel*
a restaurant	**un restaurante**	oon res-tow-*rahn*-tay
the toilet	**el servicio**	el ser-*vee*-the-o
To the right	**A la derecha**	ah lah day-*ray*-chuh
To the left	**A la izquierda**	ah lah eeth-*kyayr*-duh
Straight ahead	**Adelante**	ah-day-*lahn*-tay
I would like	**Quiero**	kyehr-oh
to eat	**comer**	ko-*mayr*
a room	**una habitación**	oo-nah ah-bee-tah-*thyon*
How much is it?	**Cuánto?**	*kwahn*-toh
The check	**La cuenta**	la *kwen*-tah
When	**Cuándo?**	*kwan*-doh
Yesterday	**Ayer**	ah-yayr
Today	**Hoy**	oy
Tomorrow	**Mañana**	mahn-*yah*-nah
Breakfast	**Desayuno**	deh-sai-*yoo*-noh
Lunch	**Comida**	co-*mee*-dah
Dinner	**Cena**	*thay*-nah

NUMBERS

1 **uno** (*oo*-noh)
2 **dos** (dose)
3 **tres** (trayss)
4 **cuatro** (*kwah*-troh)
5 **cinco** (*theen*-koh)
6 **seis** (sayss)
7 **siete** (*syeh*-tay)
8 **ocho** (*oh*-choh)
9 **nueve** (*nway*-bay)
10 **diez** (dyeth)
11 **once** (*ohn*-thay)
12 **doce** (*doh*-thay)
13 **trece** (*tray*-thay)
14 **catorce** (kah-*tor*-thay)
15 **quince** (*keen*-thay)

16	**dieciseis** (dyeth-ee-*sayss*)	20	**veinte** (*bayn*-tay)	70	**setenta** (say-*ten*-tah)
17	**diecisiete** (dyeth-ee-*sye*-tay)	30	**trienta** (*trayn*-tah)	80	**ochenta** (oh-*chen*-tah)
18	**dieciocho** (dyeth-ee-*oh*-choh)	40	**cuarenta** (kwah-*ren*-tah)	90	**noventa** (noh-*ben*-tah)
19	**diecinueve** (dyeth-ee-*nyway*-bay)	50	**cincuenta** (theen-*kween*-tah)	100	**cien** (thyen)
		60	**sesenta** (say-*sen*-tah)		

B. MENU SAVVY

Alliolo Sauce made from garlic and olive oil

Arroz con costra Rice dish of chicken, rabbit, sausages, black pudding, chickpeas, spices, and pork meatballs—everything "hidden" under a layer of beaten egg crust

Arroz empedrado Rice cooked with tomatoes and cod and a top layer of white beans

Bacalao al ajo arriero Cod-and-garlic dish named after Leonese mule drivers

Bacalao al pil-pil Cod with garlic and chili peppers

Bacalao a la vizcaína Cod with dried peppers and onion

Bajoques farcides Peppers stuffed with rice, pork, tomatoes, and spices

Butifarra Catalonian sausage made with blood, spices, and eggs

Caldereta Stew or a stew pot

Caldereta extremeña Kid or goat stew

Caldo gallego Soup made with cabbage, potatoes, beans, and various meat flavorings (ham, chorizo, spareribs)

Chanfaina salmantina Rice, giblets, lamb sweetbreads, and pieces of chorizo

Chilindrón Sauce made from tomatoes, peppers, garlic, chorizo, and spicy sausage

Cochifrito navarro Small pieces of fried lamb

Cocido español Spanish stew

Cocido de pelotas Stew of minced meat wrapped in cabbage leaves and cooked with poultry, bacon, chickpeas, potatoes, and spices

El arroz amb fessols i naps Rice with beans and turnips

El caldillo de perro "Dog soup," made with onions, fresh fish, and orange juice

El cocido madrileña Chickpea stew of Madrid, with potatoes, cabbage, turnips, beef, marrow, bacon, chorizo, and black pudding

El pato a la naranja Duck with orange, an old Valencian dish

Empanada Crusted pie of Galicia, with a variety of fillings

Escudella Catalan version of chickpea stew

Fabada White bean stew of Asturias

Habas a la catalana Stew of broad beans, herbs, and spices

Judías blancas Haricot beans

Judías negras Runner beans

Lacón con grelos Salted ham with turnip tops

La cassolada Potato-and-vegetable stew with bacon and ribs
La salsa verde Green sauce to accompany fish
Las magras con tomate Slices of slightly fried ham dipped in tomato sauce
La trucha a la navarra Trout fried with a piece of ham
Le pericana Cod, olive oil, dry peppers, and garlic
Mar y cielo "Sea and heaven," made with sausages, rabbit, shrimp, and fish
Merluza a la gallega Galician hake with onions, potatoes, and herbs
Merluza a la sidra Hake cooked with cider
Morcilla Black sausage akin to black pudding
Paella alicantina Rice dish with chicken and rabbit
Picada Sauce made from nuts, parsley, garlic, saffron, and cinnamon
Pilota Ball made of meat, parsley, bread crumbs, and eggs
Pinchito Small kebab
Pisto manchego Vegetable stew from La Mancha
Pollos a la chilindron Chicken cooked in a tomato, onion, and pepper sauce
Romesco Mediterranean sauce, with olive oil, red pepper, bread, garlic, and maybe cognac
Samfaina Sauce made from tomatoes, eggplant, onions, and zucchini
Sangría Drink made with fruit, brandy, and wine
Sofrito Sauce made from peppers, onions, garlic, tomatoes, and olive oil
Sopas castellanas Bread, broth, ham, and sometimes a poached egg and garlic
Sopa de ajo castellana Garlic soup with ham, bread, eggs, and spices
Tapas Small dishes or appetizers served with drinks at a tavern
Tortilla de patatas Spanish omelet with potatoes
Turrón Almond paste
Zarzuela Fish stew

C. GLOSSARY OF ARCHITECTURAL TERMS

Alcazaba Moorish fortress
Alcázar Moorish fortified palace
Ayuntamiento Town hall
Azulejo Painted glazed tiles, popular in Mudéjar work and later architecture, especially in Andalusia, Valencia, and Portugal
Barrio (Barri in Catalán) City neighborhood or district
Churrigueresque Floridly ornate baroque style of the late 17th and early 18th centuries in the style of Spanish sculptor and architect José Churriguera (1650–1725)
Ciudadela Citadel
Cortijo Andalusian country house or villa
Granja Farm or farmhouse

Isabelline Gothic Architectural style popular in the late 15th century, roughly corresponding to the English perpendicular

Judería Jewish quarter

Lonja Merchants' exchange or marketplace

Medina Walled center of a Moorish city, traditionally centered around a mosque

Mezquita Mosque

Mirhab Prayer niche in a mosque, by Koranic law facing Mecca

Mirador Scenic overlook or belvedere, or a glassed-in panoramic balcony sheltering its occupants from the wind

Mudéjar Moorish-influenced architecture, usually "Christianized" and adopted as Spain's most prevalent architectural style from the 12th to the 16th century

Plateresque Heavily ornamented Gothic style widely used in Spain and Portugal during the 16th century. Its name derives from the repoussé floral patterns hammered into 16th-century silver (*la plata*), which were imitated in low-relief carvings in stone

Plaza de Toros Bullring

Plaza Mayor Square at the center of many Spanish cities, often enclosed, arcaded, and enhanced with cafés and fountains

Puerta Portal or gate

Reja Iron grilles, either those covering the exterior windows of buildings or the decorative dividers in churches

Retablo Carved and/or painted altarpiece

D. THE METRIC SYSTEM

LENGTH

1 millimeter (mm)	=	.04 inches (*or* less than $\frac{1}{16}$ in.)
1 centimeter (cm)	=	.39 inches (*or* just under ½ in.)
1 meter (m)	=	39 inches (*or* about 1.1 yards)
1 kilometer (km)	=	.62 miles (*or* about ⅔ of a mile)

To convert kilometers to miles, multiply the number of kilometers by .62. Also use to convert kilometers per hour (kmph) to miles per hour (m.p.h.).

To convert miles to kilometers, multiply the number of miles by 1.61. Also use to convert from m.p.h. to kmph.

CAPACITY

1 liter (l)	=	33.92 fluid ounces = 2.1 pints = 1.06 quarts
	=	.26 U.S. gallons
1 Imperial gallon	=	1.2 U.S. gallons

To convert liters to U.S. gallons, multiply the number of liters by .26.

To convert U.S. gallons to liters, multiply the number of gallons by 3.79.

To convert Imperial gallons to U.S. gallons, multiply the number of Imperial gallons by 1.2.

To convert U.S. gallons to Imperial gallons, multiply the number of U.S. gallons by .83.

WEIGHT

1 gram (g)	=	.035 ounces (*or* about a paperclip's weight)
1 kilogram (kg)	=	35.2 ounces
	=	2.2 pounds
1 metric ton	=	2,205 pounds (1.1 short ton)

To convert kilograms to pounds, multiply the number of kilograms by 2.2.

To convert pounds to kilograms, multiply the number of pounds by .45.

AREA

1 hectare (ha)	=	2.47 acres
1 square kilometer (km²)	=	247 acres = .39 square miles

To convert hectares to acres, multiply the number of hectares by 2.47.

To convert acres to hectares, multiply the number of acres by .41.

To convert square kilometers to square miles, multiply the number of square kilometers by .39.

To convert square miles to square kilometers, multiply the number of square miles by 2.6.

TEMPERATURE

°C	−18°	−10		0		10		20		30		40
°F	0°	10	20	32	40	50	60	70	80	90	100

To convert degrees Celsius to degrees Fahrenheit, multiply °C by 9, divide by 5, and add 32 (example: 20°C × 9/5 + 32 = 68°F).

To convert degrees Fahrenheit to degrees Celsius, subtract 32 from °F, multiply by 5, then divide by 9 (example: 85°F − 32 × 5/9 = 29.4°C).

E. SIZE CONVERSIONS

The following charts should help you to choose the correct clothing sizes in Spain. However, sizes can vary, so the best guide is simply to try things on.

WOMEN'S DRESSES, COATS, AND SKIRTS

American	3	5	7	9	11	12	13	14	15	16	18
Continental	36	38	38	40	40	42	42	44	44	46	48
British	8	10	11	12	13	14	15	16	17	18	20

WOMEN'S BLOUSES AND SWEATERS

American	10	12	14	16	18	20
Continental	38	40	42	44	46	48
British	32	34	36	38	40	42

WOMEN'S STOCKINGS

American	8	8½	9	9½	10	10½
Continental	1	2	3	4	5	6
British	8	8½	9	9½	10	10½

WOMEN'S SHOES

American	5	6	7	8	9	10
Continental	36	37	38	39	40	41
British	3½	4½	5½	6½	7½	8½

MEN'S SUITS

American	34	36	38	40	42	44	46	48
Continental	44	46	48	50	52	54	56	58
British	34	36	38	40	42	44	46	48

MEN'S SHIRTS

American	14½	15	15½	16	16½	17	17½	18
Continental	37	38	39	41	42	43	44	45
British	14½	15	15½	16	16½	17	17½	18

MEN'S SHOES

American	7	8	9	10	11	12	13
Continental	39½	41	42	43	44½	46	47
British	6	7	8	9	10	11	12

MEN'S HATS

American	6⅞	7⅛	7¼	7⅜	7½	7⅝
Continental	55	56	58	59	60	61
British	6¼	6⅞	7⅛	7¼	7⅜	7½

CHILDREN'S CLOTHING

American	3	4	5	6	6X
Continental	98	104	110	116	122
British	18	20	22	24	26

CHILDREN'S SHOES

American	8	9	10	11	12	13	1	2	3
Continental	24	25	27	28	29	30	32	33	34
British	7	8	9	10	11	12	13	1	2

GENERAL INFORMATION

SIGHTS & ATTRACTIONS

MADRID

Note: * indicates author's favorite.

COSTA DEL SOL

EXCURSION AREAS

ACCOMMODATIONS

MADRID

Key to Abbreviations: *B* = Budget; *E* = Expensive; *I* = Inexpensive; *M* = Moderate; *VE* = Very Expensive; * = Author's favorite; *$* = Super-value choice.

COSTA DEL SOL

EXCURSION AREAS

RESTAURANTS

MADRID

Key to Abbreviations: *B* = Budget; *E* = Expensive; *I* = Inexpensive; *M* = Moderate; *VE* = Very Expensive; * = Author's favorite; $ = Super-value choice.

COSTA DEL SOL

EXCURSION AREAS

Please Send Me the Books Checked Below

FROMMER'S COMPREHENSIVE GUIDES
(Guides listing facilities from budget to deluxe, with emphasis on the medium-priced)

	Retail Price	Code		Retail Price	Code
☐ Acapulco/Ixtapa/Taxco 1993–94	$15.00	C120	☐ Jamaica/Barbados 1993–94	$15.00	C105
☐ Alaska 1990–91	$15.00	C001	☐ Japan 1992–93	$19.00	C020
☐ Arizona 1993–94	$18.00	C101	☐ Morocco 1992–93	$18.00	C021
☐ Australia 1992–93	$18.00	C002	☐ Nepal 1992–93	$18.00	C038
☐ Austria 1993–94	$19.00	C119	☐ New England 1993	$17.00	C114
☐ Austria/Hungary 1991–92	$15.00	C003	☐ New Mexico 1993–94	$15.00	C117
☐ Belgium/Holland/ Luxembourg 1993–94	$18.00	C106	☐ New York State 1992–93	$19.00	C025
☐ Bermuda/Bahamas 1992–93	$17.00	C005	☐ Northwest 1991–92	$17.00	C026
☐ Brazil, 3rd Edition	$20.00	C111	☐ Portugal 1992–93	$16.00	C027
☐ California 1993	$18.00	C112	☐ Puerto Rico 1993–94	$15.00	C103
☐ Canada 1992–93	$18.00	C009	☐ Puerto Vallarta/ Manzanillo/ Guadalajara 1992–93	$14.00	C028
☐ Caribbean 1993	$18.00	C102			
☐ Carolinas/Georgia 1992–93	$17.00	C034	☐ Scandinavia 1993–94	$19.00	C118
☐ Colorado 1993–94	$16.00	C100	☐ Scotland 1992–93	$16.00	C040
☐ Cruises 1993–94	$19.00	C107	☐ Skiing Europe 1989–90	$15.00	C030
☐ DE/MD/PA & NJ Shore 1992–93	$19.00	C012	☐ South Pacific 1992–93	$20.00	C031
☐ Egypt 1990–91	$15.00	C013	☐ Spain 1993–94	$19.00	C115
☐ England 1993	$18.00	C109	☐ Switzerland/ Liechtenstein 1992–93	$19.00	C032
☐ Florida 1993	$18.00	C104	☐ Thailand 1992–93	$20.00	C033
☐ France 1992–93	$20.00	C017	☐ U.S.A. 1993–94	$19.00	C116
☐ Germany 1993	$19.00	C108	☐ Virgin Islands 1992–93	$13.00	C036
☐ Italy 1993	$19.00	C113	☐ Virginia 1992–93	$14.00	C037
			☐ Yucatán 1993–94	$18.00	C110

FROMMER'S $-A-DAY GUIDES
(Guides to low-cost tourist accommodations and facilities)

	Retail Price	Code		Retail Price	Code
☐ Australia on $45 1993–94	$18.00	D102	☐ Israel on $45 1993–94	$18.00	D101
☐ Costa Rica/ Guatemala/Belize on $35 1993–94	$17.00	D108	☐ Mexico on $50 1993	$19.00	D105
			☐ New York on $70 1992–93	$16.00	D016
☐ Eastern Europe on $25 1991–92	$17.00	D005	☐ New Zealand on $45 1993–94	$18.00	D103
☐ England on $60 1993	$18.00	D107	☐ Scotland/Wales on $50 1992–93	$18.00	D019
☐ Europe on $45 1993	$19.00	D106	☐ South America on $40 1993–94	$19.00	D109
☐ Greece on $45 1993–94	$19.00	D100	☐ Turkey on $40 1992–93	$22.00	D023
☐ Hawaii on $75 1993	$19.00	D104			
☐ India on $40 1992–93	$20.00	D010	☐ Washington, D.C. on $40 1992–93	$17.00	D024
☐ Ireland on $40 1992–93	$17.00	D011			

FROMMER'S CITY $-A-DAY GUIDES
(Pocket-size guides with an emphasis on low-cost tourist accommodations and facilities)

	Retail Price	Code		Retail Price	Code
☐ Berlin on $40 1992–93	$12.00	D002	☐ Madrid on $50 1992–93	$13.00	D014
☐ Copenhagen on $50 1992–93	$12.00	D003	☐ Paris on $45 1992–93	$12.00	D018
☐ London on $45 1992–93	$12.00	D013	☐ Stockholm on $50 1992–93	$13.00	D022

FROMMER'S TOURING GUIDES
(Color-illustrated guides that include walking tours,
cultural and historic sights, and practical information)

	Retail Price	Code		Retail Price	Code
☐ Amsterdam	$11.00	T001	☐ New York	$11.00	T008
☐ Barcelona	$14.00	T015	☐ Rome	$11.00	T010
☐ Brazil	$11.00	T003	☐ Scotland	$10.00	T011
☐ Florence	$ 9.00	T005	☐ Sicily	$15.00	T017
☐ Hong Kong/Singapore/ Macau	$11.00	T006	☐ Thailand	$13.00	T012
			☐ Tokyo	$15.00	T016
☐ Kenya	$14.00	T018	☐ Venice	$ 9.00	T014
☐ London	$13.00	T007			

FROMMER'S FAMILY GUIDES

	Retail Price	Code		Retail Price	Code
☐ California with Kids	$17.00	F001	☐ San Francisco with Kids	$17.00	F004
☐ Los Angeles with Kids	$17.00	F002			
☐ New York City with Kids	$18.00	F003	☐ Washington, D.C. with Kids	$17.00	F005

FROMMER'S CITY GUIDES
(Pocket-size guides to sightseeing and tourist accommodations
and facilities in all price ranges)

	Retail Price	Code		Retail Price	Code
☐ Amsterdam 1993–94	$13.00	S110	☐ Minneapolis/St. Paul, 3rd Edition	$13.00	S119
☐ Athens, 9th Edition	$13.00	S114			
☐ Atlanta 1993–94	$13.00	S112	☐ Montréal/Québec City 1993–94	$13.00	S125
☐ Atlantic City/Cape May 1991–92	$ 9.00	S004			
			☐ New Orleans 1993–94	$13.00	S103
☐ Bangkok 1992–93	$13.00	S005	☐ New York 1993	$13.00	S120
☐ Barcelona/Majorca/ Minorca/Ibiza 1993–94	$13.00	S115	☐ Orlando 1993	$13.00	S101
			☐ Paris 1993–94	$13.00	S109
☐ Berlin 1993–94	$13.00	S116	☐ Philadelphia 1993–94	$13.00	S113
☐ Boston 1993–94	$13.00	S117	☐ Rio 1991–92	$ 9.00	S029
☐ Cancún/Cozumel/ Yucatán 1991–92	$ 9.00	S010	☐ Rome 1993–94	$13.00	S111
			☐ Salt Lake City 1991– 92	$ 9.00	S031
☐ Chicago 1993–94	$13.00	S122	☐ San Diego 1993–94	$13.00	S107
☐ Denver/Boulder/ Colorado Springs 1990–91	$ 8.00	S012	☐ San Francisco 1993	$13.00	S104
			☐ Santa Fe/Taos/ Albuquerque 1993–94	$13.00	S108
☐ Dublin 1993–94	$13.00	S128	☐ Seattle/Portland 1992– 93	$12.00	S035
☐ Hawaii 1992	$12.00	S014			
☐ Hong Kong 1992–93	$12.00	S015	☐ St. Louis/Kansas City 1993–94	$13.00	S127
☐ Honolulu/Oahu 1993	$13.00	S106			
☐ Las Vegas 1993–94	$13.00	S121	☐ Sydney 1993–94	$13.00	S129
☐ Lisbon/Madrid/Costa del Sol 1991–92	$ 9.00	S017	☐ Tampa/St. Petersburg 1993–94	$13.00	S105
☐ London 1993	$13.00	S100	☐ Tokyo 1992–93	$13.00	S039
☐ Los Angeles 1993–94	$13.00	S123	☐ Toronto 1993–94	$13.00	S126
☐ Madrid/Costa del Sol 1993–94	$13.00	S124	☐ Vancouver/Victoria 1990–91	$ 8.00	S041
☐ Mexico City/Acapulco 1991–92	$ 9.00	S020	☐ Washington, D.C. 1993	$13.00	S102
☐ Miami 1993–94	$13.00	S118			

Other Titles Available at Membership Prices

SPECIAL EDITIONS

	Retail Price	Code		Retail Price	Code
☐ Bed & Breakfast North America	$15.00	P002	☐ Where to Stay U.S.A.	$14.00	P015
☐ Caribbean Hideaways	$16.00	P005			
☐ Marilyn Wood's Wonderful Weekends (within a 250-mile radius of NYC)	$12.00	P017			

GAULT MILLAU'S "BEST OF" GUIDES
(The only guides that distinguish the truly superlative from the merely overrated)

	Retail Price	Code		Retail Price	Code
☐ Chicago	$16.00	G002	☐ New England	$16.00	G010
☐ Florida	$17.00	G003	☐ New Orleans	$17.00	G011
☐ France	$17.00	G004	☐ New York	$17.00	G012
☐ Germany	$18.00	G018	☐ Paris	$17.00	G013
☐ Hawaii	$17.00	G006	☐ San Francisco	$17.00	G014
☐ Hong Kong	$17.00	G007	☐ Thailand	$18.00	G019
☐ London	$17.00	G009	☐ Toronto	$17.00	G020
☐ Los Angeles	$17.00	G005	☐ Washington, D.C.	$17.00	G017

THE REAL GUIDES
(Opinionated, politically aware guides for youthful budget-minded travelers)

	Retail Price	Code		Retail Price	Code
☐ Able to Travel	$20.00	R112	☐ Kenya	$12.95	R015
☐ Amsterdam	$13.00	R100	☐ Mexico	$11.95	R016
☐ Barcelona	$13.00	R101	☐ Morocco	$14.00	R017
☐ Belgium/Holland/Luxembourg	$16.00	R031	☐ Nepal	$14.00	R018
			☐ New York	$13.00	R019
☐ Berlin	$11.95	R002	☐ Paris	$13.00	R020
☐ Brazil	$13.95	R003	☐ Peru	$12.95	R021
☐ California & the West Coast	$17.00	R121	☐ Poland	$13.95	R022
			☐ Portugal	$15.00	R023
☐ Canada	$15.00	R103	☐ Prague	$15.00	R113
☐ Czechoslovakia	$14.00	R005	☐ San Francisco & the Bay Area	$11.95	R024
☐ Egypt	$19.00	R105			
☐ Europe	$18.00	R122	☐ Scandinavia	$14.95	R025
☐ Florida	$14.00	R006	☐ Spain	$16.00	R026
☐ France	$18.00	R106	☐ Thailand	$17.00	R119
☐ Germany	$18.00	R107	☐ Tunisia	$17.00	R115
☐ Greece	$18.00	R108	☐ Turkey	$13.95	R027
☐ Guatemala/Belize	$14.00	R010	☐ U.S.A.	$18.00	R117
☐ Hong Kong/Macau	$11.95	R011	☐ Venice	$11.95	R028
☐ Hungary	$14.00	R118	☐ Women Travel	$12.95	R029
☐ Ireland	$17.00	R120	☐ Yugoslavia	$12.95	R030
☐ Italy	$13.95	R014			